ORDEAL BY ICE

PEREGRINE SMITH LITERARY NATURALISTS

ORDEAL BY ICE

The Search for the Northwest Passage

FARLEY MOWAT

VOLUME I
of The Top of the World trilogy

PEREGRINE SMITH BOOKS
SALT LAKE CITY

Printed in the United States of America
92 91 90 89 6 5 4 3 2

Library of Congress Cataloging-in-Publication Data

Ordeal by ice : the search for the Northwest Passage / [edited by] Farley Mowat.
p. cm.—(Peregrine Smith literary naturalists)
Reprint. Originally published: Rev. ed. Toronto : McClelland and Stewart, c1973. (The Top of the world trilogy ; v. 1)
Bibliography; p.
Includes index.
ISBN 0-87905-321-6 ; $12.95
1. Northwest Passage. I. Mowat, Farley. II. Series. III. Series; Top of the world trilogy ; v. 1.
G640.073 1989 88-31838
910'.09163'404—dc19 CIP
(Rev.)

The paper used in this publication meets the minimum requirements of American National Standard for Information Sciences—Permanence of Paper for Printed Library Materials, ANSI Z39.48-1984. ∞

Books by Farley Mowat

People of the Deer (1952, rev. 1975)
The Regiment (1955, new ed. 1973)
Lost in the Barrens (1956)
The Dog Who Wouldn't Be (1957)
The Grey Seas Under (1958)
Coppermine Journey (1958)
The Desperate People (1959, rev. 1975)
Ordeal by Ice (1960, rev. 1973)
Owls in the Family (1961)
The Serpent's Coil (1961)
The Black Joke (1962)
Never Cry Wolf (1963, new ed. 1973)
Westviking (1965)
The Curse of the Viking Grave (1966)
Canada North (1967)
The Polar Passion (1967, rev. 1973)
This Rock Within the Sea, *with John de Visser* (1968, reissued 1976)
The Boat Who Wouldn't Float (1969, illustr. 1974)
Sibir (The Siberians—U.S.A.) (1970, new ed. 1973)
A Whale for the Killing (1972)
Tundra (1973)
Wake of the Great Sealers, *with David Blackwood* (1973)
The Snow Walker (1975)
Canada North Now (The Great Betrayal) (1976)
And No Birds Sang (1979)
The World of Farley Mowat, *ed by Peter Davison* (1980)

How dangerous it is to attempt new discoveries; either for the length of the voyage, or the ignorance of the language, the want of interpreters, new and unaccustomed elements and airs, strange and unsavoury meats, danger of thieves and robbers, fierceness of wild beasts and fishes, hugeness of woods, dangerousness of seas, dread of tempests, fear of hidden rocks, steepness of mountains, darkness of sudden falling fogs, continual pains-taking without rest, and infinite others.

How pleasant and profitable it is to attempt new discoveries; either for the sundry sights and shapes of strange beasts and fishes, the wonderful works of nature, the different manners and fashions of diverse nations, the sundry sorts of government, the sight of strange trees, fruit, fowls, and beasts, the infinite treasure of pearl, gold, and silver, the news of new found lands, and many others.

From George Beste's introduction to his account of the voyages of Martin Frobisher, published in 1578.

Maps Tracing Routes of the Explorers

Illustrations

A 32-page section of illustrations appears after page 333.

Contents

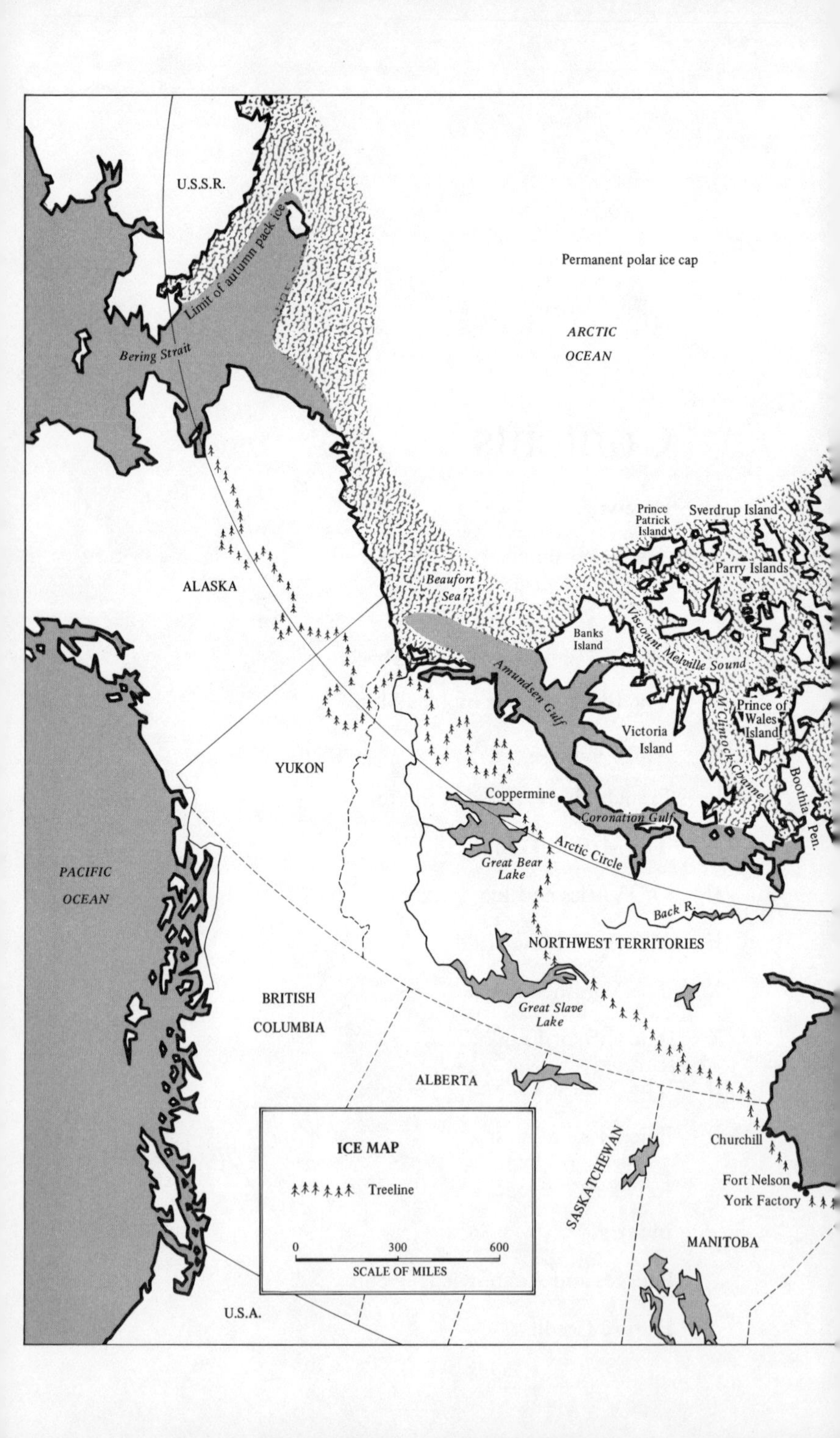

U.S.S.R.
Limit of autumn pack ice
Permanent polar ice cap
ARCTIC
OCEAN
Bering Strait
ALASKA
Beaufort
Sea
Prince
Patrick
Island
Sverdrup Island
Parry Islands
Banks
Island
Viscount Melville Sound
Amundsen Gulf
Prince of
Wales
Island
Victoria
Island
M'Clintock Channel
Boothia
Pen.
YUKON
Coppermine
Coronation Gulf
Arctic Circle
Great Bear
Lake
PACIFIC
OCEAN
Back R.
NORTHWEST TERRITORIES
BRITISH
COLUMBIA
Great Slave
Lake
ALBERTA
ICE MAP
Treeline
0
300
600
SCALE OF MILES
SASKATCHEWAN
Churchill
Fort Nelson
York Factory
MANITOBA
U.S.A.

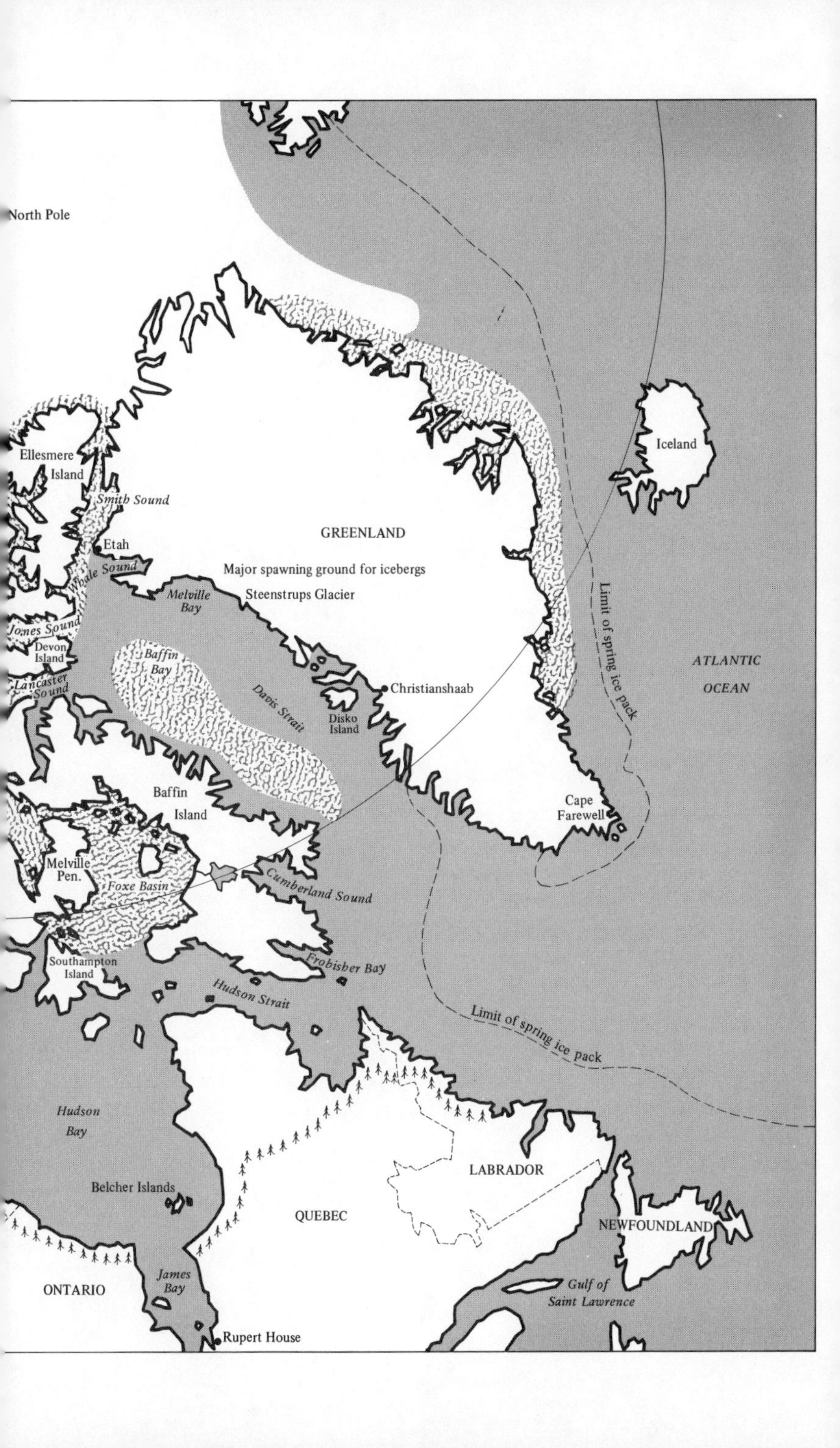
North Pole
Ellesmere Island
Smith Sound
Etah
Whale Sound
Jones Sound
Devon Island
Lancaster Sound
GREENLAND
Major spawning ground for icebergs
Steenstrups Glacier
Melville Bay
Baffin Bay
Davis Strait
Christianshaab
Disko Island
Iceland
Limit of spring ice pack
ATLANTIC OCEAN
Baffin Island
Melville Pen.
Foxe Basin
Cumberland Sound
Cape Farewell
Southampton Island
Frobisher Bay
Hudson Strait
Limit of spring ice pack
Hudson Bay
Belcher Islands
LABRADOR
QUEBEC
NEWFOUNDLAND
ONTARIO
James Bay
Gulf of Saint Lawrence
Rupert House

Foreword

In recent times North Americans have tended to ignore the almost limitless expanse of sea and land which comprises the northern reaches of their continent except to think of it as a frozen treasure house of natural resources.

It has not always been so. Until fifty or sixty years ago the Arctic was a living reality to North Americans of every walk of life. It had become real, and it stayed real for them because men of their own kind were daring its remote fastnesses in search of pure adventure, unprotected by the elaborate mechanical shields that we now demand whenever we step out of our air-conditioned sanctuaries. Press and magazines followed the fortunes of these men with a good deal more honest enthusiasm than that with which they now follow the exploits of space travellers. Personal accounts of Arctic voyages and journeys lined the shelves of book shops. Those who stayed at home identified themselves with Arctic travellers, as they can no longer truly identify themselves with the mechanical heroes of modern times.

Most of those great tales of human venturing into the Arctic (and they are legion) are no longer current or available. The majority of the original books are out of print and a good many of them are so rare they are not even to be found on public library shelves but are kept in special rooms where they are available only to the eyes of scholars.

It has long been my belief that these chronicles of high endeavour retain a powerful and essential validity for modern man. In the late 1950's I set myself the task of shaking the dust from some of them and of finding a way to restore them to the mainstream of human experience. The answer seemed to lie in gathering, editing and publishing a coherent collection of the most meaningful accounts of exploration and travel in the North American Arctic regions. This collection – which now comprises the trilogy, *The Top of the World* – was designed to provide us with an insight into the true nature of the northern world, while at the same time demonstrating the magnitude and grandeur of human endeavour in that hard environment. It was not, and is not, intended to be a history of the exploration of the North American Arctic. Rather it is the varied tale of how many individual men grappled with and came to terms with the great polar adversary. It brings the quality of these men into sharp focus so that we recognize them as superb animals, imbued with that innate strength derived from struggle with physical adversity, to which we owe ascendancy over all other forms of life.

This is an ascendancy we may be throwing away. Almost insensibly we appear to be drifting toward a biological condition which can make of us a species of unshelled blobs of protoplasm relying wholly for our survival on the mechanical maintenance of a grossly artificial, and fearfully vulnerable, environment. Witness one of our new supermen – an astronaut, the hero of our times – wombed in his gleaming layers of machinery and about as essential to the success of the electronically controlled robot that carries him as was the chimpanzee that so recently preceded him. If he is not yet completely superfluous to the machine, he is nearly so; and in the near future will be totally so. This is a matter of the flesh, but it is also becoming very much a matter of the spirit. When, and if, man comes to regard himself as being in effect an alien entity in the ancient world that formed him, then he will have become the ultimate egomaniac, imprisoned in an infinitely fragile bubble-world of his own contriving – and unquestionably doomed.

Although the selections in my trilogy are not intended to persuade modern man that he must completely divest himself of his technical proficiency and crawl back into a neolithic cave, they *are* designed to remind him, through the lips, eyes and ears of his fellows of a few short decades ago (fellows who are already beginning to have a strangely foreign look about them), that he dare not put all his future into the keeping of the machine. I hope they will suggest to him that he would be wise to retain the primal virtues of a tough, unflinching, physically competent, durable and daring animal in his own right, and *of* the world that spawned him. It is certain that we need a recognition of this truth if we are not to go over the evolutionary peak and down the sharp decline leading to the immense graveyard of other species that armoured themselves too heavily against the physical dangers and challenges, and the reality, of the world around them.

Ordeal by Ice deals with man's efforts, between 1576 and 1906, to force a sea passage through the ice barriers blocking the water routes to the north of the continent, and to find a way to link Europe with Cathay and the East. This ancient dream was one of surprising strength and viability. It gripped the imaginations of Europeans through at least four centuries and it impelled innumerable men and ships into the north-western reaches to endure the trials posed by a frozen ocean.

The Polar Passion begins shortly before *Ordeal by Ice* leaves off. By about 1850 the dream of finding a usable Northwest Passage was almost dead. Interest in the Arctic had shifted to the pursuit of a new chimera – the North Pole. This also was a development from a much older dream – that of being able to sail direct to China across the very top of the world. The search for the Northwest Passage had been rooted in commercial motives; the struggle to reach the Pole was fuelled by national pride – chauvinism, really – coupled with a burning sense of mission on the part of a handful of almost unbelievably intrepid seekers after fame.

Tundra deals with the European penetration of the gigantic Arctic land mass stretching north from the timber line and occupying the top of the continent west of Hudson Bay. This vast expanse of frozen wastes posed almost as great a challenge to the passage of European man as did the polar seas, or the ice-clogged channels between the Arctic islands.

The stories in these three books are linked by many common elements, but one of them in particular deserves special mention. The European explorers were never the first arrivals on the scene. Ages before their coming the Arctic had become an abiding home to men – to the Eskimos and the high latitude Indians, and to their forbears who, as early as six thousand years ago, had mastered the

Arctic environment despite (or it may have been because of) the limitations imposed by a stone-age technology. Their story remains unwritten, for they had no written language; but elements of it are reflected in the accounts of all European ventures into the northern regions. Their story is integral to the other accounts since, without the physical assistance of the native peoples, and without the object lessons in adaptation provided by them, most European accomplishments in the Arctic would have been impossible. This is by no means a minor theme. The Eskimo and the Indian were, and are, living symbols of the tremendous flexibility and the enduring qualities which are man's birthright, and which any species, whether man or mouse, must nurture if it is to maintain its place on the implacable and unforgiving evolutionary treadmill.

The problems involved in assembling the materials for this project have been formidable. One was the fact that we have been so careless with the stuff of history that we have allowed many of the original accounts of Arctic venturing prior to the sixteenth century to vanish utterly. I have therefore had the choice of ignoring this vast section of the story or of overtly intruding myself into it by writing my own account of the events of that obscure period. I chose the second solution. By gathering the facts that do exist, and by filling in the gaps, I have provided at least a shadow picture of the achievements of many long-forgotten men.

Another problem was that some of the older chroniclers wrote in a style that is hard for a modern reader to follow. I have therefore presented such accounts using modern spelling, phraseology and punctuation, wherever there was the possibility that the style or idiom would make easy comradeship between the original author and the modern reader difficult, if not impossible.

Still another difficulty lay in the fact that there was a good deal of repetition in the chronicles. If I had reprinted each account in full, the sheer bulk of the material would have required scores of volumes, and many of the stories would have differed, one from the other, only in detail. So I have selected those parts of each chosen voyage which are particularly revealing, and have condensed or eliminated repetitive material, sometimes substituting brief bridging paragraphs to maintain the narrative flow.

Then there was the primary problem of deciding which of the many accounts I was to include. My decision in every case is arbitrary. I have never hesitated to ignore famous voyagers in favour of little-known ones who I felt were particularly deserving of recognition.

The foregoing is in no sense an apology for the liberties I have taken with other men's works. It is merely a warning that these selections are to be read for what they are – the moving, sometimes humorous, often tragic accounts of enduring men in conflict. Scholars, and those who are interested in the minutiae of history, should go to the original sources.

Editor's Note: Throughout this volume the author's commentary has been set in italics, with the exception of the Foreword, The Forerunners, and the Epilogue.

The Forerunners

In the spring of the year 325 B.C. a bireme merchant ship put out from the Greek city-state of Massilia on the Mediterranean shores of what is now southern France, slipped past the Carthaginian warships guarding the Pillars of Hercules at Gibraltar, and turned her prow northward on a voyage of exploration into the unknown.

This Massilian bireme was a partly decked galley of about 200 tons, propelled by squaresail and by the arms of a double bank of a hundred oarsmen. She was not built for northern navigation, nor did she have any special devices or equipment to aid her, except for the knowledge and intelligence of her commander, a Greek mathematician named Pytheas. Pytheas was a philosopher, and an eminently practical one, who was perhaps the first man in history to devise a successful method of establishing an accurate latitude. He also possessed a considerable theoretical understanding of geography, including the knowledge that the world was round, that consequently there must be a north polar region, and that, in all likelihood, it was a frozen world.

Pytheas reached northern Scotland without much difficulty, and there the local seamen told him of the existence of another land lying six days' sail to the north-west. After having probably shipped a Scots pilot, Pytheas sailed on for six days until he raised the coast of a land which we now call Iceland, but which he named Thule.

Pytheas continued to sail north; but a hundred miles or so from Iceland his epochal voyage was brought to an abrupt halt. His bireme encountered the Arctic ice. Greenland, the island outpost of an undiscovered western continent, lay less than a day's sail away and its towering mountains were within easy visual range of Pytheas' position. But the ice lay in between, and the bone-chilling murk of the almost perpetual ice-fog hid the new land from his sight. This far-ranging Mediterranean Greek had come within a hair's breadth of making one of the greatest discoveries of all time, the discovery of the New World. But the ice had denied it to him, even as it was to deny to almost every succeeding Arctic voyager the full realization of his potential destiny in those high latitudes.

Since the voyage of Pytheas' bireme the struggle to achieve mastery over the ice in the north-west has never ended. The story of that struggle is the chronicle of countless men who chose to try themselves against imponderable odds in the most inimical environment on earth, who were nurtured by that trial, who sometimes died of it, but who endured what, for lesser men, would have been the unendurable. Through more than two thousand years the world of the Arctic ice was *the* ultima Thule of men eager to explore the unknown.

And what a world it was.

It was remote, not only in distances (and until very recently the sheer physical magnitude of it was enough to daunt men's hearts), but it was peculiarly and terribly remote also by virtue of its defences. Something of the quality of those defences can be seen in the ease with which they kept the Arctic almost inviolate during most of the long ages when the rest of the world was succumbing to the curiosity of western man and was being inexorably fixed on the charts of the cartographers, and in the books of scholars.

The defences of the Arctic were legion. They included such uncanny elements as the terrifying single night of winter which, in the more northern latitudes, endures for months, with only the stars, the moon and the northern lights for illumination. They included the immense glaciated mountains and lunar rock barrens of vast, frozen islands or of the illimitable continental tundra where no trees grew and where the perpetual frosts struck deep into the solid rock. They included the presence of what was, to European eyes, as strange and inexplicable (and therefore fearsome) a race of men as any in the world – the Eskimo. They included fit subjects for a bestiary as awe-inspiring as anything the mediaeval imagination could devise – the great-horned sea unicorn, the long-tusked walrus, the gigantic Greenland whale, the fearsome killer whale, the snake-necked and amphibious polar bear, and the antediluvian musk-ox. They included a climate which leapt from a summer heat that seared men's flesh to a winter frost that seared it more deeply still. It was a climate that could congeal the ocean at the height of a northern hurricane; and that could raise black ice-fogs which, for days on end, shrouded land, sea, and ice alike in a cold, palpable, and almost total darkness. It was a world that could, and did, inflict on intruders the agonies of starvation, of inevitable scurvy, and even of fatal thirst, in what was too often a frozen desert.

Yet none of these deterrents could compare with the terrible efficacy of the prime defender: the ice itself.

The disintegrating sea-cliffs of the glaciers, and their offspring, the irresistible and ponderous bergs; the drifting pack that could encompass a vessel at a moment's notice and which, if it did not crush her outright, could carry her helplessly imprisoned for a thousand miles and more; the broken floe ice lifting and lunging in the gales, and easily capable of piercing the sides of the stoutest ship afloat; the fixed ice of winter that trapped vessels like flies in amber and held them prisoner while scurvy and starvation killed their crews – these were all manifestations of the power of that one defender.

To most people ice is simply frozen water, a simple substance that preserves our food, cools our drinks, and makes the Canadian national sport of ice-hockey possible. But in fact there is nothing in the least simple, even in the chemical sense, about sea ice. Its physical forms and qualities are so amazingly complex that even today we know all too little about them. However, the men who through the centuries ventured against the ice in ships were never much concerned with its more subtle complexities. They were concerned, and remain so today, with the almost infinite variety of its manifestations – and with its habits. Ice-pilots who have lived with it through much of their lives have come to feel that it is almost sentient, as if imbued with a quality of active hostility which is certainly inhuman, but none the less real for all that. We modern acolytes of science like to believe we can demonstrate the truly mechanical nature of all aspects of the natural world, and we laugh at such superstitious nonsense. But, even in our time, men who go to the ice and who know it in all its many moods do not laugh at the suggestion that it is almost animate in its actions. They cannot afford our comfortable scepticism and our easy assumption of superiority.

In the superficial view, the Arctic sea ice can be divided into two main categories: the permanent ice which fills most of the polar basin, and its offshoots, the great southward-driving rivers of pack ice. But the permanent polar pack itself is not simply one homogenous frozen plain, for it consists essentially of innumerable individual islands, some of them of immense size and thickness, tenuously bound to their fellows by congealed slush and new ice which fills the multitude of dividing channels. And this whole, flexible continent is always in motion, revolving slowly about the top of the world, in the grip of the Arctic currents. Surrounding this relatively compact continent there is a band, of varying width, of looser polar pack ice which has a much more rapid motion, except where it lies trapped amongst the high Arctic islands. As for the ice-rivers, these are composed of fragments cast off from the fringes of the central ice continent and strongly reinforced by the annual ice which is formed in the outer reaches of the polar region and which each summer moves southward to die in the warmer waters of the North Pacific and North Atlantic Oceans. This mixture is stiffened by countless icebergs which are calved from the faces of the gigantic glaciers of Greenland and from the smaller ones on the eastern islands of the Canadian Arctic.

The general position occupied by the rotating polar ice continent is relatively static, but the ice-rivers are mutable, changing their patterns not only with the seasons of the year, but also from one year to another. They dominate, or strongly affect, an immense coastal area and a staggering portion of the northern oceans. Thus it is obvious that man's conflict with the ice in the Western Sea (as the ancients called the northern extremity of the North Atlantic) has not been, and it not, strictly limited to the arena bounded by that arbitrary and largely meaningless line, the Arctic Circle. In fact, men and vessels have undergone ordeal by ice as far south as the latitude of New York. The Arctic ice has taken its toll of ships and men all the way from latitude 38 degrees to the vicinity of the pole itself, a north-and-south distance of almost four thousand miles. Since prehistoric times men have encountered sporadic Arctic ice in almost every part of the Western Sea (icebergs have frequently floated south even to the Azores), but it was when they turned their ships' heads north-west from Europe that they entered the real domain of the ice.*

According to our written records, the tale of man's north-west venturing into this ice begins with Pytheas; but there is reason to believe that, centuries before his time, the coastal peoples of Scotland and Ireland, at least, were already venturing deep-sea into sub-Arctic waters and there encountering the ice. The vessels of those prehistoric sailors were probably very similar to the *curraghs* used during the early years of the Christian era by the people of North Ireland, Scotland, and the Faeroe and Shetland Islands. These *curraghs* consisted of hides tightly stretched over a skeleton of wood. They were *not* the little coracles of Roman Britain, but were real ships, the largest of which were capable of carrying up to sixty people, with their goods and essential supplies, on voyages of several weeks' duration. They seem to have been closely akin to the great skin *umiaks* of the Eskimos which are still being used, and which are so seaworthy that it was nothing out of the ordinary for them, a few decades ago, to traverse broad stretches of open sea in the face of heavy gales and encroaching ice, with as many as seventy people and their belongings on board. Whether rowed or fitted with crude sails, the *umiak* type of vessel could have travelled into the northern reaches of the Western Sea with relative ease and safety.

In any event it seems certain, and the assumption is accepted by such authorities as Vilhjalmur Stefansson, who made a life-long study of the subject, that when Pytheas reached Northern Scotland, he met local sailing men who were already familiar with the ocean routes north-westward at least as far as Iceland.

Although there may never be proof positive of voyages having been made into the Arctic seas in prehistoric times, there is substantial evidence to show that a Celtic priest named Brendan sailed from Ireland about 550 A.D. in one of the big skin *curraghs*, and not only visited Iceland and southern Greenland but cruised far enough north to discover Jan Mayen Island. In the Brendan accounts specific mention is made of ice; and icebergs are described in quaint but convincing language.

Less than two centuries after Brendan's time, other Celts were arriving in Iceland seeking sanctuary from Viking pirates who

* An "ice map" of the North American Arctic regions will be found on pages 10-11.

had begun to raid the outlying islands off Scotland and Ireland. For the most part, the immigrants were farmers and fishing folk who established settlements on a permanent basis. Mention of them is found in mediaeval writings of the period, and barely a century later, ancient church documents speak of Iceland *and* Greenland as being Christian countries, so that it appears that the Celts had reached and occupied the habitable parts of Greenland (the south-western regions) by the middle of the ninth century.

The westward extension of the Celtic settlements was no accident. It resulted from the appearance off the coasts of Iceland of the double-ended Viking vessels whose square sails were emblazoned with fearsome symbols of the seafaring race who had by then become the scourge of Europe. Being no match for the newcomers, the Celts fled and by 879 Iceland was Norse. Thirty years later the Vikings in their turn reached the east coast of Greenland. Then, in 981, an exiled Nordic Icelander named Erik the Red rounded the southern tip of Greenland and spent three years exploring its western coast together with a portion of the opposite coast of Baffin Island. The Norse settled south-western Greenland, and these settlements were destined to endure until the end of the fifteenth century, during which time the Norsemen explored most of Baffin Bay, the coast of Labrador, part of Newfoundland, Ungava Bay, Hudson Strait, and probably Hudson Bay as well.

Much of this vast region belongs to the domain of the Arctic ice and was the preliminary battlefield whereon the seekers after the Northwest Passage fought their first skirmishes with the white foe. But when the Greenland Norse were voyaging to the north-west – roughly between 1000 and 1250 A.D. – a unique climatic situation existed. About 800 A.D. the climate of the North Atlantic region began to experience a phenomenal moderation. This warming trend, known to scientists as the Little Climatic Optimum, reached its peak about 1000 A.D. and brought such balmy weather that the great ice-stream that normally bars the east Greenland coast vanished entirely; the pack ice which normally fills much of Baffin Bay even in midsummer also vanished; and it is possible that, during the warmest years, the polar ocean itself became partially ice-free.

The Greenland Norse, sailing into Baffin Bay during this period, apparently encountered no ice unless they went very far north indeed. I have dealt with some of their high-latitude voyages in the second volume of this trilogy, *The Polar Passion*; but one aspect of their Arctic voyaging bears directly on the Northwest Passage. This is their explorations of Hudson Strait, which many later voyagers took to be the gateway to the far western seas.

The first knowledge the Norse had of the existence of Hudson Strait was obtained during an involuntary voyage of exploration by Bjarni Herjolfsson up the Labrador coast to Cape Chidley in the year 985. Bjarni seems to have seen the mouth of the Strait, but thought it was open sea sweeping west and south to make an island out of Labrador, or *Helluland*, as that region came to be called.

The next Greenland Norse to see this region were the members of a colonizing expedition under Thorfinn Karlsefni in search of Vinland, about 1004. A four-ship flotilla crossed Davis Strait to the Cumberland Peninsula, then coasted south across the mouth of Hudson Strait before sailing on down the Labrador coast. There is no record of what the Norse sailors thought of the great stretch of open water running off to the west between Baffin Island and Labrador, but they were seamen and they would have noted the remarkable tidal stream pouring out of the great inlet – evidence that it connected with a vast, possibly oceanic, body of water far to the west.

Later Norse voyagers called the Strait *ginungagap*, meaning a mighty channel connecting the Atlantic Ocean with the mythical *Mare Oceanum* which was supposed to surround all known lands. And, after all, this was not such a wild conclusion. It expressed the first concrete belief by Europeans in the existence of a north-west passage around the land mass that much later became known as North America.

The Greenland Norse continued to visit the Hudson Strait region for several centuries. Part of the proof of this is contained in fragments from a number of sagas. One of these, the Saga of Arrow-Odd, is an epic novel which was committed to parchment in the late thirteenth or early fourteenth century; but it probably had considerably greater antiquity as an oral saga.

The story concerns a Norwegian hero named Arrow-Odd and his son Vignor, who were trying to track down a fleeing enemy named Ogmund. Here are the relevant sections, with my comments in brackets.

I will tell you where Ogmund has gone. He has gone into that fiord which is called Skuggi. It is in Helluland's obygdir [uninhabited regions]. . . . *He has gone there because he wishes to escape you. But now you may track him to his house if you wish, and see what comes of it.*

Odd decided that this is what they would do. Thereupon he [and his son Vignor, in separate ships] *sailed until they came into the Greenland Sea* [which lay between Iceland and Greenland] *when they turned south and sailed around the land* [Cape Farewell] *and to the west. . . . They sailed then until they came to Helluland* [north Labrador, perhaps Cape Chidley] *and laid their course into Skuggifiord* [Hudson Strait – Ungava Bay]. . . . [After entering Skuggifiord] *they saw two rocks rising out of the sea. Odd was very curious about this and they sailed between the two rocks. Toward evening they saw a large island. Odd brought his ship to its shore. Vignor asked why he did so, but Odd ordered five of his men to go ashore to look for water. Vignor said this was not necessary and did not allow any of the men from his ship to accompany the others.*

Not long after Odd's men had gone ashore on the island it sank and they were all drowned. This island was covered with vegetation [some translators say heather, others say weeds; the meaning may be synonymous with kelp or heavy sea vegetation which is notable on the tidal islands and rocks of Ungava Bay.] *They did not see it come up again. The rocks had all disappeared when they looked in that direction. . . .*

When they reached the land [which they were seeking in Skuggifiord], *father and son went ashore and walked there until they saw a fortified place, and it seemed very strongly built. . . .*

The course Odd and his son followed is the correct course from Iceland to north Labrador, or *Helluland* – and we are specifically told that the two men made a *Helluland* landfall. The events that follow, although they sound fabulous, and probably appeared wonderful enough to the Norse, are not really so improbable.

The tidal ranges in Hudson Strait and Ungava Bay are among the greatest in the world. At the entrance to the Strait, near the

Button Islands, the greatest range is of the order of twenty-five feet. However, inside the mouths of the Strait and of Ungava Bay the range is forty feet, while a range of fifty-two feet has been reported from the south-west shore of Ungava Bay. Islands of very considerable extent – some of them embracing several hundred acres – are periodically drowned and then exposed again by these phenomenally high tides. When Odd and his companions entered the Strait they would have been startled to see islands, which looked as if they should always be high and dry, rapidly disappearing beneath the fast-rising waters which, in some parts of the Strait, flow at speeds of as much as seven knots. While we do not need to believe that Odd's five men actually drowned on one of these disappearing islands (the saga-teller must be allowed poetic licence), it need not strain our credulity to believe that men landed to explore one of these strange, kelp-covered islands, and were forced to beat a hurried retreat to their ships when it became obvious that the whole of the island was about to disappear beneath the sea.

It should be noted that there is no other place on the east coast of North America with such a great tidal range, with the possible exception of the Bay of Fundy.* Furthermore, tidal ranges on the Greenland and Iceland coasts are of a much lower order, often averaging less than three feet. It is not hard to see how men who were used to such small tides would be mightily impressed by thirty- or forty-foot ones, and might in fact find it hard to believe that what they were witnessing was normal tidal action rather than some cataclysmic submergence of a type that was well known in Iceland where volcanic subsidence occurred often in Norse times.

Skuggifiord is mentioned by name in one other source; the saga known as *Gunnars Saga Keldugnupsfifils. Helluland* is not mentioned here, but the context of the story makes it clear that Skuggifiord had the same location assigned to it as in Arrow-Odd's saga.

In two other sagas that are related to each other and that appear also to have a relationship with the Arrow-Odd story, Skuggifiord is not mentioned by name – but *Helluland* is. One of these is the

* From the *Labrador and Hudson Bay Pilot*, 1954. "The western side of Ungava Bay is shallow for a considerable distance off shore. . . . A. P. Low describes the (tidal) appearance of the northern part of this coast as 'startling.' The bottom was exposed for about three miles outside high water and was formed of low rocky ridges while everywhere boulders of all sizes were strewn about . . . the tide rises (and falls) an inch a minute. . . ."

Saga of Bard the Snow-fell-God and it includes the following passages. (Again, the notes in brackets are mine.)

> *There was a king named Fog who ruled over those gulfs which extend north around Helluland and which are now called the Fog Seas.**

[This Fog king was not Norse. The character was probably based on the local inhabitants, who would have been either Dorset or Thule Eskimos. That they were probably Dorsets is suggested in another saga, soon to be quoted. A little further on, the present saga refers to another king who *was* Norse and of whom the saga narrator says:]

> *I have never seen him, but I have been told by my relatives that this king was called Ragnor and, from their account, I believe I recognize him. He at one time ruled over Helluland and many other countries and after he had ruled these lands a long time he caused himself to be buried alive together with five hundred men at Raknslodi. . . . It seems to me to be probable, from the reports of other people, that his burial place is in Helluland's obygdir. . . .*

[A man named Gest goes in quest of this mound. He sails to the obygdir of south Baffin Island – where, having spent three days traversing a "lava-field" on foot, he at length discovers the burial mound on an island near the sea coast.]

> *Some men say* [adds the saga narrator] *that this mound was situated to the northward of Helluland. . . . .*

[To this we add a fragment from the Saga of Halfdan Eysteinsson.]

> *Ragnor brought Helluland's obygdir under his sway and destroyed all the giants there.*

* The incidence of fog at the Cape Hopes Advance meteorological station on Ungava Bay is phenomenally high with fog being recorded on an annual average of 50 days between June 1 and Sept. 30. Fog conditions are even worse (in fact the worst in the entire Eastern Arctic) at the mouth of Hudson Strait. The average incidence of fog for June through September at Resolution Island is 65 days!

In these two fragments we are dealing with a fictionalized story of great antiquity which had an original basis in fact. It is clear that the two Ragnors of the Saga of Bard the Snow-fell-God and the Saga of Halfdan Eysteinsson are one and the same man. Ragnor was a Norseman who came out to *Helluland's* northern regions (perhaps as an outlaw, like Erik the Red before him) and there established himself. He did not succeed in doing so without a struggle with the natives of the area, who are significantly referred to as giants. This is the same term used in various other sagas, notably the Saga of Thorgisl Orrabeinsfostri, in reference to an Arctic people who were almost certainly Dorset Eskimos, rather than the smaller Thule Eskimos who *themselves* referred to the Dorsets as giants.*

If Ragnor and his supporters chose to settle anywhere in the *Helluland* region, it would not have been on the east coast of the north Labrador peninsula since this area is, and we may believe always has been, a "worthless land" even as it was categorized by the earliest Norse to visit it. On the other hand, parts of Ungava Bay (and the west coast in particular) are still noted for their excellent sea and land hunting. Throughout the historic period a large Eskimo population has existed on the west coast, and archaeology has shown that this area was once inhabited by a sizeable population of Dorsets.

Ogmund, who was probably associated in legend with Ragnor, was pursued by Arrow-Odd to *Helluland* and into Skuggifiord. The fortified building found by Odd might be identified with Ragnor's house, or even with his grave mound. In any event, the grave of Ragnor became a celebrated thing and there was a great deal of speculation about it by the Norse and several later attempts to find it.

My reconstruction can only be confirmed by archaeological evidence, and it now appears that such evidence exists. In July of 1957 an archaeological field party from the National Museum of Canada, under the leadership of Dr. William Taylor, was guided by an Eskimo to Pamiok Island in Payne Bay† on the west coast of Ungava Bay. The scientists were being taken to see some peculiar ruins reported by the local people.

* The Dorsets were an Eskimoan people of large stature who became extinct before 1200 A.D. and were replaced in the Eastern Arctic by Thule culture Eskimos.

† The tidal range at Payne Bay is forty-two feet.

The site (called by Taylor *Imaha* – Eskimo for "maybe") lay a short distance inland from a small harbour on the south-west part of the island. It consisted of innumerable burial vaults, ancient food caches, cairns, and house ruins of several types, some of which were clearly Eskimoan and rather recent, but including others which were startlingly unlike any aboriginal ruins previously found in North America. The most imposing ruin was a rectangular stone structure measuring roughly 85 feet long by 31 feet wide, enclosing a floor area about 75 feet by 20 feet and showing traces of at least two partitions, dividing the building into three separate rooms. The walls, which were originally of turf heavily ballasted with great stones, had collapsed, but the long side walls were obviously slightly curved, which is a diagnostic feature of the ancient Scandinavian long house hall known as a *scala*.

Taylor was primarily interested in discovering relics of the Dorset culture, and he did not excavate the big ruin. However, in a conversation with me in 1965, he gave it as his personal opinion that the big ruin was not Eskimoan and he added: "If I was looking for Norse ruins in America, I would head straight back to *Imaha*." He never did, but in 1966 Thomas Lee, an archaeologist with Laval University, independently investigated the ruins on Pamiok Island. A preliminary examination convinced him that he had stumbled on an extraordinary site, and he began systematic excavation which still continues in 1973. Lee is completely convinced that Pamiok was a Greenland Norse site. He has since found several more of the giant long houses and has excavated one that is more than 100 feet in length. Proof positive, by the standards of the archaeological hierarchy, may still be lacking to ascertain that these were indeed Norse buildings, but negative proof establishes beyond any doubt that they were not Eskimoan, Dorset or Thule. Scores of Icelandic-type eider-duck nesting shelters have been found in the vicinity. The whole west Ungava Coast is studded with huge cylindrical stone beacons unlike anything ever built by the Eskimos, but indistinguishable from early Scandinavian navigational beacons. On the Payne River, not far upstream from Pamiok, stands a huge stone monument in the shape of the Hammer of Thor. Much farther inland, on the shore of Payne Lake, Lee has excavated an entire village of rectangular houses constructed with stone walls, and including a structure which is very similar to early Christian churches built by the Norse in Iceland in the twelfth century. A series of skulls taken by Lee from grave vaults on Pamiok range from Eskimoan to north European in their characteristics, and an axe head found by Lee on Pamiok is of thirteenth- or fourteenth-century origin.

Lee's discoveries, coupled with the fragmentary bits of historical information buried in the ancient sagas, seem to establish with a high degree of certainty that ancient Scandinavians – possibly including the vanished settlers of Greenland – not only were familiar with Hudson Strait and Ungava Bay, but very probably had settlements, even if only of a transient nature, in the region. In 1967 I visited the sites at Pamiok, Payne Lake and points along the coast; and having carefully studied Lee's voluminous and meticulous reports, I am convinced that it was the Norse who unwittingly opened the first gate of the many that barred off the fabulous Northwest Passage of later times.

The answer to the question of how far the Norse penetrated into Hudson Bay itself has to be largely conjectural. We know, from Icelandic records, that the Greenlanders were making voyages to the Labrador coast as late as 1347. A few years later – about 1360 – an expedition from Norway under command of Paul Knutsson was commissioned by the King of Norway to reclaim the erring Greenlanders (who were reported to have relapsed into paganism) for the Holy Faith. This expedition seems also to have been entrusted with the task of finding out what had happened to the Greenland western settlement in the vicinity of Godthaab which by 1350 had been abandoned by its occupants.

No documentary evidence from European sources remains to tell us what happened to the Knutsson expedition; but there may be documentation of a sort from North America. In 1898 a stone inscribed with runic characters was found enmeshed in the roots of a tree near Kensington, Minnesota. The inscription translates as follows:

> *8 Goths* [Swedes] *and 22 Norwegians on exploration journey from* [or for] *Vinland across West. We had camp by two skerries* [islands] *one day's journey north from this stone. We were and fished one day. After we came home found 10 men red with blood and dead. AVM* [ave Maria] *save from evil. Have 10 men by the sea to look after our ships 14 days journey from this island. Year 1362.*

The Kensington Stone has been the centre of bitter controversy ever since it came to light. Some scholars insist it must be a forgery. Others point out that, considering all the circumstances, it is more difficult to believe it is a forgery than to accept it as genuine.

The Kensington Stone may bear a relationship to the Beardmore Find. This discovery, preserved in the Royal Ontario Museum at Toronto, was made near Lake Nipigon on the north shore of Lake Superior. It consists of a broken iron sword, an axe blade, and some fragments including part of a shield boss. All are unquestionably Norse, and dateable to the fourteenth century. However, the suggestion has been made that they too were "planted" in modern times. A careful analysis of the circumstances surrounding the find does not support the fraud theory, but the mere mention of the word has thrown the find into some disrepute.

If the Norse knew about Hudson Bay, it does not seem at all far-fetched to suppose that the Knutsson expedition sailed there, either with a knowledgeable Greenland or Ungava Bay pilot, or equipped with sailing directions supplied by Greenlanders. If the party landed at the mouth of the Albany River, it would have been able to proceed by boat to within a short distance of Lake Nipigon, and could then have made the short portage over the watershed, and so reached Lake Superior.

But supposition is not history, and if this were the only evidence pointing to Norse knowledge of Hudson Bay we would have to refuse to credit it. However, about a century after Knutsson's expedition, King Christian of Denmark (who had by then acquired sovereignty over Greenland from the Norwegians), also commissioned a western voyage. It sailed circa 1476 under the leadership of two ex-pirates named Pining and Pothorst, but piloted by a Scandinavian called Johannes Scolvus, who may even have been a Greenlander.

Our information about this voyage is scanty and mainly indirect. Baron de Lahontan, Lord Lieutenant of Newfoundland and Acadia near the end of the seventeenth century, tells us that Labrador (by which the French of that period meant northern Labrador, including Ungava) was initially discovered by the Danes and that Henry Hudson made his famous voyage into Hudson Bay as a direct result of his having seen a "memoir" of a Danish voyage into the Bay. According to Lahontan, a man named Anschild or Anskoeld entered Hudson Strait, followed it into Hudson Bay, and wintered there, being furnished with food and skins by certain savages.

G. M. Asher, the chief authority on Henry Hudson, was convinced that Lahontan's Anskoeld (Hans Skoeld) was the Johannes Scolvus of the 1476 expedition, and this identification is generally accepted.

There is also a cryptic comment by John Oldmixon in his *The British Empire in North America* (London, 1709): "*We know 'tis pretended* [claimed: in the usage of the times] *that a Dane made the discovery of this Streight* [Hudson Strait] *and that he called it Christiana, from the King of Denmark. . . .*"

Another scrap of evidence is found on the Gemma Frisius Globe, engraved by the famous Mercator around 1536. It shows a rather amorphous land mass to the west of Greenland, bearing the inscription: "*Quij: the people to whom the Dane Johannes Scolvus penetrated about the year 1476.*"

Still another indication that a voyage to Hudson Bay was made lies in the fact that in 1619 another King Christian of Denmark dispatched an expedition under Jens Munk into Hudson Bay, nine years after Hudson's voyage, with the declared intention of claiming the region for Denmark. The implication is clear: Christian had reason to feel that he had a prior claim upon the Bay.

The knowledge acquired by the Greenlanders about the northwestern reaches of America assuredly did not pass into limbo with the disappearance of the Greenland colonies. The knowledge may have been lost to historians – but it was not lost to Danish, Bristol, Basque and Portuguese sailors, all of whom are known to have frequented Greenland waters before the death of the Greenland colonies and who must have come to share the Norse knowledge. They made use of the information they garnered from the Greenlanders and kept it viable and current throughout the general seafaring community of Europe.

As early as the late 1300's a clandestine trade existed between the Greenland Norse and enterprising merchant-traders sailing out of Bristol. The trade was necessarily clandestine because the Norwegian kings, who then claimed sovereignty over Greenland, were extremely jealous of any encroachments on their Greenland trade monopoly – so much so that they negotiated a treaty with England designed to stop English ships from trading with Greenland. The treaty was honoured mainly in the breach, but the secrecy imposed by its illegal nature has blinded most historians to its importance. European ships were in touch with the Greenland settlements from their beginning in 985 until the last recorded appearance in history of a Norse Greenlander, whose body was discovered by the crew of a north European whaling ship not far north of Cape Farewell in 1540. Until 1350 these were mainly Norwegian ships. Thereafter ships of several nations joined in the far western voyages. The Basques were in Greenland waters by 1420, following the whale. By the middle of the fifteenth century Basque, Breton, and probably English ships had passed on to *Helluland* and were whaling in Belle Isle Strait and filling their little ships with codfish from the Grand Banks off Vinland (Newfoundland). These early voyagers seem to have sailed via Iceland and Cape Farewell – following the old Norse courses; and it is a foregone conclusion to anyone who knows anything of the sea, and of the nature of seaman, that these early mariners had their sailing directions from the Norsemen who had preceded them and blazed the way.

By the last half of the fifteenth century, European seamen knew a great deal about the north-western approaches to the New World. When, during the final decades of that century, men began to think seriously about the possibility of finding a sea passage to the north of the new continent they already had an idea – no matter how hazy it may have been – of where to begin the search. They already knew of the existence of the Norse *ginungagap* which seemed to promise a passage west. Hudson Strait, by whatever name, was already within the ken of western man.

John Cabot seems to have been the first "modern" explorer to try the gate. In 1498 he sailed from Bristol on his second voyage to the New World, with a fleet of six ships. But this time his destination was not the known lands of Labrador and Newfoundland. Instead he was sailing into the north-west, and thereby initiating the search for one of the greatest of all geographical chimeras – the passage around the top of the world.

Very little has been preserved concerning this voyage. Cabot seems to have sailed into the mouth of Davis Strait and then turned west for Hudson Strait. But things had changed since the Norse had been used to following this route. The balmy days of the Little Climatic Optimum were at an end and the Arctic weather had become uniformly bad. Davis Strait was choked with gigantic rafts of drift ice. Hudson Strait, fed by all the winter ice of Foxe Basin and Hudson Bay, spewed out its millions of tons of drifting floes on a current that occasionally reached a velocity of six knots, to form a crushing maelstrom at its mouth – one which any vessel entered at its peril. A passage of the Strait in those years seems only to have been possible very late in the season, if at all. And Cabot sailed early in the season. His flagship was destroyed and he himself perished with it. The first attempt to crash the gate had failed.

In 1509 his son Sebastian renewed the attempt, but we know little of what happened on this voyage. Then there seems to have been a hiatus until 1527 when the Englishman Robert Thorne made a trial of the north-west. All we know of his attempt is that Thorne lost one of his two ships, presumably to the ice of Hudson Strait.

The opaque mists which, through fifteen hundred years, obscure the details of man's venturings into the north-west retain their powers to conceal the past up to Thorne's time, almost as effectively as the fogs of the polar seas concealed the mysteries and hazards of that strange world. Not until 1576 do the mists at last begin to clear.

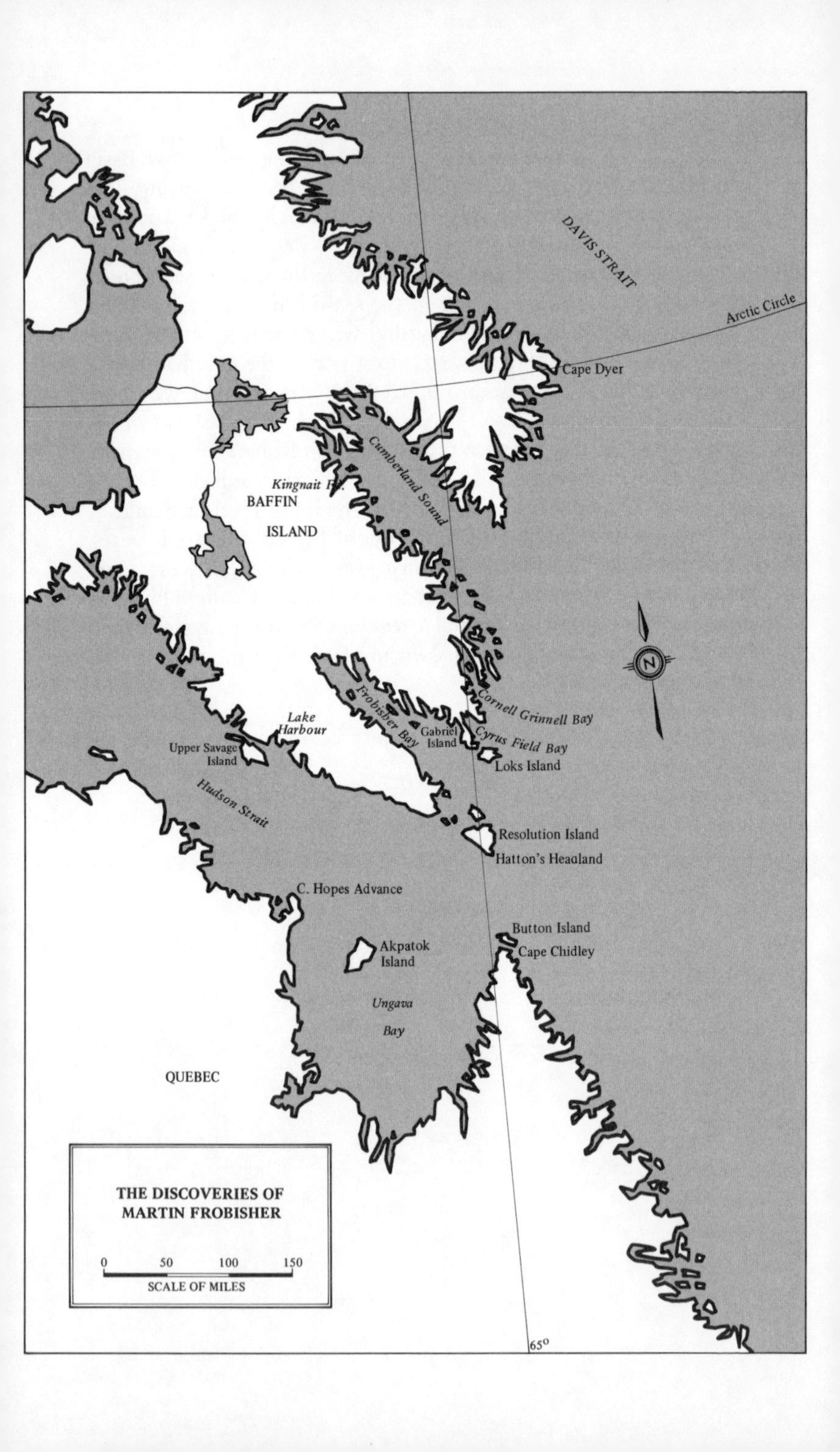
DAVIS STRAIT
Arctic Circle
Cape Dyer
Cumberland Sound
Kingnait
BAFFIN
ISLAND
Cornell Grinnell Bay
Lake
Harbour
Frobisher Bay
Gabriel
Island
Cyrus Field Bay
Upper Savage
Island
Loks Island
Hudson Strait
Resolution Island
Hatton's Headland
C. Hopes Advance
Button Island
Cape Chidley
Akpatok
Island
Ungava
Bay
QUEBEC
THE DISCOVERIES OF
MARTIN FROBISHER
0
50
100
150
SCALE OF MILES
65°

I

The Icie Seas

In 1540, when Martin Frobisher was born, the Elizabethan era was already in the making and a great maritime ferment which was soon to send English vessels into every ocean of the world was well begun.

Hailing from Yorkshire, but of Welsh ancestry, Frobisher had the West Englishman's penchant for the sea and he wasted little enough time in going down to it. By the time he was fourteen he was making commercial voyages to Guinea, perhaps as a cabin boy, but more probably before the mast as a seaman, since boys grew into men in something of a hurry in those days. In 1558, when Elizabeth's accession to the throne brought a new spirit to the age, Frobisher entered into it with gusto. He may even have been a little over-enthusiastic, for in 1566 he was being called upon to answer to charges of outright piracy committed on the Guinea coast.

But piracy was a minor peccadillo in those times. Once the transient unpleasantness of an official inquiry was behind him, Frobisher's restless mind began to turn to the prospects of a different kind of adventure – and in a different clime.

As one of his contemporaries has described it, Frobisher concluded that there was "only one thing in the world that was left undone whereby a notable mind might be made famous and fortunate," and the personal accomplishment of this one thing became his obsession. Thus he began, "first with himself to devise, and then with his friends to confer, and laid a plain chart unto them showing that a voyage was not only possible to the north-west, but also, as he could prove, easily performed."

Where John Cabot and his successors had failed, Frobisher was convinced that he would succeed in finding a short route across the frozen top of the world to Cathay and the Indies.

Unfortunately, there had already been too many failures, and in any case the temper of the times was more easily inflamed by prospects of Spanish loot than by the doubtful possibilities of a conquest of the northern ice, so for ten years Frobisher tried stubbornly but vainly to gain support for his attempt. "Although his will was great to perform this notable voyage, whereof he had conceived in his mind great hope, yet he wanted the means to set forward and perform the same. Long time he conferred with private friends, and made also many offers to sundry merchants of our country; but perceiving that hardly was he harkened to by the merchants (which never regard virtue without sure, certain, and present gains) he repaired to the Court. Here he received some comfort of his cause and by little and little, with no small expense and pain, drew together so many adventurers and such sums of money as to furnish him to sea withal."

It was mainly through the help of the Earl of Warwick that Frobisher's long planning came to fruition. But the "adventurers" (of their money, not of their lives and limbs) who paid the shot seem to have been as penurious as is usual in such cases. Frobisher was given two ships and a pinnace with which to make his voyage; but the two "ships" were only thirty-tonners, not much larger than good-sized pleasure boats of today, while the pinnace was a mere cockleshell of ten tons burthen. The total crew to man all three vessels was only thirty-five, so it was obvious that even such little ships as these were not over-manned. From the evidence implicit in the narrative, it is clear that the ships were ill-found, both as regards supplies and as to their condition. They were probably distinctly inferior, as sea-boats, to the bireme of Pytheas, and to the ships of the early Norse. Inordinately clumsy, slow through the water, and almost disastrously ill-suited for the struggle with the ice, they were nevertheless better than nothing in the eyes of Martin Frobisher.

The account of his first voyage, which follows, is adapted from a manuscript by Michael Lok, one of Frobisher's backers.

MICHAEL LOK'S ACCOUNT OF THE FIRST VOYAGE

Of the matters that chiefly moved me to enterprise and advance this voyage of Captain Frobisher and to venture my money therein so largely; I will say briefly that two things moved me thereto. First: The great hope to find our English seas do open into the seas of East India by the north-west way, whereby we might have passage by sea to those rich countries for traffic of merchandise, which was the thing I chiefly desired. Secondly: I was assured by manifold good proofs of divers travellers and histories that Canada, and the new found lands thereto adjoining, were full of people and full of such commodities and merchandise as are found in the countries of Lapland, Russia, and Muscovia, which are furs, hides, wax, tallow, oil, and other. Whereby if it should happen those new lands should stretch to the north pole, so that we could not have passage by sea that way, yet in those same new lands to the north-westward might be established trade of merchandise.

Now, in this voyage of which I write, Captain Martin Frobisher, being furnished with two ships of thirty tons burthen, the *Michael* and the *Gabriel*, and one pinnace of ten tons, and all other things necessary, in as ample manner as the funds supplied would reach, he set sail from England on the 19th day of June, anno domini 1576.

On the 30th day of June, the weather grew to a great storm which continued until the 8th day of July, in which time they could bear no manner of sail. In this great storm they lost sight of their small pinnace (she having three men therein) which they could never since hear of, though they used all possible diligence and means that the weather would suffer to seek and save the same.

When the storm ceased they passed along on their way again, and on the 11th day of July they had sight of land unknown to them.* They could not come close enough to set foot thereon because of the marvellous abundance of monstrous great islands of ice which lay driving all along the coast thereof.

Bearing in nearer, in order to explore the same, they found it marvellous high, and full of high ragged rocks all along the coast, and some of the islands of ice near it were of such height as the clouds hung about the tops of them, and the birds that flew about them were out of sight.

Here they lost the ship *Michael*, to their great discomforture, for the people of that ship, being loath to make discovery of new lands, set their course back again homeward to London.

In the meantime the said Captain Frobisher, in his remaining ship the *Gabriel*, was overset with a sea which they shipped on the thirteenth day of July during the rage of an extreme storm which cast the ship flat on her side. And being open in the waist, she filled with water so that she lay as good as sunk; and would not wear nor steer.

In this distress, when all the men in the ship had lost their courage and did despair of life, the Captain, with valiant courage, stood up and passed along the ship's side on the gunwale of her flat side, and caught hold on the weather leach of the foresail thereby to help her to her feet. And to lighten the ship, they cut away the mizzen mast. And the mariners also would have cut over the main mast, which the Captain refused to allow. At last the ship became upright again, but being full of water, with the rolling of the seas, the water issued out of her and withal many things floated over the ship's sides. And so they put the ship to run before the sea all that day and next night in the storm. Also they broke their main mast afterward, but mended it again.

The storm being ceased, and being now out of hope any more to meet with his other ship the *Michael*: still the Captain determined to follow his enterprise and voyage, according to the uttermost of his power, and rather to make a sacrifice unto God of his

* Greenland.

life than to return home without the discovery of Cathay, except by compulsion of extreme force and necessity.

And so they returned to a course according to their commission. And on the 29th day of July the Captain himself first had sight of a new land of a marvellous great height, the headland whereof he named Elizabeth Foreland* in memory of the Queen's Majesty.

When they approached near they found the seashore full of monstrous high islands and mountains of ice, floating and driving with the winds and tides so as they durst not yet approach with their ship to land thereon. Nevertheless, remaining still in hope to find a safe place to enter with the ship, they passed to and fro along the coast, still in the sight of land, for sixteen days, until the ice was well consumed and gone.

On the 19th day of August they found an island which they liked, in a great strait which they named Frobisher's Strait. The Captain and six of his men landed thereon and went to the top of a high mountain thereof to discover the land about them: and there they espied seven strange boats with men therein rowing toward the island.† Whereupon in great haste they ran down again to recover their own boat, which hardly had they recovered before the arrival of those seven boats. The Captain returned to his ship with his boat to put all in readiness for defence if need should be; but sent his skiff crew to view the strange men and have speech with them if they could.

The strangers made offer of friendship, whereupon, by signs, it was agreed that one of their men should come in the skiff aboard the ship, while in pledge for him, one of our men went on land.

This stranger being in the ship made great wondering at all things: and the Captain gave him to taste of the ship's meat and drink and wine, but he made no countenance of liking these. Then the Captain gave him some trifles, which he liked well and took them with him to land where he was delivered, and our man received back again.

Hereby the Captain, perceiving these strange people to be of countenance and conversation proceeding from a nature given to fierceness and rapine, and he being not yet well prepared in his

* The present Resolution Island.
† Eskimos of Baffin Island.

ship for defence, he set sail presently and departed thence to take more time to prepare for defence.

They passed to the southern side of the strait, and there anchored and prepared to defend themselves the best they could as need should be; which was not easily to be done, having so small a ship, and she now armed with so few and weakened men, who had so great labours and diseases suffered at the sea.

On this southern shore the Captain with some of his men went on shore on an island, and climbed to the top of a high mountain to discover what he could of the straits, of the sea, and of the land about. From there he saw two headlands at the furthest end of the straits and a great opening between them which, by reason of the great flooding tides which they found coming out of the same, they judged to be the West Sea, whereby to pass to Cathay and to East India.

Withal they also espied in a valley right under them three houses covered with leather of seal skins, like tents, and also two dogs. And presently, to avoid danger, Captain Frobisher with his men repaired to the boat at the sea shore, but as soon as they had entered it they espied a great boat* of that country, with men therein, hard by them, who made signs of friendship. But the Captain would not trust them, and made signs to one of them to come into his boat, which the stranger did. Thereafter the master of our ship went on land to the people who received him and led him by the hand into their houses, or rather cottages.

Thus, having got the master among them, some of them made secret signs to the savage who was held for pledge in our boat that he should escape into the water; which signs Captain Frobisher perceived. And, therefore, having in his hand a fair long dagger, he held the point thereof to the strange man's breast threatening by signs to kill him if he did once stir.

Meantime the master was led into their houses and there saw their manner of food and life, which is very strange and beastly. And the master being returned to the boat and entered therein, the stranger kept for pledge was delivered on land, and presently another of those strange men went willingly in the Captain's boat aboard the ship to see the same: to whom was given many trifles of haberdashery, which pleased him well.

* The Eskimos possessed two types of boats; large, open, skin boats called *umiaks;* and the one-man, decked canoes called *kayaks.*

And he being in the ship, Captain Frobisher had talk with him by signs that he should be their pilot through the straits into the West Sea, which he agreed unto. This strange pilot was then carried back again to land to prepare himself and his own boat. But because the Captain did wisely foresee that these strange people were not to be trusted, he told the boat crew that they should set that strange pilot on the point of a certain rock of an island which he assigned them: which was within his own sight so he might have rescued them if any force should have been offered against them.

But these foolish men (being five of them in all in the boat) having set on land this stranger at the place appointed, immediately, and contrary to the Captain's commandment, rowed further beyond that point and out of his sight. And after that the Captain never saw them again, nor could hear anything of them.

Thus the Captain, having lost his boat and five of his best men (to his great discomfort) still remained with the ship there at anchor all that day and next night hoping to hear of them again. But he could not hear or know anything of them, and thereby he judged they were taken and kept by force.

Wherefore the next morning, which was the 20th day of August, he set sail with the ship and passed along by their houses, as near as he could, and caused his trumpet to sound and shot a piece of ordnance over the houses. But with all this he could see nothing nor hear of his boat or men. But he heard the people of the land laugh, and then he swore not to make peace again with them, but rather to depart from thence to other places, there to try and find some other people of that land to whom these late doings were unknown, and of them to take some prisoners in reprisal for his own men.*

He sailed for the space of three days, and finding no other people, he then returned again to the same place where he lost his boat and men.

Being come there he perceived that all the men of the land were gone from thence, and their houses also, which was to his greatest discomfort: for now he was in despair of the recovery of his boat and men any more.

* It is quite possible that the seamen deliberately deserted to the Eskimos. Frobisher was a fierce disciplinarian and even desertion on the Baffin coast might have been preferable to suffering his displeasure.

Also being thus maimed by the loss he had suffered, he utterly despaired how to proceed further on his voyage towards Cathay. And most of all he was oppressed with sorrow that he should return back again to his country without bringing any evidence or token of any place whereby to certify to the world where he had been.

So, remaining in this great perplexity and sorrow, more willing to die than to live in that state; suddenly he espied a number of the boats and men of that country coming towards the ship. Whereat he was pleased (though, his ship's weak state being duly considered, he had the more cause to be afraid). But he presented, armed and prepared his ship with all things necessary for defence; and also he covered the chainways and shrouds, and all other places where the enemy might take hold to clamber into the ship. And in the waist of the ship he placed a piece of ordnance, intending to shoot and sink one of their great boats, of which some had twenty men therein, and to have recovered some of them for prisoners with which to redeem his own men.

But when their great boats approached and perceived the defence made against them, only one small boat with one man therein (which was he that first of all came into the ship) dared approach very near to the ship's side, making signs of friendship the while. Whereat the Captain likewise made him signs of friendship, and thus entertained the stranger while he placed himself at the waist of the ship, having at his feet in secret his weapons. The Captain then caused all his men to withdraw from him, whereby he might appear to be alone and without any malice. He made offer of some small things to bring the stranger to the ship's side, but for a long time the man would not approach, which was no small grief to the Captain and the rest. Yet at the last, with the fair offers and enticement with gifts of the Captain, he approached to the ship's side, but stood upon guard with his oar in one hand ready to put off his boat again suddenly if need should be. Now Captain Frobisher called for a bell which he held toward him as a gift, but with a short arm, and when the stranger reached for it the Captain caught hold of the man's wrist and suddenly, by main force of strength, plucked both the man and his light boat out of the sea into the ship in a trice.

So the Captain kept him, without any show of enmity, and made signs to him presently that if he would bring his five men back he should go again at liberty, but he would not seem to understand the Captain's meaning, and therefore he was still kept in the ship with sure guard.

This act was done in the presence of all the rest of his fellows, they being within an arrow shot of the ship; whereat they were all marvellously amazed and thereupon presently cast themselves into council and so departed in great haste toward the land, with great hallowing or howling shouts after their manner, like the howling of wolves or other beasts in the woods.

The Captain with his ship remained there all that day and the next day, but could hear no news of his boat and men. Whereupon, having this strange man prisoner in his ship, he took counsel with the master and others what were best to be done. And they all agreed that, considering their evil and weakened state, (being but thirteen men and boys remaining, and they so tired and sick with the labours of their hard voyage) that to proceed any further would bring great danger to the utter loss of the enterprise.

Therefore on the 25th day of August they set sail with their ship, keeping their course back toward England, and so came to London the 9th day of October, and there were joyfully received with the great admiration of the people, having brought with them their strange man and his boat, which was a great wonder unto the whole city and to the rest of the realm that heard of it.

Frobisher returned to England minus five men, but bringing with him a small piece of blackish rock which had been picked up on an island in his new-found strait. He gave the rock away as a souvenir, and the recipient, apparently out of aimless curiosity, threw it into a fire. The heat brought to light flecks of shining metal the presence of which, in those gold-hungry days, resulted in a wild-eyed conviction that Frobisher had stumbled upon a fabulously rich mine in his newly discovered Meta Incognita. *Assayers tested the ore, and though some cantankerous fellows judged it worthless, there were others who claimed that it was full of gold. Queen Elizabeth, who had a long nose for gold, showed considerable interest and the upshot was that Frobisher was dispatched on a second voyage the following year. In theory he was to have pressed the exploration for the Northwest Passage, but it was understood that his real task was to bring home as much of the supposed gold-bearing ore as he could cram into his ships.*

The following account of the second voyage was written by George Beste, who sailed with Frobisher as his Lieutenant, or second-in-command.

GEORGE BESTE'S ACCOUNT OF THE SECOND VOYAGE

Being furnished with one tall ship of Her Majesty's, named the *Ayde*, of two hundred ton, and two other small barques, the one named the *Gabriel* the other the *Michael*,* and being fitly appointed with all things necessary for the voyage, the said Captain Frobisher, with the rest of his company, came aboard his ships the five and twentieth day of May in the year of our Lord God, 1577.

The eighth of June we set sail from the Orkney Islands having a merry wind by night, and lost sight of all the land, keeping our course west-north-west for the space of twenty-eight days without sight of any land, and saw many monstrous fish, and strange fowl, which seemed to live only by the sea.

The fourth of July the *Michael* (being foremost ahead) shot off a piece of ordnance and struck all her higher sails, indicating to the rest that they descried land, and about ten of the clock at night we made the land, and knew it to be Freeseland.†

It is a marvellous thing to behold, of what great bigness and depth some islands of ice be here, some seventy, some eighty fathoms under water, besides that which is above, seeming to be islands more than half a mile in circuit. All these ice islands are fresh in taste, and seem to be bred in the sounds thereabouts, or in some land near the pole, and with the wind and tides are driven along the coasts.

Having spent four days and nights sailing along this land and finding the coast subject to bitter cold and continual mists, our

* The same two he had sailed with in 1576.

† Greenland.

General determined to spend no more time therein, but to bear out his course towards the straits called Frobisher Straits, after the General's name.

Our General on the morning of the 17th day of July descried land from our main top. And about noon, we made the North Foreland perfect, which otherwise is called Hall's lesser island, whence the ore was taken up which was brought into England by Captain Frobisher this last year. At our arrival here all the seas about the coast were so covered over with huge quantities of great ice that we thought these places might only deserve the name of Mare Glaciale, and be called the Icie Sea.

God having blessed us with so happy a landfall, we bore into the straits and came as near the shore as we might for the ice, and upon the 18th day of July our General, taking the goldfinders with him, attempted to go on shore with a small rowing pinnace upon the small island where the ore was, to prove whether there were any store thereof to be found. But he could not get, in all that island, another piece so big as a walnut.

However, our men which sought the other islands thereabouts, found them all to have good store of the ore, whereupon our General with these good tidings returned aboard.

On Friday the 19th of July, in the morning early, with his best company of gentlemen and soldiers (to the number of forty persons) the General went on shore to discover the habitation of the country people, as also to find out some fit harbour for our ships.

Passing towards the shore with no small difficulty, by reason of the abundance of ice which lay along the coast so thick, we arrived at length upon Hall's greater island.

Leaving our boats here with sufficient guard, we passed up into the country about two English miles and reached the top of a high hill, on the top whereof our men made a cross of stones heaped up of a good height, and solemnly sounded a trumpet, and said certain prayers, honouring the place with the name Mount Warwick. This done, we retired our companies, not seeing anything here worth further discovery, the country seeming barren and full of ragged mountains, in most parts covered with snow. And thus marching back towards our boats, we espied certain of the country people, waving us back again, and making great noise, with cries like the bellowing of bulls, seeming greatly desirous of conference with us. Whereupon the General, being therewith better acquainted, answered them again with the like cries, whereat, and with the noise of our trumpets, they seemed greatly to rejoice, skipping, laughing and dancing for joy. And hereupon we made signs unto them, holding up two fingers, commanding two of our men to go apart from our companies, whereby they might do the like. So that forthwith two of our men and two of theirs met together a good space from the company, neither party having their weapons about them.

Our men gave them pins and such trifles as they had. And they likewise bestowed on our men two bow cases, and such things as they had. They earnestly desired our men to go up into their country, and our men offered them like kindness aboard our ships, but neither party (as it seemed) admitted or trusted the other's courtesy.

The day being thus well near spent, we retired in haste into our boats again, minding forthwith to search along the coast for some harbour fit for our ships; considering that all this while they must lay off-and-on between the two headlands, being continually subject to great danger from fleeting ice.

When the people perceived our departure, they earnestly called us back again, following us almost to our boats; whereupon our General, taking his master with him, went apart unto two of them meaning if they could to lay sure hold upon them and forcibly to bring them aboard, with intent to bestow certain toys and apparel upon the one, and so to dismiss him with all arguments of courtesy, and to retain the other for an interpreter.

The General and his master being met with the two savages, they suddenly laid hold upon them. But the ground underfeet being slippery, their handfast failed, and their prey escaping, ran away and lightly recovered their bows and arrows which they had hid not far from them behind the rocks.

Though being the only two savages in sight, they now so fiercely, desperately, and with such fury assaulted and pursued our General and his master, (who were altogether unarmed) that they chased them to their boats, and hurt the General in the buttocks with an arrow.

Our soldiers (which were before commanded to keep to their boats) perceiving the danger, and hearing our men calling for shot, came speedily to the rescue. When the savages heard the shot of one of our culivers, they ran away. But a servant of my Lord of Warwick, called Nicholas Conyer, overtook one of them and, being a Cornishman and a good wrestler, showed his victim such a

Cornish trick that he made his sides ache for a month after. And so being stayed, one savage was taken alive and brought away, but the other escaped.

Thus with their strange and new prey, our men repaired to their boats and passed to a small island where they resolved to tarry all night, for even now a sudden storm was grown so great at sea, that by no means could they return to their ships.

Here every man refreshed himself with a small portion of victuals, having neither eaten nor drunk all the day before. But because they knew not how long the storm might last, nor how far off the ships might put to sea, nor whether they should ever return to them again or not, they made great spare of their victuals. For they knew full well that the best cheer the country could yield them was golden rocks and stones (a hard food to live upon withal) and that the country people were more likely to eat them, than to give them something to eat. And thus keeping very good watch and ward, they lay there all night upon hard cliffs of snow and ice, both wet, cold and comfortless.

These things thus happening with the company on land, the danger of the ships at sea was no less perilous. Within one hour of the General's departing in the morning, by the negligence of the cook in overheating the stove, and of the workman in making the chimney, the *Ayde* was set on fire, and had been the confusion of us all if, by chance a boy espying it, it had not been speedily, though with great labour and God's help, well extinguished.

This day were divers storms, and by nine of the clock at night the storm was grown so great and continued such until the morning, that it put our ships in no small peril, for having mountains of fleeting ice on every side, some scraped us, and some happily escaped us; but the least of all of them were as dangerous to strike as any rock, and able to have split asunder the strongest ship of the world. Indeed every man on board, both better and worse, had enough to do, with his hands to haul ropes, and with his eyes to look out for danger.

The next morning, being the 20th of July, as God would, the storm ceased, and the General, espying the ships, came happily aboard and then from this northern shore we struck over towards the southerland.

The 21st of July, we discovered a bay which ran into the land, that seemed a likely harbour for our ships, wherefore our General rowed thither with his boats to make proof thereof, and with his goldfinders to search for ore. Here all the sands and cliffs did so glitter that it seemed to be all gold, but upon trial being made it proved no better than black lead and verified the proverb – All is not gold that shineth.

Upon the 22nd of July we bare farther into Frobisher's Strait and came to anchor thinking ourselves in good security. But we were soon greatly endangered with a piece of drift ice which struck on our stern such a blow that we feared lest it had struck away our rudder. Being forced now to cut our cable to escape, we were fain to set our foresail to run further up within a very narrow channel.

Upon a small island called Smith's Island (because our smith set up his forge there) was found a mine of silver, but the ore was not won out of the rocks without great labour. Here our goldfinders made assay of such ore as they had found upon the Northerland, and found four sorts thereof to hold gold in good quantities.

Upon another small island here was also found a great dead fish which, so it seemed, had been embalmed with ice. It was round like to a porpoise, being about twelve foot long, and having a horn of two yards length growing out of the snout or nostrils. This horn is wreathed and straight, like in fashion to a taper made of wax, and may truly be thought to be the sea Unicorn.* This horn is to be reserved as a jewel by the Queen Majesty's commandment, in her wardrobe of robes.

Tuesday the 23rd of July divers of the gentlemen desired our General to suffer them, to the number of twenty or thirty persons, to march up thirty or forty leagues in the country, to the end they might explore the inland and do some acceptable service for their country. But the General, well considering the short time he had in hand, and the greedy desire our country hath for gain, bent his whole endeavour only to find a mine to freight his ships, and to leave the exploration (by God's help) hereafter to be accomplished.

Therefore the twenty-sixth of July he departed over to the Northland with the two barques, leaving the *Ayde* riding in Jackman's Sound.

The barques came the same night to anchor in a sound upon the Northland, where the tides did run so swift, and the place was so subject to indrafts of ice, that by reason thereof they were

* A Narwhal.

greatly endangered. They found a very rich mine, and had got almost twenty ton of ore together when, upon the 28th of July, the ice came driving into the Sound where the barques rode, in such sort that they were therewith greatly distressed. The *Gabriel*, riding astern the *Michael*, had her cable torn asunder by a piece of driving ice, and lost another anchor. Having but one cable and anchor left (for she had lost two before) and the ice still driving upon her, she was (by God's help) well fenced from the danger by one great island of ice which came aground hard ahead of her which, if it had not so chanced, I think surely she had been cast upon the rocks with the ice.

The *Michael* moored upon this great ice and rode under the lee thereof; but about midnight, by the weight of itself, and the setting of the tides, the ice broke apart within half the barque's length, and made a sudden and fearful noise.

Toward the morning we weighed anchor and went further up the straits, leaving our ore which we had digged, behind us.

In one of the small islands here we found a tomb wherein the bones of a dead man lay and, our savage being with us, we demanded by signs whether his countrymen had slain this man and eaten his flesh. He made signs to the contrary, and indicated that he was eaten by wolves and wild beasts.

Here also was found hid under stones good store of fish, and sundry other things of the inhabitants: as sleds, bridles, kettles of fish skins, knives of bone, and such other like. Taking in his hand one of those country bridles, our savage caught one of our dogs and hampered him handsomely therein, as we do our horses, and with a whip in his hand he taught the dog to draw a sled, as we do horses in a coach. They thus use dogs for that purpose as we do our horses. And we found since that the lesser sort of dogs they feed fat, and keep them as domesticated cattle in their tents for their eating.

The 29th of July, about five leagues from Beare's Sound, we discovered a bay which was a fit harbour for our ships, and this is the furthest place that this year we have entered up within the straits. It is reckoned from the cape of the Queen's Foreland, which is the entrance of the straits, not above ninety miles.

Upon this island was found good store of the ore, which in the washing held gold plainly to be seen; whereupon it was thought best to load here, than to seek further for better ore, and spend time with jeopardy. Therefore our General, setting the miners to work, and showing first a good precedent of a painful labourer and a good captain in himself, gave good examples for others to follow him; whereupon every man, both better and worse, with their best endeavours, willingly laid to their helping hands.

The next day, being the 30th of July, the *Michael* went over to Jackman's Sound for the *Ayde* and the whole company to come thither.

Upon the main land over against the Countess of Warwick's Island, we discovered and beheld to our great marvel, the poor caves and houses of those country people, which same serve them for their winter dwellings. They are made two fathom underground, in compass round like to an oven, having holes like to a fox to enter by.

From the ground upward they build with whale bones (for lack of timber) which, bending one over another, are handsomely compacted in the top, and are covered over with seal skins which, instead of tiles, fenceth them from the rain. In each house they have only one room, having the one half of the floor raised with broad stones a foot higher than the other, whereon after strewing moss, they make their nests to sleep in. They defile these dens most filthily with their beastly feeding, and dwell only in one place until they are forced to seek a sweeter air, and a new home. They are (no doubt) a dispersed and wandering nation, as the Tartars, and live in hordes and troups without any certain abode, as may appear by sundry circumstances of our experience.

Here our captive (being ashore with us to declare the use of such things as we saw) stayed alone behind the company, and did set up five small sticks round in a circle, one by another, with one small bone placed just in the midst of all: which thing, when one of our men perceived it, he called us back to behold the matter, thinking that he had meant some charm or witchcraft therein. But the best conjecture we could make thereof was that he would thereby signify to his countrymen the memory of our five men which they betrayed the last year, and also that he himself was taken and kept prisoner.

Thereupon, we calling the matter to his remembrance, he gave us plainly to understand by signs that he had knowledge of the taking of our five men the last year. And when we made him signs that they were slain and eaten, he earnestly denied it, and made signs to the contrary.

The first of August, Captain Yorke, with the *Michael*, came into Jackman's Sound and declared unto us that the last night past he came to anchor in a certain bay where he discovered tents of the country people. Going with his company ashore, he entered into them, but found the people departed, as it should seem, for fear of their coming. But amongst sundry strange things which they found in these tents there was raw and new killed flesh of unknown sort, with dead carcasses and bones of dogs, and I know not what. They also beheld (to their greatest marvel) a doublet of canvas made after the English fashion, a shirt, a girdle, three shoes for contrary feet and of unequal bigness, which they well conjectured to be the apparel of our five poor countrymen which were intercepted the last year by these country people.

Which informations, when he had delivered them to the company, we determined forthwith to investigate the matter. Hereupon Captain Yorke, accompanied by thirty or forty persons in two small rowing pinnaces, made towards the place where they had discovered the tents of those people and here he set some of the company ashore under the mate, to encompass the savages on the one side, whilst the Captain and his boats might entrap them on the other side. Landing at last at the place where the people had been, they found the tents removed. Notwithstanding this, our men marched up into the country, passing over two or three tedious mountains, and by chance espied certain tents in a valley and, besetting them about, determined to take the people if they could. But the savages, having descried our company, launched one great and another small boat, being about sixteen or eighteen persons, and very narrowly escaping, put themselves to sea.

Whereupon our soldiers on the shore discharged their pieces and followed them, thinking the noise, being heard by our boats at sea, would bring our boatmen to that place. And thereupon, indeed, our men which were in the boats did come and forced the country people to put themselves ashore again upon a point of land. Our men so speedily followed that they had little leisure left them to make any escape. So soon as the savages landed each of them broke his oar, thinking by that means to prevent us carrying away their boats, for want of oars. Then, desperately turning upon our men, resisted them manfully in their landing, so long as their arrows and darts lasted, and after that, by gathering up those arrows which our men shot at them, yes, and even plucking our arrows out of their bodies, so they encountered us afresh and maintained their cause until both weapons and life utterly failed them. When they found they were mortally wounded (being ignorant what mercy meaneth) with deadly fury they cast themselves headlong from the rocks into the sea, lest perhaps their enemies should prey off their dead carcasses (for they supposed us to be eaters of man's flesh).

In this conflict one of our men was dangerously hurt in the belly with one of their arrows, but of the savages five or six were slain. The rest escaped among the rocks, saving two women, whereof the one being old and ugly, our men thought she had been a devil or some witch, and therefore let her go. The other, being young and encumbered with a sucking child at her back, hiding herself behind the rocks, was espied by one of our men who, supposing she had been a man, shot through the hair of her head and pierced through the child's arm, whereupon she cried out and was taken. Our surgeon, meaning to heal her child's arm, applied salves thereto. But she was not acquainted with such kind of surgery and plucked those salves away, and by continual licking with her own tongue (not much unlike our dogs) healed up the child's arm.

And now considering their sudden flying from our men, and their desperate manner of fighting, we began to suspect that we had heard the last news of our men, which last year were betrayed of these people. And considering also their ravenous and bloody disposition in eating any kind of raw flesh or carrion, however stinking, it is to be thought that they had slain and devoured our men. For the doublet which was found in their tents had many holes therein, being made with their arrows and darts.

Having now got a woman captive, for the comfort of our savage man, we brought them both together, and every man desired to behold the manner of their meeting, the which was more worth the beholding than can be well expressed by writing. At their first encounter they beheld each the other for a good time without speech or word uttered, with great change of colour and countenance, as though it seemed the grief and disdain of their captivity had taken away the use of their tongues and utterance. The woman at the first turned away and began to sing, as though she thought upon another matter; but being again brought together, the man broke up the silence first, and with stern countenance began to tell a long solemn tale to the woman, whereunto she gave good hearing. Afterwards, they being grown into more familiar acquaintance I think the one would hardly have lived without the comfort of the other. Yet, insofar as we could perceive (albeit they lived continually together) yet did they never use each other as man and wife. The woman did all necessary things that appertained to a good housewife, as in making clean their cabin, and every other thing that appertained to his ease. When he was seasick, she would make him clean, she would kill and flay the dogs for their eating, and dress his meat. Only I think it worth the noting that the man would never shift himself, except he had first caused the woman to depart out of his cabin; and they both were most shameful lest any of their private parts should be discovered either of themselves or any other person.

On Monday, the 6th of August, the Lieutenant, with all the soldiers, for the better guard of the miners, pitched their tents in the Countess' Island, and fortified the place for their better defence as well as they could; when, being all at labour, they perceived upon the top of a hill a number of the country people waving with a flag and making great outcries unto them. These were of the same company which had lately encountered our men, being come to complain of their late losses and to entreat (as it seemed) for restitution of the woman and child. Whereupon the General, taking the savage captive with him, and setting the woman where they might best perceive her, in the highest place of the island, went over to talk with them.

This captive, at the first encounter with his friends, fell so into tears that he could not speak a word for a great space; but after a while, overcoming his weakness, he talked with his companions and bestowed upon them such toys and trifles as we had given him. Whereby we noted that they are very kind one to the other, and greatly sorrowful for the loss of their friends.

Our General, by signs, required his five men back which they took captive the last year, and promised them not only to release those which we had taken, but also to reward them with great gifts and friendship. Our savage made signs in answer from them, that our men should be delivered us, and were yet living, and made signs likewise unto us that we should write letters unto them.

The next morning early, being the 7th of August, they called again for the letter which, being delivered unto them, they speedily departed, making signs with three fingers, while pointing to the sun, that they meant to return within three days.

I thought the Captain's letter well worth the remembering,

and therefore have repeated here the same, as by himself it was hastily written.

> *In the name of God, in whom we all believe, who, I trust, has preserved your body and souls amongst these infidels, I commend me unto you. I will be glad to seek by all means you can devise, for your deliverance, either with force or with any commodities within my ships, which I will not spare for your sakes, or anything else I can do for you. I have captive of theirs a man, a woman, and a child, which I am contented to deliver for you; but the man I carried away from hence last year is dead in England. Moreover, you may declare unto them that if they deliver you not, I will not leave a man alive in their country. And thus unto God, whom I trust you do serve, in haste I leave you, and to Him we will daily pray for you. This Tuesday morning, the seventh of August, anno 1577.*
>
> *Yours to the uttermost of my power.*
>
> *Martin Frobisher.*
>
> *I have sent you by these bearers pen, ink and paper, to write back unto me again, if personally you cannot come to certify me of your estate.*

Saturday, the 11th of August, the people showed themselves again, and called unto us from the side of a hill over against us. The General (with good hope to hear of his men) went over unto them. There were only three in sight, but greater numbers were hid behind the rocks and our men, justly suspecting them, kept aloof. In the meanwhile, others of our men who stood on the Countess' Island saw divers of the savages creeping behind the rocks towards our men; whereupon the General presently returned without tidings of his missing men, nor did we ever after hear aught of them.

Now our work was growing towards an end. Though having only five poor miners, and the help of a few gentlemen and soldiers, we had brought aboard almost two hundred tons of gold ore in the space of twenty days. And upon Wednesday, being the 21st of August, we fully finished the whole work. And it was now good time to leave; for, as the men were well wearied, so their shoes and clothes were well worn, their basket bottoms torn out, their tools broken, and the ships reasonably well filled.

Some, with over-straining themselves, received hurts not a little dangerous, some having their bellies broken, and others their legs made lame. And about this time the ice began to congeal and freeze about our ship's sides at night, which gave us a good argument of the sun's declining southward, and put us in mind to make more haste homeward.

The arrival home of the three ships with their cargoes of ore resulted in a frenzy of gold fever. Michael Lok, in particular, seems to have believed that the fortunes of all the adventurers were made, and he was instrumental in the establishment of furnaces where relatively large batches of the ore were smelted. Gold in worthwhile quantities was produced from the ore — or at least it was produced from somewhere. Enthusiasm for the mines of Meta Incognita *knew no bounds, and Frobisher was the man of the hour. The excitement took tangible form in the outfitting of a fleet of fifteen ships to proceed to the mines the following year.*

Beste again accompanied Frobisher, commanding the Anne Frances, *and wrote the following account of the voyage.*

GEORGE BESTE'S ACCOUNT OF THE THIRD VOYAGE

Having received our articles of direction, we departed from Harwich the 31st of May with a fleet of fifteen vessels. We at length came by the coast of Ireland at Cape Cleare, the 6th of June, and gave chase there to a small barque which was supposed to be a pirate or rover on the seas; but it fell out indeed that they were poor men of Bristol who had met with a company of Frenchmen who had spoiled and slain many of them, and left the rest so sore wounded that they were like to perish in the sea, having neither hand to help themselves withal, nor victuals to sustain their hungry bodies. Our General, who well understandeth the office of a soldier and an Englishman, and knoweth well what the necessity of the sea meaneth, pitying much the misery of the poor men, relieved them with surgery and salves to heal their hurts, and with meat and drink to comfort their pining hearts. Some of them having neither eat nor drink more than olives and stinking water in many days before (as they reported). And after this good deed done, having a large wind, we kept our course upon our voyage.

The last of June the *Salamander*, being under both her courses and bonnet sails, happened to strike a great whale with her stem with such a blow that the ship stood still and stirred neither forward nor backward. The whale thereat made a great and ugly noise and cast up his body and tail, and so went under water, and within two days after there was found a great whale dead, floating above water, which we supposed was that the *Salamander* struck.

The second day of July, meeting great quantities of ice early in the morning, we had sight of the Queen's Foreland, and one of our fleet, named the barque *Dennys*, being of a hundred ton burden, seeking a way amongst this ice, received such a blow with a block of ice that she sunk down therewith, in the sight of the whole fleet. However, having signified her danger by shooting off a piece of great ordnance, the succour of other ships came so readily unto them that the men were all saved.

Now this was a more fearful spectacle for the fleet to behold, for the ships being encompassed on every side with ice, there arose a sudden and terrible tempest at the southeast, which brought together all the ice to seaward of us upon our backs, and debarred us of recovering sea room again.

Being thus encompassed with danger on every side, sundry men with sundry devices sought the best way to save themselves. Some of the ships, where they could find a place more clear of ice, and get a little berth of sea room, did take in their sails and there lay adrift. Others fastened and moored anchor upon a great island of ice, and rode under the lee thereof. And again some were so fast shut up and encompassed that they were fain to submit themselves and their ships to the mercy of the unmerciful ice. These crews strengthened the sides of their ships with chunks of cables, beds, masts, planks, and such like, which being hanged overboard on the sides of their ships, might the better defend them from the outrageous sway and strokes of the said ice. Some other men, having pikes, pieces of timber, and oars in their hands, stood by almost all day and night, without any rest, bearing off the force and breaking the sway of the ice, with such incredible pain and peril that it was wonderful to behold; which ice otherwise no doubt had striken quite through and through the sides of their ships. And yet many of the ships, even those of greatest burdens, were heaved up between islands of ice a foot out of the sea above their watermarks, having their knees and timbers within board both bowed and broken therewith.

Amidst these extremities, whilst some laboured for defence of the ships and sought to save their bodies, others of more milder spirits sought to save the soul by devout prayer and mediation to the Almighty.

Thus all the gallant fleet and miserable men, without hope of ever getting forth again, distressed with these extremities, remained here all the whole night and part of the next day.

The seventh of July, as men nothing yet dismayed, we cast about towards the inward and made a point of land which some mistook for a place in the Frobisher Straits, but how we should be so far shot up so suddenly within the said straits, the expertest mariners began to marvel, thinking it a thing impossible that they could be so far wrong in their accounts and navigation. Howbeit, many confessed that they found a swifter course of flood tide here than they had observed the previous year. And truly it was wonderful to hear and see the rushing and noise that the tides do make in this place, with so violent a force that our ships were turned sometimes round about even in a moment, after the manner of a whirlpool; and the noise of the stream was no less to be heard afar off than the waterfall of London Bridge.*

The tenth of July, the weather still continuing thick and dark, some of the ships in the fog lost sight of the Admiral† and the rest of the fleet and, wandering to and fro' with doubtful opinion whether it were best to seek back again to seaward through great store of ice, or to follow on a doubtful course in a sea, bay, or straits, they knew not, or along a coast whereof by reason of the dark mists they could not discern the dangers, if by chance any

* Frobisher's fleet was now well into Hudson Strait, and to him must go (though the history books do not acknowledge it) credit for the discovery which was later exploited by Henry Hudson.

† The leader of this type of expedition was called the General, while the ship he sailed in was called the Admiral.

rock or broken ground should lie off the place, as commonly in these parts it doth.

Some hoped to save themselves on chests, and some determined to tie the hatches of the ships fast together and to bind themselves fast thereunto and so to be towed with the ship's boat ashore, which otherwise could not receive half of the company. But if by these means they had happily arrived ashore, they should either have perished for lack of food to eat, or else should themselves have been eaten by those ravenous, bloody, and man-eating people of the land.

Most of the fleet followed the course of the General, who led them the way and passed up above 180 miles into these doubtful and supposed straits, having always a fair continent upon their starboard side, and a continuance still of an open sea before them.

Some of our company affirm that they also had sight of a continent upon their larboard side at 60 leagues within the supposed straits. All the aforesaid tract of land seemeth to be more fruitful and better stored of grass. There were to be seen more deer, wild fowl, such as partridges, larks, seamews, gulls, guillemots, falcons, ravens, bears, hares, foxes, and other things, than any other part we have yet discovered. And here Luke Ward, a gentleman of the company, traded merchandise and did exchange knives, bells, looking-glasses, etc. with the country people who brought him fowl, fish, bear-skins, and such like, as their country yieldeth. Here also they saw some of those greater boats of the country, with twenty persons in apiece.

Now, after the General had bestowed many days here, not without many dangers, he turned back again. And sailing along this coast (it being the back side of the supposed continent of America), he perceived a great sound to go through into Frobisher's Straits. And so he departed towards these straits, thinking it were high time now to recover his port of the last year and to provide the fleet of their loading of ore.

Now the report of the dangers experienced by divers ships, published amongst the fleet, with the remembrance of the perils past, and those present before their face, brought no small fear and terror into the hearts of many considerate men; so that some began privily to murmur against the General for this wilful manner of proceeding. Some desired to discover some harbour thereabouts to refresh themselves and reform their broken vessels for a while, until the north and northwest winds might disperse the ice and make the place more free to pass. Others, forgetting themselves, spoke more undutifully in this behalf, saying: that they had as leave be hanged when they came home, as without hope of safety, to seek a pass, and so to perish amongst the ice.

In the meantime, whilst the fleet lay thus doubtful and without any certain resolution what to do, being close upon the leeshore, there arose a sudden and terrible tempest at the south south-east, whereby the ice began marvellously to gather about us.

Whereupon every man, as in such case of extremity he thought best, sought the wisest way for his own safety. The most part of the fleet, which were further shot up within the straits, followed the course of the General who led them the way, took in their sails and laid amongst the ice, and so passed over the storm. Howbeit, the other ships which plied out to seaward had an extreme storm for a longer season.

In this storm, being the 26th of July, there fell much snow, with such bitter cold air that we could scarce see one another for the same, nor open our eyes to handle our ropes and sails. The snow was above half a foot deep upon the hatches of our ship, which did so wet through our poor mariners' clothes that he that had five or six changes of apparel, had scarce one dry thread left upon his back; which kind of wet and coldness, together with the over labouring of the poor men amidst the ice, bred no small sickness amongst the fleet. This somewhat discouraged some of the poor men, who had not experienced the like before, every man persuading himself that the winter there must needs be extreme, where there be found so unseasonable a summer.

The General, notwithstanding the great storm, followed his own former resolution and sought by all means possible to recover his port. Where he saw the ice ever so little open, he got in at one gap, and out at another, and so himself valiantly led the way through to induce the fleet to follow after, and with incredible pain and peril, at length got through the ice. Upon the 31st of July he recovered his long wished-for port after many attempts, and sundry times being put back, and came to anchor in the Countess of Warwick's Sound. But in the entrance thereof (when he thought all peril past) he encountered a great island of ice which gave the *Ayde* such a blow that it forced the anchor fluke through the ship's bows under the water, which caused so great a leak that only with much ado did they preserve the ship from sinking.

Now, whilst the mariners were clearing their ships and mending that which was amiss, the miners followed their labours for getting together of sufficient ore.

The seventeenth of August the Captains with their companies chased and killed a great white bear, which same adventured against them and made a fierce assault upon twenty armed men. And he served them for good meat many days after.

In the middle of the month the General with two boats and good numbers of men went to Beare's Sound to see if he could encounter or apprehend any of the cannibals, for sundry times they showed themselves busy thereabouts, as though minded to encounter our company who were working there at the mines in no great numbers. But when the savages perceived any of our ships to ride there, never did they show themselves there at all.

The thirtieth of August, the masons finished a house of lime and stone upon the Countess of Warwick's Island, to the end that we might prove against the next year whether the snow could overwhelm it, the frosts break it up, or the country people dismember it. And the better to allure those brutish and uncivil people to courtesy against the time of our returning, we left therein divers of our country's toys, as bells and knives (wherein they specially delight); also pictures of men and women in lead, men on horseback, looking-glasses, whistles and pipes. Also in the house was made an oven, and bread left baked therein for them to see and taste.

We buried the timber of a fort we had intended to build, with many barrels of peas, meal, grist and sundry other good things which were to have been the provisions for those we had intended to inhabit the place, had this not been made impossible by the loss of part of their house timbers with the barque *Dennys.* Instead of these things we freighted our ships full of ore, which we hold of far greater price.

Having now received directions for our voyage homeward, the last day of August the whole fleet departed from the Countess' Sound excepting the *Judith* and the *Anne Frances* who stayed for taking in fresh water, and the two barques *Michael* and *Gabriel* with the *Busse* of Bridgewater, who stayed for their loading of ore.

The first of September I went to Beare's Sound in my pinnace to fetch my men aboard who had been upon the shore. But the wind grew so immediately, upon our landing, that the ships at sea were in great danger and greatly feared to be utterly lost. The ships were not able to tarry amongst the mighty rocks threatening on one side and driving islands of cutting ice on the other side, and our small pinnaces could not recover their ships.

The General willed me and my company to lodge aboard the *Busse* and himself with the rest of his men went aboard the two barques. The morning following, the storm was far worse, the sea being more swollen, and the fleet gone quite out of sight. So now our doubts began to grow great, for the *Busse*, which was most heavily laden, rode so far to leeward of the harbour mouth that we were not able, for the rocks, to lead it out by sail.

In the morning the General departed to sea in the barque *Gabriel* to seek the rest of the fleet (the *Judith* having already gone) leaving the *Busse* and the *Michael* behind. Then the *Michael* set sail to follow the General, and could give the *Busse* no relief, though they earnestly desired the same.

I was left in hard election of two evils; either to abide my fortune with the *Busse*, which was doubtful of ever getting out, or else being towed in my small pinnace at the stern of the *Michael* through the raging seas, for that barque was not able to receive half of the company I had with me.

Resolving to commit myself to the fortunes of God and sea, I was dangerously towed at the stern of the barque for many miles until at last we espied the *Anne Frances* under our lee; the master of which, because of his good regard of duties toward his General and his Captain honestly abode to hazard a dangerous road all the night long, notwithstanding the stormy weather when all the rest of the fleet departed. And the pinnace no sooner came alongside the ship and the men entered, when she presently shivered and fell all to pieces and sunk with the poor men's furniture.

There were lost in the whole fleet about twenty boats during this storm, and some men stricken overboard into the sea and utterly lost. Yet thanks be to God, all the fleet arrived safely in England about the first of October. Even the *Busse* got away, who being abandoned by the others, and in great danger of ever getting forth, was forced to seek a way northward through an unknown channel, a very dangerous attempt.

There died in all this voyage not above forty persons, which number is not great considering how many ships were in the fleet, and how strange the fortunes we passed.

Neither Frobisher nor any of his companions were destined to return to Meta Incognita. *Shortly after their arrival home, the sickening discovery was made that there was, after all, little real gold in the ore, though there was much fools' gold. What happened to the sponsors of the expedition is not clear, but as they had undoubtedly incurred the not inconsiderable wrath of Elizabeth, their fate was probably hard. The fate of the 1300 tons of ore which had been brought home was unknown until quite recently, when dredging operations in an English harbour brought up quantities of iron pyrites which had originated on Baffin Island.*

Even the physical discoveries were lost. For some inscrutable reason, the geographers and map-makers of the time transplanted Frobisher's Sound to the south-east coast of Greenland, and it was not fully restored to its rightful place until a young American, Charles Hall, who wintered in the area in 1860-61, discovered relics of the Frobisher expeditions and heard from the Eskimos a most accurate recital of the encounters their ancestors had had with the white men. Hall showed that the sound was in reality only a deep bay, but it is now one of the most important places in the Canadian Arctic, being the site of the town of Frobisher Bay and of a great airport used by modern airliners on the circumpolar routes between Europe and North America.

Hall also unravelled the mystery of the missing five men of Frobisher's first expedition. The Eskimos gave him a circumstantial account of how the five white men had eventually returned to the Countess of Warwick's Island and there built themselves a small sailing vessel from materials left behind by the third expedition. Hall later found physical evidence of the building of this little vessel, and there is no reason to doubt the Eskimo account of how the five men, despite the well-meant advice of the natives amongst whom they had evidently been living amicably for four years, tried to set sail for England far too early in the season. But sail they did, and this time they vanished without a trace, and for all time.

As for Frobisher, his was a lucky star. Joining the naval service he rose so rapidly that, by the time the Spanish Armada threatened England, Frobisher commanded one of the three largest of the English ships which, in company with John Hawkins' and Francis Drake's two vessels, led the spectacularly successful attack upon the Spaniards. He was knighted for this, and his popularity was so great that it rivalled Drake's. He continued to display his fighting prowess until 1594 when, after successfully leading an assault on a Spanish fort at Brest, he was mortally wounded. In the register of St. Andrew's Parish Church in Plymouth there is this entry, marking the end of a magnificently adventurous life:

"November 22nd. (1594). Martin Frobisher, knight, being at the fort built against Brest by the Spaniards, deceased at Plymouth this day, whose entrails were here interred, but his corpse was carried hence to be buried in London."

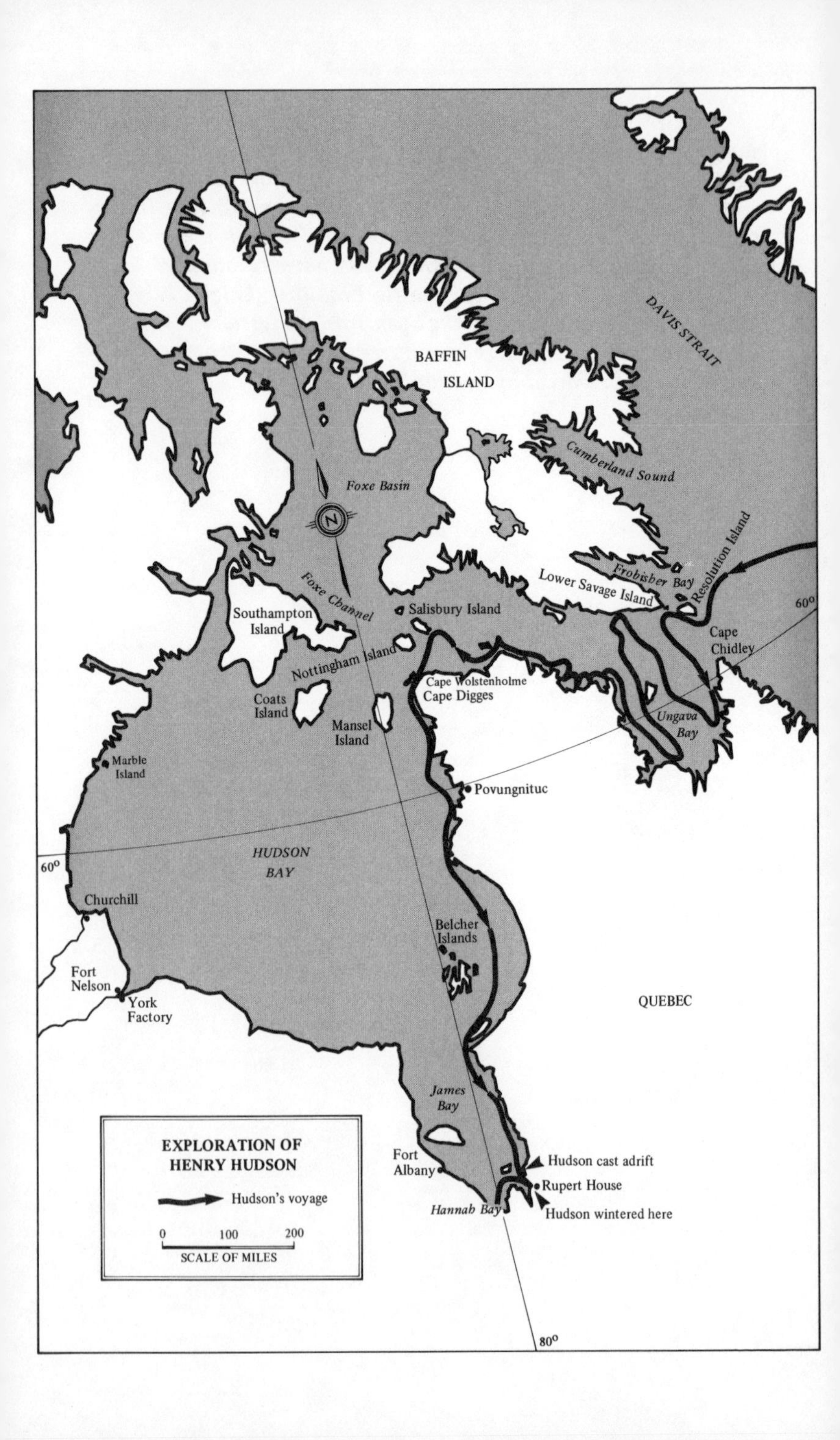
BAFFIN
ISLAND
DAVIS STRAIT
Cumberland Sound
Foxe Basin
Foxe Channel
Frobisher Bay
Resolution Island
Lower Savage Island
Salisbury Island
Southampton Island
Nottingham Island
Cape Chidley
Cape Wolstenholme
Cape Digges
Coats Island
Mansel Island
Ungava Bay
Marble Island
Povungnituc
60°
HUDSON BAY
Churchill
Belcher Islands
Fort Nelson
York Factory
QUEBEC
James Bay
Fort Albany
Hudson cast adrift
Rupert House
Hannah Bay
Hudson wintered here
80°
EXPLORATION OF HENRY HUDSON
Hudson's voyage
0
100
200
SCALE OF MILES

II

Henry Hudson's Fateful Voyage

The ignominious end to Frobisher's Arctic ventures did not dampen the enthusiasm of Elizabethan mariners for north-western discovery. Though Frobisher's brave dream had been subverted by the general lust for gold, both he and other seamen of his time were convinced that the Northwest Passage did exist, and that a determined and single-minded effort would reveal it. However, the failure of the two Cabots, of Thorne and finally of Frobisher himself, to force the ice barriers of Skuggifiord temporarily turned men's thoughts away from that potential gateway to the west.

Seven years after the return of the great flotilla from Frobisher's Meta Incognita, *John Davis, another west-of-England mariner, took up the search. Under the auspices of a new company, and supported by the government, he sailed in 1585 with two small vessels. Choosing a more northerly path than Frobisher's, he coasted west Greenland to the Godthaab area and then sailed west, straight through the southern bulge of the Baffin pack, to raise Cape Dyer on Baffin Island, where he turned south, discovered Cumberland Sound, and then made sail for home. His passage through the south Baffin pack barrier was an amazing exploit, and in a sense it was the first major victory by seamen of his period against the ice barriers of the north.*

Davis himself seems to have looked upon this voyage primarily as a successful reconnaissance, and to have felt confident that the passage would now readily be found to the north and west of the strait which is named for him. In the event, his intuitive conviction turned out to be well founded, but he was not to know this. Though he made two more voyages during the two succeeding years, in a dogged attempt to break past the ice which guards the approaches to Baffin Bay and to the north, the ice defeated him each time. His defeats were taken to heart in Europe, with the result that for more than two and a half centuries no more attempts (with one notable exception) were made to find the Northwest Passage by way of Davis Strait.

With Davis' failure to find a passage farther to the north, interest in what was to become known as Hudson Strait was renewed. In 1602 George Weymouth was commissioned by the East India Company to explore this strait and to determine if it indeed offered a passage to Cathay.

Weymouth's ship was to become the most enduring, and deserves to have become the most famous, of all Arctic ships. She was the Discovery, *a barque of only fifty-five tons burthen, but so well built of English oak that she was destined to outlive many of the men who sailed her into the north-western ice on her six Arctic voyages.*

She carried Weymouth across the ice of Davis Strait and, turning her blunt prow northward, might have taken him farther up the coast of Baffin Island than Davis had reached, had not the chaplain threatened to lead a mutiny, and forced Weymouth to turn south again. Passing Frobisher's "Strait," without recognizing it, Weymouth forced the Discovery *through the maelstrom of tide-driven pack ice that blocks the entrance to Hudson Strait; but though the* Discovery *sailed well to the west she was not yet destined to reach the inland sea beyond, for her people were not equal to her strength, and they turned her head for home. Still, Weymouth had seen no land barriers ahead of him, and so the voyage confirmed the belief held in England that this might well be the passage to the distant East.*

Henry Hudson, who was to give his name to this strait, and to the land-locked sea beyond it, lived in the world's eye for only four short years. He came out of total obscurity in 1607, and vanished just as totally in 1611. But during those four years he demonstrated an unequalled passion for the conquest of the icy seas; and his too-brief tale is one unmatched by that of any explorer of the Arctic world through all of history.

Like Frobisher, he was seized by the vision of the Northwest Passage, and in 1607 he persuaded the powerful Muscovy Company of England to support him in a fantastical endeavour to reach Cathay by sailing straight across the top of the world. To accomplish this dramatic objective the generous merchants gave him the forty-ton* Hopewell, *which had been with Frobisher twenty-nine years earlier, and supplied him with a crew of ten men – and one boy.*

Disdaining cautious feints amongst the Arctic islands Hudson sailed directly for the pole. He drove the Hopewell *up to and into the ice to the east of Greenland, and after a bitter struggle with the pack he achieved the phenomenal north latitude of eighty degrees, a point only six hundred miles from the pole itself. But he could go no farther. His ship, already rotten when he sailed from England, was now not much better than a battered hulk. There was no other course but retreat open to Hudson. Yet he did not sail directly, and ignominiously, for home and safety. On the way he explored the Spitzbergen Islands, and in so doing provided the genesis of the greatest Arctic whaling activity of all time, the Spitzbergen fishery, which was soon to draw uncounted vessels into the struggle with the northern ice.*

Hudson had failed in his polar venture, but he still had other strings to his bow. In 1608 he again persuaded the Muscovy Company to sponsor an Arctic voyage, and this time he chose to try to find a passage to Cathay by the north-east, around the top of Russia. This voyage, too, was a heart-breaking battle against the unyielding barriers of ice, and though he reached Novaya Zemlya on the shores of the Kara Sea, he could not force his small and awkward vessel any farther to the east.

On his return home, bearing this second disappointment, he found a third one waiting for him. The Muscovy Company, delighted with the whaling profits that could be made at Spitzbergen, was no longer interested in financing a further search for a northern passage to the Far East.

A lesser man would have accepted this rebuff. Not Henry Hudson. If no one in England would support him, then he would

* At this time it was believed that the central polar sea itself might be ice-free – a belief that lingered into the late nineteenth century.

sail from a foreign port. He went to Amsterdam, and after a harrowing struggle, persuaded the stolid burghers of the Dutch East India Company to back another expedition into the north-east.

The Dutch merchants proved to be as parsimonious as their English contemporaries. They gave Hudson a tiny vessel called the Half Moon, *and found him an unsavoury crew of eighteen men, most of them dockyard scum. Still, it was enough for Hudson. In the early spring of 1609 he sailed to the north, entered the Norwegian Sea, and fought his way through the ice to Novaya Zemlya for a second time. But here he was again brought to a halt, not by the ice this time, but by a mutiny amongst his men. They had had enough of Arctic voyaging; and that was that.*

Hudson might reasonably have returned to Amsterdam, but, being Henry Hudson, this did not even occur to him. He would *find a passage to Cathay, and if his crew would not let him seek it in high latitudes, then he would look for it elsewhere. Remembering that Richard Hakluyt, and other theoretical geographers of the time, contended that North America must be divided into two parts by a "strait" in latitude forty degrees (which lies just south of New York), Hudson extricated the* Half Moon *from the Russian ice and set course south-west across the Atlantic to Newfoundland, and then coasted south. He found no "strait" but he did discover the present site of New York, and he discovered and explored the Hudson River – discoveries that were, to him, only one more disappointment.*

That autumn he sailed the Half Moon *back to England, where she and her whole crew were arrested at the instigation of angry English merchants who were outraged that Hudson had dared to serve a foreign company. Hudson, instead of admitting that he was beaten, and relinquishing the pursuit of his chimera, returned at once to the attack. Calming the merchants down, he managed somehow to persuade them to finance one final Arctic voyage.*

This time his sponsors were three wealthy individuals, Messrs. Smith, Digges, and Lord Wolstenholme, and they provided Hudson with Weymouth's old Discovery, *and a crew of twenty-two weirdly assorted men. On April 17th, 1610, the* Discovery *departed from the Thames; her objective, the western strait lying north of Labrador.*

With Hudson sailed a most mysterious individual (apparently an unfrocked priest) bearing the unlikely name of Abacuk Pricket, who was the sponsors' representative, and who was also a man of singular parts. It is to Pricket that we owe the survival of the only material account which we possess of Henry Hudson's final, fateful voyage.

A LARGE DISCOURSE OF THE SAID VOYAGE, AND THE SUCCESS THEREOF, WRITTEN BY ABACUK PRICKET, WHO LIVED TO COME HOME

In the month of May we reached the Isle of Orkney, and from thence passed to the Faeroes. From thence we sailed to raise the Snowhill-foot, a mountain on the north-west part of Iceland. And in that course we saw the famous Mount Hecla, which cast out much fire, a sign of foul weather to come.

We coasted along betwixt west and north-west until we saw Desolation, which is a great island on the north-west part of Greenland. Here we saw great store of whales, some of which came about and under the ship, but did no harm.

About the last of June we raised land to the north of us and we took the same to be that island which Captain Davis set in the chart at the west side of this strait for which we sought.* We passed this island into a great rippling or overfall of a current. Into the current we went and made our way northward of west until we met with ice which hung upon this island, wherefore we cast about to the south and cleared ourselves, and then stood to the west into a great sound,† amongst a store of floating ice upon which there was a store of seals.

We still made our way north-west, meeting sometimes with ice, and then again clear water. Thus, proceeding betwixt ice and

* Resolution Island.

† Ungava Bay.

ice, we see a great island of ice tumble over, which was a good warning to us not to come near them.

The next day we had a great storm and were driven to put in amongst the ice and there to lie. Some of our men fell sick; I will not say from fear, though I saw no other symptoms to explain their sickness.

The storm ceasing we stood on to the west as the sea and the ice would suffer us. The Master tried to seek to the south, but the more he strove, the worse he was, for he was fast enclosed by ice and began to despair, and (as he afterwards told me) he thought we should never have got out of this ice, but there have perished.

Wherefore he showed us by his chart that we were 100 leagues further than ever any English man was before us in this place and asked us our choice whether to proceed further, or no. Whereupon some of our people wished themselves at home; others wished themselves anywhere else so long as it was away from among the ice; and in this perplexity there passed hot words between some of the people, which words were thought upon a long time after.

There was one man told the Master that, if he had 100£, he would give 90£ thereof to be at home. But the Carpenter made answer to him and said that if *he* had 100£ he would not give 10£ for the same purpose, but that he would consider all his money safe and would, by God's leave, bring it *all* home upon due time.

Well, to work we went and with much labour got the ship clear of the ice. Returning into the strait we stood along on the south shore until, meeting with ice, we stood into the shore and found a harbour in an island. Here we sailed over a rock, at two fathoms and a half depth, which same was completely bare at low water; and on account of this escape we named the place the Isle of God's Mercy.

The Master sent me over to explore this island, where I met with a covey of partridge, but killed only the old one. It was barren land, having nothing thereon but little ponds and torn rocks, as though it had been subject to earthquakes.

We still stood to the west along the south shore until we raised an island having a very fair headland to the west which the Master named Cape Digges. On the other side of it, to the east, was another cape which he called Cape Wolstenholme.

We sent a boat ashore to Digges His Island. Her people came to the north-east side which, being high land, gave them much ado to get to the highest part, where they found some level ground, and deer, of which there were sixteen in one herd; but they could not come nigh them within musket shot.

Thus, walking from place to place, they see to the west a hill higher than all the rest. In this place bred great quantities of wild fowl, and here also our people found the best grass they had seen since their coming from England. They found sorrell and scurvy-grass in great abundance. Also they found huts built by the country people and like to haycocks, within which were great stores of fowls hanged by the necks. They took many of these fowls and carried them down a valley to their boat.

During this time Master Hudson had brought the ship in between the two headlands and had shot off some pieces of ordnance to call the boat on board, for a fog had come down. Our people tried to persuade him to stay here for a time so that we might refresh ourselves with sorrell grass and fowl, but he would not, and sailed down to the south.

The land now bore away to the east and we lost sight thereof. After we had sailed 25 or 30 leagues we came to shallow water, broken ground and rocks, which we passed to the south, in a storm of wind.

Full many days later, we came into the bottom of a bay,* in six or seven fathoms of water, and thence we stood to the north along the western shore until we came to an island where we anchored and took in water and ballast.

Now we continued north, but some two of three days later there fell some arguments about the reasons for our coming into this last bay, and the Master took occasion to revive old matters of the following nature, which were writ down by one Thomas Woodhouse, mathematician, who was of our company.

> *The 10th of September, 1610, after dinner, the Master called all the company together to hear and bear witness, it having been the request of Robert Juet, the Mate, that the Master should redress some abuses and slanders (as he called them) made against himself by our Master.*
>
> *After the Master had heard what Juet could say for himself, there were proved — by others of the company — so many great abuses and mutinous matters and actions, by*

* James Bay.

Juet against the Master, that there was danger in suffering them any longer, and it was therefore a fit time to punish Juet and cut off further occasions of his mutinies.

It was first proved to his face by Bennet Mathew, our Trumpeter, that, upon our first sight of Iceland, Juet confessed that he expected the outcome of the voyage would be manslaughter, and would prove bloody to some.

Secondly, at our coming from Iceland, he did, in the hearing of the company, threaten to turn the ship's head home; but at that time he was pacified by the Master in hopes of amendment of his conduct.

Thirdly, it was deposed by Phillip Staffe, our carpenter, and Arnold Lodly, to Juet's face and upon the Holy Bible, that he had persuaded them to keep muskets charged with powder, and swords ready in their cabins, and that he said the muskets would be charged with shot before the voyage was over.

Fourthly, at the time we were driven to lie amongst the ice and were sore beset thereby, he had used many words tending to mutiny, discouragement and slander of the voyage, which easily took effect on those who were timorous. And, had not the Master in time prevented it, it might easily have overthrown the voyage. And now, being embayed in a deep bay which the Master had desire to see, for some reasons known to himself, Juet's words tended altogether to put the company into a fright of extremity.

For these and divers other base slanders against the Master, Juet was therefore deposed, and Robert Bylot, who had showed himself honest respecting the good of the voyage, was placed Master's Mate in his stead.

Also the Master promised that, if the offenders yet behaved themselves honestly, he would be a means for their good and would forget the injuries.

On Michaelmas Day, (October 11th), we came in and went out from certain islands and from thence we stood to the north and came into shoal water. The weather being thick and foul, we anchored in 6 or 7 fathoms and lay eight days, during which time there was not one hour in which we could have got up our anchor. Then, the wind ceasing, (but the seas still running very high) the Master would have up the anchor, against the opinions of all who knew what would follow thereunto. And when the anchor was on peak, the ship took such a sea that it threw them all from the capstan, and divers of them were hurt. Thus we lost the anchor, but saved most of our cable, for the carpenter had laid his axe ready to cut the cable if occasion should so fall out.

From hence we stood to the south-west for a time until we came to the westernmost bay of all that we had yet discovered.*

In this bay we anchored, and sent on shore our boat. We found the land flat, and our men saw the footing of a savage man and of a duck upon the snowy rocks, and found good store of wood.

We weighed anchor at midnight and thought to stand forth as we came in, but it fortuned that we ran upon the rocks and sat there for twelve hours; but by God's mercy we got off again unhurt, though not unafrighted.

We then stood up to the east, into a bay and anchored, and the Master sent the carpenter and I to look for a place to winter; it being the last of October, the nights long and cold, the earth all covered with snow, and ourselves wearied, having spent three months in the labyrinth of this bay.

The next day we found a place unto which we brought the ship and hauled her on shoal ground, and on the 10th day of November, she was frozen in.†

Now we looked to the lengthening of our provisions. We had been victualled for six months, with good provisions, and might have brought more from home had the Master wished. But these he did not bring, and now we were forced to pinch, for we knew of no new supply until we came the next year to Cape Digges where the wild fowl breed, for that was all our hope. Wherefore the Master proposed a reward to him that killed either beast, fish or fowl.

Our gunner, John Williams, died about the middle of the month; and note what followed:

The Master had kept in his house at London, a young man named Henry Greene, born in Kent of worthy parents; but by the way he lived and spoke he had lost the love of all his friends, and spent all that he had. This Henry Greene was not known to the Adventurers who sent out our ship, but came privily aboard at

* Probably Hannah Bay.

† In Rupert Bay.

Gravesend. At Harwich he and one Wilkinson, of our company, would have deserted. At Iceland he fell out with the surgeon in *Dutch,* and when they went on shore, beat him in *English,* which set all the company in a rage against him, and they had much ado to get the surgeon to come back on board again. I told the Master of it, but he bade me let the matter alone, for (said he) the surgeon had a tongue that would wrong the best friend he had. But Juet, the Master's Mate, must needs put *his* fingers in the embers and told the carpenter a long tale (when he was drunk) that the Master had brought Greene along to spy on those who should displease him.

When the Master heard this tale he would have gone back to Iceland (though we were forty leagues therefrom) and sent Juet home in a fishing vessel. But being otherwise persuaded, all was well; and Greene stood upright, and was very inward with the Master, and was a serviceable man in every way, (though as for religion, he would say that he was like white paper, whereon he could write whatever he would).

Now the gunner being dead, and (as the order is in such cases) if the company stands in need of anything belonging to the man that is deceased, then these things are brought to the main-mast and there sold to them that will give the most for them. Now this gunner had a gray cloth gown and Greene prayed the Master to befriend him so much as to let him have it, being willing to pay for it as much as any other would give. The Master said he should have it, and therefore answered some others who sought for it, that Greene should have it and no one else.

Now, though it was past the time and season, the Master called upon the carpenter to put in hand the building of a house on shore which, on our first coming here (and when it might have been done) the Master would not hear of it. The carpenter told him that the snow and frost was such that he neither could nor would go ahead with such work. When the Master heard this he ferreted the carpenter out of his cabin and struck him, calling him by many foul words and threatening to hang him. The carpenter told the Master that he knew his own place better than the Master did, and that he was no house carpenter, but a ship's carpenter.

The next day after the Master and Philip Staffe, the carpenter, fell out, the carpenter took his fowling-piece and Henry Greene with him, and went off a-hunting. This did anger Master Hudson so much against Greene that he decided Robert Bylot, the mate, must have the gunner's gown, and he had it delivered to him. Henry Greene, seeing this, charged the Master to keep his promise. Then the Master did rail against Greene, telling him that all his friends dared not trust him with twenty shillings, and therefore why should he? And as for wages, he was to have none (yet the Master had promised him as good wages as any man in the ship, and was to have made him one of the Prince's Guard at his homecoming). But you shall see hereafter how the Devil so wrought out of this that Greene did the Master what mischief he could.

God dealt mercifully with us in this time, for in the space of three months we killed at least one hundred dozen of one kind of fowl which was a sort of partridge, but white as milk.* In the spring this fowl left us and in its place came others of divers sorts such as swans, goose, duck and teal, but they were pretty hard to come by.

We searched the woody hills and valleys for all things that had any show of substance for food, however vile. The moss on the ground and the frog in his engendering time were not spared. Amongst divers sorts of buds it pleased God that Thomas Woodhouse found the buds of one kind of tree that were full of turpentine substance, and of this the surgeon made a decoction to drink, and applied the buds hot to them that was troubled with ache in any part. And from this treatment they received present ease.

Now about the time the ice began to break out of the bays there came a savage to the ship, as it were to see and to be seen. He was the first that we had seen in all that time. We treated him well, and used him kindly, hoping for great results from this.

To this savage the Master gave a knife, a looking-glass and buttons, and he received them thankfully and made signs that after he had slept, he would come back again. This he did, and brought with him a sled which he drew after him, and upon it were two deer skins and two beaver skins. He had a bag under his arm out of which he drew those things the Master had previously given him, and laid the knife upon one of the beaver skins, and the glass and buttons on the other, and so gave the whole to the Master, who received them. The savage then took those things back which the Master had given him, and put them into his bag again.

Then the Master showed him a hatchet, for which the savage

* Ptarmigan.

would have given him one of his deer skins, but the Master would have both, and so he got both, although not willingly. After many signs telling us of people to the north and to the south, and signing to us that after so many sleeps he would come again, the savage went his way; but he came back no more.

Now the ice being broken so that a boat might pass, the Master appointed Henry Greene and some others to go fishing. The first day they went, these men caught 500 fish as big as good herring, and also some trout. Here was good hope to have our wants supplied, but these were the most fishes that ever they got in one day, and on many days they got not a quarter so many.

In this time of their fishing, Henry Greene and William Wilson, with others, plotted to take the net and the shallop and so shift for themselves. But the Master first got himself into the shallop, for he would discover to the south and south-west to see if he could meet people, for in that direction he could see the woods had been set on fire by them.

So the Master took the net and shallop, and so much victuals as would serve for nine days, and went to the southward. They that remained on board were appointed to take in water, wood and ballast, and to make the ship ready against his return. He was persuaded that, if he met with the savages, he should have from them a good store of fresh meat. But in the event he returned worse than he went out, and though the inhabitants set the woods on fire before him, yet they would not come to him.

Being at length returned, the Master made ready for the homeward voyage, and first he delivered to the company all the bread in the foreroom, which came to a pound apiece for every man's share, and he wept when he gave it unto them that it was so little. To help themselves to some relief the boat went to fish from Friday morning until Sunday noon, but brought back only 80 small fish for eighteen hungry bellies. Whereupon we weighed anchor and came away from our wintering place, into the sea.

Our bread being gone, that store of cheeses which we had must stop the gap, though they were but five. The company grumbled of this, for they had made account that there were nine cheeses. But those five were equally divided by the Master, though some counselled him to the contrary for there were some who, having it, would make haste to be rid thereof, because they could not govern their appetites.

I know that at another time Henry Greene gave half his bread (of which he had 14 days supply) to a companion to keep, and prayed him not to let him have any until the next Monday. But by Wednesday night he took it back again, having eaten up his first week's bread. Likewise Wilson, the bosun, ate his 14 days bread in one day, and thereafter lay in his bed for two or three days for his pains.

The reason why the Master delivered all of the cheeses was because they were not all of one goodness, and therefore we should see that we had not been done wrong, but that every man had the best and worst together, which was three pounds and a half to last for seven days.

The wind serving, we stood to the north-west and on Monday night, the 18th of June, we fell into the ice and lay fast within sight of land until the following Sunday.

Now the Master told the boy Nicholas Simmes that there would be a breaking open of sea-chests, and a search for bread, and willed him if *he* had any, to bring it to him, which he did, and he delivered to the Master thirty cakes, in a bag.

Being thus in the ice, on Saturday, the one and twentieth of June, at night, Wilson the Bosun, and Henry Greene, came to me where I was lying lame in my cabin, and told me that they and the rest of their associates would turn the Master and all the sick men into the shallop and let them shift for themselves; since there were not fourteen days victuals left aboard the ship, even at the poor allowance we were getting. They further said that here we lay in the ice, the Master not caring to go one way or the other, and that they had not eaten anything these three days past. Therefore they were resolute, either to mend or end, and what they had begun they would go through with, or die.

When I heard this I told them I marvelled to hear so much from them, considering that they were married men and had wives and children, and that they should commit so foul a thing in the sight of God and man as this would be; for why should they banish themselves from their native country by thus putting themselves outside the law?

Henry Greene bade me hold my peace, for he said he knew the worst of it, which was to be hanged when he came home; and therefore, of the two, he would rather be hanged at home than starved abroad. But, considering the goodwill they bore me, they would let me stay in the ship.

I gave them thanks, but told them that I came into the ship

not to foresake her, nor yet to hurt myself and others by any such a deed. Henry Greene then told me that I must take my fortune in the shallop. "If there be no remedy," quoth I, "the will of God be done."

Then away goes Greene in a rage, swearing to cut the throat of any who tried to thwart him; leaving Wilson by me, with whom I had some conference, but to no avail, for he was persuaded to go on with the action while it was hot, lest some of their party should fail them and the mischief they intended to others should fall upon their own shoulders.

Greene came back again and demanded to know what I had said. Wilson answered, "He is in his old song," (not having changed his tune).

Then I again spoke to Greene to persuade him to delay three days, in which time I said I would so deal with the Master that all would be well. Being refused this, I begged with him for two days, nay, for twelve hours. But they still said there was no way for it, but to do it out of hand.

Then I told them that if they would delay till Monday I would join them and I would also justify the action to the authorities when we came home. But this would not serve either, wherefore I told them it must be some worse matter they had in hand than they admitted, and that it was blood and revenge Greene sought, else he would not undertake such a deed at such a time of night. With that Greene took my Bible, which lay before me, and swore that he would do no harm, and whatever he did was for the good of the voyage and for nothing else, and that the rest should swear the like. The like did Wilson swear.

Greene went away and presently in comes Juet who, because he was an ancient man, I hoped to have found some reason in him; but he was worse than Greene, and swore plainly that he would justify the deed upon our homecoming. After him came John Thomas and Michael Pierce, birds of a feather indeed, but I shall let discussion of them pass. Then came Motter and Bennet, of whom I demanded if they were well advised in what they had taken in hand. They answered that they were, and had therefore come to take their oath.

Now because I was later much condemned for preparing this oath, as one that plotted with them, and that by an oath I should bind them together to perform what they had begun, I think it good to set down in writing to the view of all men, to see how well their oath and words agree. And thus it was.

> *You shall be true to God, your Prince, and Country. You shall do nothing but to the glory of God, and to the good of the voyage in hand, and harm to no man.*

I now looked to see more of those companions in mutiny, although there were already too many, but there came no more.

It was dark, and they in readiness to put this deed of darkness into execution. I called Greene and Wilson to me and prayed them not to go on with it in the dark, but to stay until morning, for now, I told them, every man should get his rest. But wickedness sleepeth not.

I asked Henry Greene whom he would put out of the ship, with the Master. He said Philip Staffe the carpenter, John King, and the sick men. I said they would not do well to part with the carpenter. The reason why Philip Staffe was in no high regard with them was that he and his friend John King were condemned for wrong-doing in the victuals, but the chiefest cause was because the Master loved John King and had made him mate, thereby displacing Robert Bylot. This change the company begrudged since King could neither read nor write, and therefore, said they, the Master and his ignorant new mate will carry the ship whither the Master pleases, the Master having forbidden any man to keep account or reckoning of courses sailed, and having taken from all men whatever might serve them for that purpose.

However, I obtained consent of Henry Greene and Wilson that the carpenter should stay, by whose help I hoped that, after the company had satisfied themselves with mutiny, the Master and the rest might be taken back into the ship again. I further hoped that someone or other would give some warning to Philip Staffe, John King, or the Master. And so it might have come to pass had not some of us who were the most forward in this design been prevented from so doing.

This night John King was late up, and they thought he had been with the Master, but he was with the carpenter, who lived in the poop. Coming back he was met by his cabin-mate, Robert Bylot, as if by chance, and they went to their cabin together.

It was not long ere it was day, and then came Bennet to me for water for the kettle. I went into the hold to get the water and when I was in it they shut the hatch on me.

In the meantime Henry Greene and another went to the carpenter and held him in talk, until the Master should come out of his cabin, which he soon did. Then John Thomas and Bennet appeared before the Master while Wilson came behind and seized and bound his arms behind his back. The Master asked what they meant to do, and they told him that he should know when he was in the shallop.

While this was doing, Juet followed John King into the hold, but King was prepared for him and had got a sword, and kept Juet at bay and might have killed him had not others come to help him. So John King was brought up beside the Master.

Then was the shallop hauled up to the ship's side and the poor sick and lame men were called upon to get them into the shallop.

The Master then called to me, for I had come up as well as I could to the hatchway to speak to him. On my knees I besought them, for the love of God, to remember themselves, and do as they would be done unto. They bade me get myself into the cabin, not suffering the Master to speak to me.

The carpenter, Philip Staffe, being at liberty, asked them if they wished to be hanged when they came home. As for himself, he said he would not stay in the ship unless they forced him so to do. They bid him go then, for they would not stop him. "I will," said he, "if I may have my chest and all that is in it." They put it in the shallop and he came to take his leave of me.

I tried to persuade him to stay aboard, saying that if he would, he might so work that all might be well. But he answered that he thought the mutineers would be glad to take them back aboard in any case, for the Master had convinced him that there was no one else in all the ship who could tell them how to sail her home. "But," said he, "if the ship and the shallop should separate – which we will not willingly allow, for we will follow the ship – then, when you come to Cape Digges, leave some token that you have been there, near to the place where the fowls breed." He said that he would do the like for us, if he should come there first, and so I parted from him with tears.

Now were the sick men driven out of their cabins into the shallop; but Francis Clements had been a friend of John Thomas, and the cooper a friend of Bennet's, and so there were words between these two and Henry Greene, he swearing the two sick men must go, and Bennet and Thomas swearing that they should stay, until at last Henry Greene was forced to give way to them.

In the meantime there were some that acted as though the ship had been entered by force and they had free leave to pillage, breaking up chests, and rifling all places.

Now were all the poor men loaded in the shallop, being Henry Hudson, Master; John Hudson, his son; Arnold Ladlo, Sydrack Fenner, Philip Staffe, Thomas Woodhouse, Adam Moore, John King and Michel But. The carpenter had persuaded the villains to give them a musket, powder and shot, some pikes, an iron pot with some meal, and a few other things.

Now the ship stood out of the ice (the shallop still being fast to the stern of the ship) but when they were almost clear of the ice they cut the line from the stern of the ship and then out went the topsails and she stood to the east in a clear sea until we lost sight of the shallop. Then they took in the topsails, righted their helm and lay under foresails only, while they ransacked and searched the ship.

In the hold they found one whole vessel of meal and another half-spent. They found also two firkins of butter; some 27 pieces of pork and half a bushel of peas. But in the Master's cabin they found 200 biscuit cakes, a peck of meal and a butt of beer. But now the lookout said the shallop was again within sight and so they let fall the main sail and broke out the topsails and fled as if before an enemy.

At last, coming near the east shore, they anchored in 16 fathoms and tried with the net for fish, but could not seine with it because of rocks. Michael Pierce killed two fowl, and here we found a good store of cockle grass, some of which we gathered and brought on board. We lay there that night and most of the next day, in which time we did not see the shallop, nor did we see it ever after.

Now Henry Greene came and told me that it was the company's will that I should go up to the Master's cabin and take charge thereof. I told him that it was more fit for Robert Juet, but Greene said Juet should not come into it, or meddle with the Master's chart nor journals. So up I went and Greene gave me the key to the Master's chest and told me that he had laid the best of the Master's things together, which he would use himself when time did serve. The bread was also delivered into my keeping.

The wind serving, we stood north-east and this was Bylot's

course, contrary to Juet who would have gone north-west. We had the east shore in sight and during the night had a stiff gale of wind and stood before it until we met the ice, which we stood amongst until we were held fast in it. The ice was so thick ahead, and the wind brought it so fast from astern, that we could not stir; and so laid there fourteen days in worse plight than ever we had been.

At length, being clear of the ice, we continued our course in sight of the east shore.

Now they began to talk that England was no safe place for them, and Henry Greene swore that the ship should not come in any place, but should keep the sea until he had the King's hand and seal to show for his safety. Henry Greene was now the Captain, and so the others called him.

Keeping the east land still in sight we came athwart of low land and struck upon a rock that lay underwater; but without any harm that we could see. Now we raised land ahead which stretched to the north, whereupon the company said plainly that Robert Bylot, by following his course, had left Cape Digges to the south, and thither we must return for relief, having but small store of victuals left. But Bylot would still follow the land. So we still stood to the east, and leaving the mainland to the north, came to a narrow gut between two lands and anchored.

We went ashore on the west side and found a great sea-unicorn's horn, and much cockle grass, which was a great relief to us, for without it we could not have continued, for want of victuals.

Not long after, with great joy, we raised the Capes of Wolstenholme and Digges; but bearing in on them we ran upon a rock and stood fast for eight or nine hours. Being afloat again we stood to the eastward and anchored.

This day, July 27th, the boat was sent ashore to kill fowl. The boat made directly for the place where the fowls breed. Now we saw seven boats filled with savages come about the eastern point toward us; but when the savages saw us they drew their little boats into their bigger ones, and then they came rowing toward us, making signs to the west.

Our men made ready for anything, but the savages came to us and we grew familiar so that we took one of their men into our boat, and they took one of ours into theirs. Then they carried our man to their tents, where he remained until their man was returned to them.

Now our boat went to the place where the fowls breed and their man showed us the manner whereby the savages killed fowls. They took a long pole with a snare on the end which they cast about the fowl's neck and so pulled them down. But our men knew of a better way, and so showed the savages the use of our pieces, which at one shot would kill seven or eight.

At last we returned to the cove to receive our man back, and to deliver theirs. When we came to them they made great joy, dancing, leaping and beating their chests, and offering divers things to our men. But we only took some walrus tusks in exchange for a knife and two glass buttons.

Now, after receiving back our man, we came aboard the ship, rejoicing that we had met the most simple people in the world. And Henry Greene, more than the rest, was so confident (of gulling them) that by no means would he have us take care and stand upon our guard. God blinded him, so that where he thought to receive great matters from this people, he did receive more than he looked for.

On July 29th, we made haste ashore again while the ship weighed and stood as near as possible, (but that was not very near) to where the fowls breed.

Now, because I was lame, it was agreed that I was to stay in the boat and take charge of such things as we had for trading. So, with more haste than good speed (and not without much swearing) away we went. Those in the boat being Henry Greene, William Wilson, John Thomas, Michael Pierce, Andrew Motter and myself.

When we came near the shore the people were on the hills dancing and leaping. We brought our boat to the east side of the cove and made it fast to a great stone on shore. The people came to us and each had something in his hand to barter, but Henry Greene swore they should have nothing from us until we had some venison from them.

Now Henry Greene, John Thomas and William Wilson stood on the shore hard by the boat's head while Michael Pierce and Andrew Motter climbed upon the rocks to gather sorrel grass. Not one of them had any weapon about him, save Henry Greene, who had a piece of a pike in his hand. Greene and Wilson had looking-glasses, jews-harps, and bells which they were showing to the savages.

Now one of the savages came into the boat and I made signs to him to get out again but he made as though he had not understood and drew my attention to the shore by pointing. While I was thus distracted, another savage stole to the stern of the boat and suddenly I saw the legs and feet of a man beside me. I at once cast up my head and saw this savage with a knife in his hand, with which he was striking down over my head, aiming at my breast. I cast up my arm and the knife wounded me in the arm and then struck into my breast under the right pap.

Now the savage struck a second blow which I warded with my left hand, but it struck into my thigh, and also nigh cut off my little finger. But now I got hold of the string which hung from the knife, and wrapping it around my left hand, so pulled the savage down that his side lay open to me, and I, remembering the dagger at my side, reached down for it, and therewith struck the savage in the body and in the throat.

Meantime, the men ashore had been assaulted. John Thomas and William Wilson had their bowels cut, and Michael Pierce and Henry Greene (he being mortally wounded) came tumbling into the boat together.

When Andrew Motter saw this melee he came running down the rocks, leapt into the water, and swam to the boat's stern. The while, Michael Pierce manfully defended the boat's head against the savages, who pressed sore upon him, by means of a hatchet.

Henry Greene now laid about him with a truncheon, while I cried to them to clear the boat's head, and Andrew Motter cried to be taken in.

The savages then betook themselves to their bows and arrows and sent so many arrows amongst us that Greene was slain outright and Pierce received many wounds, as did the rest of us. But Pierce had cleared the boat, and now he put it from the shore, then helped Andrew Motter into it. Only Pierce and Motter had strength to row the boat, for I had received a cruel arrow wound in my back.

Now the savages came to their own boats and we feared they would launch them, but they did not. When we had rowed a good way from the shore Pierce fainted. Then Motter stood in the bow and waved to the ship which at first saw us not. But at last they saw us, and stood in, and took us up.

Greene was then thrown into the sea, he being dead. That same day Wilson died, cursing and swearing in a most fearful manner. Michael Pierce lived two days more, then died. And thus you have the tragical end of Greene and his three mates (for John Thomas also had expired of his wounds), being the lustiest men in all the ship.

With the poor number we had left aboard we stood to and fro in the straits, for we dared not leave until we had procured more fowl. And this we did, though it was a great danger because of the savages, yet we had needs to have these fowl else we should not have had victuals wherewith to make our way to England.

So we killed 400 fowls, and then a west wind drove us homeward but not without many days of troubles with the fogs and rocks before ever we came clear of the strait and into the sea.

And before we had come out to the sea we were reduced to an allowance of half a fowl a day, and we were glad to burn off the feathers from the skin (the feathers could on no account be pulled free) and eat the skin; nor was any of the garbage of the fowls thrown away.

Now Robert Bylot was the Master, and he shaped course for Ireland, though Juet spoke for Newfoundland, thinking that we would there find relief amongst our countrymen upon the fisheries.

So we sailed many days, and none knew with certainty whereat we were, and in this time we were fain to fry the bones of the fowls in candle tallow, putting vinegar thereto, and every man had a pound of candles allowed each week to eat, as a great dainty.

Then Robert Juet died, and the rest despaired, saying we were past Ireland. The last fowl in the ship was eaten and then the men cared not which end of the ship went down first. The Master had needs do all their labour as well as his own, for none now hoped to live, nor cared to save themselves.

In this extremity it pleased God to give us sight of land and to espy a boat which piloted us into Bear Haven in County Cork. Here we stayed several days hoping to deal with the Irish for relief, but we found none, neither bread nor drink, for these people were so cold in kindliness that they would do nothing without having money first.

But in the month of September we came at last to Gravesend, and so brought our voyage to its end.

On their return to England, the survivors were arrested and confined in prison where they were to remain until Hudson and his fellow castaways returned, or if they did not return, then the survivors were to remain in prison until their lives were at an end.

However, it happened that depositions were taken from each of the survivors before the officials of Trinity House and, although the records are scanty, it must be assumed that the officials saw sufficient justification for the actions of the mutineers, for the following report was issued, and the survivors of the unlucky voyage were freed.

24 October. 1611.

By examination of the seamen of the company of that ship which endeavoured to make the north-west discovery, it plainly appeareth that the Master and the rest of those men who are lost, were put out of the ship by consent of all such as are come home, and who were then in health.

It appeareth further that the plot was begun by Henry Greene and Wm. Wilson, but that Juet, whom they presumed on to be their pilot, was privy to the plot.

Some of them confess that Robert Bylot, who came home Master, was acquainted with the plot in the beginning. But Pricket clears him thereof, and saith he was only chosen to take charge after the Master was put away.

They all charge Master Hudson to have stolen the victuals by means of a scuttle or hatch cut between his cabin and the hold; and it appears that he fed his favourites, such as the surgeon, etc. and kept the others at only ordinary allowance, which led those who were not so favoured to make the attempt and to perform it so violently.

But all conclude that, to save some from starving, they were content to put away so many.

Of Hudson and his companions, nothing more was ever heard. However, there is some reason to believe that they landed safely on one of the islands in James Bay (later making their way to the mainland), and that they may have survived for many months or even years before death came to them.

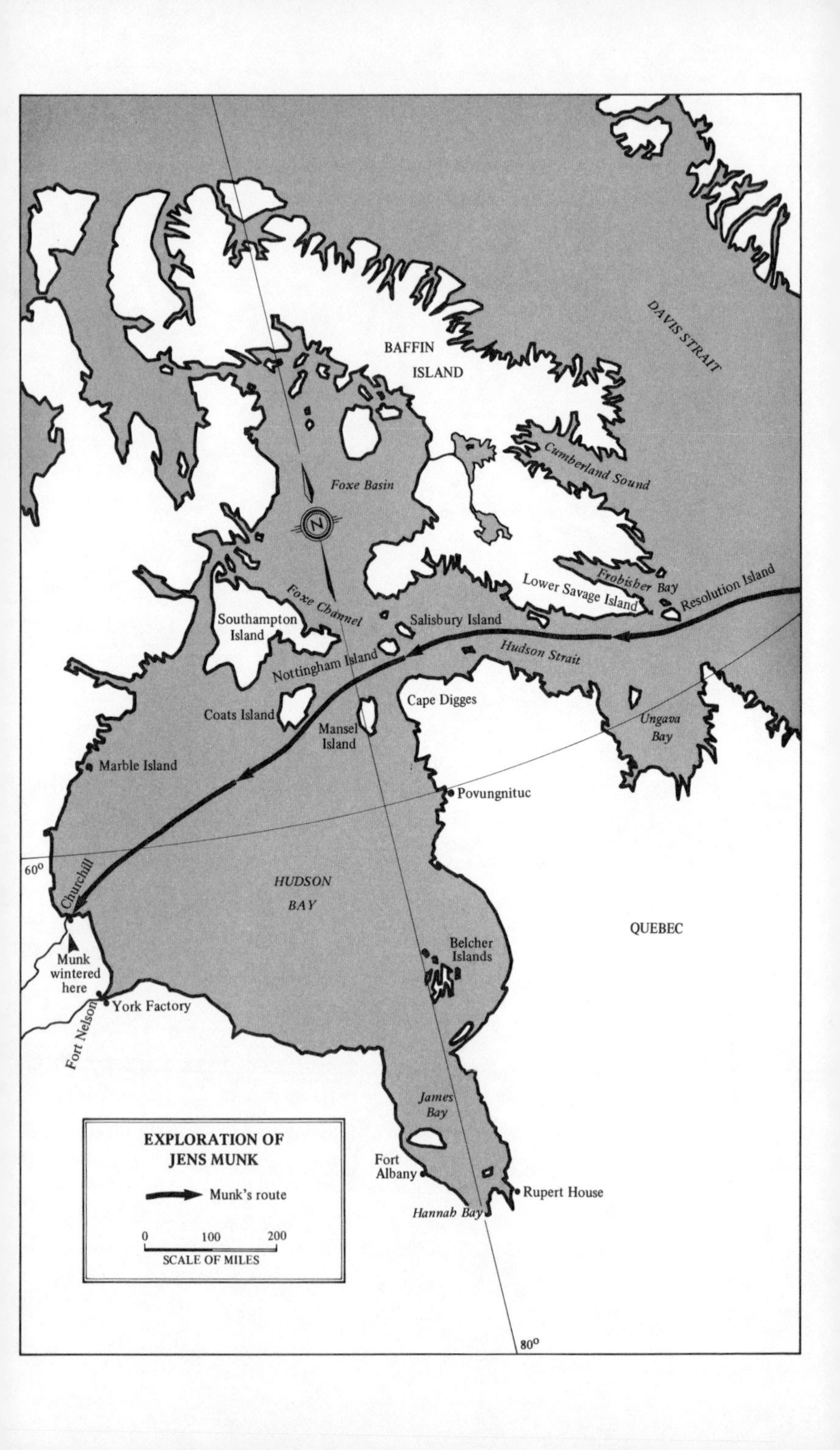

BAFFIN ISLAND
DAVIS STRAIT
Cumberland Sound
Foxe Basin
Frobisher Bay
Lower Savage Island
Resolution Island
Foxe Channel
Southampton Island
Salisbury Island
Hudson Strait
Nottingham Island
Cape Digges
Coats Island
Mansel Island
Ungava Bay
Marble Island
Povungnituc
60°
Churchill
HUDSON BAY
QUEBEC
Belcher Islands
Munk wintered here
York Factory
Fort Nelson
James Bay
EXPLORATION OF JENS MUNK
Munk's route
0
100
200
SCALE OF MILES
Fort Albany
Rupert House
Hannah Bay
80°

III

The Black Winter of Jens Munk

During the next few years several of the survivors of Hudson's voyage took part in further expeditions into the north-west. Thus, in 1612, when Thomas Button was sent to Hudson Bay, ostensibly to search for Hudson, one of the two vessels he was given was the stout old Discovery, *again commanded (but legally this time) by Robert Bylot, and accompanying Bylot was none other than that ill-omened bird, Abacuk Pricket.*

This expedition discovered, and wintered at, Port Nelson on the west coast of the Bay; but it seems to have wasted little, if any, time looking for Hudson. In fact, an aura of mystery hangs over the whole Button voyage. The logs of the two vessels and Button's personal account were never made public, so that we know little about the details of the endeavour or about its real objectives. Its primary interest lies in the fact that it included Bylot and Discovery *and is therefore a part of the prologue to a venture which these two were destined to undertake together, and which constitutes one of the most remarkable passages into the ice of which any record still survives.*

In 1615 Bylot completed the prologue to his great adventure by making a third voyage into Hudson Bay in an attempt to find a north-western outlet from what is now called Foxe Basin. He worked Discovery *into new waters beyond Cape Comfort on the north shore of Southampton Island, but here the ice became impassable and the ship had to be turned for home. It was not a* spectacular voyage, but it serves to introduce a new and most enduring name to north-west venturing, that of William Baffin, who was Bylot's pilot – a position roughly equivalent to that of chief officer today.

In the early spring of the following year Discovery sailed once more, with Bylot still commanding and with Baffin again serving as pilot. This time the task was to exploit Davis' discoveries and to determine what lay beyond his Strait, to the north and west of Greenland. The incomparable Discovery, scarred by her several previous battles with the ice, (she had also been out in 1614, under command of an incompetent who nearly lost her), was nothing loath to try again.

Rounding Cape Farewell she pushed north along the Greenland coast until, by May thirtieth, she had equalled Davis' farthest point north. Then she really began to show her mettle.

Reaching Melville Bay she shouldered her way through the pack which congests this infamous death-trap, pounding the ice under her bluff bows, wedging her way through narrow leads, and somehow avoiding the proliferating bergs which filled the Bay. By July fifth she had wormed and wiggled her way to seventy-six degrees north latitude, and was poking her nose into Smith Sound. But here the ice rallied its defences and finally turned her back. Still she sailed new waters, coasting the west shore of this new sea and discovering the mouths of Jones and Lancaster Sounds enroute. South of Lancaster the fast shore ice held her off the land until she reached Cumberland Sound and known waters again, then Bylot squared her off for home, her task completed.

This was Discovery's sixth, and Bylot's fourth, or possibly fifth, voyage into the ice – and it was the final recorded one for both of them. But what a period it makes to the career of ship and man: the complete circumnavigation of that ice-bound sea which we now call Baffin Bay; and the discovery of the two channels, by one of which (Smith) men would eventually reach the Pole itself, while through the other (Lancaster) they would find the long-sought Northwest Passage. The quality of this achievement is revealed by the fact that two centuries had to pass before another ship could gain a comparable victory over the ice of Baffin Bay and, in fact, before the northern two-thirds of the Bay were even approached by another ship, or seen again by western men.

So startling was the voyage of the Discovery that future generations concluded it was an impossible feat, and that the whole *voyage had been no more than a hoax. As late as 1812 the charts of this portion of the Arctic did not even show Baffin Bay at all, but only a dotted bulge north of Davis Strait in which the legend was printed:* Baffin's Bay according to the relation of W. Baffin in 1616, but not now believed.

When the Bay was at last rediscovered, and the old charts of Bylot's voyage were found to be amazingly accurate and entirely truthful, something very odd took place. Under the aegis of the Royal Navy's Arctic voyagers, and of the historians at home, the entire credit for the original discovery was given to William Baffin; while Bylot was condemned to complete obscurity. There were probably two reasons why this happened. In the first place Bylot appears to have been extremely self-effacing and inarticulate, and all *the surviving accounts of the voyages of 1615 and 1616 are of Baffin's authorship, so that it was easy for an uncritical, or biased, historian of the nineteenth century to dispose of Bylot. These historians* were *biased, and heavily so. They could never forgive Bylot for the part he had played during the last voyage of Henry Hudson. They felt, and many still seem to feel, that it would actually be immoral to allow Bylot his due place in the sun, in view of the fact that he chose to remain with, and eventually save, the* Discovery *and those aboard her, rather than to volunteer for a futile death with Hudson in an open boat. But no man bearing even the suspicion of anything so heinous as mutinous conduct against an officer could ever have been accepted at his real worth by the Victorians of yesterday — or of today.*

Bylot's fate is by no means unique in the annals of the Arctic, but it must surely be one of the most glaring examples of the injustice which can result when we leave the evaluation of such a man's achievements in the hands of those professional arbiters of immortality who censor history on our behalf.

Although it was the English who were most actively engaged in the struggle to master the ice defences of the north-west during the early part of the seventeenth century, they were not entirely alone. Between 1605 and 1612, King Christian IV, the Sailor King of Denmark, despatched four expeditions into Greenland waters under the direction of James Hall. Ostensibly these voyages were intended to discover the lost Norse settlements. In fact, they were intended to be profitable, and it was expected that Hall would find mines, sources of furs and narwhal ivory, and perhaps the

Northwest Passage. Hall found no surviving Norsemen (though if he had looked closely at the Eskimo inhabitants of Greenland he might have noticed blonde hair, blue eyes, and other evidence of what had happened to the lost colonists). He found no mines, either, though he thought he had done so. Instead he found his own death at the hands of the Eskimos, whom some of his men had savagely mistreated. As for King Christian, he acquired a new land which has remained under the Danish flag into our time.

It was not enough for the Sailor King.

In 1619 he undertook to follow the English into Hudson Bay and do what they had so far failed to do – discover an outlet from it into the western seas. The man he chose to carry out his wishes was a forty-year-old adventurer named Jens Munk.

Munk's personal history is an epic in itself. While he was still a small child his wealthy father was jailed for life as a result of some shady manipulations of public funds, and the boy was forced to grow up in a hurry. At the age of eleven he went to Portugal where he spent a year learning the language (it was then the language of the richest merchants in the world) in order to have a head start on the road to fortune. At thirteen he shipped aboard a Dutch vessel bound for Bahia in Brazil, as cabin boy. Outward bound again from Bahia for Europe, Jens' ship sailed in company with twelve other merchant vessels for mutual protection – but it was not adequate protection. A French squadron fell upon them off the Brazil coast and sank or seized the entire fleet. Munk's ship was burned, and her crew clung to floating wreckage until a French man-of-war picked them out of the water. It was hardly an act of mercy. The Frenchman promptly landed the survivors on an untamed part of the Brazilian coast where most of them seem to have died of disease, starvation, or from the attacks of Indians. But not young Munk. He made his way back to Bahia where he maintained himself for the first year of exile as a shoemaker's apprentice.

When he was eighteen, two Dutch vessels entered Bahia harbour without a trading permit from the King of Spain, and the Spanish authorities prepared to seize both ships. Seven vessels were manned with soldiers for the attempt, but Munk's then protector, a merchant called Miguel Duez, decided to warn the Dutchmen. Jens was chosen for the task. In darkness, and with the Spanish vessels all about him, he swam across the harbour, clambered aboard the nearest Dutch vessel and gave the alarm. The two merchantmen cut their cables and made sail just in time, for the Spaniards were already upon them. There was a sharp skirmish before they were clear of the harbour and free to sail for home, carrying with them the boy who had given them their freedom.

Back in Copenhagen Jens put his hard-won experience to work. By the time he was twenty-five he was a merchant captain, and, more than that, owned his own vessel. Now the north began to draw him, and he made at least one voyage to Iceland, followed by an exploratory voyage toward the bitter lands of Novaya Zemlya in Barents Sea. On this voyage he explored the island of Kulguew to the north of Russia, but his ship was lost on the island's shores and it was only after a long and harrowing journey in a small boat that he and his crew reached safety.

In 1611 he was commissioned a Captain in the Danish Navy and was immediately engaged against the Swedes. In 1615 he was chasing (and catching) pirates in the North Sea and off the coast of Norway; but two years later he had turned back to the Arctic to establish the first Danish whaling enterprise in Spitzbergen waters.

By this time he had established himself as a fellow after Christian's own heart, and when the King decided to lead the English through the Northwest Passage, Munk was the inevitable choice to command the expedition.

NAVIGATIO SEPTENTRIONALIS

Anno Domini, 1619: His Royal Majesty's ship *Unicorn*, and the sloop *Lamprey*, having been properly made ready, provisioned, and prepared with other necessaries for the voyage to search for the Northwest Passage, I, Jens Munk, in the name of God, sailed with the said two ships from Copenhagen on the 9th of May with forty-eight men aboard the *Unicorn* and sixteen aboard the *Lamprey*.

On the 18th of May it happened, early in the morning, while we were sailing along, that one of my men who was walking on the deck suddenly jumped overboard and plunged his head under water without, however, so it appeared, sinking as quickly as he desired. But, as it was blowing hard, no one could save him; which I should much have wished. He therefore went down and was lost.

On the 25th of May, while off southern Norway, the *Lamprey* sprang a leak so that I was obliged to run into Karmsund. On examination I found that three bolt-holes had been left open by the carpenters and afterwards filled with pitch. While I stayed at Karmsund one of my two coopers died, wherefore I caused three young men to be engaged so as to maintain my full complement of men.

On the 30th of May I sailed from Karmsund and shaped our course for Shetland. On the 4th of June we sailed round the east end of the Faeroe Islands and shaped our course west and west-by-north.

Now I ascertained what quantities of stores had been consumed, and gave orders how these stores should be served out. In this way I secured always an accurate account of what had been consumed and of what still remained in store of all kinds of provisions and drinks.

Thus we sailed on in a Westerly direction until the 20th of June when we encountered much ice, so that we were obliged to turn eastward again toward the open sea. We kept sailing back and forth, with gales and bad weather, until June 30th, when we sighted the southern cape of Greenland which the English call Cape Farewell. Doubtless whoever named that place did not intend to return thither.

We had then arrived at Davis Strait and when I had got free of this ice I shaped my course west by north on which track we encountered much more ice.

On the 8th of July we sighted the land on the American side but could not reach the shore for the quantity of ice, so we sailed to and fro outside the ice and could effect nothing.

On July 9th there was such a fog in the night, and so great a cold, that icicles were hanging from the rigging six inches long, and none of the men could stand the cold. But before three o'clock on the same day the sun was shining so hotly that the men threw off their overcoats, and some of them their jackets as well.

Then I stood in among the ice into a great bay which, according to my English pilots, ought to have been the proper entrance to Hudson's Strait, but which after long investigation we found not to be the right entrance.*

Leaving this bay we shaped our course southerly along the coast which we found to consist everywhere of broken land and high rocks, until we came to Resolution Island on the north side of the entrance into Hudson's Strait.

On the 12th I sent my Lieutenant with some of the crew on shore at this island in order to fetch water and to ascertain what was to be found there, because it seemed a likely place for finding harbours and for obtaining water. In the evening they returned with water, but reported that there was no anchorage. On the same day I shot two or three birds with a gun; but at the last discharge the same gun burst into pieces and took the brim clean off the front of my hat.

On the 13th of July, towards evening, we were in the greatest distress and danger in the Strait of Hudson, and did not know what counsel to follow, because we could not advance any farther by tacking, the ice pressing us hard on all sides. Being in such a perilous situation we took in all the sails and fastened the *Lamprey* to the *Unicorn.* We then commended all into the hand of God and drifted along and into the ice again.

While we thus drifted forward and backward in the ice, in great danger of our lives, the ice displaced a large knee which was in the head of the ship and fastened with six long iron bolts. I set all my carpenters to work to set that knee straight again, but it was too much for them. I therefore had the ship swung round and then ordered the rudder to be worked so as to turn the ship against the ice in order that the pressure against the damaged knee would make it right itself. And this was effected as perfectly as if twenty carpenters had been engaged in refitting it.

On the 17th of July I ordered the *Lamprey* to sail ahead of us to find where we could anchor, and followed after with the *Unicorn.* We then found a good harbour where we cast anchor in the name of God.

The following day I sent men out with orders to search whether any people were to be found on the land, and toward midday they returned without having noticed any people. They had, however, found many places where people had been.

On the 18th of July we observed that there were people on the

* This was probably Frobisher Bay.

southern side of the harbour, wherefore I at once had my boat manned and went myself thither in it.

When the natives saw that I was coming on shore they remained standing, having laid down their arms and implements behind some stones. When I approached them they returned whatever salutations I offered them; but were careful to keep between me and the place where their arms were laid.

I took up some of their arms and implements and examined them, upon which they at once made me understand that they would rather lose all their garments and go naked, than lose their arms and implements; and they pointed to their mouths thereby signifying that it was by means of their arms and implements that they obtained their food. When I again laid down their things they clapped their hands, looked up to heaven, and showed themselves very merry and joyful. Thereupon I presented them with knives and all sorts of iron goods. One of my men, who had a very swarthy complexion and black hair, they embraced, no doubt thinking that he was one of their own nation and countrymen.

On the 19th of July I had hoped to have had further intercourse with the natives, but it was altogether in vain for, though I remained lying here until July 22nd, none of the natives came to me, from which it is to be concluded that they are doubtless subject to some authority which must have forbidden them to come to us again.

On the 23rd of July we found ourselves so entirely surrounded by ice on all sides that we could not get away from it. We therefore made the *Lamprey* fast to the *Unicorn*, brought down the topmasts (as a violent gale was commencing) and then drifted whither the wind or the ice might carry us. In the next night the ice pressed on us so hard and we were so firmly fixed in it that we could not give way, and the ice crushed four anchors to pieces on the bow of the *Lamprey*. At the same time the ice forced itself under the *Lamprey*'s keel so that one might pass one's hand along the keel from stem to stern.

On the 25th I nearly lost two men who were ordered to fetch back a grapnel which had been thrown onto a large mass of ice in order to turn the ship. On the same day the rudder head of the *Unicorn* was broken to pieces. The following day the ships remained in the same place, drifting neither outward nor inward, so that we were now in the greatest distress and danger. We did not know of any measures we could take, but commended the whole matter into the hand of God.

On July 31st we were carried inward by the flood tide over some rocks, and thus came into a small bay where we were somewhat more secure against the ice. The men were now so entirely worn out that they could not any longer have sustained the hard work entailed in pushing great quantities of ice from the ship, and by the incessant veering and hauling.

During August 5th the ice commenced to thin somewhat and drift away; wherefore I had the hold trimmed and ordered the beer to be put into fresh casks, water fetched, and everything made ready to proceed. But on August 8th so much snow fell that all the mountains were covered with it and, on the deck, the snow was more than six inches deep. On this same day we buried one of our seamen named Anders Staffuanger in this place, which we have called Haresund because we caught many hares here.

Thus did our journey proceed for many days until in time we came out of Hudson's Strait and set our course south-west-by-south for three days and three nights sailing, to reach the land again at Jens Munk's Wintering-place,* as I have called the river mouth which we discovered on the western shore of the great bay.

September 7th. Now that I had come into the harbour aforesaid, though with great difficulty on account of wind and storm, snow, hail and fog, I ordered a watch on the land, and maintained a fire in order that the *Lamprey*, which had strayed from us during a great gale, might find us again. She joined us on the 9th of September.

The crews having suffered much from the aforesaid gale, and other hardships and trouble, and a part of them in consequence being down sick, I caused the sick people to be brought on shore and we gathered cloud-berries, gooseberries and other berries for them. I also had a good fire made on the shore every day for the sick, whereby they were comforted and in time nicely regained their health.

On the 10th and 11th of September there was such a terrible gale and snowstorm that nothing could be done.

Early the next morning a large white bear came down to the water near the ship and began eating the flesh of a white-whale which I had caught the day before. I shot the bear, and the men

* The present site of Churchill.

all desired its flesh for food, which I allowed. I ordered the cook just to boil it slightly and then to keep it in vinegar for a night, and I myself had two or three pieces of this bear's-flesh roasted, for the cabin. It was of good taste and did not disagree with us.

On the 16th of September Jan Peterson, who had been investigating the localities on the western side of the harbour in the shallop, returned to say that, where he had been, no harbours were to be found; the land was low, flat and wooded, and there was scarcely any safe place to protect a boat. On this same day there was a terrible snowstorm from the north-east.

By the 18th we were experiencing nothing but frost and snow and so we deliberated together as to what measures to take. Then all the officers thought it best, and it was so resolved, that inasmuch as the winter was coming on us very hard and severe, increasing and getting worse day by day, we should have the ships brought into the best place, though all seemed equally unfavourable, where they might at least be safe from the drift ice. Thus, on the following day we sailed up the river as far as we could, and on that night the new drift ice cut into both sides of the ship and sloop to the depth of about two fingers' breadth, so that I was obliged to have the ship brought closer to the shore across a tidal flat. It was a distance of nearly a mile across the flat and the ship was in great danger because the ground was covered with stones and the ship could not well rest on it on account of her being sharp-built. As the ice got the upper hand the ship struck on a stone and became quite leaky, so that all the carpenters had enough to do to make her tight again before the return of the flood tide.

By the 25th we had secured the ship close under the land and had brought the sloop on shore, by means of a high tide. I now caused the ship's keel to be dug into the ground of the tidal flats and branches of trees to be spread under the bilge, packed together with clay and sand, in order that she might rest evenly and thus suffer less damage.

While we now thought that the ship was well protected against drift ice and bad weather, such a tremendous drift of ice came upon us on the 27th, with the low ebb tide, that if the ship had not been resting so firmly on the ground, we should have been carried away. We were obliged to let go all four hawsers by which the ship was moored, and part of them went to pieces. The ship also became so leaky that at flood tide we pumped out 2,000 strokes of water. I ordered the carpenters, and others who could ply an axe, to make five bridge-piles while the other men hauled timber and stones for these piles which I caused to be placed before the bow of the ship in order to turn off the ice so it would not hurt us.

Everything being now well finished and the ship and sloop protected against the ice and tempest, I ordered the cannon to be placed in the hold and a part of our goods to be brought on shore, in order that the deck might be clear and that the ship should not suffer so much from the great weight resting on her deck. I also distributed to the crew clothes, shirts, shoes and boots and whatever else could be of use as a protection against the cold.

On the 5th of October I caused two large fireplaces, around each of which twenty men might easily sit, to be arranged on deck; one before the mast, the other behind the mast; as well as a fireplace in the steerage; these being in addition to that in the cook's galley where he did his cooking, and which he required to have to himself.

The weather being fine on the 7th I journeyed up the river to see how far I could get with a boat but there were so many stones in it that I could not advance beyond a mile and a half. On my return I came to a promontory and found there a picture on a stone, drawn with charcoal, and fashioned like the half of a devil: wherefore I called the place Devil's Cape.

In many places where we came we could quite well see where people had been and had had their summer abodes.* In the forest there are in many places great heaps of chips where they have cut wood or timber, and the chips look as if they have been cut off with curved iron tools. I am of the opinion that the said people have some kind of idolatry connected with fire and, if that is so, it is to be wished that these poor, blinded pagans might come to the profession of the true Christian Faith. As regards their food and mode of living, it would seem they use much in a half-cooked state because, wherever we found that they had had their meals, the bones did not seem to have been very well roasted.

On the 10th of October I began to give the men rations of wine; but beer they were allowed to drink according to their want, as much as every man himself liked. At the same time I made regulations for keeping a watch, the fetching of wood, and burning of

* These people were probably Eskimos who came here for wood for weapons and implements.

charcoal, so that everyone knew what he was to do and how to conduct himself.

On October 22nd the ice became very firm and there was a terribly hard frost, and on the same night we caught a black fox. The crew now commenced to go ashore in the daytime in pursuit of game. A part went into the forest to set traps to catch animals, and some of these built a hut wherein to lie in ambush for animals. Another part of the men betook themselves to open country for shooting, because there was plenty of ptarmigan and hares as long as the snow was not too deep. At this time, and until Christmas, the men liked to go ashore when the weather was fine, because they never went without they carried home something good to eat, which was a sufficient inducement to them to move about.

On November 10th, which was St. Martin's Eve, the men shot some ptarmigan, with which we had to content ourselves instead of the traditional St. Martin's goose. I ordered a pint of Spanish wine be given to each of the men beside their daily allowance, wherewith the whole crew were satisfied, even merry and joyful. And of the ship's beer there was given them as much as they liked. But afterwards, when the frost got the upper hand, the beer froze to the bottom so that I was afraid to let the men drink of it before they had well melted and boiled it again. However in this matter I let the men follow their own inclination because the common people, after all, are so disposed that, whatever is most strongly forbidden them, they are most apt to do on the sly without considering whether it be beneficial or hurtful to them.

In the middle of the month two of the men commenced to use the ambush hut and in the first night they caught two black foxes and a cross fox, which were very beautiful. This same night a large black dog came to the ship on the ice; but the man on watch, not knowing but that it was a black fox, shot him and with much exultation dragged him into the cabin thinking that he had got a great prize. But when we examined it, we found it to be a large dog which no doubt had been trained to catch game because it had been tied round the nose with small cords so that the hair was rubbed off. His right ear was cleft, and perhaps his owner was not very pleased to lose him. I should myself have been glad to have caught him alive, in which case I should have made a pedlar of him and have let him go home to where he had come from, carrying a pack of small goods.

On November 27th there was a very sharp frost by which all

the glass bottles we had (which contained all kinds of precious waters) were broken to pieces; wherefore it is observed that whoever intends to navigate such cold seas should supply himself well with tin bottles, or other such that are able to resist the frost.

On December 12th one of my two surgeons, David Velske by name, died and his corpse had to remain on the ship unburied for two days because the frost was so very severe that nobody could get ashore to bury him; and even on the 14th the cold was so intense that many of the men got frost-bites when they met the wind with uncovered face.

On Christmas Eve I gave the men wine and strong beer, which they had to boil afresh, for it was frozen to the bottom. Nevertheless, they had quite as much as they could stand, and were very jolly, but no one offended another with as much as a word.

The Holy Christmas Day we all celebrated and observed solemnly, as a Christian's duty is. We had a sermon, and after it we gave the priest an offertory, according to ancient custom, each in proportion to his means. There was not much money among the men but they gave what they had. Some of them gave white foxskins, so that the priest got enough wherewith to line a coat. However, sufficiently long life to wear it was not granted to him.

During all the Holy Days the weather was rather mild; and, in order that the time might not hang on hand, the men practised all kinds of games, and whoever could imagine the most amusement was the most popular. The crew, most of whom were at that time in good health, consequently had all sorts of larks and pastimes. And thus we spent the Holy Days, with the merriment that was got up.

Anno Domini 1620.

On New Year's day there was a tremendously hard frost and I ordered a couple of pints of wine to every bowl to be given to the people, over and above their allowance, in order that they might keep themselves in good spirit. During these days we had the sharpest frost that we had yet experienced during the whole winter, and we suffered more severely from that terrible frost than from anything else.

On January 10th, the priest, Mr. Rasmus Jensen, and the surgeon, M. Casper Caspersen, took to their beds having for some time felt unwell. And after that time violent sickness commenced among the men, which day by day prevailed more and more. The illness which then raged was peculiar, and the sick were generally attacked by dysentery about three weeks before they died. On this same day my head cook died.

On the 21st of January it was fine, clear weather and sunshine, and on that date thirteen of us were down with sickness. Then, as I had often done before, I asked the surgeon, M. Caspersen (who was also lying mortally ill), whether he knew of any good remedy that might be found in his chest and which might serve for the recovery or comfort of the crew; requesting him to inform me of it. To this he answered that he had already used as many remedies as he had, to the best of his abilities, and that if God would not help, then he could not employ any further remedy at all that would be useful for recovery.

On the 23rd of January died one of my two Mates, Hans Brock by name, who had been ill and in and out of bed for nearly five months. On this day it was fine weather and beautiful sunshine and the priest sat up in his berth and gave the people a sermon, which sermon was the last he ever delivered in this world.

On the 25th, I had the body of Hans Brock buried, and ordered two falconets* to be discharged, which was the last honour I could show him. But the trunnions burst off both falconets and the man who fired them very nearly lost both his legs, so brittle had the iron become on account of the sharp and severe frost.

Two days later Jens Helsing, seaman, died and on the same day my Lieutenant, the well-born Mauritz Stygge, took to his bed for good, after having been ailing for some time. Also on this day the men saw tracks of five reindeer which had been chased by a wolf, wherefore I sent a party after them. But on account of a great fall of snow which overtook the men, they could not trace the animals and returned without catching any.

The next day the cold was so severe that a tin pot with water in it, which the boy had forgotten in the cabin, burst in the night by frost. So I do not know in what kind of vessels any precious waters may be preserved on voyages to such cold seas as these.

On February 5th a seaman named Laurids Bergen died, and I again sent to the surgeon with an urgent request that, for God's sake, he would do his utmost if he knew of any remedy or good advice. Or, inasmuch as he was himself very ill and weak, if he

* Small cannon.

would let me know what medicine or remedy I could use for the benefit of the crew. To which he answered as before that, if God would not help, he could not help either.

February 10th. During these past days the weather was rather mild, but there was much sickness and weakness amongst the crew. Two of them died on this day.

On the 12th we caught two ptarmigan which were very welcome for the use of the sick; and on the following day I ordered for each person at each meal, one-third of a pint of wine and, in the morning, a whole measure of whisky, beyond the ordinary allowance.

During these days there was nothing but sickness and weakness and every day the number of the sick was continuously increased so that by the 17th, there were only seven persons in health that could fetch wood and water and do whatever work there was to be done on board. On this day also, there died a seaman who had been ill the whole voyage and of whom one may truly say that he was as dirty in his habits as an untrained beast.

On the next day Rasmus Kiobenhauffn died and, of the crew, there had then already died twenty persons. On this day we got a hare, which was very welcome.

On the 20th died the priest.

On the 29th of February the frost was so severe that nobody could get on shore to fetch water or wood, and that day the cook was obliged to take for fuel whatever he could find. I was obliged to mind the cabin myself, for this day my servant had also fallen ill and taken to his bed altogether.

On March 4th the weather was mild and we caught five ptarmigan in the open country, which was very welcome to us. I ordered broth to be made of them and had that distributed amongst the sick. But of the meat they could eat nothing because of their mouths being badly afflicted by the scurvy.

On the 8th died Oluf Boye who had been ill nearly nine weeks; and on the 9th died Anders, the cooper, who had been ill since Christmas.

March 21st. During the past days the weather had been changeable, being sometimes fine and clear, at other times sharp and severe. As regards the crew, most of them were, alas, down with illness, and it was very miserable and melancholy either to hear or see them. On this day died the surgeon, and Povel Pedersen, both of whom had been ill almost since Christmas. Now, and afterwards, the sickness raged more violently every day, so that we who were still left suffered great trouble before we could get the dead buried.

March 24th. These days were fine and mild, without frost. One of the men who got on shore and climbed a high rock, saw open water outside the inlet, which filled us with confident expectations of release. But on the following day the skipper, Jan Ollufsen, died.

I was myself now much ashore collecting herbs where the snow had melted off. They were as fresh in such places as if it had been autumn, but one had to be careful to gather them as soon as they appeared from under the snow, because otherwise they withered speedily. I also gathered a quantity of berries which I distributed among the men.

On the 27th of March I looked over the surgeon's chest and examined its contents in detail because, no longer having a surgeon, I had now to do the best I could myself. But it was a great neglect and mistake that there was not some list supplied by the physicians, indicating what the various medications were good for and how they were to be used. I am certain, and would venture my life on it, that there were many kinds of medicaments in that chest which my surgeon did not know – much less did he know for what purpose, and in what way, they were to be employed. All the names on them were written in Latin, of which he had not forgotten much in his lifetime, for want of ever knowing any. Whenever he was going to examine any bottle or box, the priest had to read the label for him.

On March 29th died Ismael Abrahamsen and Christen Gregersen, whose dead bodies were buried according to our opportunity and ability at that time.

On March 30th there was a sharp frost and on this date died Suend Arffuedsen, carpenter. And at this time commenced my greatest sorrow and misery, and I was then like a wild and lonely bird. I was now obliged myself to run about in the ship, to give drink to the sick, to boil drink for them, and get for them what I thought might be good for them, to which I was not accustomed, and of which I had but little knowledge.

The next day my second mate, Johan Pettersen died, and the following day my nephew Erich Munk; and his and Pettersen's dead bodies were placed together in one grave.

On April 3rd it was a fearfully sharp frost, so that none of us could uncover himself for cold. Nor had I anyone now to command, for they were all lying under the hand of God, so that there was great misery and sorrow. On this day died Iffuer Alsing.

On the 5th died Christoffer Opsloe, Rasmus Clemendsen and Lauritz Hansen, but the number of men in health was now so small that we were scarcely able to bury the bodies of the dead.

On the 8th died William Gordon, our English pilot, and towards evening Anders Sodens died so that these two were also buried in one grave, which we who were then alive could only manage with great difficulty, on account of the miserable weakness which was upon us, in consequence of which not one of us was well enough to go into the forest and fetch wood or fuel. Thus we were obliged to collect everything that was in the ship which would serve as fuel, and when that was consumed, we were obliged to burn our shallop for fuel.

On the 10th of April died the honourable and well-born Mauritz Stygge, my Lieutenant, and I took some of my own linen wherewith to wrap his body as well as I could. It was with great difficulty that I got a coffin made for him.

Three days after this I took a bath in a wine-cask which I had caused to be prepared for the purpose. And I utilized all the kinds of herbs which we found in the surgeon's chest and thought serviceable. After that my men likewise had a bath, as many of them as could move about and were not too weak; which bath (thanks be to God) did us much good, myself in particular.

On the 14th there was a sharp frost. On that day only four besides myself had strength enough to sit up in the berths and listen to the homily for Good Friday. Then, on Easter Day, died Anders Aroust and Jens the cooper and, as the weather was fairly mild, I got their bodies buried. I also promoted the captain of the hold to be my skipper, even though he too was ill, in order that he might assist me as far as his strength was able, because I was myself then quite miserable and abandoned by all the world. And in the night died Hans Bendtsen.

The next day died my servant Olluff Andersen who during seven years had served me faithfully and well, and after him died Peter Amundsen.

On the 21st of April the sunshine was beautiful, wherefore some of the sick crawled forth from their berths in order to warm themselves by the sun. But as they were so very weak, some of them swooned, so that it did not do them any good, and I had enough to do before I got them back again, each to his bunk.

On the 25th the wild geese began to arrive, at which we were delighted, hoping that the summer would now come soon. But in this expectation we were disappointed for the cold lasted on much longer.

May 4th. By this day many others had died, and now not a man left his berth save myself and the under-cook who still could do a little. And on this day died Anders Marstrand and Morten Marstrand who had both been long ill.

On May 7th the weather became a little milder and we three poor men who still had a little strength left could get the dead men buried but, on account of our extreme weakness, it was so difficult for us that we could not carry the dead bodies to their burial in any other way than by dragging them on a little sledge which had been used in the winter for the transport of wood.

May 10th. The foregoing days were very severe with cold and and frost which greatly weakened and hindered us, but on this day the weather was fine and numbers of geese arrived. We got one of them, which sufficed for two meals. We were, at that time, eleven persons alive, counting the sick. On the following day it was very cold and we remained quietly in our bunks because, in our extreme weakness, we could not stand any cold; our limbs being paralyzed and, as it were, crushed with cold.

On the next day died Jens Jorgensen the carpenter, and Suend Marstrand. And God knows what misery we suffered before we got their bodies buried. And these were the last that were buried in the ground.

On the 16th died the new skipper Jens Hendrichsen, and on the 19th died Erich Hansen Li who, throughout the voyage, had been very industrious and willing and had neither offended anyone or deserved any punishment. He had dug many graves for others, but now there was nobody who could dig his, and he had to remain unburied.

On the 22nd of May the sunshine was as fine and warm as anyone could wish from God and, by Divine Providence, a goose which three or four days before had had a leg shot off, came near the ship. We caught and cooked it, and we had food for two days off it.

Until the 28th there was nothing to write about, except that we seven miserable persons who were still lying there alive, looked mournfully at each other, hoping every day that the snow would thaw and the ice drift away.

As regards the symptoms of the illness which had fallen upon us, it was a rare and extraordinary one. All the limbs and joints were so miserably drawn together, with great pains in the loins, as if a thousand knives were thrust through them. The body, at the same time, was blue and brown as when one gets a black eye; and the whole body was quite powerless. The mouth also was in a very bad and miserable condition, as all the teeth were loose and we could not eat any victuals.*

During these days when we were lying in bed, so altogether bad, there died Peder Nyborg, carpenter, Knud Lauritzen Skudenes, and Jorgen, the cook's boy, all of whom remained on the steerage, for there was then nobody that could bury their bodies or throw them overboard.

On June 4th, which was Whitsunday, there remained only three alive, besides myself; all lying down unable to help one another. The stomach was ready enough, and had appetite for food, but the teeth would not allow it. The cook's boy lay dead beside my berth, and three men on the steerage. Two of the living were on shore, and would gladly have been back on ship but it was impossible for them to get there as they had not sufficient strength. We had now, for four days, had nothing for the sustenance of the body. Accordingly I did not now hope for anything but that God would put an end to this my misery; and thinking that it would have been the last I wrote in this world, I penned as follows:

> *Inasmuch as I have now no more hope of life in this world, I request for the sake of God, if any Christian men should happen to come here, that they will bury in the earth my poor body, together with the others which are found here, expecting their reward from God in Heaven. And, furthermore, that this, my journal, may be forwarded to my most gracious Lord and King (for every word that is found herein is altogether truthful) in order that my poor wife and children may obtain some benefit from my great distress and miserable death. Herewith, goodnight to all the world; and my soul into the hand of God.*
>
> *Jens Munk.*

* The disease was undoubtedly scurvy.

June 8th. As I could no longer stand the bad smell and stench from the dead bodies, I managed as best I could to get out of the berth, considering that it would not matter where, or among what surroundings I died. I spent that night on the deck using the clothes of the dead. Next day, when the two men who were on shore saw me and perceived that I was still alive (I had thought that they were dead long ago) they came out on the ice to the ship and assisted me to the land.

Then for some time we had our dwelling on shore, under a bush, and there we made a fire in the daytime. We crawled about everywhere near, wherever we saw the least green growing out of the ground, which we dug up and sucked the main root thereof. This benefited us and, as the warmth now commenced to increase nicely, we began to recover. But while we thus continued on the shore, the sailmaker who had remained aboard the ship now died.

June 18th. After the ice had drifted away from the ship we got a net for catching flounders, out of the sloop, and when the ebb had run out one-quarter, we went out dryshod and set it. When the flood returned, God gave us six large trout which I cooked myself, while the other two men went aboard the *Lamprey* to fetch wine, which we had not tasted for a long time, none of us having any appetite for it.

We now every day got fresh fish which was well cooked. It comforted us much, although we could not eat any of the meat, but only the broth, with which we drank wine, so that by degrees we recovered somewhat. At last we got a gun on shore and shot birds, from which we obtained much refreshment; so that day by day we got stronger and fairly well in health.

On the 26th of June we set to work to bring the *Lamprey* off the shore and alongside the ship, and worked as diligently as we could, getting sails ready for her. But herein we encountered a great difficulty and much anxiety, because the *Lamprey* stood high on shore, having been carried up by the winter flood. We were consequently obliged first to unload all that was in her and then to look for a high spring tide in order to haul her out. In this we succeeded, and at last brought her alongside the *Unicorn*.

When we boarded the *Unicorn* we threw overboard the dead bodies, which were then quite decomposed, as we could not move about or do anything there for bad smell and stench. Yet we required to take out of the *Unicorn*, and place aboard the *Lamprey*, victuals and necessaries for our use in crossing the sea.

It was not until the 16th of July that we were able to set sail from that place. At that time it was as warm as it might have been in Denmark, but there was such a quantity of mosquitoes that in calm weather they were unbearable. Before setting out I drilled some holes in the *Unicorn* in order that the water would rise in her, with the tide, and so keep her always firm on the ground in this harbour which I have called Jens Munk's Bay.

On the 17th we met much ice and stood off and on in front of it until later when we stuck firm in it and were so held for several days. On the 20th, while we were drifting in the ice, a large white bear came close to the ship. When he saw us he took flight across the ice and through the water, followed by a large dog which I had with me. The dog strayed from the vessel in consequence and never returned, though for a couple of days we could still hear him howl.

On the 22nd of July there was a severe gale and the ship drifted with great speed, and each time it struck against the ice it was as if it had struck against a rock. At that time the ice broke the rudder, and if I had not succeeded in throwing a grapnel on a large mass of ice, by which I could turn the ship so as to prevent her from drifting too fast, both ship and we would have been lost that day.

On the 26th we got clear of the ice and I stood to the east between the ice and the southern land, and for three days kept tacking between the ice and the land until I concluded that it was vain to hope to get past the ice on the southern side, and so on the 29th I stood again to the north-west and the following day again became fixed in the ice.

So we sailed in this great bay, with fog, gales and ice, until the 14th of August when we came at last to the entrance into Hudson's Strait. There was then so much ice in the channels between the Digges Islands that there was nothing to do but grapnel to the ice. Much snow fell on the 15th and the wild geese commenced briskly to fly south again.

Thus did we sail eastward through Hudson's Strait into the sea where we met storm and tempest. On the 4th of September we had tremendous rain, and wind amounting to a gale, and we could not at all leave off pumping. Toward evening the wind commenced to be more favourable and, as we were quite exhausted with pumping, we drifted the whole night without sails, in order to get some rest – as far as the pump would allow us to rest. On the 11th we had yet another gale and our foresail was torn from the bolt-rope so that we three men had plenty to do to get it in, and by then the sloop was half full of water.

On September 13th I conjectured we were in the longitude of Shetland, and we then descried a ship. We approached so near that we could speak to the people on board and I requested them to assist us; but though I got alongside him twice, he could not help me because the wind was too high.

Thus we bore on until the 20th of September when we saw Norway, and toward evening of the next day I steered into a bay, where I dropped anchor and thus remained without being moored as I had no boat wherewith to carry a hawser on shore. Later in the evening a peasant came there by accident, and I was obliged to threaten him with a gun to make him come with his boat and assist me in getting a hawser on shore.

As I had now seen the ship safe, and had returned into a Christian country, we poor men could not hold our tears back, for the great joy; and we thanked God that he had graciously granted us this happiness at the end of our journey.

The frightful experiences of this voyage, during which sixty-one of Munk's men died before his eyes, would have subdued the spirit of an ordinary man. But they did not make a landlubber out of Munk. The Thirty Years War was now well started and almost immediately after his return from Hudson Bay he was again at sea as a Naval Commander. He served with such effect that by 1628 he was Admiral of the Danish Fleet, and it was at this pinnacle of his career, and in his forty-ninth year, that he died.

He died unsatisfied. Until the last he had it in mind to make another expedition to the north-west. Had he not been such a good Naval Commander, and had the war not engrossed King Christian's interest and money, he would indubitably have made the second voyage, for his plans were drawn and complete. And if he had voyaged once again into the ice, perhaps the dark memories of his tragic first venture might have been overlaid by a success that he so well deserved.

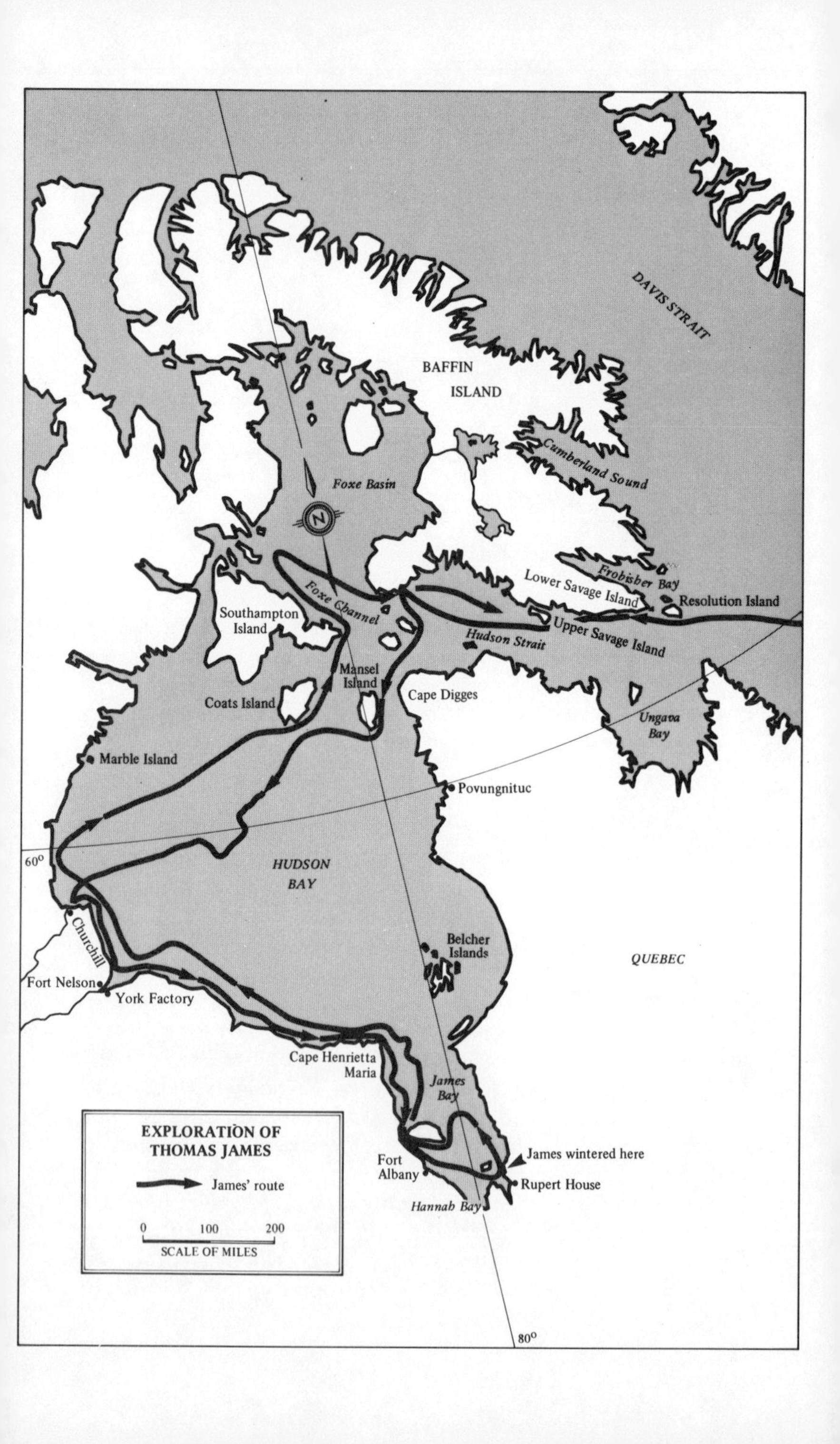

DAVIS STRAIT
BAFFIN
ISLAND
Cumberland Sound
Foxe Basin
N
Frobisher Bay
Lower Savage Island
Resolution Island
Foxe Channel
Southampton
Island
Upper Savage Island
Hudson Strait
Mansel
Island
Cape Digges
Coats Island
Ungava
Bay
Marble Island
Povungnituc
60°
HUDSON
BAY
Churchill
Belcher
Islands
QUEBEC
Fort Nelson
York Factory
Cape Henrietta
Maria
James
Bay
EXPLORATION OF
THOMAS JAMES
James' route
0
100
200
SCALE OF MILES
Fort
Albany
James wintered here
Rupert House
Hannah Bay
80°

IV

The Venturesome Voyage of Captain James

After Munk there was a ten-year hiatus in exploration to the north-west (and, considering what had happened to Munk, the wonder is that the hiatus was not five times as long); but in 1631 two expeditions were dispatched from England, both directed into Hudson Bay and both aiming at the discovery of the passage west.

One of these was supported by a group of London merchants who employed Captain Luke Foxe — Northwest Foxe, as he preferred to call himself — while the other was backed by the Company of Merchant Venturers of Bristol. The Bristol men seem to have decided on their voyage primarily to spite the London merchants for, then as now, there was nothing a Londoner could do that a Welshman did not feel he could do better. The Bristol faction hired Captain Thomas James to prove their point.

Very little is known of James before the date of his voyage. He was Welsh, that much is certain, and he was clearly an educated man. One source says that he was a "rich barrister-at-law," a peculiar qualification for an Arctic adventurer. Fortunately, he was also a good navigator, as well as being a good raconteur; but he must have been one of the world's most persistently unlucky explorers, as his journal demonstrates.

James and Foxe left England within a month of one another and by immense coincidence met briefly off the west shores of Hudson Bay. Foxe did not winter, but hurried home again where he wrote an acidulous and amusing book, in the course of which he backs poor James to ribbons both as a navigator and as an explorer. But his judgment of James, and that of many historians since then, is not particularly just. James at least realized that there was little or no prospect of a practicable north-west passage leading out of Hudson Bay, a fact that the rest of the world refused to credit until well into the nineteenth century. And in his own right he explored and mapped as great a part of the shores of Hudson and James Bays as any of his contemporaries, Foxe included.

Here then is his own account of the calamitous voyage of the seventy-ton Henrietta Maria, *which, after an almost catastrophic passage through Hudson Strait, reached the Bay in late July. We take up the story at this point.*

THE STRANGE AND DANGEROUS VOYAGE OF CAPTAIN THOMAS JAMES

In Hudson's Bay

On July 28th and 29th, 1631, we were so fast enclosed in the ice that, notwithstanding we put abroad all the sail, and that it blew a very hard gale of wind, the ship stirred no more than if she had been in a dry dock.

This was the first day that our men began to murmur, thinking it impossible to get either forward or backwards. The nights were getting long, and every night it did so freeze that we could not sail amongst the ice by night, nor in the thick foggy weather. I comforted and encouraged the men the best I could; and, to put away these cogitations, we drank a health to His Majesty on the ice – not one man remaining in the ship, and she still under all her sails. I most ingeniously confess that all their murmuring was not without reason; wherefore I ordered that fire should be made but once a day, the better to prolong our fuel, whatsoever should happen.

On the 30th we made some way through the ice, we heaving the ship with our shoulders and, with mawles and crow-bars of iron, breaking the corners of the ice to make way.

6th of August. In the morning the wind came up at North-West, and we weighed with much joy, hoping now to get into an open sea to the southward. This, by noon, we had done.

The 13th in the afternoon (it being something hazy) we saw some breakers ahead of us and, luffing to clear ourselves of them, we suddenly struck upon the rocks. In this fearful accident, we struck all our sails amain; but it did please God to send two or three good swelling seas which did heave us over the rocks into three fathoms, where we chopped to an anchor and tried the pumps; but we found she made no water, although she had three such terrible blows that we thought her mast would have sheered to pieces, and that she had been assuredly bilged.

We hoisted the boat overboard and double manned her, to go seek and sound a way out of this perilous place. But she was no sooner gone than there rose a fog, so that we were fain to spend some powder that she might hear whereabouts we were. The wind dropped a little; otherwise it had been doubtful whether she could ever have recovered to us again. After she had been absent two hours, she brought us word that it was all rocks and breakers round about us; but that withal she had found a way where there was not less than two fathoms and a half, and that afterwards the water did deepen. We did presently weigh and follow the boat. It being now night, we came to an anchor, where we did ride indifferent well all the night.

The 20th of August at six in the morning, we saw the western mainland, it being a very low flat land. We named it The New Principality of South Wales;* and drank a health in the best liquor we had to Prince Charles, His Highness, whom God preserve. We stood along it and came to a point where it trends to the southward, and here we came to an anchor.

About nine at night it was very dark and it did blow hard. We did perceive by the lead the ship did drag her anchor, wherefore we brought the cable to the capstan to heave in our cable, but the anchor caught the bottom again and, upon the chopping of a sea, threw the men from the capstan. A small rope, in the dark, had got foul about the cable and about the Master's leg too, but with the help of God, he did clear himself, though not without sore

* The present vicinity of Churchill.

bruising. The two Mates were hurt; the one in the head, the other in the arm. One of our lustiest men was struck on the breast with a capstan bar, so that he lay sprawling for life. Another had his head betwixt the cable, and hardly escaped. The rest were flung where they were sore bruised. But our gunner (an honest and diligent man) had his leg taken betwixt the cable and the capstan, which wrung off his foot, and tore all the flesh off his leg, and crushed the bone to pieces, and sorely withal bruised all his whole body; in which miserable manner he remained crying till we had recovered ourselves, our memory, and strengths to clear him. Whilst we were putting him and the rest down to the Surgeon, the ship drove into shoaler water, which put us all in fear, we being so sorely weakened by this blow, which had hurt eight of our men. But it pleased God that the anchor held again, and she rode it out all night. By midnight the Surgeon had taken off the gunner's leg at the gartering place, and dressed the others that were hurt and bruised, after which we comforted each other as well as we could.

The 29th in the morning, we made account we had drifted back again some sixteen or eighteen leagues; and in the morning, to our great surprise, we saw a ship to leeward of us, some three or four leagues. So we made sail and bore up with her. It was His Majesty's ship (the *Charles*), and Captain Foxe commanded in her.

In the morning Captain Foxe and his friends came aboard of me, where I entertained them in the best manner I could. I told him how I had named the land The South Principality of Wales. I showed him how far I had been to the Westward, where I had landed; and, in brief, I made known to him all the dangers of this coast, as far as I had been. He told me how he himself had been in Port Nelson, and that he had not been on land, nor had not many times seen the land. In the evening, after I had given his men some necessaries with tobacco and other things which they wanted, he departed aboard his ship and, the next morning, stood away South-South-West, since which time I never saw him.

The month of August ended with snow and hail, the weather being as cold as at any time I have felt in England.

September 1st. We coasted along the shore in ten fathoms, in sight of land.* At length the water shoaled; and we saw it all breakers to leeward. So we hauled off, but we had much ado to get safely out of this dangerous bay. This day was the first time

* They were now in James Bay.

the Surgeon told me that there were divers of the men tainted with sickness.*

The fourth, the weather was very thick, and we sounded continually. In the evening, there came a great rolling sea and, by reason of the encounter of the wind and this great sea, the sea was all in a breach; and to make up a perfect tempest, it did thunder and lightning, snow, rain, and blow all the night long, that I was never in the like. We shipped many seas, but one most dangerous which racked us fore and aft, that I verily thought it had sunk the ship, it struck her with such a violence. The ship did labour most terribly in this distraction of wind and waves, and we had much ado to keep all things fast in the hold and betwixt decks.

The fifth, in the morning, the wind continued in his old anger and fury. In the afternoon it shifted to the North-West and there showed his uttermost malice; and in a tearing violence that not I, nor any that were then with me, ever saw the sea in such a breach. Our ship was so tormented, and did so labour, with taking it in on both sides and at both ends, that we were in a most miserable distress in this so unknown a place.

At eight o'clock in the evening the storm broke up, and we had some quietness in the night following, not one having slept one wink in thirty hours before. If this storm had continued Easterly, as it was at first, without God's goodness, we had all perished.

The sixth, we spent the time in trimming our ship. Others did pick our bread,† whereof there was much wet, for do what we could, we shipped abundance of water betwixt decks, which ran into the hold and into our breadroom; for the sea, indeed, so continually over-racked us that we were like Jonas in the whale's belly. This evening, our boatswain was very sick, swooning away three or four times; insomuch that we thought verily he would presently have died.

The eleventh, in the morning, I went in the boat ashore and, whilst I was aland, I sent the boat about amongst the broken grounds to sound. I found an island utterly barren of all goodness; yea, of that which I thought easily to have found, which was scurvy-grass, sorrell, or some herb or other, to have refreshed our sick people.

The twelfth of September, in the morning, it began to blow

* Scurvy

† "Hard-tack" biscuits.

hard at South-East, which was partly off the shore, and the ship began to drive, it being soft oozie ground. We heaved in our anchor thereupon and came to sail. Whilst the most were busy in heaving out of topsails, some that should have had special care of the ship ran her ashore upon the rocks, out of mere carelessness in not looking out, or heaving of the lead, after they had seen the land all night long, and might even then have seen it if they had not been blinded with self conceit, and been enviously opposite in opinions. The first blow struck me out of a dead sleep; and I, running out of my cabin, thought no other, at first, but I had been awakened (when I saw our danger) to provide myself for another world.

After I had controlled a little passion in myself, and had checked some bad counsel that was given me to revenge myself upon those that had committed this error, I ordered what should be done to get off these rocks and stones. First we hauled all our sail aback; but that did no good, but made her pound the harder. Whereupon we struck all our sails amain, and furled them up close, tearing a hole in our stern to bring the cable through the cabin to the capstan in the bow, and so laid out an anchor to heave her astern. I made all the drinking water in the hold to be pumped out, and did intend to do the like with our beer. Others I put to throw out all our coals, which was soon and readily done. We coiled out our cables into our long boat, all this while the ship beating so fearfully that we saw some of her sheathing swim by us. Then stood we, as many as we could, to the capstan, and heaved with such good will that the cable broke, and we lost our anchor. Out, with all speed, therefore, we put another. We could not now perceive whether she did leak or no, though we much expected that she had received her death's wound. Wherefore we put into the boat the carpenter's tools, a barrel of bread, a barrel of powder, six muskets with some match and a tinder-box, fish hooks and lines, pitch and oakum, and, to be brief, whatever could be thought on in such an extremity. All this we sent ashore to prolong a miserable life for a few days.

We were five hours thus beating on the rocks, in which time she struck one hundred blows; insomuch that we thought every stroke had been the last that it was possible she could have endured. At length, it pleased God, she beat over all the rocks, though yet we knew not whether she were staunch. Whereupon to pumping go all hands till we made the pumps suck, and then we saw how much water she did make. We found her to be very leaky, but we went to prayer and gave God thanks it was no worse, and so fitted all things again, and got further off, and came to an anchor.

In the evening it began to blow very hard at W.S.W.; which, if it had done whilst we were on the rocks, we had lost our ship without any redemption. With much ado we weighed our anchor and let her drive to the Eastward amongst the broken grounds and rocks, the boat going before sounding. At length we came amongst breakers, and the boat made signs to us that there was no going further. Amongst the rocks, therefore, we again came to anchor, where we did ride all night, and where our men, which were tired out with extreme labour, were indifferent well refreshed, for we did pump almost continually.

The 13th of September at noon, we weighed and stood to the Westward; but, in that course, it was all broken grounds, shoals, and sunken rocks, so that we wondered with ourselves how we had found our way in amongst them, and that in a thick fog. Then we shaped our course to the Northward; and, after some consultation with my associates, I resolved to get about this island, and so to go down into the bottom of Hudson's Bay, and see if I could discover a way into the River of Canada;* and, if I failed of that, then to winter on the main land, where there is more comfort to be expected than among rocks or islands.

In the evening of the 14th, it began to blow a storm not sail-worthy; and the sea went very high and was all in a breach. Our shallop, which we did now tow at stern in case of shipwreck, was sunken, and did spin by her moorings with her keel up, twenty times in an hour. This made our ship to veer very broad, so that the sea did continually over-rake us, yet we endured it, and thought to recover the shallop.

All night the storm continued with violence. The water shoaled apace, with such an over-grown sea withal that a sail was not to be endured; and, what was as ill, there was no trusting to an anchor. Now, therefore, we began to prepare ourselves how to make a good end of a miserable tormented life. About noon, as it cleared up, we saw two islands under our lee, whereupon we bare up to them; and seeing an opening betwixt them, we endeavoured to get into it before night; for there was no hope of us if we con-

* The St. Lawrence River.

tinued out at sea that night. Therefore, come life, come death, we must run this hazard.

We found it to be a good sound, where we rode all night safely, and recovered our strength again, which was much impaired with continual labour. But before we could get into this good place our shallop broke away and we lost her, to our great grief. Thus now had we but the ship's boat, and she was all torn and bruised.

Seeing the winds continue so Northerly that we could not get about to go into the bottom of Hudson's Bay, we considered again what was best to do to look out for a wintering place. Some advised me to go for Port Nelson, because we were certain that there was a cove where we might bring in our ship. I liked not that counsel; for that is a most perilous place, and that it might be so long ere we could get thither that we might be debarred from it by the ice. Moreover, seeing it was so cold here as that every night our rigging did freeze, and that sometimes in the morning we did shovel away the snow half a foot thick off our decks, I thought it far worse in Port Nelson, it being much farther North. I resolved thereupon to stand again to the Southward, there to look for some little creek or cove for our ship.

The last night and this morning, the 23rd of September, it did snow and hail, and was very cold; nevertheless I took the boat and went ashore to look for some creek or cove to hove in our ship; for she was very leaky and the company become sickly and weak with much pumping and extreme labour. This island, to which we had now come, was nothing but ledges of rocks and banks of sand, and there went a very great surf on them. Nevertheless, I made them row through it; and ashore I got with two more, and made the boat row off outside the surf, and there to come to an anchor and to stay for me.

I made what speed I could to the top of a hill to discover about, but could not see what we looked for; thus, because it began to blow hard, I made haste towards the boat again. I found that the tide had ebbed so low that the boat could not by any means come near the shore for me, so that we were fain to wade through the surf and breakers to her, in which some took such a cold that they did complain of it to their dying day.

Now it began to blow hard, so that we could not get but little to windward toward our ship; and return to the shore we could not, by reason of the surf. Well, we rowed for life; they in the ship let out a buoy by a long warp; and, by God's assistance, we got to it, and so hauled up to the ship, where we were well welcomed and we all rejoiced together.

The 25th we weighed, and thought to get to the Eastward, but, as we tacked to and again, the wind shifted so in our teeth that it put us within a quarter of a mile of the shore, where we chopped to an anchor and rid out for life and death. Such miseries as these we endured amongst these shoals and broken grounds or, rather, more desperate than I have related (very unpleasant perchance to be read), with snow, hail and stormy weather, and colder than ever I felt it in England in my life. All this lasted with us until the 30th of this month of September, which we thought would have put an end to our miseries; for now we were driven amongst rocks, shoals, overfalls, and breakers round about us, that which way to turn we knew not, but there rode amongst them in extremity of distress.

The third of October, about noon, the wind dulled and we had up our anchor, standing in further in the bay. I took the boat and went presently ashore on an island* to see what comfort I could find. I found the tracks of deer, and saw some fowl; but what did rejoice me most was that I did see an opening into the land, as if it had been a river. To it we made all speed, but found it to be barred; and not two foot water at full sea on the bar; and yet within a most excellent fine harbour. In the evening I returned aboard, bringing little comfort for our sick men, more than hopes.

The 4th it did snow and blow very hard, yet I got ashore and went some four or five miles up into the country, but could find no relief all that way for our sick, but a few berries only. Thus we returned aboard with no good news. It continued foul weather, with snow and hail and extreme cold, till the 6th, when, with a favouring wind, we stood in nearer to the shore, and here moored the ship.

October 7th it snowed all day, so that we were fain to clear it off the decks with shovels; and it blew a very storm withal. It continued snowing and very cold weather, and it did so freeze that all the bows of the ship, with her beak-head, was all ice. Afterwards the sun did shine very clear, and we tore the top-sails out of the tops, which were hard frozen in them into a lump, so that there they hung a-sunning in a very lump, the sun not having power to thaw one drop of them.

* Probably Charlton Island.

After the boat was fitted, we rowed towards the shore, but could not come near the place where we were used to land, for it was all thickened water with the snow that had fallen. This made it so difficult to row that we could not get through it with four oars; yet something higher to the westward we got ashore. Seeing now the winter to come thus extremely upon us, and that we had very little wood aboard, I made them fill the boat, and went aboard and sent the carpenter and others to cut wood, others to carry it to the water side, whilst the boat brought it aboard, for I expected that we were likely to be debarred the shore, and that we should not go to and fro' again with the boat.

It was miserable and cold already aboard the ship; everything did freeze in the hold and by the fire side. Seeing therefore that we could no longer make use of our sails (which be the wings of a ship) it raised many doubts in our minds that here we must stay and winter.

After we had brought so much wood aboard as we could conveniently stow, the sick men desired that some little house or hovel might be built ashore, whereby they might be the better sheltered, and recover their healths. I took the carpenter (and others whom I thought fit for such a purpose) and, choosing out a place, they went immediately to work upon it. In the meantime, I myself, accompanied with some others, wandered up and down in the woods to see if we could discover any signs of savages, that we might the better provide for our safety against them. We found no appearance that there was any on this island, nor near unto it. The snow by this time was half-leg high; and, stalking through it, we returned comfortless to our companions, who had all this time wrought well upon our house.

The 12th of October we took our main sail from the yard, which was hard frozen to it, and carried it ashore to cover our house withal, being first fain to thaw it by a great fire. By night, they had covered it, and the six builders did desire to lie in it ashore that night, which I condescended unto, having first fitted them with muskets and other furniture and a charge to keep good watch all night. Moreover, they had ashore two greyhounds (a dog and a bitch) which I had brought out of England to kill us some deer, if happily we could find any.

The 14th betimes in the morning, being fitted with munition some of our men went hunting, and on the 15th in the evening, returned very weary, and brought with them a small, lean deer which rejoiced us all, hoping we should have had more of them to refresh our sick men withal. They reported that they had wandered about twenty miles, and had brought this deer above twelve mile, and that they had seen nine or ten more. The last night they had a very cold lodging in the woods; and so it appeared, for they looked almost frozen, nor could they recover themselves in three or four days after. They saw no sign of savages, nor of any ravening wild beasts, nor yet any hope of harbour.

The 17th my Lieutenant and five more desired they might try their fortunes in travelling about the island. But they had far worse luck than the others, although they endured out all night and had wandered very far in the snow (which was now very deep) and returned comfortless and miserably disabled with the coldness. But, what was worse than all this, they had lost one of their company, John Barton, our gunner's mate, who, being very weary, had attempted to go over a pond where, when he was in the very middle, the ice broke and closed over him, and we never saw him more.

Considering these disasters, I resolved to fish no more with a golden hook, for fear I weakened myself more with one hunting than twenty such deer could do me good. Being now assured that there were no savages upon the island, we comforted and refreshed ourselves by sleeping the more securely. We changed our island garrison every week; and, for other refreshing, we were like to have none till the spring.

From this to the 29th of October it did (by interims) snow and blow so hard that the boats could hardly adventure ashore, and but seldom land, unless the men did wade in the thick congealed water, carrying one another. We did sensibly perceive withal how we did daily sink into more miseries. The land was all deep covered with snow, the cold did multiply, and the thick snow water did increase; and what would become of us, our most merciful God and preserver only knew.

The 4th of November, the men found a place to get ashore, and so brought beer to our men ashore, in a barrel, which would freeze firmly in the house in one night. This ice beer, being thawed in a kettle, was not good, and they did break the ice of the ponds of water to come by water to drink. This pond-water had a most lothesome smell with it, so that thinking it might be infectious, I caused a well to be sunk near the house. There we had very good water which did taste (as we flattered ourselves with it) even like milk.

The 12th of November our house took afire, but we soon quenched it. We were fain to keep an extraordinary fire, night and day; and this accident made me order a watch to look to it continually; seeing that, if our house and clothing should be burnt, all would be in a woeful condition.

I lay ashore till the 17th, all which time our miseries did increase. It did snow and freeze most extremely. At which time, we looking from the shore towards the ship, she did look like a piece of ice in the fashion of a ship, or a ship resembling a piece of ice. The snow was all frozen about her, and all her fore-part firm ice, and so was she on both sides also. Our cables froze in the hawse, wonderful to behold.

I got me back aboard, where the long nights I spent with tormenting cogitations; and, in the day time, I could not see any hope of saving the ship. This I was assured of; that it was most impossible to endure these extremities long. Every day the men must beat the ice off the cables, while some with the carpenter's long calking iron did dig the ice out of the hawse pipes; in which work, the water would freeze on their clothes and hands, and would so benumb them that they could hardly get into the ship without being heaved in with a rope.

The 19th our gunner (who, as you should remember, had his leg cut off) did languish unrecoverably, and now grew very weak, desiring that, for the little time he had to live, he might drink sack altogether, which I ordered he should do.

The 22nd in the morning, he died; an honest and a strong-hearted man. He had a close-boarded cabin in the gunroom, and as many clothes on him as was convenient (for we wanted no clothes) and a pan with coals afire continually in his cabin. For all which warmth, his plaster would freeze at his wound, and his bottle of sack at his head. We committed him at a good distance from the ship unto the sea.

The three and twentieth, the ice did increase extraordinarily, and the snow lay on the water in flakes as it did fall; much ice withal drove by us. In the evening, after the watch was set, a great piece came athwart our hawse, and four more followed after him, the least of them a quarter of a mile broad; which, in the dark, did very much astonish us, thinking it would have carried us out of the harbour upon the shoals which was full of rocks. It was newly congealed, a matter of two inches thick, and we broke through it, the cable and anchor enduring an incredible stress, sometimes stopping the whole ice. We shot off three muskets, signifying to our men ashore that we were in distress, who answered us again, but could not help us.

And now I resolved to bring the ship aground, for no cables nor anchors could hold her against the ice. We brought the ship into twelve foot water, and laid out one anchor in the offing, and another in shoal water, to draw her to land at command. We then being about a mile from the shore, about ten o'clock in the dark night, the ice came driving upon us, and our anchors came loose. She drove some two cables length and, the wind blowing on the shore, by two o'clock she came aground.

On the 25th the wind came up at North-West, and blew a very storm. The wind was off the shore, which blew away all the ice from about us. Then there came in a great rolling sea withal, accompanied with a great surf on the shore. And now were we left to the mercy of the sea, on the ground. By ten, she began to roll and, soon after, began to beat against the ground. We stood at the capstan, as many as could, others at the pumps, for we thought that every fifth or sixth blow would have staved her to pieces. We heaved to the uttermost of our strengths, to keep her as near the shore as we could. By reason of this wind it flowed very much water, and we drew her up so high that it was doubtful if ever we should get her off again. She continued thus beating till two o'clock the next morning, and then she again settled; whereupon we went to sleep, to restore nature, seeing the next tide we expected to be again tormented.

The sixth and twentieth, in the morning tide, our ship did not float, whereby we had some quietness. After prayers I called a consultation of the Master, my Lieutenants, the Mates, carpenter, and boatswain, to whom I proposed that now we were put to our last shifts, and therefore, they should tell me what they thought of it; namely, whether it were not best to carry all our provisions ashore, and that, when the wind should come Northerly, it were not safest to draw her further off and sink her as the best way to preserve her. After many reasonings, they allowed of my purpose, and so I communicated it to the company who all willingly agreed to it. And so we fell to getting up of our provisions, first our bread, with a hogshead of beef, having much ado to get the boat through the thick congealed water.

The 28th, I made the carpenter prepare the ship against all sudden extremities; for that, with the first North-West or Northerly wind, I meant to effect our last project. On the starboard side he cut away the sealing and the plank to the sheathing, some four or five inches square, so that it might be bored out at an instant. We brought our remaining bread up into the great cabin, and likewise all our powder, setting much of our light dry things betwixt decks.

The nine and twentieth, at five o'clock in the morning, the wind came up. By seven o'clock, it blew a storm at North-West, our bitter enemy. The ship was already bedded some two foot deep in the sand, and whilst that tide was flowing, she must beat. Yet we had been so frighted by her last beating that I resolved to sink her right down, rather than run that hazard. By nine o'clock she began to roll with a most extraordinary great sea that was come. And this was the fatal hour that put us to our wits end. Wherefore, I went down in the hold with the carpenter, and took his auger and bored a hole in the ship, and let in the water. Thus, with all speed, we began to cut out other places to bore through, but every place was full of nails. By ten, notwithstanding, the lower tier was covered with water; despite which she began so to beat more and more, that we could not work nor stand to do anything in her. Nor would she sink so fast as we would have her, but continued beating double blows, first abaft, and then before, that it was wonderful how she could endure a quarter of an hour with it. By twelve o'clock the water inside her surged so that it beat the bulkheads of the bread-room, powder-room and fore peak all to pieces; and, when it came betwixt decks, the chests fled wildly about, and the water did flash and fly wonderfully, so that now we expected every minute that the ship would open and break to pieces.

At one o'clock, she beat off her rudder, and that was gone, we knew not which way. Thus she continued beating till three o'clock, and then the sea came up on the upper deck; and, soon after, she began to settle. In her, we were fain to sink the most part of our bedding and clothes, and the Surgeon's chest with the rest. Our men that were ashore stood looking upon us, almost dead with cold and sorrow, to see our misery and their own. We looked upon them again, and both upon each other, with woeful hearts. Dark night drew on, and I bade the boat to be hauled up, and commanded my loving companions to go all in her, who expressed their faithful affections to me, as loth to part from me, until I told them that my meaning was to go ashore with them. And thus, lastly, I foresook the ship.

We were seventeen poor souls now in the boat, and we now

imagined that we were leapt out of the frying pan into the fire. The ebb was made, and the water extraordinary thick congealed with snow, so that we thought, assuredly, it would carry us away into the sea. We thereupon double-manned four oars, appointing four more to sit ready with oars, and so, with the help of God, we got to the shore, hauling up the boat after us. Being arrived upon the land, we greeted our fellows the best we could, at which time they could not know us, nor we them, by our clothing nor voices, so frozen all over we were, faces, hair, and apparel.

The Wintering

After we had hauled up the boat, we went along in the dark towards our house, where we made a good fire and, with it and bread and water, we thawed and comforted ourselves, beginning after that to reason one with another concerning our ship. I required that every one should speak his mind freely. The carpenter (especially) was of the opinion that she was foundered and would never be serviceable again. He alleged that she had so beaten that it was not possible but that all her joints were loose and seams open, and that, by reason of no creek nor cove being near wherein to bring her aground, he could not devise how he might come to mend it. Moreover, her rudder was lost, and he had no ironwork to hang on another. Some alleged that we had heaved her up so high upon the sands that they thought we should never have her off again. Others, that she lay in the tides way, and that the ice might tear her to pieces; besides which, two of our anchors we could not now get from under the ice which, when the ice broke (which would be of a great thickness by the spring) would break our anchors to pieces, and then we should have no anchors to bring us home withal, supposed we got the ship off and that she proved sound also.

I comforted them the best I could with such like words: "My Masters and faithful companions, be not dismayed for any of these disasters, but let us put our whole trust in God. His will be done. If it be our fortunes to end our days here, we are as near heaven as in England; but, in my judgement we are not yet so far past hope of returning into our native countries but that I see a fair way by which we may effect it. Admitting the ship be foundered (which God forbid: I hope the best), yet have those of our own nation, and others, when they have been put to these extremities, even out of the wreck of their lost ship built them a pinnace, and recovered to their friends again. It may be objected that they have happened into better climates, yet there is nothing too hard for courageous minds."

They all protested to work to the uttermost of their strength, and that they would refuse nothing that I should order them to do, to the uttermost hazard of their lives. I thanked them all; and, to the carpenter, for his cheerful undertaking to construct a pinnace, I promised to give him so much plate presently as should be worth ten pound sterling; and, if so be we went to England in the pinnace, I would give her him freely, and fifty pounds in money over and above, and would, moreover, gratify all those whom I should see painful and industrious. Thus we then resolved to build us the frame of a new pinnace with the timber we should get upon the island, that so, in the spring, if we found the ship not serviceable, we might tear her up and plank the pinnace with the ship's planks. And so, for this night, we settled ourselves close about the fire, and took some rest till daylight.

The thirtieth, betimes in the morning, I caused the Surgeon to cut the hair of my head short, and to shave away all the hair of my face, for that it was become intolerable and that it would be frozen so great with icicles. The like did all the rest, and we fitted ourselves to work.

The first thing we were to do was to get our clothes and provisions ashore. In the afternoon the water veered to so low an ebb that we thought we might get something out of our ship's hold. We launched our boat, therefore and set through the thick congealed water. It did freeze extreme hard, and I did stand on the shore with a troubled mind, thinking verily that, with the ebb, the boat would be carried into the sea and that then we were all lost men. But, by God's assistance, they got safely to the ship and made a fire there to signify their arrival aboard. They fell presently to work and got something out of the hold upon the decks; but, night coming on, they durst not adventure to come ashore, but lay on the bed in the great cabin, being almost frozen.

The first of December was so cold that I walked the same way over the ice to the ship where the boat had gone yesterday. This day we carried upon our backs in bundles 500 of our dried fish, and much of our bedding and clothes, which we were fain to dig out of the ice inside the vessel.

The 2nd was mild weather, and some of the men, going over

the ice, fell in, and very hardly recovered, so that this day we could land nothing, neither by boat nor back. I put them therefore to make us a store-house ashore.

In the evening the wind came up at West and the ice did break and drive out of the bay. And on the next day there were divers great pieces of ice that came athwart the ship, and she stopped them, yet not so that we could walk over them. We found a way for the boat; but when she was laden she drew four foot water, and could not come within a flight-shot of the shore. The men, therefore, must wade through the thick congealed water and carry all things out of the ship upon their backs. Every time they waded in the ice, it so gathered about them that they did seem like a walking piece of ice, most lamentable to behold.

The fifth and sixth were extremely cold, and we made bags of our store shirts and in them carried our loose bread over the ice ashore upon our backs. We also dug our clothes and new sails, with hand-spikes of iron, out of the ice, and carried them ashore, which we dried by a great fire.

The tenth of December our carpenter found timber to make a keel and a stern for our pinnace. The rest wrought about our provisions until the 13th day, which we spent in digging our boat out of the ice (where she lay frozen by the ship), which we were fain to do to the very keel, and dig the ice out of her; and then we got her up on the ice, in which doing many had their noses, cheeks and fingers frozen as white as paper. The cold now increased most extremely. By the 19th we could get no more things out of our hold, but were fain to leave five barrels of beef and pork, all our beer, and divers others things, which were all firm frozen in her.

The three and twentieth, we went to haul our boat ashore, running her over our oars but, by 10 o'clock, there came such a thick fog that it was as dark as night. I made them give over, and make what haste we could to the shore which we had much ado to find, for the time losing one another. At the last we met all at the house, the miserablest frozen fellows that can be conceived. Upon many the cold had raised blisters as big as walnuts. This we imagined to come by reason that they came too hastily to the fire.

Long before Christmas our mansion house was covered thick over with snow, almost to the very roof of it. Thus we seemed to live in a heap and wilderness of snow; forth out of doors we could not go, but upon the snow, in which we made us paths, middle-deep in some places.

The cold was as extreme through February as at any time we had felt it this year, and many of our men complained of infirmities; some of sore mouths, all the teeth in their heads being loose, their gums swollen, with black rotten flesh, which must every day be cut away. The pain was so sore on them that they could not eat their ordinary meat. Others complained of pain in their heads and their breasts; some of weakness in their backs; others of aches in their thighs and knees; and others of swellings in their legs.* Thus were two thirds of the company under the Surgeon's hands. And yet, nevertheless, they must work daily and go abroad to fetch wood and timber, notwithstanding the most of them had no shoes to put on. Their shoes, upon their coming to the fire, out of the snow, were burnt and scorched upon their feet, and our store-shoes were all sunk in the ship. In this necessity they would make this shift; to bind clouts about their feet, and endeavoured by that poor help, the best they could, to perform their duties. Our carpenter likewise is by this time fallen sick, to our great discomfort.

Since now I have spoken so much of the cold, I hope it will not be too coldly taken if I, in a few words, make it someway to appear unto our readers.

We made three differences of the cold, all according to the places. In our house; in the woods; and in the open air upon the ice in our going to the ship.

For the last, it would be sometimes so extreme that it was not endurable; no clothes were proof against it; no motion could resist it. It would, moreover, so freeze the hair on our eyelids that we could not see; and I verily believe that it would have stifled a man in a very few hours. We did daily find by experience that the cold in the woods would freeze our faces, or any part of our flesh that was bare, but it was yet not so mortifying as the other. Our house, on the outside, was covered two third-parts with snow and, on the inside, frozen and hung with icicles. The clothes on our beds would be covered with hoar frost which, in this little habitation, was not far from the fire. But let us come a little nearer to it. The cook's tubs, wherein he did soak his salt meat, standing about a yard from the fire, and which he did all day ply with melted snow-water, yet in the night season, whilst he slept but one watch, would they be firm frozen to the very bottom. And, therefore, was he

* All symptoms of advanced scurvy.

fain to soak his meat in a brass kettle, close adjoining the fire, and I have many times both seen and felt, by putting my hand into it, that the side which was next the fire was very warm, and the other side an inch frozen. I leave the rest to our cook who will almost speak miracles of the cold. Also the surgeon, who had hung his bottles of syrups and other liquid things as conveniently as he could to preserve them, had them all frozen. Our vinegar, oil, and sack, which we had in small casks in the house, was also all firm frozen.

The fifteenth of March, one of our men thought he had seen a deer, whereupon he, with two or three more, desired that they might go to see if they could take it. I gave them leave; but in the evening they returned so disabled with cold, which did rise up in blisters under the soles of their feet, and upon their legs, to the bigness of walnuts, that they could not recover their former estate (which was not very well) in a fortnight after.

The six and twentieth, three more desired that they also might go out to try their fortunes, but they returned worse disabled, and even almost stifled with the cold.

In brief, all this month had been very cold; the wind about the N.W.; the snow as deep as it hath been all this winter; but, to answer any objection that may be made: "You were in a wood" (some men may say unto us) "and therefore you might make fire enough to keep you from the cold." It is true, we were in a wood and under a south bank too, or otherwise we had all perished. But I must tell you withal how difficult it was to get wood even in a wood; and first I will make a muster of the tools we had. The carpenter had two axes indeed; but one of them was spoiled in cutting down wood to pile about our house before Christmas. When we came first a-land, we had but two whole hatchets (apart from those three belonging to the cooper), which in a few days broke two inches below the sockets. The carpenter's axe and the cooper's best hatchet I caused to be locked up, and the blades of two broken hatchets to be put into cleft pieces of wood, and then to be bound about with rope yarn as fast as might be, which must be repaired every day. And these were all the cutting tools we had; moreover, the 6th of February, the carpenter had out his remaining axe about something, and one of the company, in his absence, by his indiscreet handling of it, broke that too. We had henceforth to order these pieces of tools the best we could; wherefore I gave order that the carpenter should have one of the cooper's hatchets; they that looked for timber to build the pinnace, the other; and they that cut down wood to burn were to have the two broken hatchets. And this was before Christmas.

The three that were appointed to look for crooked timber for the pinnace must stalk and wade (sometimes on all fours) through the snow; and, where they saw a tree likely to fit the mould, they must first heave away the snow, and then see if it would fit the mould, if not, they must seek further. If it did fit the mould, then they must make a fire to it, to thaw it; otherwise it could not be cut. Then they must cut it down and then, with other help, get it home a mile through the snow.

Now, for our firing, we could not burn green wood; it would so smoke that it was not endurable, for we had but an open fire; yea, the men had rather freeze without in the cold than sit by it. As for the dry wood, that also was bad enough; for it was full of turpentine and would send forth such a thick smoke that would make abundance of soot, which made us all look as if we had been free of the company of chimney-sweepers. Our clothes were quite burnt in pieces about us; and for the most part we were all without shoes. But to our fuellers again. They must first go up and down in the snow till they saw a standing dry tree, for the snow covered any that were fallen. Then they must hack it down with their pieces of hatchets, and then others must carry it home through the snow. The boys with cutlasses must cut boughs for the carpenter's fire; for every piece of timber that he did work must first be thawed in the fire, and he must have a fire by him, or he could not work. And this was our continual labour throughout the fore-mentioned cold, besides our tending of the sick and other necessary employments.

The first of April, being Easter-day, we solemnised as religiously as God did give us grace. Both this day and the two following Holy-days were extremely cold, and now, sitting all about the fire, we reasoned and considered together upon our estate. We had five men (whereof the carpenter was now one) not able to do anything. The boatswain, and many more, were very infirm; and, of all the rest, we had but five that could eat of their ordinary allowance. Our pinnace was in an indifferent forwardness, but the carpenter grew worse and worse. The ship lay all full of solid ice, which was weight enough to open the seams of any new and sound vessel, especially of one that had lain so long upon the ground as she had done. In brief, after many disputations, and laying open of our miserable and hopeless estates, I resolved upon this course;

that, notwithstanding it was more labour, and though we declined weaker still and weaker, yet that, with the first warm weather, we would begin to clear the ship.

This being ordered, we looked to those tools we had to dig the ice out of her; we had but two iron bars ashore, the rest were sunk in the ship, and one of them was broken too. Well, we fell to fitting of those bars, and of four broken shovels that we had, with which we intended to dig the ice out of her, and to lay that ice on a heap beside the larboard bow, and to sink down that ice to the bottom so far that it should be a barricade to us when the bay ice broke up, which we feared would tear the ship to pieces.

The nineteenth, we continued our mining work aboard the ship, and returned in the evening to supper ashore. This day, the Master and two others desired that they might lie aboard, which I condescended to; for indeed they had lain very discommodiously all the winter, and with sick bed-fellows, as I myself had done. By lying aboard they avoided the hearing of the miserable groanings and lamenting of the sick men all night long, enduring (poor souls) intolerable torments.

By the one and twentieth, we had laboured so hard that we came to see a cask and could likewise perceive that there was some water in the hold. This we knew could not be thawed water, because it did still freeze night and day very hard aboard the ship, and on the land also.

By the three and twentieth, in the evening, we came to pierce the aforementioned cask, and found it was full of very good beer, which did much rejoice us all, especially the sick men, notwithstanding that it did taste a little of bilge-water.

The four and twentieth, I put them to work on the outside of the ship, that we might reach the lower hole which we had cut in the stern-sheets to sink her. With much labour, by night, we dug down through the ice to it, and found it unfrozen (as it had been all the winter); and, to our great comforts, we found that on the inside the water was ebbed even with the hole, and that on the outside it was ebbed a foot lower. Hereupon I made a shot-board to be nailed on it, and to be made as tight as might be, to try if the water came in any other way. To the other two holes, we had dug on the inside and found them frozen.

Our carpenter was by this time past hope, and therefore little hope had we of our pinnace. But, which was worst of all, we had not four men able to travel through the snow over the ice; and in this miserable estate were we at this present.

The 25th we satisfied our longing; for the water rose outside the ship (where we had dug down) a foot and more above the hold, and yet did not rise within board. This did so encourage us that we fell very lustily to digging, and to heave out the ice out of the ship. I put the cook and some others to thaw the pumps, who, by continual pouring of hot water into them cleared one of them, which we found did deliver water very sufficiently.

The one and thirtieth of April was very cold, with snow and hail, which did pinch our sick men more than any time this year. This evening, being May evening, we returned late from our work to our house and made a good fire, and chose Ladies, and did ceremoniously wear their names on our caps, endeavouring to revive ourselves by any means. And now, because you hear us in this merry humour, I will make known to you what good cheer we kept and how we had dieted ourselves all the winter.

At our coming forth of England, we were stored with all sort of sea provisions, as salt beef, salt pork, dry fish, etc. which our cook did order in this manner:

The beef which was to serve on Sunday night to supper, he did boil on Saturday night in a kettle full of water, with a quart of oatmeal, about an hour. Then, taking the beef out, he boiled the rest till it came to half the quantity. And this we called porridge which, with bread, we did eat as hot as we could; and after this we had our ordinary portion of fish. Sunday dinner, we had pork and peas, and at night the former boiled beef made more porridge. In this manner our Tuesday's beef was boiled on the Monday nights, and the Thursday's upon the Wednesdays; and thus all the week (except Friday night) we had some warm thing in our bellies every supper. And (surely) this did us a great deal of good. But soon after Christmas many of us fell sick, and had sore mouths, and could neither eat beef, pork, fish, nor porridge. Their diet was only this: they would pound bread or oatmeal in a mortar to meal, then fry it in a frying pan with a little oil, and so eat it. Some would boil peas to a soft paste, and feed as well as they could upon that. For the most part of the winter, water was our drink. In the whole winter we took not above a dozen foxes, many of which would be dead in the traps two or three days, oftentimes, and then when the blood was settled they would be unwholesome. But if we took one alive that had not been long in the trap, him we boiled and made broth for the weakest sick men. The flesh of it, being soft boiled, they did eat also.

Some white partridge were killed, but not worth the mentioning towards any refreshing.

We had three sorts of sick men; those that could not move, nor turn themselves in their beds, who must be tended like an infant; others that were, as it were, crippled with scurvy aches; and others, lastly, that were something better. Most of all had sore mouths.

You may now ask me how these infirm men could work? I will tell you. Our Surgeon (which was diligent, and a sweet conditioned man as ever I saw) would be up betimes in the mornings and, whilst he did pick their teeth, and cut away the dead flesh from their gums, they would bathe their own thighs, knees and legs. The manner whereof was this: there was no tree, bud, nor herb but we made trial of it; and this, being first boiled in a kettle, and then put in small tubs and basins, they put it under them, and this would so mollify the grieved parts that, although when they did rise out of their beds they would be so crippled that they could scarce stand, yet after this was done half an hour, they would be able to go (and must go) to the wood through the snow, to the ship, and about their other business. By night they would be as bad again, and then they must be bathed, annointed, and their mouths again dressed, before they went to bed. And with this diet, and in this manner, did we go through our miseries.

Spring Suns

I expected that we should be weakest in the spring, and therefore had I reserved a tun of wine unto this time. Of this, by putting seven parts of water to one of wine, we made some weak beverage which (by reason that the wine, by being frozen, had lost his virtue) was little better than water. The sicker sort had a pint of this wine pure a day; and of such poor aqua vitae as we had, they had a little dramme allowed them next their hearts every morning; and thus we made the best use of what we had, according to the seasons.

The 6th of May, John Wardon died, whom we buried in the evening (in the most Christian-like manner we could) upon the top of a bare hill of sand which we called Brandon Hill.

The 11th we were aboard betimes, to heave out ice. By the 12th at night, we had cleared all the ice out of the hold, and found likewise our store-shoes which had lain soaked in the water all the winter; but we dried them by the fire, and fitted ourselves with them.

We could find no great defect in the ship, and therefore well hoped that she was staunch. The carpenter, nevertheless, did earnestly argue to the contrary, alleging that the ice had filled her defects, and that the ice was the thing that kept out the water; but when she should come to labour in the sea, then doubtless she would open. And, indeed, we could now see quite through her seams betwixt wind and water. But that which did trouble us as ill as all this was the loss of her rudder, and that she now lay in the very strength of the tide which, whenever the ice drove, might tear her to pieces. But we still hoped the best.

The 14th we began a new sort of work. The boatswain and a convenient number sought ashore the rest of our rigging (which was much spoiled by pecking of it out of the ice), and this they now fell to fitting and to serving of it. I set the cooper to fit our casks although (poor man) he was very infirm, my intent being to pass some cables under the ship, and so to buoy her up with these casks, if otherwise we could not get her off. Some others I ordered to go see if they could kill some wild-fowl for our sick men, who now grew worse and worse. And this is to be remembered; that we had no shot except what we did make of the lead aprons of our cannons and of some old pewter that I had; for the carpenter's sheet-lead we dare not use, it being needed to repair the ship.

The 15th I manured a little patch of ground that was bare of snow, and sowed it with peas, hoping to have some of the herbs of them shortly to eat; for, as yet, we can find no green thing to comfort us.

The 18th our carpenter, William Cole, died, a man generally bemoaned of us all, as much for his innate goodness as for the present necessity we had of a man of his quality. He had endured a long sickness with much patience, and made a very godly end. In the evening we buried him by Master Wardon.

Before his extreme weakness he had brought the pinnace to that pass that she was ready to be bolted and trenneled, and to be joined together to receive the planking, so that we were not so discouraged by his death but that we did hope of ourselves to finish her, if the ship proved unserviceable.

In the evening the Master of our ship, after burial, returning aboard ship and looking about her, discovered some part of our gunner under the gunroom ports. This man we had committed to the sea at a good distance from the ship, and in deep water, near six months before.

The 19th in the morning, I sent men to dig him out. He was fast in the ice, his head downwards and his heel upward (for he had but one leg) and the plaster was yet at his wound. In the afternoon they had digged him clear out, and he was as free from noisomeness as when we first committed him to the sea. This alteration had the ice and water and time only wrought on him; that his flesh would slip up and down upon his bones like a glove on a man's hand. In the evening we buried him by the others.

The four and twentieth was very warm sunshine and the ice did melt by the shore's side, and cracked all over the bay with a fearful noise. About three in the afternoon we could perceive the ice, with the ebb, to drive by the ship. Whereupon I sent two with all speed unto the Master with order to sink the ship else she would drift away; and likewise to look for the rudder betwixt the ice. This he presently performed and a happy fellow, one David Hammon, pecking betwixt the ice, struck upon the rudder, and it came up with his lance, who, crying that he had found it, the rest came and got it up on the ice and so into the ship.

In the meantime the ice began to rise and mount into high heaps against the shoal shores and rocks, and likewise against the heap of ice which we had put for a barricade to our ship, but with little harm to us. Oh! this was a joyful day to us all, and we gave God thanks for the hopes we had of it.

The last of May we found, on the beach, some green vetches to appear out of the ground, which I made the men to pick up and to boil for our sick men.

This day we made an end of fitting all our rigging and sails; and it being a very hot day, we did dry and new-make our fish in the sun, and aired all our other provisions. There was not a man of us at present able to eat of our salt provisions, but myself and the Master of my ship.

The ninth of June, betimes in the morning, we fell to work. We hoist out our casks of beer and cider from the hold, and made a raft of them, fastening it to our shore anchor. The beer and cider sunk presently, which was nothing strange to us, for any wood or barrel-staves that had lain under the ice all the winter would also sink down so soon as ever it was heaved overboard. This day we heaved out ten ton of ballast.

Here I am to remember God's goodness towards us, in sending those aforementioned green vetches. For now our feeble sick men that could not for their lives stir these two or three months, can endure the air and walk about the house; our other sick men gather strength also, and it is wonderful to see how soon they were recovered. We used them in this manner: Twice a day we went to gather the herb or leaf of these vetches, as they first appeared out of the ground; then did we wash and boil them, and so, with oil and vinegar that had been frozen, we did eat them. It was an excellent sustenance and refreshing; the most part of us ate nothing else. We would likewise bruise them and take the juice of them, and mix that with our drink. We would eat them raw also with our bread.

The eleventh was very warm weather, and we did hang our rudder.

The fourteenth, we had heaved out all the ballast and carried all our yards and everything else of weight ashore, so that we now had the ship as light as possible it could be.

The fifteenth, we did little but exercise ourselves, seeing that by this time our men that were most feeble are now grown strong, and can run about. The flesh of their gums became settled again, and their teeth fastened, so that they can eat beef with their vetches.

The sixteenth of June was wondrous hot, with some thunder and lightning, so that our men did go into the ponds ashore to swim and cool themselves; yet was the water very cold still.

Here had lately appeared divers sorts of flies, as butterflies, horseflies, and such an infinite abundance of bloodthirsty mosquitoes that we were more tormented with them than ever we were with the cold weather. These (I think) lie dead in the old rotten wood all the winter, and in summer they revive again. Here be likewise infinite company of frogs in the ponds upon the land; but we durst not eat of them, they looked so speckled, like toads.

The seventeenth I took all that were able to do anything, aboard with me; and, at high water (although she wanted something to rise clear out of her trough) yet we heaved with such a good will that we heaved her through the sand into a foot and a half deeper water. Further than so we durst not yet bring her, for that the ice was all thick about us.

The 20th the tide rose so high that our ship floated, and we drew her further off. This we did by little and little, for that the ice was still wonderful thick about us.

At low-water on the 23rd we sounded all about the ship and found it very foul ground; we discovered stones three foot high above the bottom, and two of them within a ship's breadth of the ship; whereby did more manifestly appear God's mercies to us; for if, when we forced her ashore, she had struck one blow against those stones, it had bilged her. In the evening we towed off the ship unto the place she rid last year, and there moored her.

Whereas I had formerly cut down a very high tree and made a cross of it, to it I now fastened the King's and Queen's Majesties pictures, drawn to the life, and doubly wrapped in lead, and so close that no weather could hurt them. Betwixt both these I affixed His Majesty's Royal Title, viz: Charles the First, King of England, Scotland, France and Ireland, as also of Newfoundland, and of these Territories, and to the Westward as far as Nova Albion, and to the Northward to the Latitude of 80 degrees, &c.

On the outside of the lead I fastened a shilling and a sixpence of His Majesty's coin; under that we fastened the King's Arms, fairly cut in lead; and under that the Arms of the City of Bristol. And this being Midsummer-Day, we raised it on top of the bare hill where we had buried our dead fellows; formally (by this ceremony) taking possession of these Territories to His Majesty's use.

About ten o'clock on the 25th, when it was already something dark, I took a lance in my hand, and a fellow with me with a musket and some fire, and went to our watch-tree to make a fire on the eminentest place of the island, to see if it would be answered. Such fires I had formerly made to discover if there were any savages on the mainland or the islands about us. Had there been any, my purpose was to have gone to them to get some intelligence of some Christians or some ocean sea thereabouts.

When I was come to the tree, I laid down my lance and, whilst myself climbed up to the top of the tree, I ordered my consort to put fire unto some low trees thereabouts. He (unadvisedly) put fire to some trees that were to windward, so that they (and all the rest too, by reason it had been very hot weather) being sear and dry, took fire like flax or hemp; and the wind blowing the fire towards me, I made haste down the tree. But before I was half way down, the fire took in the bottom of it and blazed so fiercely upwards that I was fain to leap off the tree and down a steep hill and, in brief, with much ado, escaped burning. The moss on the ground was as dry as flax; and the fire would run through it most strangely, and like a powder train, along the earth.

My consort at last came to me, and was joyful to see me for he thought verily I had been burned. And thus we went homeward together, leaving the fire increasing, and still burning most furiously. We could see no answer of it. I slept but little all night after; and at break of day, I made all our powder and beef to be carried aboard. This day I went to the hills, to look to the fire, where I saw how it did still burn most furiously, both to the Westward and Northward. Leaving one upon the hills to watch it, I came home immediately and made them take down our new suit of sails and carry them to the seaside, ready to be cast in if occasion were, and to make haste to take down the canvas roofs from off our houses. About noon the wind shifted Northerly and our sentinel came running home, bringing us word that the fire did follow him at hard heels like a train of powder.

The fire came towards us with a most terrible rattling noise, bearing a full mile in breadth; and by the time we had uncovered our houses and begun to carry away our last things, the fire was come to our Town and seized on it, and (in a trice) burnt it down to the ground. We lost nothing of any value in it, for we had brought everything away into a place of security. Our dogs, in this combustion, would sit down on their tails and howl, and then run into the sea, and there stay. The wind shifted Easterly and the fire ranged to the Westward, seeking what it might devour. This night we lay altogether aboard the ship, and gave God thanks that had shipped us in her again.

The mosquitoes, upon our coming away, were most intolerable. We tore an old ship's flag in pieces, and made us bags of it to put our heads in; but it was no fortification against them. They would find ways and means to sting us so that our faces were swollen hard out in pimples which would so itch and smart that we must needs rub and tear them. And these flies, indeed, were more tormenting to us than all the cold we had heretofore endured.

The Homeward Voyage

Monday, being the 2nd of July, we were up betimes, stowing and fitting our ship and weighing of our anchors.

This being done, we came cheerfully to sail and stood over to Danby Island to take in more wood, and there to be ready to take the opportunity of fair wind. I went ashore myself with the boat, for that some of the company had told me they had seen some stakes the last year, driven into the ground. When we came ashore, I went to the place, where I found two stakes driven into the ground about a foot and a half, and firebrands where a fire had been made. I pulled up the stakes, which were about the bigness of my arm, and they had been cut sharp at the ends with a hatchet or some other good iron tool, and driven in, as it were with the head of it. They were distant about a stone's throw from the water-side. I could not conceive to what purpose they should be there set, unless it were for some mark for boats. This did augment my desire to speak with the savages; for without doubt they could have given notice of some Christians with whom they had some commerce.*

The 22nd we again saw the mainland, and at the instant had a good observation; whereby we knew it to be Cape Henrietta Maria. I made the Master stand in with it; and, in the meantime, we fitted a cross and fastened the King's Arms and the Arms of the City of Bristol to it. We came to an anchor within a mile of the shore, so we hoist out the boat, and took our arms and our dogs and went ashore.

Upon the most eminent place we erected the cross, and then, seeking about, we soon saw some deer, and by and by more and more. We stole to them with the best skill we had, and then put our dogs on them; but the deer ran clear away from them at pleasure. We tired the dogs, and wearied ourselves, but to no purpose; neither could we come to shoot at them.

We took half a dozen young geese on the pools, by wading in to them; and so returned to our boat, vexed that now we had found a place where there was fresh meat, and we could get none of it. Whereas, therefore, we had kept our dogs with a great deal of inconvenience aboard the ship all the winter, and had pardoned them many misdemeanours (for they would steal our meat out of the steeping tubs) in hope they might hereafter do us some service; and, seeing they now did not, and that there was no hope they could hereafter, I caused them to be left ashore. They were a dog and a bitch, buck dogs, of a very good race. The dog had a collar about his neck which, it may be hereafter, may come to light. I

* It has been suggested that these "marks" may have been erected by Henry Hudson after his abandonment.

did see no sign at all of any savages, nor could we find any herbs or other refreshing here.

The great deep ice withal, driving on these uncertain depths, did so distract the tides and deceive us so much in our accounts that by the thirtieth we were driven back so far to the Eastward and to the Southward of the Cape that, at five o'clock in the evening, it bare North-West of us, some three leagues off, contrary to our expectations. With all these mischiefs, our ship is now become very leaky, that we must pump every half watch. Here I called a consultation and, after consideration of all our experience, we were all of the same opinion, that it was impossible to get to the Northward, or to the Eastward, by reason of the ice. Wherefore I resolved upon this course: When the wind blew from South, it would blow the ice off the South shore; then we would seek to get to the Westward, betwixt it and the shore. I must confess that this was a desperate resolution, for all this coast we knew to be shoal and foul ground, all rocks and stones; so that, if the wind should shift to the Northward there would be (without God's mercies) little hope of us. But here we must not stay. The nights grew long; the cold already so increased that, betwixt the pieces of ice, the sea would be frozen.

I caused the ship to be again prepared to sink her the second time, if so be we were put to extremities.

We presently put our hope into execution (the wind being at South) and got about the shoals of the Cape, standing then into the shoreward, to get betwixt it and the ice. The wind increasing, we endured a most dangerous dark night of it. In the morning we fell to work to get the ship out of the ice into some clear water, which we saw West by South of us; some of our company out upon the ice, to heave her with their shoulders, whilst others stood aboard with poles. The rest stood to spill and fill the sail. By nine in the morning we had gotten into some clear water.

About midnight there came a great piece of ice (which we could not avoid) athwart of our cable, and made the ship drive and drag her anchor. This drove her into shoal water, it being very rocky and foul ground. We brought the cable to capstan, and heaved with such a courage that we heaved home our anchor from under the ice. It then pleased God that the wind blew along the shore; otherwise it had gone far worse with us.

During the following thirty-three days James struggled to escape from the ice of Hudson Bay; but it was not until September 3rd that he finally raised Resolution Island and again saw the open, and ice-free ocean. The worst was over.

The two and twentieth of October, we arrived in the Road of Bristol, having been hindered and crossed with much contrary tempestuous winds and weather. The ship being brought into harbour and hauled dry aground to look to her, it was there found that all her cut-water and stern were torn and beaten away, together with fourteen feet of her keel, much of her sheathing cut away, her bows broken and bruised and many timbers cracked within board, and under the starboard bilge a sharp rock had cut through the sheathing, the plank, and an inch and a half into a timber that it met withal. Many other defects there were besides, so that it was miraculous how this vessel could bring us home again.

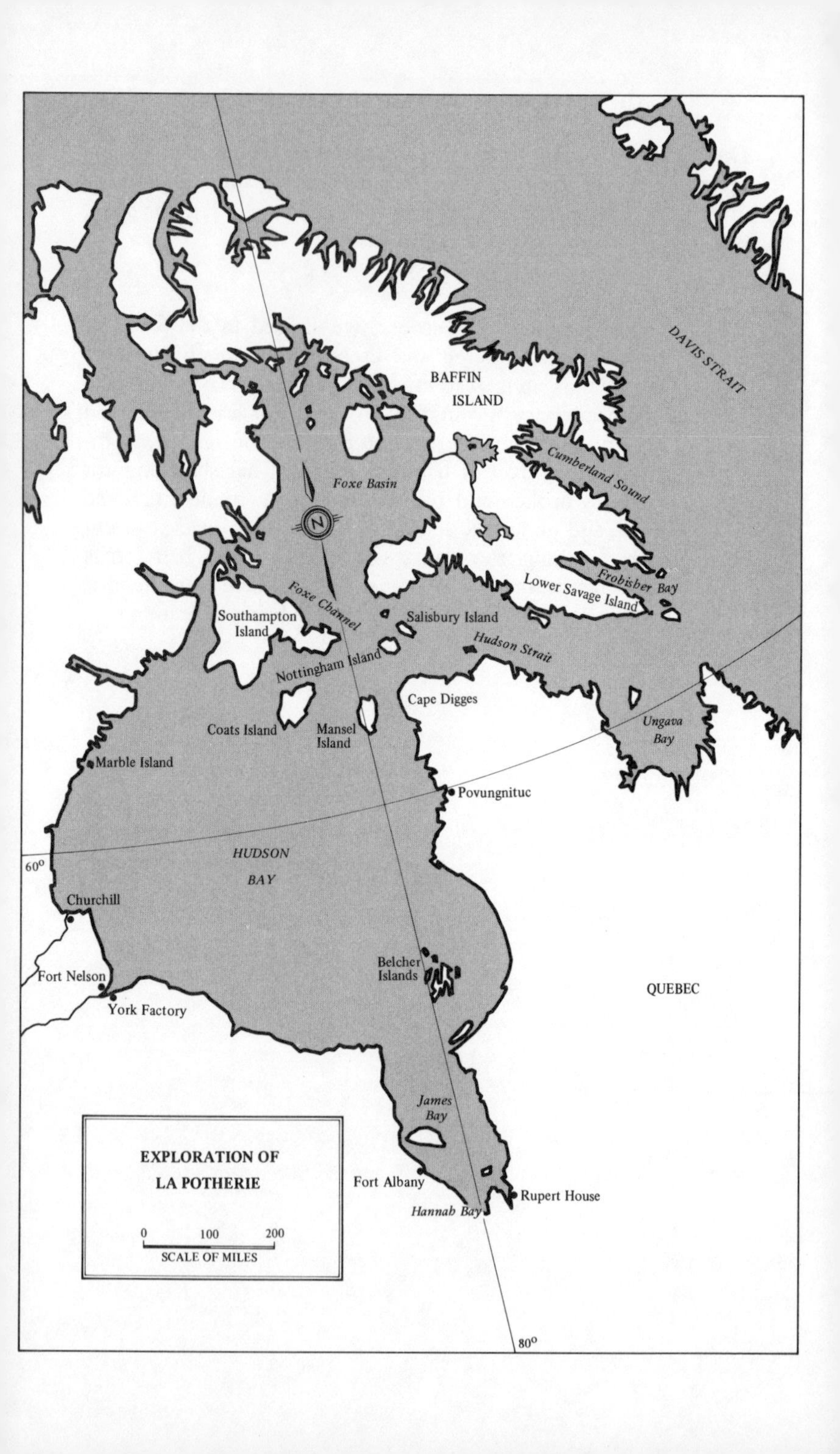

DAVIS STRAIT
BAFFIN
ISLAND
Cumberland Sound
Foxe Basin
N
Frobisher Bay
Lower Savage Island
Foxe Channel
Southampton
Island
Salisbury Island
Hudson Strait
Nottingham Island
Cape Digges
Coats Island
Mansel
Island
Ungava
Bay
Marble Island
Povungnituc
HUDSON
BAY
60°
Churchill
Belcher
Islands
Fort Nelson
York Factory
QUEBEC
James
Bay
EXPLORATION OF
LA POTHERIE
Fort Albany
Rupert House
Hannah Bay
0
100
200
SCALE OF MILES
80°

V

French Guns Amongst the Ice

After the departure of James, Hudson Bay and the rest of the North American Arctic enjoyed a rest from Europeans for more than thirty years. But shortly after the middle of the seventeenth century Prince Rupert, and a number of other mercenary Englishmen, banded together to put discovery in the north-west on a paying basis. The motto was no longer exploration, but exploitation. Inspired by the disreputable and indefatigable Sieur des Groseilliers and Pierre Radisson, two renegade fur-traders from French Canada, they formed the Company of Gentlemen Adventurers Trading Into Hudson's Bay – now known more familiarly as the Hudson's Bay Company.

In 1668 des Groseilliers sailed west in the little Nonsuch *and established the first trading post for the new company at Rupert's River. Then, as beaver pelts began to flow into the company warehouses, the Gentlemen Adventurers lost any faint interest they might have had in exploration for its own sake (or for any sake except their own, perhaps) and north-west exploring voyages came to a full stop.*

For more than a century Hudson Bay remained the private lake of the company, and interlopers, whether engaged in exploration or any other activity, were greeted with a frigidity greater than that of snow and ice.

There was, however, one group of interlopers who did not give a tinker's damn for the majesty and might of the Gentlemen Ad-

venturers. These were the French. Pushing north by land from Montreal they were able to seize several Company posts on James Bay; but it was by water that they committed lèse-majesté *on the grand scale, for in a series of naval operations in Hudson Bay they eventually captured all but one of the Company's posts.*

In 1697 Louis XIV decided to administer the coup de grace *to the English on the northern part of the new continent, and to this end he despatched a naval squadron under command of M. d'Iberville. Although d'Iberville was nominally in charge, he had to put up with the presence of a King's Commissioner who was evidently a kind of seventeenth-century political commissar (a monarchical one, of course), one of whose duties was to report to the King on the conduct of the expedition.*

This Commissioner was the Sieur de la Potherie, and while we know little of his personal history from other sources, he manages to tell us some of it in his account of the voyage.

The expedition had two phases. The first was the reduction of Newfoundland, and the second, the capture of the Hudson Bay posts.

Newfoundland presented no problem. Faced by a force of seven hundred professional soldiers from France, augmented by a number of Canadiens *and an efficient contingent of Indians, the largely unarmed settlers and fishermen of Newfoundland were easy meat. Within a few months the French had burned most of the tiny settlements, had captured seven hundred prisoners, and had slaughtered two hundred fishermen. The French losses were two men wounded. La Potherie righteously suggests that the Newfoundlanders needed just such a salutary lesson, for: "the inhabitants of this colony were living without any religion and . . . their sexual morality was corrupt to a degree."*

Having brought a little religious light to the darkness of Newfoundland, the King's fleet sailed north, there to engage the formidable forces of the English, which amounted to about a hundred and eighty fur-traders, their clerks and apprentices, scattered along nearly a thousand miles of coast.

After the sometimes dour and lugubrious accounts of the early English voyages to the Arctic, la Potherie's tale stands in bold, if somewhat improbable, contrast; but who is to blame him if he made the most of his opportunity to impress an impressionable king?

THE LETTERS OF THE SIEUR DE LA POTHERIE, TO MONSEIGNEUR THE DUKE OF ORLEANS, REGENT OF THE KINGDOM OF FRANCE

Monseigneur,

The expedition to Hudson Bay, an account of which I have the honour to present to Your Royal Highness, is one of the most singular which has yet appeared; Your Highness will find in it nothing but storms, battles, and ship-wrecks.

The royal squadron fitted out for this enterprise in 1697, has had to contend not so much with the savages who inhabit this extreme northern part of America as with waves, storms, ice, sand banks, and mountains of snow. It was here that the French showed their full courage and triumphed over the most terrible obstacles that nature could present to the most famous heroes. In fact, to arrive in Hudson Bay we had to pass through a great sea rendered inaccessible, even in the dog-days of summer, by currents, sand banks, continued storms and icebergs. These difficulties, insuperable by any other people, served only to excite the valour of the French, who, like the heroes that govern them, find nothing that can repel their attack.

What a joy it is for the members of this expedition to see their country again after passing through such perils, and to hear that Your Royal Highness has been pleased to listen to their tale! No one can better appreciate the extraordinary deeds recorded in these narratives than those who have themselves performed heroic deeds. Wherefore I am in duty bound to dedicate to Your Royal Highness this work, which having been written by the Sieur de la

Potherie, the King's commissioner in the fleet, who took part in all the expeditions described in it, cannot be suspected of being untrue.

We set sail from Newfoundland to the northward on July 8, and on the 17th we perceived, three leagues to windward, a floating iceberg three hundred feet in height, in the shape of a sugar loaf.

Now nothing is more disagreeable than to find yourself in a storm, but it is much worse when storms happen in these northern places. On the 24th, in latitude 60° 9′, we met a gale from the north-north-west which lasted eight hours. All our rigging was covered with ice and our crews suffered a great deal. The *Palmier* had her bowsprit broken. This, however, was but the beginning of the difficulties and hardships we were to endure in the course of the most dangerous navigation. On the 25th, we knew from the current that we were approaching the frigid zone; and on that day we saw nothing but terrifying sights for, as we were making our way north-north-west, we began about eight o'clock in the morning to run into a field of ice.

The first land in this clime that we became acquainted with was Resolution Island at the mouth of Hudson's Strait.

Nothing could be more frightful than to see ourselves in this vast strait where we could scarcely discern the water for the many ice-floes against which our ships struck every moment. The *Pelican*, which was always ahead (the three others following us in line), did her utmost to lessen the difficulties. She made openings crossways by main force, but the others, not being able to follow us, often found themselves shut in. It was very distressing, Sir, to find ourselves unable to give them any assistance. They anchored at once; so did we, drawing alongside an iceberg four or five hundred feet in length, on which we landed some sailors with anchors to make fast our vessel. At that time there was no night. We had the pleasure of seeing the sun set and rise almost at the same time, and you could read with ease at midnight.

On one occasion, while we were moored to the ice, we put in forty barrels of fresh water, very good to drink. This, Sir, is not surprising, for the rain, falling upon the ice, makes a kind of cistern and, when the snow melts, the water formed has none of the acrid and salty taste of sea water. Still we had to put brandy in the casks in order to remove its crudeness; otherwise it would be dangerous to drink it pure and one would run the risk of having violent colics.

At times there occur such sudden movements of the ice, that, just as you think yourself properly moored, the whole pack opens up. Once, as we were waiting for a favourable moment to continue our journey, the ice to which we were moored was unfortunately broken up by great currents. Our ship was carried away, without any possibility of steering her, and ran poop to poop against the *Palmier* at four o'clock in the morning. This mishap was followed by a far more cruel accident, for our brigantine, the *Esquimaux*, of thirty tons, which had always followed us through the ice, was crushed near the *Palmier* and the twelve men on board barely saved their lives.

However, after being carried along the coast and constantly flung from side to side of the strait for many days, we at last found ourselves quite close to Cape Digges.

For a long while we had been longing to see Eskimos. They are a very cruel people with whom, up to that time, no one had had any commercial dealings. On the 19th, however, we saw some of them on the ice, crying aloud to us from a great distance and leaping up with dresses of caribou and other skins which they were showing to us.

The opportunity was too good to be lost. M. Martigny, after taking all precautions not to be made their victim, embarked in a skiff with four or five well armed men. Landing on the ice where they were, he found nine of them, with their canoe which they had drawn up on the ice. On landing, he presented the calumet to two who had come forward while the others remained at the edge of the ice.

The calumet is something very mysterious among the savages of the north; it is the symbol of peace. It is a kind of large pipe made of red, black, or white stone. The head is well polished and made in the form of a war club. The stem is ornamented with porcupine quills and little threads of skins of various colours.*

So, at this meeting, Martigny presented them with a pipe like a calumet and a tobacco-pouch, smoked for a little, and then gave them the pipe to smoke. The seven other natives, who had kept away, when they saw the good faith in which we were acting, came to him with exclamations of joy, crying out in very clear tones, leaping and rubbing their stomachs as most convincing signs

* The Eskimos were never familiar with the calumet, which was a purely Indian artifact, and their surprise at being presented with one must have been considerable.

of friendship and of the good trade they wished to carry on with us. They gave him to understand that they were well enough off to trade. But, as he wished to have them on our ship, he told them he had nothing and asked them to come with him. But no matter how he insisted and welcomed them, they would not trust him. Martigny finally lay down on the ice to indicate that he would give himself as a hostage on condition that one of them would be sent. They wished to have two for one, and Grandville, a marine guard, remained also as a hostage.

When this Eskimo was at the top of the ladder of our ship, he saw one of our men dressed in black, of whom he was so much afraid that he hestitated whether to throw himself into the sea. The man, seeing his terror, offered him a knife, after which he decided to come aboard. On finding himself surrounded by a crowd of the crew, he did not seem at all put out but kept dancing and crying out in amazement at a machine which seemed to him so surprising. But when he saw the fire burning in the kitchen, he gave a dreadful cry, not being able to conceive how such a flame should not cause a conflagration. For, as far as we could conjecture, these people must rarely warm themselves at a fire for there was not an inch of soil in the strait, nor the smallest shrub. If they make a fire, they must burn the fat of seals and walruses.

We gave a pie to the Eskimo! He did his utmost to show his gratitude. I think there is no other nation that speaks faster. His accent resembled the Basque; he hardly opened his teeth, and yet he articulated quite distinctly. They gave him a small piece of bread which he slipped adroitly under his chin between his coat and his skin, pretending to eat it. We pretended not to notice, but we saw that he was afraid of being poisoned. We therefore tasted another piece, which we gave him, and he ate it afterwards. However, we neglected to taste a glass of wine, which he, as a result of our neglect, poured again under his chin. We had to drink some, and to taste beforehand everything we wished to give him. The sound of a silver fork pleased him so much that he hid it very cunningly between a piece of pie and a bit of bread. I embarked with him, and, when we had arrived on the ice where his comrades were, they all crowded around me, crying and jumping. I made them several presents, and, willy-nilly, they insisted on stripping themselves naked in order to give me their clothes, and I grew anxious to know if they were sensitive to the cold.

The reception we gave them led them to send two others on

board. They met with as agreeable a reception as the first. They stripped themselves as bare as my hand, and I observed that, when looked at in this condition, they had a sense of modesty. They were given knee-breeches and they showed no sign of suffering from cold. Yet they had to go three leagues to get to Digges Islands. One of them, as he was going, gave me a piece of the raw flesh of a sea-fowl which I had to eat in his presence. He gave a cry of joy, and, at the same time, sucked a raw beef heart which we had given to him.

Two others came in the afternoon to the ice-field where we were hunting. These also traded their clothing for knives, scissors, needles, bells, farthings, playing cards, old sheet music, and, in general, everything we gave them was precious to them. As these people have no trade with anybody, they did not bring any skins, but they must have the finest furs in the world in those regions.

Although we were now at the entrance of Hudson's Bay, we could not get into it. All the ice in that vast body of water was passing out into this strait. The continual movements of the icebergs in the current forced us also to take a capricious course and the currents drove the *Pelican* back more than eight leagues into the strait. On August 25 we made all sail through the ice because we were quite a distance behind the other three ships which were by then at the end of the strait, and we were anxious to join them.

Now the *Profond* saw three vessels approaching. Dugue, who was in command of her, thought at first that they were the other three ships of our squadron. They came up to him gradually with the currents. Then he was surprised to see such a sudden change, for they were three English ships of fifty-six, thirty-six, and thirty-two guns. He ungrappled from the ice immediately and ran at all hazards into a field of ice rather than surrender, for he had on board all our munitions and provisions for the Fort Nelson expedition. The English gave chase. Serigny and Chartrier in the *Weesph* and *Palmier* wanted to go to his assistance but they were fast in the ice. The *Profond* was now also fast and close to the English ships *Dering* and *Hudson's Bay*. Then, on August 26, at about nine in the morning, the battle began. Dugue attacked them; the enemy riddled him with balls, cutting his rigging in pieces, because he could only fight with two cannon which had been placed in the rear of the gunroom.

The *Hampshire** of fifty-six guns was not able to join the other English ships till the evening. After ten hours of intermittent fighting all three fired broadsides at the *Profond* and left her, thinking she was certain to go down. Four men were killed on the *Profond.* The English must also have lost some, because several human arms were found on the ice. As to our own ship, we were not in this glorious battle, which may be said to have been the first sea fight ever waged amid the ice.

The currents now brought the *Pelican* out into Hudson's Bay, and our sailors had reason to be pleased at seeing themselves freed from the ice. A fresh breeze arose which helped us greatly as we sailed to the south-west.

On September 3, 1697, we in the *Pelican* arrived within sight of Fort Nelson, from which the English fired some cannon-shots, which were apparently signals for the ships they were expecting from England. We anchored three leagues and a half to the south-west of this fort, in the open sea. We were surprised not to find there the *Palmier*, the *Weesph*, and the *Profond*, which ought to have arrived before us, as they had been off Cape Digges while we were still detained in the ice.

At daybreak on the 5th we perceived three vessels to leeward that we took to be ours. After weighing anchor about seven in the morning, we sailed down on them and made signals to which they made no response. This made us think they were English and so they were, being the *Hampshire*, the *Dering*, and the *Hudson's Bay*.

Every man was at his post. La Salle, the ship's ensign, and Grandville, a marine guard, commanded the lower battery; Bienville, the brother of M. d'Iberville, and the Chevalier de Ligondez, a marine guard, the upper battery. M. d'Iberville asked me to take command of the forecastle and, with a detachment of *Canadiens* that he gave me, to meet the enemy as they tried to come on board.

The enemy drew up in line. The *Hampshire* was at the head, the *Dering* followed, and the *Hudson's Bay* came behind, all three close together. The fight began at half past nine in the morning. We made straight for the *Hampshire*, which, thinking we were going to board her, let fall her mainsail and shook out her topsails. After this refusal, we went to the *Dering* and our fire cut the tackle

* *Hampshire* was the only English naval vessel. The *Dering* and *Hudson's Bay* were light-armed merchantmen.

of her mainsail, and then, the *Hudson's Bay* coming in front, we sent her the rest of our broadside. The *Hampshire*, putting about to windward, fired a volley of musketry on our forecastle and sent a broadside of grape which cut the halliards of our fore-topsail, a back stay of our top gallant mast, and our mizzen stay. The fight grew stubborn, the three vessels keeping up a continual fire on us, with the object of dismasting our ship.

Now the *Hampshire*, seeing that she could not engage us between a shoal and their own two vessels, and that all the efforts they had made during two hours and a half were useless, determined to run us down, and, for that purpose, tried to get to windward of us (which she was unable to do), but we ran alongside of her, yard-arm to yard-arm. As we were so close to each other, I ordered a volley of musketry to be fired at her forecastle where there were many sailors who called out for us to leap aboard. They immediately returned our volley with a discharge of grape which cut nearly all our rigging in pieces and wounded many of our men. As they ran along by our ship, we fired our batteries, which were so well aimed that they proved most effective, for we were no sooner separated from one another than the *Hampshire* immediately foundered. The *Dering*, which was close to us, sent us her broadside, but the encounter was a cruel catastrophe for the English, because the *Hudson's Bay* lowered her flag, and the *Dering* took to flight.

We had fourteen men wounded by two discharges of shot from the last broadside of the *Hampshire*, which fell in the lower battery. We had seven shots below the water-line and the water came pouring in, not to speak of several shots which passed through the *Pelican* from side to side. We had been so overwhelmed with their musketry fire and the discharges of grape-shot which they fired at us from pistol range, that our mizzen mast was filled with musket balls on all sides to the height of ten or twelve feet; and if I had not looked after my men we should not have had four people left on the forecastle. I got off very cheaply myself with having my coat all tattered, and my cap pierced by a ball. In fact I was in as good condition and with as much coolness after the battle as when M. d'Iberville bade us enter the lists, except that one would have mistaken me for a veritable blackamoor, my face was so peppered with powder. I think the English took me for some prince of Guinea, for I heard someone crying out: "Fire at that fine-looking darkey from Guinea."

We gave chase to the *Dering*, and we should have captured her if we had not, three days before, had our mainyard broken in half by a squall. In any case our prize, the *Hudson's Bay*, which was a league distant, might have got away into the mouth of the river on which Fort Nelson is situated, so we put about and, after having put a prize crew on board, we went towards the *Hampshire* in order to save her sailors. We found that she had stranded on the shoal where the enemy had wished to engage us, and the weather became so rough after the battle that it was impossible for us to lower a boat. We anchored close to the *Hampshire* with the chagrin of being unable to aid her in so dangerous and unfortunate a situation.

The east-north-east wind, which was then blowing, kept getting stronger and stronger. A frightful sea arose, driving us steadily towards the shore till the next morning between nine and ten o'clock, when our rudder struck bottom a couple of times. We were obliged to cut our cable at midday so as to make sail, and drove before the wind till four o'clock in the afternoon. The bitter cold, the snow, and the ice which covered our rigging were cruel obstacles. As we could not reach the shore, we anchored in nine fathoms of water. Our anchors held till nine in the evening, when the great anchor broke. I cannot express to you the sad state of the crew. Some were suffering from disease. The very strongest were in desperate straits. It was night, and the horror of darkness was added to the fear of death. The tossing and the disorder reacted quickly upon people in so downcast a state, and when the panic spread we could not reassure them.

The vessel was headed into the wind and anchored again, but the kedge anchor broke. As the small remaining anchor could not hold, we had to cut the cable and get under way again. A wave swept off our stern galley, and broke the table and benches which were in the main cabin. At ten o'clock in the evening our rudder was carried away and we thought ourselves utterly lost. As the tide rose, our ship, which was drawn along in the current, went aground. All these various movements made the hair of the most careless stand on end. Finally, about midnight, the ship split along the middle of the keel and filled with water above the between-decks. We spent the night in this wretched state and, at daybreak, we saw the land two leagues away.

In our cruel situation we did not lose hope of saving our lives. M. d'Iberville, who had all the forethought possible in such a catastrophe, was bent on saving his crew. He begged me to take the canoe and try where we could make a landing in some safety.

So, on September 8, the Nativity of the Virgin, I embarked in a canoe with some *Canadiens,* and after we had leapt into the sea, which was up to our shoulders, with our muskets and powder-horns on our heads, and some balls, I sent the canoe back to the ship. Meanwhile, rafts and floats were being made to save the sick. We drew ourselves as well as we could out of the water, which was extremely cold.

For all my vigour and presence of mind, I felt myself suffering keenly and, as I was utterly exhausted, I wished to find somewhere to rest. I was suddenly overcome with hunger which forced me, in my despair, to eat the weeds floating on the sea.

After having crossed more than a league of sea, we came to a snow bank more than two feet thick under which was mud. Our passage was very rough and cost the lives of eighteen soldiers who died of cold, and I myself should have succumbed but for the help of some *Canadiens* who found me lying on the snow.

The next day, we crossed over a marsh which would have been impassable for horses and then we made another camp at a place we called the "Outpost." I forgot to state that the *Hudson's Bay* had met the same fate as ourselves, having foundered eight leagues further south.*

In the meantime, the *Palmier*, the *Weesph*, and the *Profond* arrived at the mouth of the river. The first had lost her rudder forty leagues to the west of this, having been steered these forty leagues with oars and outriggers.

M. d'Iberville with some others of us went to reconnoitre Fort Nelson about eleven o'clock in the morning. We could not manage it without drawing the musket fire of the English, and they would have fired grape-shot at us if we had not defiled by narrow paths. We kept under cover till we were almost at the foot of the fort. Then d'Iberville sent for Martigny and ordered him to go and demand two Iroquois and two Frenchmen whom he knew to be in this place for they had not been able to get away last year before it had been recaptured by the English from the *Canadiens.*

When Martigny arrived with the white flag at the gates of the fort, the governor had his eyes bandaged and had him led into the place. He held a council of war. It was decided that the four men

* The *Hampshire* was also a total wreck, with a loss of about 250 lives.

could not be given up under such circumstances. Some of the men from the *Hudson's Bay* had taken refuge in the fort after their shipwreck, and this had strengthened the garrison.

That afternoon we set up a mortar battery in the wood two hundred paces from the fort, without letting the enemy become aware of what we were doing. When the platform was almost finished, they heard the noise of two or three blows of a sledge-hammer, which quickly brought upon us three cannon-shots, one of which came near killing M. d'Iberville.

On the night between the 11th and the 12th, we cut off some English who were going to and fro to fetch the sailors of the *Hudson's Bay*, who kept arriving every now and then. The clerk of the Hudson's Bay Company was killed in this encounter.

We began our bombardment of the fort at ten in the morning of the 12th. When we saw the third bombshell fall at the base of the fort, Serigny went to summon the governor to surrender. The latter declared that he did not wish to have his throat cut, and that he preferred to see the place burned rather than give it up. He admitted that there was no chance of his receiving any aid from England, and that, if he were forced to capitulate, it would be due to his bad luck.*

We began to fire anew between one and two o'clock. They kept up a continual fire on us with cannon and with two mortars. They had very able cannoneers. They had nothing but the sound of our bombs to enable them to conjecture where we were, because the thick copse, in which our battery was, prevented them from getting an accurate knowledge of its position. This did not prevent two of their cannon-balls from hitting the parapet and another from covering us with earth.

Serigny summoned the English again at four o'clock and told the governor that it would be the last time he would do so. We had resolved to make a general assault and, if he should then make any proposals, they would not be received. We had surrounded their fort and with storming axes we would have cut down their palisades and bastions, and they might have expected that, had we stormed them sword in hand, they would have had no chance of escape. Serigny even assured the governor that, although the sea-

* There were only a handful of soldiers in the Fort, the rest of the garrison consisting of clerks, artisans and other civilian employees of the Hudson's Bay Company.

son would not allow our ships to remain more than ten or twelve days, forces would be left more than sufficient to capture the fort in the winter.

The English governor told Serigny that he was not wholly his own master and that he would give him an answer at sundown. We did not cease setting up a new battery on the south-south-west side, which would have thrown them into utter disorder, but, at six o'clock, the governor sent a Protestant minister, Mr. Morison, to bring a capitulation, in which he asked to keep all the beavers that belonged to the Hudson's Bay Company.

I was willing to act as interpreter, but I soon saw that I was wasting my Latin on this minister who could scarcely decline Musa. I was not surprised at it afterwards as there are very few Scottish ministers who know Latin.

This proposal of theirs was too advantageous for people who were at our mercy, and our gentle dealing with them was rather due to our natural French generosity. So we refused their demand.

They held a council of war, and at eight p.m. the governor sent Mr. Henry Kelsey, a King's Lieutenant, and the deputy governor with a letter in which he asked to be allowed to retain two mortars and four cannon (five-pounders), which they had brought last year from England. We would not let them have these. Finally, on the next day, the 13th, the governor sent us three hostages to tell us that he would surrender the place and to ask permission to evacuate it at an hour after midday.

The governor at the head of the garrison and part of the crew of the *Hudson's Bay* left the fort an hour after with drums beating, muskets loaded, matches lighted, banner waving (they had lowered it very quickly at the third bombshell we had fired at them, perceiving that we were using it as a target), and their arms and baggage.

I had the skins that were in the fort put on board the Hudson's Bay Company sloop *Albemarle,* which we had also captured. As our pilots were not well acquainted with the river, this vessel ran on a little rock which made a hole in her. There was a panic among our own people and the English who were on board. The barque filled with water. They tried to lighten her by jettisoning many cases and packages. It was a very dark night. Some threw themselves into the water, others, in trying to get safely to land, found themselves fast in the mud.

We left Fort Nelson on September 24, 1697, which is the date when the rivers and the sea begin to freeze over, or very fierce winds prevail.

We set sail with the wind south-south-west, at an hour after midday. The *Profond* – to which our crew had been transferred from the wreck of the *Pelican*, as well as a party from the *Hudson's Bay*, and from the garrison of the fort – went aground an hour later on the bank or shoal on the north side. However, as we still had an hour of flood tide, we got clear and continued our course. Otherwise, we should have been obliged to transfer some of our three hundred men to the *Weesph*, which had escaped our mischance, and to send back the rest to the fort. We should certainly in that event have suffered a famine there, and also on the *Weesph*, for the latter had only enough provisions for her own crew, and the fort no more than was necessary for the garrison we had left behind in it.

Next day the wind blew very hard. The cold increased because we were getting nearer the pole. The days became very short. The sun no longer was visible, so we could not get an altitude. A storm was indicated. We advanced without knowing where we were, and yet we had to get into Hudson's Strait. To enter it was a stumbling-block for us, as we were enclosed in a bay, the northern shore of which was quite unknown. We were wandering in a region full of dangers.

The constant working of our rigging exhausted our sailors. The wretched condition we were all in, owing to lack of linen and other clothes, due to our shipwreck, suddenly brought about an epidemic of scurvy; and I hardly venture to tell you, Sir, that we were all tormented with vermin to such an extent that some of our scurvy patients, who had become paralytics, actually died from this pest. When the sailors came down from the yards, they fell stiff with cold on the deck, and it required the use of fomentations to bring them round again.

We were running east when we found ourselves by good fortune in Hudson's Strait. We found no more ice-packs in the strait. There were still some icebergs of great height which had stranded a league or two from the land and had not been able to follow the current. The ice-packs in the bay and in the strait extend more than four hundred leagues. When they begin to break up, they pass out into the sea. These fragments are so large that five or six thousand men could be drawn up in order of battle upon them with ease. They usually break up in the month of July and they sometimes travel two hundred leagues in the open sea before being completely melted.

At this time the sea was clear, but the cold was so piercing that our crew could not endure it and nearly all the sailors took the scurvy. So few of us escaped that we were obliged to make use of our English prisoners in order to run the ship.

On October 5, at midday, we saw the Savage Isles to the north-east of us. They are on the north coast of the strait a mile or two distant from the mainland.

We began then to find ourselves out of danger, freed from those anxieties which had kept us in dread of perishing every moment.

As the winds drove us along we found ourselves suddenly in another and even harsher climate. This sudden change caused so many deaths in our vessels that we threw five or six sailors into the sea every day.

It was a plague that had infected our ships. Perhaps you will not be displeased if I give you an idea of it. You will see that I have become a great doctor on this voyage, and that I have not altogether forgotten the study I made of anatomy while I was taking my course in philosophy.

You must know, then, that the sudden change which takes place in the temperature, after leaving the mildest and most agreeable season of the year, brings about an entire revolution, all at once, in the human body, which contracts a disease peculiar to those regions, called the scurvy.

The extreme cold, and especially the tremendous quantity of nitre that exists in the straits, form fixed salts which arrest the circulation of the blood. These corrosive spirits give rise to acids, which, little by little, undermine the part where they occur; and the chyle, which becomes viscous, acid, salt, and earthy, causes the thickening of the blood, which, being thus impeded in its circulation, gives rise at the same time to pains in the lower extremities, as in the legs, thighs and arms, which are the first parts to be attacked.

The parts affected become insensible, blackish, and, when one touches them, there remains a hollow such as one would make in a piece of dough.

It was most pitiful to see people completely paralysed, so that they could not move themselves in their hammocks, and yet their minds were perfectly sane and clear.

The food that one is obliged to take at sea contributes not a little to the malady. Thus the quantity of acid in the salt beef and pork that they give the sailors causes a swelling in the gums and an obstruction in the salivary glands, which are intended to filter the lymph with the blood and carry it into the mouth by little ducts so as to serve as the first solvent in digestion. And, as all these little passages are blocked up by the excess of these penetrating salts, there is then spread through the mouth a thick, gluey, and viscous humour. Then the blood, finding these ducts stopped, forms a mass of putrid matter which corrupts the gums, loosens the teeth and causes them all to drop out.

Some have a flux at the mouth, others have dysentery. The former drivel. The viscous matter which flows from the mouth causes gangrene in the glands and in the gums. They must then be given strong detergent gargles which can separate this thick matter. Lemon juice is very helpful.

Those who have dysentery are more liable to die. In these patients, there is formed in the region of the intestines an extremely corrosive humour. As soon as this juice is found to be corrupt, it follows of necessity that there are faintings and heart failures. For, as the heart can only exist by the circulation of a pure, clean, and active blood, any other matter that forms in it cannot help hindering its ordinary course. And the gangrene, which forms in these patients, arrests the laws of the circulation of the blood.

The brain, being no longer bathed in its mild influences, receives vapours which cause delirium, madness, and then death. I have seen several who seemed to have a strong voice, a clear eye, and a clear tongue without any blackening or excoriation, and yet died while they were speaking.

One must use foods, therefore, which can dissolve the mass of the blood and by their sulphurous and volatile parts carry off the acids. These foods, by an insensible transpiration, dissipate the crudities of the mass, and are able to rally together the fibres of the blood. One should give the patients very little salt meat, but rice, peas, dried beans, detersivent injections, and astringent opiates into which cordials enter; giving them plenty of fresh linen, which is a great relief in such cases.

This sickness only increases the appetite. The patients are as ravenous as dogs. I was not surprised, Sir, that this sudden change of climate on our return voyage should have caused so many deaths on our ships. There was a fermentation going on in the mass of the blood, which caused a gangrenous corruption. The heat wished to dilate what the cold had contracted; there was bound to be a combat. And nature, enfeebled by the dilation of the pores, caused an overflow which threw the whole machine out of gear.

Finally, after so many pains, labours, and misfortunes, we arrived at Belle Isle in Newfoundland on November 8. We proceeded to put our scurvied patients in the hospital of Port Louis, and we set out from there for Rochefort, where we discharged our ship.

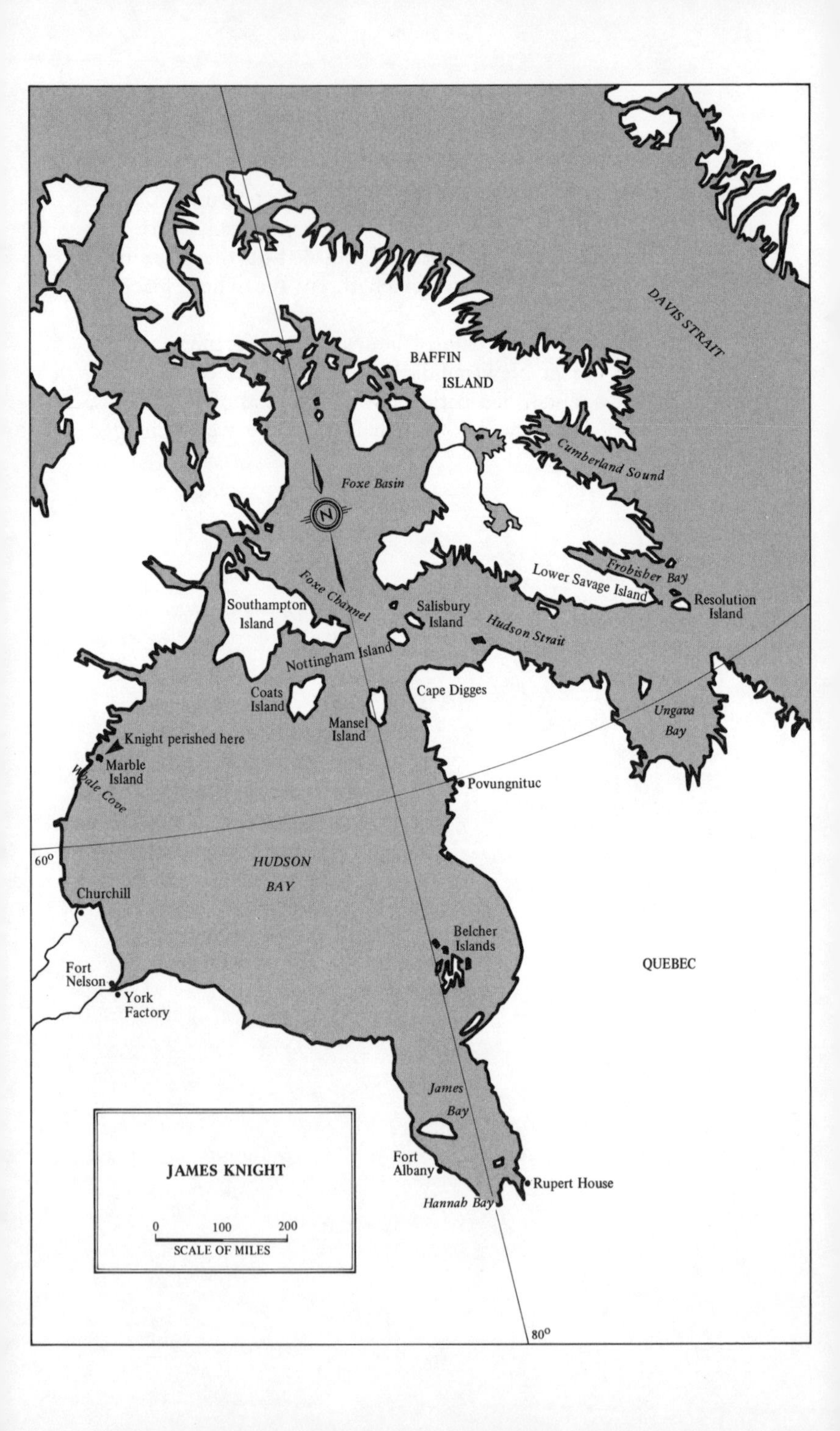

DAVIS STRAIT
BAFFIN
ISLAND
Cumberland Sound
Foxe Basin
N
Frobisher Bay
Lower Savage Island
Resolution
Island
Foxe Channel
Southampton
Island
Salisbury
Island
Hudson Strait
Nottingham Island
Coats
Island
Cape Digges
Mansel
Island
Ungava
Bay
Knight perished here
Marble
Island
Whale Cove
Povungnituc
60°
HUDSON
BAY
Churchill
Belcher
Islands
Fort
Nelson
York
Factory
QUEBEC
James
Bay
JAMES KNIGHT
0
100
200
SCALE OF MILES
Fort
Albany
Rupert House
Hannah Bay
80°

VI

The Marble Tomb

During the early eighteenth century, exploration in the waters and amidst the ice of the North American Arctic was at a standstill. The quest for the Northwest Passage had all but been forgotten in the hectic and often unscrupulous scramble of European merchants to make the most of the obvious riches of the new continent.

Nevertheless, the spirit of exploration was not quite dead. James Knight, who had long served the Company of Gentlemen Adventurers, was obsessed with the idea of discovery to the north-west. Time after time he begged the Company to outfit him for a north-west voyage, but the Gentlemen had hardened in their resolution to discourage any new discovery which might lead to a threat against their fur-trade monopoly; and they remained deaf to his pleas until Knight was approaching his eightieth year. Then, and apparently partly in the hopes of being rid of him, they gave permission for a voyage to explore the north-western corner of the Bay.

No record of Knight's voyage survived him; but there is an almost contemporary notice of it in the narrative of another Company servant who was, in his own right, one of the great overland explorers of all time. In the preface to the narrative of his own journey from Churchill to the Coppermine River, Samuel Hearne provides the single extant account of James Knight's venture to the north.

THE VOYAGE OF CAPTAIN KNIGHT

Accounts of a grand River to the north-west of Hudson's Bay, which some have turned into a Strait, together with samples of copper from it, were brought to the Company's Factory at Churchill River immediately after its first establishment in 1715. It does not appear, however, that any attempt was made to discover the river or the mines till 1719, when the Company fitted out a ship called the *Albany Frigate*, Captain George Barlow, and a sloop called the *Discovery*, Captain David Vaughan.

The sole command of the expedition, however, was given to Mr. James Knight, a man of great experience in the Company's service, who had been many years Governor at the different Factories in the Bay, and who had made the first settlement at Churchill River.

Notwithstanding the experience Mr. Knight had in the Company's business, and his knowledge of the parts of the Bay where he had resided, it cannot be supposed that he was well acquainted with the nature of the business in which he then engaged, having nothing to direct him but the slender and imperfect accounts which he had received from the Indians, who at that time were little known and less understood.

Those disadvantages, added to his advanced age (he being then near eighty) by no means discouraged this bold adventurer; who was so prepossessed of his success and of the great advantage that would arise from his discoveries, that he procured and took with him some large iron-bound chests to hold gold dust and other valuables which he fondly flattered himself were to be found in those parts.

Mr. Knight soon left Gravesend and proceeded on his voyage. The ship not returning to England that year, as was expected, it was judged that she had wintered in Hudson's Bay. Having on board a good stock of provisions, a house in frame, together with all necessary mechanics, and a great assortment of trading goods, little or no thoughts were entertained of their not being in safety. But as neither ship nor sloop returned to England in the following year, the Company were much alarmed for their welfare.

By the Company ship which went to Churchill in 1721, they sent orders for the sloop called the *Whale-Bone*, John Scroggs, Master, to go in search of them. But the ship not arriving in Churchill till late in the year, those orders could not be put in prosecution till the following summer.

The North West coast of Hudson's Bay being little known in those days, and Mr. Scroggs finding himself greatly embarrassed with shoals, he returned to Churchill River without making any certain discovery respecting the above ship or sloop. Some marks he saw amongst the Esquimaux at Whale Cove scarcely amounting to the spoils which might have been made from a trifling accident to the expedition, and consequently could not be considered as signs of total shipwreck.

The strong opinion which then prevailed in Europe respecting the probability of a Northwest Passage by the way of Hudson's Bay, made many conjectures that Messrs. Knight and Barlow had found that passage, and had gone through it into the South Sea by way of California.

Many years elapsed without any convincing proof to the contrary, except that no one had been able to find any such passage. And, notwithstanding a sloop was annually sent northward from Churchill River to trade with the Esquimaux, it was the summer of 1767 before we had proof positive that poor Mr. Knight and Captain Barlow had been lost in Hudson's Bay.

The Company was then carrying out a black whale fishery, and Marble Island was made the place of rendezvous, not only on account of the commodiousness of the harbour, but because it had been observed that whales were more plentiful about that island than on any other part of the coast.

This being the case, the boats, when on the look-out for whales, had frequent occasion to row close to the island; by which means they discovered a new harbour near the east end of it. At the head of this harbour they found guns, anchors, cables, bricks, a smith's anvil and many other articles which the hand of time had not defaced, and which, being of no use to the natives, or too heavy to be removed by them, had not been taken from the place in which they were originally laid.

The remains of a house, although pulled to pieces by the Esquimaux for the wood and iron, were yet very plain to be seen, and indeed I have myself seen the remains of this house several times. They are on the west side of the harbour and in all probability will be discernible for many years to come.

Also the hulls, or more properly speaking the bottoms of the sloop and ship, which lie sunk in about five fathoms of water, were observed. The figurehead of the ship, and also the guns, etc., were sent home to the Company and are certain proofs that Messrs. Knight and Barlow had been lost on that inhospitable island, where neither stick nor stump was to be seen, and which lies near sixteen miles from the mainland. Indeed the mainland itself is little better, being a jumble of barren hills and rocks, destitute of every kind of herbage except moss and grass.

In the summer of 1769, while we were prosecuting the fishery, we saw several Esquimaux at this new harbour. Perceiving that one or two of them were greatly advanced in years, our curiosity was excited to ask them some questions concerning the above sloop and ship; which we were better able to do by the assistance of an Esquimaux who was then in the Company's service as a linguist.

The account we received from them was full, clear and unreserved, and the sum of it was to the following import.

When the two vessels arrived at this place it was very late in the fall and, in getting them into the harbour, the largest received much damage. But on being fairly in, the English began to build a house. Their number at that time seeming to be about fifty.

As soon as the ice permitted, in the following summer (1720), the Esquimaux paid them another visit, by which time the number of English was greatly reduced, and those that were living seemed very unhealthy. According to the account they were then very busily employed but, about what, the Esquimaux could not easily describe. Probably they were busy lengthening the long-boat, for at a little distance from the house there is now lying a great quantity of oak chips, which had been most assuredly made by the carpenters.

However, sickness and famine occasioned such havoc among the English that, by the setting in of the second winter, their number was reduced to twenty. That winter some of the Esquimaux took up their abode on the opposite side of the harbour to where the English had built their house, and frequently supplied them with such provisions as they had, which chiefly consisted of whales' blubber, and seals' flesh and oil.

When the spring advanced, the Esquimaux went to the continent, and on their visiting Marble Island again in the summer of 1721, they only found five of the English still alive. These were in such distress for provisions that they eagerly ate the seals' flesh and whales' blubber quite raw, as they purchased it from the natives. This disordered them so much that three of them died in a few days, and the other two, though very weak, made shift to bury them.

Those two survived many days after the rest and frequently went to the top of an adjacent rock and earnestly looked to the South and East, as if in expectation of some vessels coming to their relief. But nothing appearing in sight they sat down together and wept bitterly.

At length one of the two died and the other's strength was so far exhausted that he fell down and died also, in attempting to dig a grave for his companion.

VII

Of Whales and Ice

The white cliffs of Marble Island gleam across the grey waters of Hudson Bay, a monument not only to Knight's men, dead these two centuries of scurvy and starvation, but to an era which died with them.

The days when brave men in ill-found little sailing vessels were ready to voyage, almost totally unprepared, into the virtually unknown waters of the Arctic, depending only on their own courage and faith, were at an end. Though that courage and that faith had brought their victories, the price was one which men of a newer age were not inclined to pay.

After Knight's pathetic failure, there was an almost total and century-long hiatus in ship-borne ventures to the north-western ice. The Elizabethan spirit was in decay. In its place there was the thundering beat of money in the hearts of the successors of the old adventurers, and they were dulled and sickened by it. Annual commercial voyages through the ice of Hudson Bay were undertaken by the Hudson's Bay Company, but these were generally as devoid of interest as are most commercial voyages in our day. Only in Davis Strait was there a sense of adventure, and that only in the final years of the eighteenth century when the whalers began to crowd the Greenland whale up to and into the Baffin pack.

The majority of Arctic historians pay little or no attention to these most daring of northern venturers. Nevertheless, if their achievements against the ice were not of the kind to win them fame, they were certainly equal to anything of which the professional explorers could boast. And it is a seldom acknowledged fact that much of the exploration of North American Arctic waters during the eighteenth and nineteenth centuries was lighted on its way by the original discoveries made by whalers. These discoveries were seldom publicized, for it was part of the game that a skipper who found new fishing grounds attempted to keep the information to himself. It was whales, or "fish" as they were always known, that mattered, and not some sterile geographical discovery. All the same, most Arctic expeditions (when northern exploration was resumed in 1818) made it a point to consult the whalers before setting out, and from them obtained semi-secret information without which some of the more famous voyages of discovery would probably have failed. The whalers not only supplied invaluable information, they also supplied most of the ice-pilots accompanying Arctic expeditions, and in some cases they supplied the ships and crews as well.

In the north-western seas the Basque whalers had begun fishing off Labrador and southern Greenland as early as 1560, but it was not until a century and a half later, when the great whale fishery off Spitzbergen was almost exhausted, that whaling ships appeared in numbers in the north-western waters. In 1719 the Dutch sent their first whalers into Davis Strait, and they found the place full of ice – but also full of whales. The rush was on. Three years later there were three hundred and fifty-five whaling vessels of several nationalities operating in Davis Strait and along the Baffin Island coast. Some of the more daring skippers had even worked well into Baffin Bay decades before it was officially rediscovered by John Ross in 1818. That they anticipated the discoveries of recognized explorers in many parts of the Eastern Arctic is not to be doubted, but the full extent of their penetrations cannot now be known, for not only were the whaling captains close-mouthed, but their owners took good care that the ship's logs never fell into public hands.

The hazards of the Arctic whaling trade were frightful. More than five hundred whaling ships are known to have been lost in the north-western waters alone, and many more undoubtedly went down of which no record now exists. Of the whaling ships sailing to the Arctic from a single English port, Hull, eighty out of the one hundred and ninety-four employed in the trade were lost, mainly to the ice, between 1772 and 1852. In 1819 fourteen whalers were caught and crushed in Melville Bay, while the year 1830 was fatal to twenty ships in that same place. In that year the Princess of Wales *and the* Letitia *were stove in by ice passing completely through them and almost literally cutting them in half. The* Resolution, *of Peterhead, had her counter pierced by ice, and quickly sank. The* Laurel *and* Hope *were squeezed flat and then thrown on their sides on the floe. The* Commerce *was lifted bodily up onto the ice, and sank when the ice parted. The* Baffin, Achilles, Ville de Dieppe *and* Rattler *were crushed to pieces, and the* Progress *was destroyed by an iceberg.*

They were great men to take risks, the whalers, and they paid for it often enough; yet individual whale fishermen went back into the ice time after time. There is a record of a Scots fisher named Peter Ramsay who died aboard the famous whaler Erik *in 1874, having made* fifty-six consecutive annual whaling voyages into Arctic waters.

The whalers gained no fame and found no place in history, for they did not write and publish accounts of their activities. There was only one exception, but he bore one of the greatest names of the whaling trade — William Scoresby. He and his father fished for whale between 1785 and 1823, and there was hardly a year throughout this period when one or other of them, and often both, did not command a ship in the Greenland whale fishery. In 1820 William published a little volume called The Northern Whale-Fishery *in which he recalled some of his own experiences, and some of the experiences of his fellow skippers. The brief episode from Scoresby's book which follows serves to give some indication of the nature of the struggle between the whalers and the icy seas.*

THE NORTHERN WHALE-FISHERY

(CAPTAIN WILLIAM SCORESBY)

The ship *Esk*, which I then commanded, sailed from Whitby on the 29th of March, 1816. We entered the frigid confines of the Icy Sea and killed our first whale on the 25th of April. On the 30th of April we forced our way into the ice with a favourable wind, and after passing through a large body of it, entered an extensive open sea. The wind then blowing hard south-south-east, we kept our reach to the eastward until three o'clock in the afternoon when we unexpectedly met with a quantity of ice which interrupted our course. We then wared, by the way of avoiding it, but soon found, though the weather was thick with snow, that we were completely embayed in a situation that was truly terrific.

In the course of fourteen voyages in which I had before visited this inhospitable country, I passed through many dangers wherein my own life, together with those of my companions, had been threatened; but the present case far surpassed in awfulness, as well as actual hazard, anything that I had before witnessed. Dangers which occur unexpectedly and terminate suddenly, though of the most awful description, appear like a dream when they are past; but horrors which have a long continuance leave an impression on the memory which time itself cannot altogether efface. Such was the effect of the present scene. Whilst the wind howled through the rigging with tempestuous roar, the sea was so mountainous that the mastheads of some accompanying ships, within the distance of a quarter of a mile, were intercepted and rendered invisible by the swells, and our ship frequently rolled the lee-boats into the water, that were suspended by their keels above the rough-tree rail!

At the same time we were rapidly approaching a body of ice, the masses of which, as hard as rocks, might be seen at one instant covered with foam, the next concealed from sight by the waves, and instantly afterwards reared to a prodigious height above the surface of the sea. It is needless to relate the means by which we attempted to keep the ship clear of the threatened danger because those means were without avail. At eleven p.m. we were close to the ice, when perceiving through the mist an opening a short distance within, we directed the drift of the ship towards it. In this place the pieces of ice were happily of smaller dimensions; at least all the larger masses we were able to avoid, so that after receiving a number of shocks we escaped without any particular accident into the opening or slack part of the ice above noticed. This opening, as far as we could see, promised a safe and permanent release.

But in this we were grievously disappointed: for when we attempted to ware the ship, which soon became necessary, she refused to turn round, notwithstanding every effort. In consequence of this accident, which arose partly from the bad trim of the ship, and partly from the great violence of the wind, she fell to leeward into a close body of ice, to which we could see no termination. The *Mars*, of Whitby, and another vessel which closely followed us as we penetrated the exterior of the ice, being in better trim than the *Esk*, performed the evolution with ease, and were in a few minutes out of sight. In this dreadful situation we lay beating against the opposing ice with terrible force, during eight successive hours, all which time I was at the top-gallant masthead directing the management of the sails in order to avoid the largest masses of ice, any one of which would have perforated the side of the ship. By the blessing of God, we succeeded wonderfully; and at eight a.m. the 2nd of May, gained a small opening where we contrived to navigate the ship until the wind subsided, and we had the opportunity of forcing into a more commodious place. On examining the ship we found our only apparent damage to consist in the destruction of most of our rudder works, a few slight bruises on the sides, and a cut on the lower part of the stern of the ship.

From this time to the 20th of May, the fishery was generally interrupted by the formation of new ice, insomuch that during this interval we killed but one whale, while few of our neighbours succeeded so well. During the succeeding week we became so fixed that we never moved except occasionally a few yards. The next twelve days were spent in most arduous labour in forcing the ship through the ice. At length, on the 12th of June, we happily escaped. On the 27th of June, we had secured thirteen fish, and our quantity of oil was about 125 tuns.

After proceeding to the westward for the greater part of the 28th, we arrived at the borders of a compact body of field-ice, consisting of immense sheets of prodigious thickness. As I considered the situation not favourable for fishing, the ship was allowed to drift to the eastward all night. In the morning of the 29th I found, however, that she was very little removed from the place where she lay when I went to bed. I perceived that the floes, between which there had been extensive spaces, were now in the act of closing, and attempted by lowering four boats to tow the ship through an opening at a short distance from us. At the moment when we were about to enter it, it closed. In attempting to get the ship into the safety of an indentation which appeared calculated to afford a secure retreat, a small piece of ice came athwart her bow, stopped her progress, and she was in a minute afterwards subjected to a considerable squeeze.

From none of the pieces of ice around us did we apprehend any danger. There was a danger, however, on the larboard quarter, of which we were totally unconscious. The piece of ice that touched the ship in that part, though of itself scarcely six yards square, and more than one yard above the water, concealed beneath the surface of the sea, at the depth of ten or twelve feet, a hard pointed projection of ice which pressed against the keel, lifted the rudder, and caused a damage that had nearly occasioned the loss of the ship. About an hour and a half after the accident, the carpenter, having sounded the pump, discovered to our great concern and amazement a depth of eight and a half feet of water in the hold. This was most alarming; with despair pictured in every face the crew set on the pumps; a signal of distress was at the same time hoisted, and a dozen boats approached us from the surrounding ships. In the space of four hours the water had lowered to nearly four feet, but one of the pumps becoming useless, and bailing being less effectual than at first, the water once more resumed its superiority and gained upon us.

As the pumping and bailing could not possibly be continued by our own ship's company, it was necessary to make use of some means to attempt a speedy remedy whilst our assistants were numerous. As there was a probability that a bunch of rope-yarns, straw, or oakum, might enter some of the larger leaks and retard the influx of water if applied near the place through the medium of a fothering-sail (that is, a sail drawn by means of ropes at the four corners, beneath the damaged or leaky part) we prepared a lower studding-sail, by sewing bunches of these materials which, together with sheets of old thin canvas, whalebone-hair, and a quantity of ashes, fitted it well for the purpose. Thus prepared it was hauled beneath the damaged place, but not the least effect was produced. We therefore set about unrigging the ship and discharging the cargo and stores upon a flat place of the floe, against which we had moored, with the intention of turning the ship keel upwards. My own sailors were completely worn out, and most of our auxiliaries wearied and discouraged; some of them evinced by their improper conduct their wish that the ship should be abandoned.

Before putting our plan in execution, we placed twenty empty casks in the hold to act against a quantity of iron ballast which was in the ship; caulked the dark lights, removed all the dry goods and provisions that would injure with the wet, secured all the hatches, skuttles, companion, etc., then, erecting two tents on the ice, one for sheltering myself, and the other for the crew, we ceased pumping, and permitted the ship to fill. At this crisis, men of whom I had conceived the highest opinion for firmness and bravery greatly disappointed my expectations. Among the whole crew, indeed, scarcely a dozen spirited fellows were to be seen.

As no ship could with propriety venture near us to assist in turning the *Esk* over, on account of the hazardous position of the ice around her, we had no other means of attempting this singular evolution than by attaching purchases to the ice from the ship. Everything being prepared, while the water flowed into the ship, I sent our exhausted crew to seek a little rest. For my own part, necessity impelled me to endeavour to obtain some repose. I had already been fifty hours without rest, and this unusual exertion, together with the anxiety of mind I endured, caused my legs to swell and become so extremely painful that I could scarcely walk. Spreading a mattress upon a few boards laid on the snow within one of the tents, and notwithstanding the coldness of the situation and the excessive dampness that prevailed from the constant fog, I enjoyed a comfortable repose for four hours, and arose considerably refreshed.

About 3 p.m. on the 1st of July, I proceeded with all hands to the ship which, to our surprise, we found had only sunk a little below the sixteenth mark externally, while the water but barely covered a part of " 'tween decks within." Perceiving that it was not likely to sink much further on account of the buoyancy of the empty casks, and the materials of which the ship was composed, we applied all our purchases; but even with the strength of 150 men we could not heel her more than five or six strakes. When thus partly careened, with the weight of two anchors suspended from the mast acting with the effect of powerful levers on the ship, I accompanied about 120 men on board. All these being arranged on the high side of the deck, ran suddenly to the lower side, when the ship fell so suddenly on one side that we were apprehensive she was about to upset; but after turning a little way the motion ceased. The tackles on the ice being then hauled tight, the heeling position of the ship was preserved until we mounted the higher part of the deck, and ran to the lower as before. At length, after a few repetitions of this manoeuvre, no further impression whatever was produced, and the plan of upsetting the ship appeared quite impracticable.

The situation of the ship being now desperate, there could be no impropriety in attempting to remove the keel and garboard strake, which prevented the application of the fothering. Whatever might be the result, it could scarcely be for the worse. These encumbrances being removed, the sail for fothering was immediately applied to the place, and a vast quantity of fothering materials thrown into its cavity, when it was fairly underneath. Over this sail we spread a fore-sail, and braced the whole as tight to the ship as the keel-bolts, which yet remained in position, would admit. The effect was as happy as we could possibly have anticipated. Some time before all these preparations were completed, our people, assisted by the crew of the *John,* commanded by my brother-in-law, who after a short rest had returned to us, put the three pumps and bailing tubs in motion and applied their energies with such effect that in eleven hours the pumps sucked! The *John's* crew on this occasion exterted themselves with a spirit and zeal which was truly praiseworthy.

As the assistance of carpenters was particularly needed, we fired a gun and repeated our signal of distress, which brought very opportunely two boats, with six men each, from the *Prescot*, and the same number from our tried friend, Mr. Allen, of the *North Britain.* As we likewise procured the carpenters of these ships, together with those of the *John,* they commenced operations by cutting through the sealing, between two frames of timbers directly across the hold; a situation which was on the fore part of the leak, or between the leak and the body of the ship. The timbers in this place were unhappily found so closely connected that we had to cut away part of one of the floors so that we might come at the outside plank, and caulk the crevices between it and the timbers. This operation, on account of the great depth of timber and the vast flow of water that issued at the sealing, was extremely difficult, tedious, and disagreeable.

Meanwhile seeing that we had good assistance, I allowed our crew four hours' rest, half of them at a time, for which purpose some of their beds were removed from the ice to the ship. Here, for the first time during four days they enjoyed their repose; for on account of the cold and damp that prevailed when they rested on the ice, several of them, I believe, never slept.

Some of the *John's* people returning to us, swayed up the topmast, and rigged most of the yards, while our men were employed stowing the mainhold which, by the floating of the casks, was thrown into a singular state of disorder. Some of the casks were found without heads and all the blubber lost, and many were found bilged, or otherwise damaged.

After the carpenters had completely cleared the space between the ribs, or frames of timbers, they drove oakum into it, along with an improved woollen sheathing substance; and occasionally, where the spaces were very large, pieces of fat pork. The spaces or crevices being then filled, all the above substances were firmly driven down by means of pine wedges, and the spaces between each of the wedges caulked. This would have been very complete had not the increased flow of the water overcome the pumps, and covered the sealing where the carpenters were at work. They were therefore obliged to wedge up the place with great expedition; and being at the same time greatly fatigued, the latter part of the operation was accomplished with much less perfection than I could have wished.

Hitherto calm weather with thick fog having constantly prevailed, was the occasion of several ships remaining by us and affording assistance, which would otherwise have left us. But the weather having now become clear, and a prospect of prosecuting the fishery being presented, every ship deserted us except the *John,* and she was preparing to leave us likewise. In the state of extreme jeopardy in which we were still placed, the love of life on the part of the crew determined them to attempt to quit the ship and take refuge in the *John* as soon as she should attempt to leave us. I was confident that unless the assistance of the *John* was secured, the *Esk*, after all the labour bestowed on her, and the progress which had been made towards her preservation, must yet be abandoned as a wreck.

At length I yielded to the request of my whole crew and made a proposal to Captain Jackson of the *John*, who agreed, on certain conditions involving the surrender of a large proportion of our cargo, to stay by us and assist us until our arrival at some port of Shetland.

These agreements being fully understood and signed, the *John* hauled alongside of the ice, which had now opened near the *Esk* for the first time since the accident, and took on board the whole of our loose blubber, together with half our whalebone, as agreed. Everything now went on favourably, and whilst our crew and assistants were in full and vigorous employment, I retired to seek that repose which my wearied frame stood greatly in need of.

On the 5th of July, assisted by all hands from the *John*, the stowing of the hold and the rigging of the ship were completed and, under a moderate breeze of wind, we left the floe; but what was our astonishment and mortification to find that the ship could not be guided! The rudder had become perfectly useless, so that the ship could not be turned round or diverted in the least from the course in which the impetus of the wind on the sails was the most naturally balanced. This was an alarming disappointment. However, as the ship was in such constant danger of being crushed in the situation where she lay, the *John*, with the greatest difficulty imaginable, towed us three or four miles to the eastward into a place of comparative safety. Here we rectified our rudder and arranged for the trimming of the ship more by the stern, to compensate in some degree for the loss of the after-keel. When these matters were completed, on account of strong wind and thick weather we could not, without imminent danger, attempt to penetrate the compact body of ice which at this time barred our escape to the sea.

However, after various other alarms, and careful attention to the leakage, together with the unremitting diligence of the crew in the use of the pumps, we eventually descried land on the 23rd of July and approached within three or four miles of the coast of

Shetland. In the evening the *John*, having fulfilled the articles of agreement as far as was required, we sent the twelve men belonging to her crew on board, and they left us with three cheers and the usual display of colours. We were now left to sail by ourselves; our progress was in consequence rather slow. At daylight on the 27th we were rejoiced with a sight of our port. We pressed towards it with every sail we could set, and having received a pilot as we approached the pier, we immediately entered the harbour and grounded at half-past five a.m. in a place of safety.

The Scoresbys left the sea before the great change came – when sails gave way to steam. But whaling in the north-west waters bridged the change and continued well into the first decade of the twentieth century. In the later years there were far fewer ships involved, but they were bigger ships, mainly from Scottish ports, and especially designed to take the ice. Through the whole period of their activity they served as auxiliaries for those vessels which were engaged in the struggle with the ice for scientific or exploratory reasons. But they also conducted exploratory voyages on their own account, and the first vessel ever to reach many of the outlying inlets and channels of the Eastern Arctic was often a steam whaler. Establishing advanced supply depots for explorers, bringing land exploration parties through the ice, rescuing the crews of wrecked exploration vessels, advising the commanders of outward-bound expeditions – all these, and more, were regular services performed by the whalers right up until the day when steel replaced whalebone in women's corsets, and the Eastern Arctic whale fishery came to an abrupt conclusion.

Of all the voyagers who dared the north-western waters, none came to know the ice so well, none engaged it more stubbornly, and none suffered so heavily from it as the whaling men.

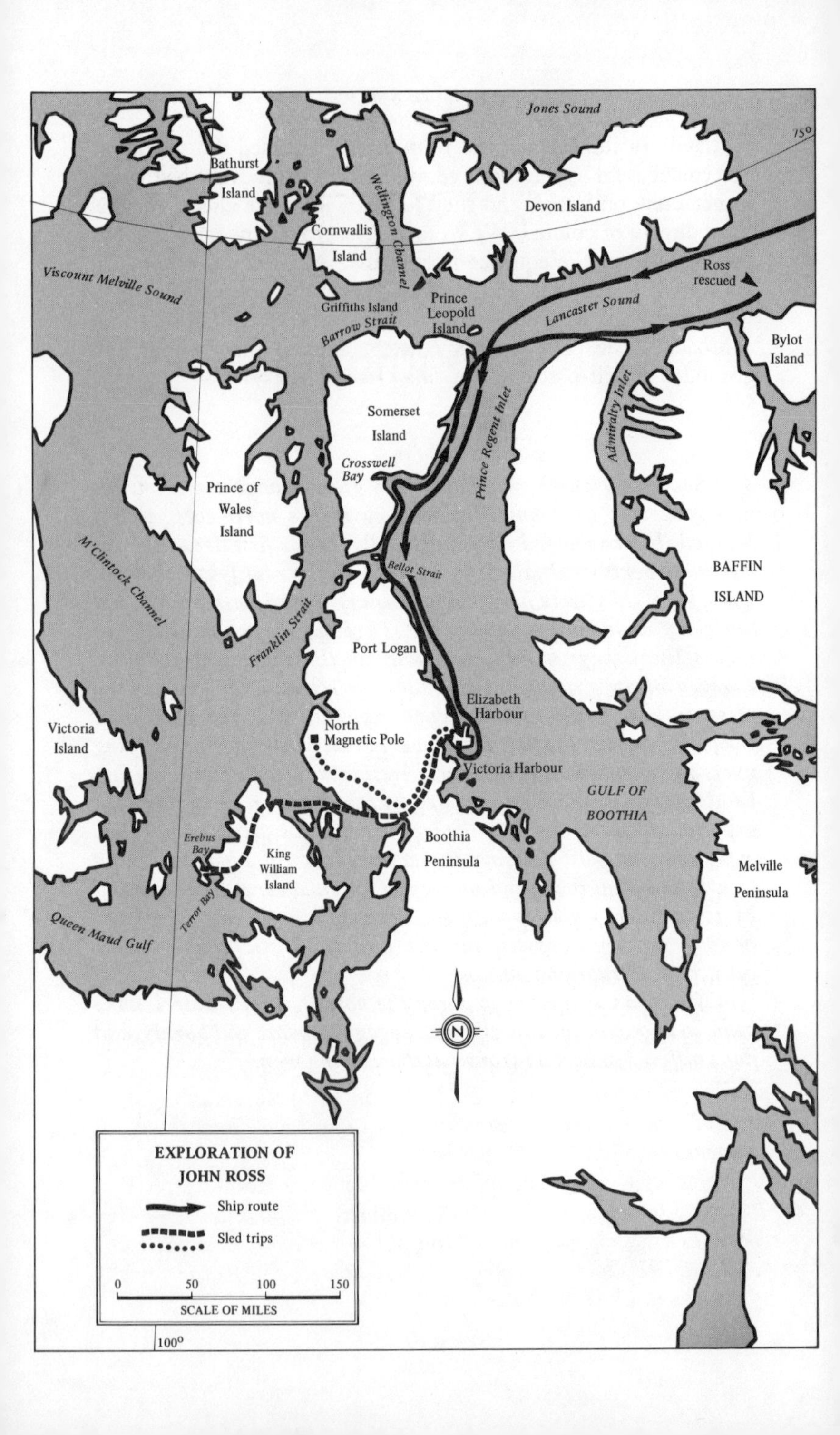
Jones Sound
75°
Bathurst Island
Wellington Channel
Devon Island
Cornwallis Island
Ross rescued
Viscount Melville Sound
Griffiths Island
Prince Leopold Island
Lancaster Sound
Barrow Strait
Bylot Island
Admiralty Inlet
Somerset Island
Prince Regent Inlet
Crosswell Bay
Prince of Wales Island
M'Clintock Channel
Bellot Strait
BAFFIN ISLAND
Franklin Strait
Port Logan
Elizabeth Harbour
Victoria Island
North Magnetic Pole
Victoria Harbour
GULF OF BOOTHIA
Erebus Bay
King William Island
Boothia Peninsula
Melville Peninsula
Terror Bay
Queen Maud Gulf
N
EXPLORATION OF JOHN ROSS
Ship route
Sled trips
0
50
100
150
SCALE OF MILES
100°

VIII

Winter Without End

An era in Arctic exploration had ended with James Knight. By late in the eighteenth century Frobisher, Hudson, Bylot, James, and Munk were all but forgotten. By the beginning of the nineteenth century Baffin's Bay had been expunged from the maps as being no more than a figment of the imagination. Frobisher's Strait had become a myth, transposed to the ice-bound southeastern coast of Greenland. Even Henry Hudson's early attempt to sail direct across the polar sea by way of Spitzbergen had been lost to memory. The men of the nineteenth century could neglect the past as thoroughly as we of the twentieth have done.

Yet in the early years of the nineteenth century a new breed of Arctic venturers was being spawned, though all unknowing, in the unlikely bed of war. The struggle with Napoleon had swelled the British Navy to immense size and power, and it had become a fully professional navy employing thousands of regular officers and hundreds of ships. When Napoleon was sent off to St. Helena there was no longer need for such a vast establishment; but then, as now, the military mind could not endure to see a waning of its empire, and so the Lords of Admiralty looked anxiously about for new means to justify their Service.

By a happy chance the Navy's need to find a raison d'etre *coincided with a national desire to consolidate and to exploit the discoveries made in earlier times. But in British North America nothing could be done to evaluate the potential of the Arctic regions*

(Hudson Bay excepted) since almost nothing was known about this immense stretch of land and sea and ice. Except for the mouths of the Mackenzie and Coppermine Rivers, which had been reached by the overland journeys of Mackenzie and Hearne, the entire Arctic coast and its vast archipelago of islands remained unknown to Europeans all the way from east Baffin Island to Icy Cape in Alaska. The whole of this vast area had been claimed by Britain, but the claims were meaningless without a physical evaluation.

In addition to the consequent compulsion to fill up the blank spaces on the charts and maps, the will-o'-the-wisp possibility of discovering a western passage to the Pacific was again stirring European curiosity, and these things combined to induce a new general interest in north-western exploration – an interest which the Royal Navy seized upon with gratitude, and attempted to make peculiarly its own province.

The new period of exploration in the Arctic began in 1818 when four Royal Navy ships, comprising two separate expeditions, were ordered north. One of these (including amongst its officers a man called John Franklin), was ordered to do what Hudson had demonstrated could not be done: to sail past Spitzbergen to the pole, thence south to Bering Strait. Here it was to rendezvous with the two ships of the second expedition which, under Captain John Ross, were to find and then sail through the Northwest Passage.

Trafalgar seems to have had a singularly heady effect upon the Admiralty. The Sea Lords apparently believed that even the Arctic ice would quail before this double onslaught.

*But the ice was proof against the victors of Trafalgar, and the Arctic surrendered nothing that it had not already given to the early voyagers. The Spitzbergen flotilla bloodied its nose against the impenetrable polar pack, and limped back home. Ross and his two ships did better – they passed through Davis Strait to rediscover and explore the whole of Baffin Bay. Had luck and time been on their side they might have done far better still, for they entered Lancaster Sound and followed it for fifty miles to the westward before turning back, primarily because of the lateness of the season, but also because they had glimpsed what they took to be a range of mountains barring further progress.**

* What Ross probably saw was the ice fog rising over the eastern edge of the Lancaster Sound ice-stream.

This was John Ross's first venture to the Arctic. Born in 1777 he had joined the Royal Navy at the age of nine, and had served with it ever since. Naval warfare was not much of an apprenticeship for an Arctic explorer, but Ross could learn from new experiences with astounding rapidity. He showed another aspect of his character after his return to England by refraining from any braggadocio about his exploits and, instead, by thanking God that he had been able to vindicate the names of Baffin and Bylot.

But during this voyage Ross had under his command a young man of a different stamp. This was William Edward Parry, and he was mightily ambitious on his own account. Gambling that he might succeed in finding a Northwest Passage where Ross had failed, he used his considerable personal influence to persuade the Admiralty that Lancaster Sound must provide a certain route to the Pacific, and he suggested that it was only Ross's timidity which had prevented the discovery of the passage in 1818.

The upshot of Parry's machinations was that Ross went under a cloud of disapproval that was not to leave him for fifteen years; while, in 1819, Parry sailed for the north-west with a naval expedition under his own command.

He was more than lucky. Unusually favourable ice conditions let him reach Lancaster Sound early in the season and then enabled him to sail with very little difficulty as far west as Melville Island. For this not inconsiderable feat he was lionized in London and he and his crew shared a Parliamentary prize of several thousand pounds – while Ross was relegated to complete disgrace.

Much encouraged, the Navy renewed its assault upon the Arctic seas with considerable vigour, but with considerably reduced success. The insatiable Parry sailed again, in 1821, to prove the existence of a usable passage west from Hudson Bay. He finally discovered the impassable Fury and Hecla Strait, but it took him two years of largely wasted effort to gain this Pyrrhic victory. Then, in 1824, he again attacked the Arctic by way of Lancaster Sound. This time his luck was completely out. Impenetrable ice forced him south into Prince Regent Inlet where the floes battered his two vessels until he lost the Fury *and was forced to beat an ignominious retreat. This, and another defeat sustained in the same year by Captain Lyon, R.N., in Roes Welcome Sound, left a sour taste in the mouth of the Admiralty. The Arctic was evidently not such an easy field of opportunity as had been thought. The attack was called off and the Navy withdrew its forces.*

Then in 1829, eleven years after Parry had doomed him to obscurity, John Ross came back to vindicate himself. Failing to obtain any support from the Admiralty (after several futile attempts to do so), he at length found a friend and a supporter in Felix Booth, the Sheriff of London. Booth provided the money for an expedition to discover the location of the north magnetic pole, and, if possible, to find a passage out of Prince Regent Inlet to the western waters.

Since this was a private expedition, the available money fell far short of the need. The ship chosen for the voyage was the Victory, *one of the first side-wheel steamers ever built. She was a small coastal packet which had been employed on the run between Liverpool and the Isle of Man, and she was most assuredly never intended for Arctic exploration. But it was a question of the* Victory *or nothing, and so Ross bought her.*

He took with him a crew of twenty-two officers and men, one of whom was his nephew, Commander James Clark Ross, who had been along on all three of Parry's expeditions.

The supplies they could afford were meagre, if not inadequate, and Ross had to trust to what he might salvage from the naval stores landed on a beach in Prince Regent Inlet from the lost Fury, *to meet the balance of his needs.*

The voyage out was a purgatory. The Victory's *primitive engine proved useless, and worse than useless, since not only did it occupy an immense amount of valuable space, but the vessel's designers had relied upon it so heavily that the ship was seriously under-rigged for sail. Ross showed his skill, and the qualities of endurance which were to stave off tragedy in the years ahead, by patiently nursing her through the ice of Baffin Bay with such effect that on August 13, 1829, he had entered Prince Regent Inlet and was in sight of Fury Beach.*

NARRATIVE OF A SECOND VOYAGE IN SEARCH OF A NORTHWEST PASSAGE

The *Victory* being securely moored in a good ice harbour, within a quarter of a mile of the place where the *Fury*'s stores were landed in 1825, we were anxious to examine the spot. It was with no common interest that we proceeded to the only tent which remained entire. This had been the mess tent of the *Fury*'s officers; but it was too evident that the bears had been paying frequent visits. There had been a pocket near the door where my nephew and present companion, Commander Ross, had left his memorandum book and specimens of birds; but it was torn down, without leaving a fragment of what it contained.

Where the preserved meats and vegetables had been deposited, we found everything entire. The canisters had been piled up in two heaps; but though quite exposed to all the chances of the climate for four years, they had not suffered in the slightest degree. The security of the joinings had prevented the bears from smelling their contents. Had the bears known what was within, not much of this provision would have come to our share and they would have had more reason than we to be thankful for Mr. Donkin's patent for preserving meat in tins. On examining the contents they were not found frozen, nor did the taste appear to have been in the least degree altered. This was indeed no small satisfaction; as it was not our luxury, but our very existence and the prospect of success, which were implicated in this discovery. The wine, spirits, sugar, bread, flour and cocoa, were in equally good condition. The lime-juice and the pickles had not suffered much, and even the *Fury*'s sails were not only dry but seemed as if they had never been wetted.

We proceeded now to the beach where the *Fury* had been abandoned, but not a trace of her hull was to be seen. No doubt she had been carried bodily off or had been ground to atoms and floated away to add to the drift timber of these seas.

We therefore returned on board and made preparations for embarking a sufficiency of stores and provisions to complete our equipment for two years and three months; being what we expected to want on the one hand, and to obtain on the other. I need not say that it was an occurrence not less novel than interesting, to find in this abandoned region of solitude and ice and rocks, a ready market where we could supply all our wants, the materials all ready to be shipped when we chose, and all free of cost.

The powder magazine, detached from the rest of the store, was unroofed and the waterproof cloth of it in tatters; but the patent cases had kept the gunpowder itself perfectly dry. We selected from it what we thought we should require, and then in compliance with Sir Edward Parry's request and our own sense of what was right, caused the remainder to be destroyed lest it should prove a source of injury to any Esquimaux who might hereafter chance to visit this spot. And with this we ended our new outfit; storing ourselves somewhat like Robinson Crusoe, with whatever could be of use to us from the wreck.

It had been nearly calm for two days; but at eight in the afternoon a fresh breeze sprung up from the northward and the ice harbour that we lay in began to break up. The boats were therefore hoisted up and secured, and casting off the ship from the ice, we made sail for Cape Garry.

It is unfortunate that no description can convey an idea of a scene like that which surrounded us; and as to the pencil, it cannot represent motion or noise. And to those who have not seen a northern ocean in winter – who have not seen it, I should say, in a winter's storm – the term ice, exciting but the recollection of what they only know at rest in an inland lake or canal, conveys no idea of what it is the fate of an Arctic navigator to witness and to feel. But let them remember that ice is stone; a floating rock in the stream, a promontory or an island when aground, not less solid than if it were a land of granite. Then let them imagine, if they can, these mountains of crystal hurled through a narrow strait by a rapid tide; meeting, as mountains in motion would meet, with the noise of thunder, breaking from each other's precipices huge fragments, or rending each other asunder till, losing their former equilibrium, they fall over headlong, lifting the sea around in breakers, and whirling it in eddies; while the flatter fields of ice, forced against these masses, or against the rocks, by the wind and the stream, rise out of the sea till they fall back on themselves, adding to the indescribable commotion and noise which attend these occurrences.

It is not a little, too, to know and to feel our utter helplessness in these cases. There is not a moment in which it can be conjectured what will happen in the next; there is not one which may not be the last; and yet that next moment may bring rescue and safety. It is a strange, as it is an anxious position; but though fearful, it often gives no time for fear, so unexpected is every event, and so quick the transitions. If the noise and the motion and the hurry in every thing around are distracting, if the attention is troubled to fix on anything amid such confusion, still must one's attention be alive that it may seize on the single moment of help or escape which may occur. Yet with all this, and it is the hardest task of all, there is nothing to be acted, no effort to be made; and though the very sight of the movement around inclines the seaman to be himself busy, while we can scarcely repress the instinct that directs us to help ourselves in cases of danger, he must be patient, as if he were unconcerned or careless; waiting as he best can for the fate, be it what it may, which he cannot influence or avoid.

Despite a constant repetition of such hair-raising struggles with the ice, Ross edged his balky vessel on toward the south, reaching Victory Harbour near the end of September.

Before proceeding with the journal I must offer some remarks on the actual condition of our ship, especially as regards the engine. The record of the last weeks has already shown that we had ceased to consider her as aught more than a sailing vessel; and it is also true that whatever advantage we had latterly derived from our machinery, it was not greater than we might have obtained from our two rowing boats, by towing. But thus rendering us no service, the engine was not merely useless, it was a serious encumbrance; since it occupied, with its fuel, two-thirds of our tonnage. It had been from the beginning a very heavy grievance in another way, and in addition to the endless troubles and vexations which I have recorded; since it demanded and employed the services of four persons who were necessarily landsmen, not sailors; thus cramping very seriously the number of our real, or nautical, crew. As the engine, moreover, had been considered the essential moving power in the original arrangement of the vessel, the masting and sailing had been reduced accordingly, since it was presumed that the sails would only be required in stormy weather; so that in fact she was almost a jury-rigged ship. To add to all these disadvantages, she had, under this imperfect power, the heavy duty of towing the *Krusenstern*, a boat of eighteen tons, a dimension equalling one-fourth of her own; the whole comprising a mass of obstruction and encumbrance which we certainly as little expected as we had foreseen when we quitted England.

If with all this, we had not less reason to be thankful for the progress we had made, than really to wonder at our success thus far, these were not things to make us shut our eyes to what it seemed now most needful to do. In future our ship was to be a sailing vessel and nothing more. I therefore determined to lighten her of the most ponderous and least expensive part of this machinery, and to apply, towards strengthening the ship, whatever might seem available for that purpose.

With this view, arrangements were made on the last day of September for taking to pieces the boilers, that we might land them as soon as the ship should be frozen in; an event that could not be far distant. It is true that we thus consented to reduce ourselves to a degree of power far inferior to that of any preceding vessel engaged in these Arctic services; but in reality that evil had already occurred against our will, and our voluntary act of self-condemnation was, after all, little more than a form.

October 1st. During the last night the thermometer fell to 17° threatening us with having reached our last position for this season; but towards daylight the weather became cloudy with a fall of snow which continued the whole day. We could do nothing more therefore than sound and survey our harbour; and were pleased to find that if we should really be frozen up in this spot, we should find it a safe place, after making some alterations in it by clearing away the heavy masses and sawing our way into the bay ice, which was now six inches thick. A very recent stone fox-trap was found on the shore; and as the seals were very shy, while numerous, it was a natural conclusion that the Esquimaux had not long quitted this place.

We were at a stand. We had indeed long suspected that the event which could not be very distant, was impending, nor could we in reason be surprised that it had arrived. Yet we had been busy and active up to the present point and our perpetual efforts had, as is usual in life, prevented us from thinking of the future; from seeing that the evil which could not for ever be protracted was drawing nearer every hour, that it was coming every minute, that it was come.

It was now that we were compelled to think, for it was now that there was nothing more to be performed; as it was now also that the long and dreary months, the long-coming year I might almost say, of our inevitable detention among this immovable ice rose full in our view. The prison door was shut upon us for the first time; leaving us feeling that we were as helpless as hopeless captives, for many a long and weary month to come.

October 6th. A fresh breeze of wind made the last night colder than any which had preceded. We now, therefore, proceeded to cut the ice so as to get the ship into what we considered the position of greatest safety for the winter; a work which occupied the whole day.

The tedium of this day, the forerunner of many far worse, was enlivened by a successful bear hunt, being the first chance of the kind which had occurred to us. The animal, having approached the ship, was turned towards an island; and in this way our party was enabled to cut it off from the land. Thus imprisoned, we turned our Greenland dogs on it; but they proved to be of no use, showing nothing of the instinctive desire to attack this animal which is so general in their race. It was then chased to the water; where, plunging into the new-formed ice, it could make little progress and was consequently overtaken by the skiff and killed.

October 8th. There could, in fact, no longer be the least doubt that we were at our winter's home, if we could indeed have reasonably doubted this some days before. We could no longer expect to lead an active life now; we did not even know that we should find anything useful to do; but it was our business to contrive employment and to make ourselves as easy and as happy as we could.

There was now not an atom of clear water to be seen anywhere; and excepting the occasional dark point of a protruding rock, nothing but one dazzling and monotonous, dull and wearisome extent of snow was visible all round the horizon in the direction of the land. It was indeed a dull prospect. Amid all its brilliancy, this land, the land of ice and snow, has ever been and ever will be a dull, dreary, heart-sinking, monotonous waste, under the influence of which the very mind is paralyzed, ceasing to care or think. Even a poetical imagination would be troubled to extract matter of description from that which offers no variety; where nothing moves and nothing changes, but all is for ever the same, cheerless, cold, and still.

The work in the ship was continued, and a place for a powder magazine selected on the island near us. The fuel was measured and found to amount to seven hundred bushels of coal and coke; being, as we computed, sufficient for the ordinary wants of the ship during the same number of days. A complete examination of the provisions also took place; and the result was to find that there was enough for two years and ten months on full allowance; a quantity easily made to cover three years' consumption. The quantity of oil and tallow was found such as to promise a duration equivalent to that of the provisions; presuming on the further assistance that we had a right to expect from our captures of bears and seals, on sea and land.

On the 13th, a part of the engine was hoisted over on the ice. The brass guns were put on the ice and the lower deck was cleared of some spare stores, by stowing these in the hold. They who valued omens were left to speculate on the prophesying of a raven which flew round the ship. How far they did speculate, and what their prognostics were I did not take the trouble to enquire.

October 22nd. It now became necessary to cut away the ice round the ship, in consequence of her having been so much lightened; that she might rise to her natural line of flotation. This being done, she rose nine inches, and we proceeded to build up a bank of snow and ice round her for shelter from the cold. The galley was also moved and placed in the centre of the men's berths, that the heat from the fire might be more equally distributed. A tank of plate iron was placed on the upper deck, over the coppers, and by this contrivance the steam, which is a constant annoyance at these low temperatures, was secured and condensed. Another raven was seen; and a fishery of whelks,* though never very productive, was continued daily.

* A kind of shellfish.

I formerly mentioned the quantity of provisions and fuel that we had remaining, but there was only one year's allowance of spirits, which was a subject rather of congratulation than otherwise, since there can be no question of their pernicious effects in these frozen climates; one of these being, I have no doubt, to increase the tendency to scurvy. It was necessary, however, that what we had should be reserved for the future parties on land excursions, where it might often prove of considerable, if temporary service; or, as might become necessary, for our use in case of shipwreck and our being condemned to take to the boats; since this article would then be valuable not merely as an article of diet, but as fuel; or finally, under the chance of our being unable to liberate the ship in the spring, and being thus compelled to continue our investigations by land. Orders were accordingly given to stop the use and allowance of grog; while it was very satisfactory to find that these were received without remonstrance.

Our roofing over the ship had been perfected in this month; but it still remained to complete our embankment and to cover the upper deck with snow. More arrangements had also been made in the interior of the ship, by constructing a room in the place of the steerage, to receive the men's chests and the apparatus for cooking and baking; while copper flues were carried from them round the whole apartment, in order to convey away the vapour. Over the steam kitchen, oven, and after passage, apertures were made in the upper deck on which were placed iron tanks with their openings downward. In these the vapour was received and became immediately condensed.

We found this last contrivance to be the best that had yet been adopted; and chiefly as, by keeping the apartment of the crew dry, it saved the necessity of forcing up the temperature, as had been done on former occasions* for the purpose of keeping the vapour afloat till it was condensed on the beams and deck. This too involved a great saving of fuel; since we found that a temperature between 40° and 50° was sufficient to make the place dry, warm and comfortable, whereas it had, in the ships that preceded us, been necessary to carry it as high as 70°.

The men slept in hammocks which were taken down at six in the morning and hung up at ten at night, being also aired twice a week. The lower deck, being the dwelling floor, was covered with

* Parry's expeditions.

hot sand every morning and scrubbed with sand till eight, when the men breakfasted. Monday was settled in future as the washing day, and this operation being finished by noon, the linen was dried at the stove. The upper deck having been at length covered with snow two feet and a half in thickness, it was trod down till it became a solid mass of ice, and was then sprinkled with sand so as to put on the appearance of a rolled gravel walk. Above this was the roof already mentioned, of which the canvas sides were continued so low as to cover those of the ship. The surrounding bank of snow reached to the ship's gunwale, so that the union of this with the roof formed a perfect shelter from all wind, and thus excluded, very materially, the impressions of the external cold.

During the day the steam kitchen was found sufficient both for warmth and cooking; and in the night the baking oven served the same purpose, while it also heated the sand for the morning's use. As it is a pernicious plan, being a very clumsy and inconvenient one even in the domestic arrangements of England, to supply from the doors the air required for the combustion of the fires, I caused a large copper pipe to be brought from without to the fireplace. Thus, not only was the external air prevented from making a cold "draught" through the room, but the pipe itself became sufficiently warmed to assist in keeping dry the air within this principal apartment.

By these means the vapour was enabled more easily to ascend and settle in the external condensers, instead of becoming water in the room itself; while, what was not less important, the fires were kept burning with a uniform degree of strength. In proof of the utility of the condensers, I may now remark that it was our practice to clear them out every Saturday, and that the quantity of ice they contained averaged about a bushel a day.

Breakfast consisted of cocoa or tea; and dinner was at noon. When the weather permitted anything to be done outside of the ship, the men worked after that meal till three or four o'clock, while, when that was impossible, they were obliged to walk for a certain number of hours on the deck, beneath the roof. Their tea was at five o'clock; and after this they attended an evening school, commencing at six, and lasting till nine; which being closed, and the hammocks slung, they retired to bed at ten.

On Sunday, no work was allowed. The men were mustered and inspected in their best clothes, after which there were prayers and a sermon. To occupy the remainder of the day there was a collection of tracts which had been presented to us by Mrs. Enderby of Blackheath, proving a judicious as well as a useful gift. At six there was a Sunday school, the occupation on this evening being the reading of portions of scripture by the men, while the day was concluded by psalms and by the lessons appointed in the liturgy. Of the good effect of this system of religious duties and of instruction I could entertain no doubt.

Our school was completely organized for instruction in reading, writing, arithmetic, mathematics, and navigation. Out of the eighteen men, three had not learned to read and write; but the want of arithmetic was very general. No compulsion was here necessary; all were volunteers, and the school hours always terminated by reading two chapters from the Bible, together with the evening psalms.

So passed the early months of the winter of 1829-30 in what Ross and his men seem to have believed was a dead and empty world. But the impression of desolation was an illusion, as the early January days soon showed.

January 9th. Going on shore this morning, one of the seamen informed me that strangers were seen. I proceeded accordingly in the direction pointed out, and soon saw some Esquimaux near a small iceberg, not far from the land and about a mile from the ship. They retreated behind it as soon as they perceived me; but as I approached, the whole party came suddenly out of their shelter, forming in a body of ten in front and three deep, with one man detached on the land side who was apparently sitting in a sledge. I therefore sent back my companion for Commander Ross to join me, together with some men, who were directed to keep at a distance behind him. Proceeding then alone to within a hundred yards, I found that each of the Esquimaux was armed with a spear and a knife.

Knowing that the word of salutation between meeting tribes was *tima tima*, I hailed them in their own language, and was answered by a general shout of the same kind.

The rest of my party now coming up, we advanced to within sixty yards and then threw our guns away, with the cry of *aja, tima;* being the usual method, as we had learned it in Greenland, of opening a friendly communication. On this they threw their knives and spears into the air in every direction, returning the shout *aja*, and extending their arms to show that they were also without weapons. But as they did not quit their places we advanced and embraced in succession all those in the front line, stroking down their dress also, and receiving from them in return this established ceremony of friendship. This seemed to produce great delight, expressed by laughing and clamour, and strange gestures, while we immediately found ourselves established in their unhesitating confidence.

Commander Ross's experience was here of great use and, being informed that we were Europeans, *Kablunae*, they answered that they were men, *Innuit*. Their numbers amounted to thirty-one. Two were lame, and, with an old man, were drawn by the others on sledges; one of them having lost a leg from a bear as we understood, and the other having a broken or diseased thigh.

They were all well dressed, in excellent deerskins chiefly; the upper garments double and encircling the body, reaching in front from the chin to the middle of the thigh, and having a cape behind to draw over the head, while the skirt hung down to the calf of the leg. The sleeves covered the fingers and, of the two sets of skins which composed all this, the inner one had the hair next to the body, and the outer one in the reverse direction. They had two pairs of boots on, with the hairy side of both turned inwards, and above them trousers of deerskin reaching very low on the leg.

With this immense superstructure of clothes, they seemed a much larger people than they really were. All of them bore spears looking not much unlike a walking stick, with a ball of wood or ivory at one end, and a point of horn at the other. On examining the shafts, however, they were found to be formed of small pieces of wood, or of the bones of animals, joined together very neatly. The knives that we first saw consisted of bone or reindeer's horn without point or edge, forming a very inoffensive weapon; but we soon discovered that each of them had, hanging at his back, a much more effective knife pointed with iron, and some also edged with that metal. One of them proved also to be formed of the blade of an English claspknife, having the maker's mark on it, which had been so fixed as to be converted into a dagger.

This was a proof of communication with the tribes that trade with Europeans, if that was not the case with themselves. Commander Ross did not indeed recognize among them any of his former acquaintances,* while he was evidently unknown to them,

* As noted, James Ross had accompanied Parry's expedition to Repulse Bay and Melville Peninsula in 1821-22.

but when he mentioned the names of places in Repulse Bay, they immediately understood him and pointed in that direction.

Having no foresight of these visitors, we had of course no presents at hand for them and we therefore sent a man back to the ship for thirty-one pieces of iron hoop, that there might be a gift for each individual. But in the meantime they consented to accompany us on board, and we soon arrived at our snow wall. At this they expressed no surprise; it was, indeed, too much like their own work to excite any; nor did they show any of those marks of astonishment at either the ship itself or the quantity of wood and iron before them, which we had found among the northern savages of Baffin's Bay in 1818. It was evident that they were no strangers to even an abundance of these materials.

The present of the iron excited universal delight. In return they offered us their spears and knives which, to their equal astonishment and satisfaction, we refused. We could now easily see that their appearance was very superior to our own; being at least as well clothed and far better fed; with plump cheeks of as rosy a colour as they could be under so dark a skin.

Their dresses were made with peculiar neatness; and some were ornamented with fringes made of sinews or with strings of small bones. Their sledges were singularly rude; the sides consisting of pieces of bone tied round and enclosed by a skin, and the cross bars on the top being made of the fore legs of a deer. One of them was but two feet long, and fourteen inches wide, the others were between three and four feet in length. On the under part of the runner there was a coating of ice attached to the skin, rendering their motion very easy.

Three of the men were introduced into the cabin where, at length, they showed abundant signs of wonder. The engravings representing their countrymen, selected from the several former voyages, gave them great delight as they instantly recognized them to be portraits of their own race. The looking-glasses, as usual, were however the chief source of astonishment as, especially, was a sight of themselves in our largest mirror. Scarcely less surprise was excited by the lamp and the candlesticks; but they never once showed a desire to possess themselves of any thing; merely receiving what was offered with signs of thankfulness that could not be mistaken. They did not relish our preserved meat; but one who ate a morsel seemed to do it as a matter of obedience, saying it was very good but admitting, on being cross-questioned by Commander Ross, that he had said what was not true; on which all the rest, on receiving permission, threw away what they had taken. But the same man on being offered some oil drank it with much satisfaction, admitting that it was really good.

Thus admirably are the tastes of all these tribes adapted to their compulsory food, and their views of happiness to the means of it which have been provided; nor, assuredly, had these men amidst their blubber and their oil, their dirty diet and villainous smells, any reason to envy the refined tables of the south; as, among those, they would not only have experienced disgust, but felt pity for our barbarism and ignorance; while if they had been induced to partake, it could have been only under the impulse of starvation.

A short race was also run between one of them and an officer of our party; but with so much and such equal politeness on both sides, that there was no victor to be declared. The violin being afterwards produced, they joined our men in dancing.

This was a most satisfactory day; for we had given up all expectations of meeting inhabitants in this place; while we knew that it was to the natives that we must look for such geographical information as would assist us in extricating ourselves from our difficulties and in pursuing our course. It was for philosophers to interest themselves in speculating on a horde so small, and so secluded, occupying so apparently hopeless a country, so barren, so wild, and so repulsive; and yet enjoying the most perfect vigour, the most well-fed health, and all else that here constitutes, not merely wealth, but the opulence of luxury.

January 10th. After Divine Service we proceeded to visit the Esquimaux village, though the thermometer had fallen to minus 37°.

The village consisted of twelve snow huts erected at the bottom of a little bight on the shore, about two miles and a half from the ship. They had the appearance of inverted basins, and were placed without any order; each of them having a long crooked appendage, in which was the passage, at the entrance of which were the women with the female children and infants. We were soon invited to visit these, for whom we had prepared presents of glass beads and needles; a distribution of which soon drove away the timidity which they had displayed at our first appearance.

The passage, always long and generally crooked, led to the principal apartment which was a circular dome, being ten feet in diameter when intended for one family, and an oval of fifteen by ten where it lodged two. Opposite the doorway there was a bank of snow occupying nearly a third of the breadth of the area, about two feet and a half high, level at the top, and covered by various skins; forming the general bed or sleeping place. At the end of this sat the mistress of the house, opposite to the lamp, which being of moss and oil, as is the universal custom in these regions, gave a sufficient flame to supply both light and heat; so that the apartment was perfectly comfortable. Over the lamp was the cooking dish of stone, containing the flesh of deer and of seals, with oil. Everything else, dresses, implements, as well as provisions, lay about in unspeakable confusion, showing that order, at least, was not in the class of their virtues.

Of these huts, built entirely of snow, I must add that they were all lighted by a large oval piece of clear ice fixed about half way up on the eastern side of the roof. We found that these huts had been but just erected; they were scarcely a day old; so that the architectural processes of this country did not occupy much time. It was also ascertained that their winter stock of seal and reindeer was buried in the snow, that this store was laid up in the summer, and that they returned to it in the winter.

The females were certainly not beautiful; but they were at least not inferior to their husbands, and were not less well behaved. All above thirteen years of age seemed to be married; and there appeared three or four such in every house, whether belonging to one establishment or not, we were not sure, but appearing to be the young wives in a house where there was one old one. Their stature was short and they were much inferior in dress and neatness to the men; their hair especially being in a matted and disordered state. Their features were mild, and their cheeks, like those of the men, ruddy; one girl of thirteen was even considered to have a pretty face. All were tattooed to a greater or less extent, chiefly on the brow and on each side of the mouth and chin.

They informed us that there were plenty of musk oxen on the hills to the southward, and that the reindeer* all came this way in April. Their method of hunting reindeer, as they described it, consists in aping the appearance of the animal, by means of two men, the foremost carrying the head and horns over his own; thus giving them unsuspected access, even within the herd.

It being then time to think of returning, many of the people

* Caribou.

offered to accompany us, and we took leave of the women and children; inviting the lame man to come on the following day that he might be examined by our surgeon. Eight of the men attended us to the ship, and while six were turned over to the care of the seamen, we invited the two leaders to our own cabin dinner.

Much astonishment was of course excited by the knives, plates, and other furniture of the table; and if their taste was not improved since the day before (when it had probably only been taken by surprise) they at least relished the soup, and with scarcely any awkwardness immediately learned the use of the spoon. They were at least good mimics; since after observing our proceedings for a little while they equally found out the management of the knife and fork, shortly using these as if they had been long accustomed to them. They seemed now to relish the preserved meat; but they did not like the salt meat, and equally rejected pudding, rice, and cheese.

As we were returning to the ship with them, before these adventures, a very cold blast of wind come down a valley, when one of them observed that the frost had seized one of my cheeks, on which he immediately made a snowball and rubbed it, thus certainly saving me from a disagreeable sore. After this he continued always near me, frequently reminding me to put my hand to the same part, for fear of a recurrence of the attack. This was good natured, and aided, with all else, to give us a favourable impression of these peoples; while they all shared the same dispositions, in aiding to carry our things, as if they could not do too much to oblige us.

At one o'clock the next day, the man who had lost his leg arrived, with another drawing him on a sledge. On examining the stump, the surgeon found it a sound one, long healed, while the knee being bent, there was no difficulty in applying a wooden leg. The carpenter was therefore sent for to measure him.

In our cabin the candle snuffers proved a great object of attraction; but still more effect was produced by a large reading-glass, through which each saw his friend's face magnified beyond all understanding. Such are the delights of novelty, and thus does the curiosity of pure ignorance ever find new gratifications. But we who know everything, knowing even what we have not seen or learned, have contrived to get rid of these pleasures.

Fortunately for our new guests, there was no penny science in this land of little light, to interfere with their admiration; it was absolute; though one bad effect at least of their ignorance was displayed in their abhorrence of plum pudding, with which we had vainly hoped to regale stomachs accustomed to find blubber a sweetmeat, and train oil preferable to maraschino. Our brandy was as odious as our pudding; and they have yet to acquire the taste which has, in ruining the morals, hastened the extermination of their American Indian neighbours to the southward. If, however, these Indian tribes must finally disappear, as seems their fate, it is at least better that they should die gradually by the force of rum, than that they should be exterminated in masses by the fire and the sword of Spanish conquests; since there is at least some pleasure, such as it is, in the meantime.

The time came to end our entertainment and send our company home; the carriage, such as it was, being in waiting. We explained that the new leg would be ready in three days, when we hoped for the pleasure of trying it on; and then presenting them each with one of the empty meat canisters, they took their departure in high glee. It is delightful to be able to overwhelm the needy with gold, not less so I imagine, when it is done at no cost; and here we had made these poor men as rich and as happy, with what was little better than an old saucepan, as if our canisters had been made of silver. Let no man imagine that he knows what a present is worth till he has found what happiness can be produced by a blue bead, a yellow button, a needle, or a piece of an old iron hoop.

January 14th. The thermometer fell from its station of minus 33° last evening, to minus 38°; and as the breeze made it very cold I doubted if our patient would keep his appointment. He came, however, accompanied by his friend Otookiu, together with two women, four men, and two boys. The wooden leg was then fitted, to ascertain whether the length was correct; and as it had, after this, to be finished, the man for whom it had been made was desired to return on the following day.

The rest of the party were called from below, and we were entertained to find that the mate had prevailed on an elderly dame to have her hair cut and combed and arranged; the result making such an advantageous change in her appearance that all of them desired to undergo the same operations. This was an unusual display of ambition and taste among these tribes; making me regret that I had not provided myself with a stock of combs as presents; but the string of beads which I gave to each of the women was probably of more value in their eyes, if of far less use.

January 15th. We tried some mercury known to be pure, and it froze. This was the test of a temperature of 39° minus. It fell afterwards to 40°, being hitherto, our lowest degree.

The two men of yesterday came alone; it was understood that the rest had gone to hunt for seals. The promised leg, being now complete, was fitted on; and there was little time lost in finding its use and value; as the disabled person soon began to strut about the cabin in apparent ecstacy; with more reason certainly to be delighted with his present than all the others united, with what they had received. All the surgery of this case lay indeed with the carpenter; not the worst operator, I believe, in this compound profession; but I doubt if any effort of surgery ever gave more satisfaction than we had thus conferred in reproducing a man fully serviceable once more to himself and his community.

The leg was inscribed with the name of the ship, and packed up in the sledge, as it was not yet sufficiently familiar for the journey of two miles through ice and snow. That we parted better friends than ever, cannot be doubted.

The twenty-first of January was calm and clear. A boy and a girl from the Esquimaux, in company with some men, paid us a visit. The latter was so wrapped up in furs that she had the figure of a globe standing on two pins; but black piercing eyes, added to ruddy cheeks and youth, produced a pretty face where our standard of beauty had ceased to be fixed at a very high degree. I imagine that this is a much more tractable standard than is commonly supposed; and that habit effects in a far shorter time than has been thought, that change in the feelings on this subject which we vainly suppose can never occur. Such at least has been the experience of all travellers; and the arrangement is unquestionably a wise one, since that which is the only accessible ought also to be the most acceptable. This young person was already betrothed, as is the custom of this country; the affiance being even settled, in many cases, during extreme infancy or almost from the birth of the female child.

January 28th. A female fox was taken in a trap, in a state of extreme starvation; displaying corresponding voracity when meat was produced. Another, in the same condition, was caught on the following day; and an unfortunate solitary raven, approaching the ship, was shot. It had been a companion of our stay all the winter and deserved to have been spared. In other days, or in minds more deeply tinctured with poetry or superstition, I know not what mental misery might not have followed an act so sacrilegious.

This month ended with a very fine day. Half the village arrived while we were engaged in our church service and we learned that they had found a bear, torpid in its den, and had killed it with their knives. We offered to buy it of them and they promised to bring it on the following day. We had a specimen of their cunning, in one who, having a sore on his leg, begged to have a wooden leg made, expecting thus to gain a piece of timber. It was easily explained that the first condition was to cut off the sore leg; which put an end to this application.

During the rest of the winter Ross and his men were busy preparing for overland explorations by sledge, and in consolidating their friendship with the Eskimos upon whose help the white men relied almost completely for the success of the expedition. But there were times when friendly relations came perilously close to a rupture, as in the following incident related by Commander Ross.

April 26th. A large party of the Esquimaux had come to the ship and one of them was engaged to conduct me on a sledge journey, and the arrangements made for our departure the next morning.

We departed accordingly, early in the morning of the 27th of April, and approaching the Esquimaux village were exceedingly disappointed at not hearing the cheerful shouts with which we had been usually greeted. That was succeeded by a very disagreeable surprise on finding that the women and children had been all sent out of the way, since we knew this to be a signal of war; a fact of which we were speedily convinced by seeing that all the men were armed with their knives. The fierce and sullen looks of these people also boded mischief; but what the cause of all this could be, it was quite impossible to conjecture.

We could see them better than they could distinguish us, as the sun was in their faces; it was the noise of our dogs which gave them notice of our arrival and proximity; and as soon as this was heard one of them rushed out of a hut brandishing the large knife used in attacking bears, while the tears were streaming down his aged and furrowed face. In an instant he lifted his arm to throw his weapon at myself and the surgeon, who were then within a few yards of him. But the sun dazzling him, caused him to suspend his arm for an instant; when one of his sons laid hold of his uplifted hand and gave us a moment's time for reflection.

The result of that was, of course, an immediate preparation for defence; though we could have done little against such odds as our unexpected enemies displayed. My two companions and I therefore retired to the sledge where I had left my gun; and not daring again to quit it, waited for the result, while losing ourselves in vain conjectures respecting the cause of offence, seeing that we had parted good friends on the preceding day.

The ferocious old man, Pow-weet-yah, was still held fast, and now by both his sons, who had pinioned his arms behind him; though he strove hard to disengage himself; while the rest of the party seemed to be standing in readiness to second any attempt which he might make on us. That there was some difference of opinion amongst them, however, and that all were not equally hostile, was plain from the conduct of these young men; so that we could still hope for some parley before matters came to extremity.

They now began to talk among themselves, and then separated in such a manner as to be ready to surround us, which they having nearly affected, and we not choosing to be so cut off from the ship, I warned those who were closing in on the rear to desist. This produced a short pause, and a still shorter conference; but they immediately again began to close in, brandishing their knives in defiance, according to their usual custom, and had nearly gained their object, when finding that further forbearance would be hazardous I placed the gun to my shoulder and was about to fire, when I fortunately saw that the threat alone was sufficient to give them a check. With little loss of time, those who had advanced nearest broke off in evident alarm and retreated towards their huts; thus leaving us an open passage in the rear.

But as I could not induce any of them to approach, or to answer my questions, we continued for nearly half an hour in this state of suspense and perplexity, when we were relieved by the courage or confidence of one of the women, who came out of a hut just as I was again raising my gun, and called to me not to fire, advancing up to our party without showing the least mark of fear.

From her we soon learned the cause of all this hubbub, which, absurd as it was, might have had a fatal termination. One of Pow-weet-yah's adopted sons, a fine boy of seven or eight years of age, had been killed on the preceding night by the falling of a stone on his head. This they had ascribed to our agency, through the supernatural powers which we were believed to possess; while the father, not very unnaturally under this conviction, had meditated revenge in the manner which we had experienced.

I had much difficulty in persuading the good woman that we were totally ignorant of this catastrophe, and that we were very sorry for the misfortune; she however repeated all that I had said to two of the men who had not taken any share in the business of the attack, and who now approached us unarmed in token of peace. Their object was to persuade us to go back to the ship and return in three days, when they offered to be our guides on our journey. But many reasons opposed this scheme; of which the chief was that it was essential to come to an understanding and to renew our friendships without any delay, as they might go away in the meantime, whether for fear of our returning in greater numbers, or for any other reason, and thus not only cause a lasting estrangement as to themselves, but a general hostility or desertion on the part of all the natives within their connexions or reach; thus rendering the whole land our enemies. I therefore objected to this proposal and declared that I would not go back till we were all once more good friends, when perceiving that the hostile party was gradually approaching our group, though probably but to hear the conversation that was passing, I drew a line on the snow and declared that none of them should cross it without putting away their knives, which they still continued to grasp in their right hands. After some conversation among themselves their grim visages began to relax, the knives were put up; and becoming at last apparently convinced that we had no concern in the death of this boy, they seemed now very anxious to remove the unfavourable impression which their conduct had made on us.

But they still urged us to return to the ship, because as they said, it was impossible for them to make use of their dogs till three days had passed away after the death of any one belonging to a family. Though in all probability this was really a funeral usage, I was unwilling to yield this point, could I possibly carry it; as the loss of even three days at this season was an important consideration.

I therefore produced a large file, offering it to any one of the party who would go with me, and assuring them at the same time that if they all refused I should go alone, and they would thus lose the reward. On this, a consultation of some minutes took place, in which I heard the word "Erk-she" (angry) frequently used, accompanied by my name; which being ended, the man called Poo-yet-tah seemed to yield to his wife's entreaties and offered to accompany me, provided I would allow Il-lik-tah, a fine lad of sixteen or seventeen, to be associated with him.

If I have dwelt on this adventure at some length, it is because this was the only occasion on which they ever showed any hostile feelings toward us, during all the years which we passed in their neighbourhood.

The baggage and provisions were then placed on two sledges, each drawn by six dogs; and by their aid we travelled very quickly over the smooth ice of the bay, we each by turns undertaking to lead on foot, and then in rotation taking his seat in the vehicle.

April 28th. We halted at five o'clock to make the necessary observations for longitude. It was not very wonderful that the sight of the instruments revived in the mind of the guide the belief in our powers of conjuration. And as the idea of eating is ever predominant in the mind of an Esquimaux, while hunting and fishing are almost the only occupation of their lives, his inquiries took this very natural turn. Should we find any musk oxen by means of this inexplicable brasswork, or see them among the hills while looking so intensely through these tubes and glasses? In fact we were in the parts frequented by these animals; and it was a very natural conclusion of the guide that we had come thus far and taken all this trouble for that most important of all purposes, a dinner or a feast. Poo-yet-tah had yet to learn that civilized Europeans must gain their dinners by operations much more circuitous than killing and eating them; and would have been puzzled to understand a system which had brought so many men in a large ship, all the way from England to his shores, that they might command the means of present and future dinners by measuring angles and looking at the moon.

I was by no means desirous of passing for a conjuror. We had found ourselves in a sufficiently awkward predicament already in consequence of this unenviable reputation; and I therefore declared my total ignorance of all musk oxen and their ways. At this he seemed greatly disappointed, and then proposed that we should build a hut in this place, to watch for them; but on my expressing my desire to go still further this day, he quickly again put on his good-tempered face and we proceeded accordingly.

In less than half an hour his sharp eyes observed the tracks of two of these animals on the face of a steep hill. We therefore went back to the sledges; and after selecting a spot to build a hut and leaving the work to be executed by the boy, he took his bow and arrows and set off; leading two of his dogs, and desiring me to follow with my gun and favourite dog Tup-to-ach-ua.

On regaining the tracks he immediately let slip the dogs, and I followed his example with mine. They went off at full speed and were very soon out of sight. His politeness, however, induced him to think me too much fatigued to accompany him in search of the dogs and the game; and he therefore slackened his pace, refusing to leave me behind, though I urged him to do so lest we should lose our expected prey.

We went on laboriously enough for two hours, over a very rugged country and through deep snow; when finding that the footsteps of the dogs no longer followed those of the oxen, he concluded that they had got up with the animals and were probably holding one or both of them at bay. We soon found this to be the fact. On turning the angle of a hill the sight of a fine ox at bay before the three dogs cured our fatigue in an instant, and we went off ourselves at full speed to the rescue.

Poo-yet-tah kept the lead and was in the act of discharging his second arrow when I came up. We saw that it had struck on a rib, since it fell out without even diverting the attention of the animal from the dogs which continued barking and dodging round it, seizing it by the heels whenever they had an opportunity, or when it turned to escape, and then retreating as it faced them. In the meantime it was trembling with rage and labouring to reach its active assailants, but unable to touch them, experienced as they were in this service.

It was easy to see that my companion's weapons were of little value in this warfare, or that the victory would not at least have been gained under many hours; as he continued to shoot without apparent effect, finding his opportunities for an aim with much difficulty, and losing much time afterwards in recovering his arrows. I was pleased, therefore, to find an opportunity of showing him the superiority of our arms, and I fired at the animal with two balls at a distance of about fifteen yards. They took effect, and it fell; but rising again made a sudden dart at us, standing close together as we were. We avoided the attack by dodging behind a large stone which was luckily near us; on which, rushing with all its force, it struck its head so violently that it fell to the ground with such a crash that the hard ground around us fairly echoed to the sound. My guide now attempted to stab it with his knife; but failing in this he sought shelter behind the dogs, which again came forward to the attack. At this time it was bleeding so profusely that the long hair on its sides was matted with blood; yet its rage and strength seemed undiminished, as it continued to advance and butt with the same ferocity as before.

In the meantime I had reloaded my gun behind the stone, and was advancing for another shot when the creature rushed towards me as before, to the great alarm of Poo-yet-tah who called to me to return to the same shelter. But I had time for a cool aim; and it immediately fell, on the discharge of both barrels, but not till it was within five yards of me. The sight of his fallen enemy made my companion scream and dance with joy. He was lost in astonishment at the effect of the fireams, first carefully examining the holes which the balls had made, and pointing out to me that some of them had passed quite through the animal. But it was the state of one broken shoulder which most surprised him; nor would it be easy to forget his look of horror and amazement when he looked up in my face and exclaimed "Now-ek-poke!" (it is broken).

We had now been eighteen hours without any refreshment, and I naturally expected that my friend would have lost no time in extracting a dinner out of the ox. I had however done him injustice; his prudence was more powerful than his stomach. He was content with mixing some of the warm blood with snow, thus dissolving as much as he required to quench his thirst, and then immediately proceeded to skin the animal; knowing very well what I might have recollected, that the operation would shortly become impossible in consequence of the severity of the cold which would soon freeze the whole into an impracticable mass. For the same reason he divided the carcass into four parts, afterwards disposing of the paunch and intestines in the same manner, their contents being previously separated. I did not know before that they did not eat these, as they do the analogous matters of the reindeer; and could only conjecture that at this season of the year the plants on which the musk ox feeds were disagreeable to their taste. In the reindeer, the matters found in the stomachs are considered a great delicacy; and however our own might revolt at a vegetable dish cooked in this manner, this forms a very useful and salutary ingredient among their gross animal diet, since it is scarcely possible for them to collect any eatable vegetables by their own exertions.

As we were unable to carry off our prize we were obliged to

build a snow hut over it, after which, setting up marks to enable us to find it again, we set out on our return to the place where we had left our companions. In the way, we discovered another ox about a quarter of a mile off, under the face of a precipice, but were far too fatigued to think of pursuing it. The guide assured me that this was of no consequence, since it would remain there for some time and we might easily go after it in the morning.

We reached the hut at five in the morning of the twenty-ninth, hungry and fatigued enough to find a very serious enjoyment in a hot supper and rest. We had brought away some of the musk ox beef, and found it exceedingly good, not having at this season of the year the least flavour of musk.

We had not been asleep more than four or five hours when we were awoke by the shouts of Poo-yet-tah and the barking of the dogs in full cry. On inquiring of the boy, he informed me that our guide and huntsman had crept out of the hut silently about an hour before, and was gone in pursuit of the ox which we had seen on the preceding day. In a short time he returned and told us that he had found the animal grazing on top of the hill, that he had advanced upon it by the only accessible road, keeping himself in the middle of his dogs, and that he had done this with so much rapidity that the creature finding no other mode of escape had thrown itself over the precipice.

On going to the spot, we accordingly found the carcass in the place which he had mentioned, exceedingly mangled by the fall, which had exceeded thirty feet.

Until mid-June, and the summer thaw, brought an end to sled travel, the white men spent most of their time on short journeys of exploration. But for the balance of the summer the whole party was restricted to the vicinity of their ship where they waited impatiently for the ice to free the Victory *and allow them to continue their voyage of discovery.*

19th August. A fine day, with a northerly breeze, was but a continuation of a now sleepy uniformity; our ship could do nothing; and we, little. The capture of some fish, and the occurrence of rain at night, scarcely varied the sameness of the following day. The twenty-first closed another week: and thus did the third week of August find us where we had been since the previous September, still fast in the ice.

August 22nd. It was the same this Sunday; though the afternoon was warmer than it had been for a considerable time. There was an open lane of water seen from the shore, lying along the land to the westward of the furthest visible point north. On Monday there was no change; but in the night the wind increased to a fresh gale from the northern quarter, and at daylight next day the ice was seen in rapid motion to the southward, and packing into the bottom of the bay. The inner part of our harbour was thus cleared, as the coast was, for about two miles to the southward; but afterwards a pack of the ice streamed in and filled all except the place where we lay.

August 26th. Both the subsequent days were equally free of any events worth noticing, beyond some indifferent success in fishing and shooting, including the taking of a seal. Another week was gone, and the night thermometer had little changed, varying between 36° and 38°.

August 30th. The ice continued moving to the southward till four o'clock, when it stopped, and remained stationary the whole day. We made ready for hauling the ship out into a pool to the northward of us, that we might be more in the way of extricating ourselves when the ice should fairly open. And with this was summed up the month of August.

The end of that month left us eleven months fixed to one spot. Whatever value voyages of discovery may have in these countries, they are certainly purchased at a high price in time. We might have circumnavigated the globe in the same period; and I imagine no one was very sanguine any longer about future north-west passages, even should we contrive to make one ourselves.

That this was a month of daily and hourly anxiety, of hopes and fears, promise, and non-performance, I need not say; while no record of feelings could give a picture of them. There were but four weeks of this never-assured summer still to come; and really, the hope of its speedy arrival was by no means great. On many past days we had more than hoped, we had almost expected that the next day, or the following, or some other not far distant, would release us; and they who reflected most were perhaps the least easy under this constantly recurring disappointment. It was my business, at any rate, to keep up the hopes of the men, and where that might be difficult, to find them occupations to prevent them from thinking too much of the future. In this, the permission to shoot and fish gave much aid, while the variety of diet this procured them was also advantageous. Of their health, indeed, there was no reason to complain.

Everything about the ship had been entirely refitted and made ready for sea – and she had never been so trim, neat, clean, and comfortable. We had obtained abundant room by the dismissal of the engine; and that was no small gain, to compensate a loss (if that machinery can be esteemed a loss) whence we had derived so little advantage and undergone so much inconvenience and vexation. It was probable that the Esquimaux would profit for a long time to come, by the caches of Messrs. Braithwaite and Erickson's machinery.

September 4th. The weather being fine, and we expecting a high tide at two in the morning, we attempted to cross the bar in front of our harbour; but before we could warp out, the tide fell so much that we remained aground in only fourteen inches of water. By this accident we profited so as to examine the ship's bottom, and thus also repaired several small damages which she had received from the ice. Having shored her up, we proceeded to lighten her by discharging four tons of water, and putting ten tons of other articles in the boats, that we might, if possible, float her off at the next tide.

September 5th. At two o'clock in the morning we attempted to heave the ship over the bar, but in vain. The wind had shifted to the southward, and the tide did not rise so high as before. It became necessary therefore, to unload the vessel, as the tides were now diminishing. A bridge was, in consequence, laid to the rocks, which were but eight yards from us, and we carried over it all our remaining stores and provisions, together with that iron-work of the engine which remained on board.

September 6th. A shift of the wind up towards the north produced such a tide as enabled us to heave off the bar very early in the morning. Yet the ice had so grounded that we could not advance far enough to avoid grounding ourselves again when the tide should fall, and did not therefore dare to bring on board much of what had been landed. During the day everything was covered with snow, which partially dissolved under an evening haze; and at night it was clear and frosty.

September 7th. It blew a gale from the northward during the night, but the ice did not move. Towards morning we contrived to heave out so as to get a foot more of water, which enabled us to proceed with the reloading of the ship; and after this we gained another foot, thus advancing about ten feet in distance. This gave us a depth sufficient to allow us to reload entirely; and that caused us work enough for two days.

September 8th. The changes in the wind and weather were trifling, and we proceeded with the reloading of our discharged stores; also cutting some ice at our bows, that we might have no obstruction to our next attempt to escape. The following day was without change or interest, except that more ice was cut and the ship hove a few feet ahead. Everything was got on board and stowed. The next day did not advance us even a foot. The lakes on shore had not yet frozen, though there was ice on the pools.

September 16th. The wind was of little service today, being light and unsteady between the south and west; but as the ice near us was becoming slack, the ship was hove out two cables' length to take advantage of any opening that might occur. Some lanes of water appeared in the evening along the shore to the northward. At daylight we could see that the ice had drifted off the land, but there was still a complete ridge between the ship and a lane of water which led to a point three miles to the northward. About two in the afternoon, however, it seemed to be breaking up; when we immediately cast off, warped through the bay ice around us, and in half an hour our ship was at length once more in clear water, and under sail.

Under sail! We scarcely knew how we felt, or whether we quite believed it. He must be a seaman, to feel that the vessel which bounds beneath him, which listens to and obeys the smallest movement of his hand, which seems to move but under his will, is a thing of life, a mind conforming to his wishes. But what seaman could feel this as we did, when this creature which used to carry us buoyantly over the ocean, had been during an entire year immovable as the ice and the rocks around it, helpless, disobedient, dead. It seemed to have revived again to a new life; it once more obeyed us, did whatever we desired; and in addition to all, we too were free. It was the first burst of enjoyment on the recovery of our liberty; but we were not long in finding, as other pursuers of other liberty have found, that it was a freedom which was to bring us no happiness.

Thus free at last, we advanced about three miles; but then finding a ridge of ice we were obliged to make fast near the point which was to the north of us; and in a sufficiently commodious harbour between two icebergs, we passed the night.

September 18th. The wind came round, unfortunately, to the southward, and by morning our passage was blocked up; so that we were compelled to remain. There was much snow today, and the land was entirely covered. Four hares that were shot did not much comfort us under this detention, however they might vary our dinners.

September 20th. The ice opened so slightly under a westerly breeze, that it rendered us no service; and as we were frozen round by new ice, we were obliged to cut around the ship. Our detention was more perfectly assured the next day by a south-easterly wind bringing the ice in upon us. After many changes, it at last settled in the north-north-west and blew a heavy gale. The ice being thus set in rapid motion, came in contact with some bergs which protected us and forced them and us together onwards, till our stern was within twenty yards of the rocks. The *Krusenstern* was at the same time forced out of the water. It was fortunate that the icebergs which protected us were not carried away, else we should have gone with them into the moving pack, or been driven on the rocks.

September 29th. The thermometer fell to 5°, and the clear water of yesterday was covered with newly formed bay ice. The surrounding hummocks were also cemented together in such a manner that nothing but a storm could separate them. Our hopes of a liberation were therefore fast passing away; and our work was now to cut through the ice so as to attain a harbour that was likely to prove our home for the better part of another year. It was found to be a foot thick; and as there were also many heavy pieces in the way, our progress was necessarily very slow, and the labour hard.

September 30th. Under the continuance of the very low temperature, the whole sea was now covered with ice. There was no longer, therefore, occasion either to hope or fear; and there was an end to all anxiety at least. The agitation under which we had so long laboured had subsided into the repose of absolute certainty. Our winter prison was before us; and all that we had now to do was to reach it, set up our amphibious house, and with one foot on sea and one on shore, "take patience to ourselves."

It had been a busy and a laborious month; but it was busy idleness, as far as any result had followed, and all the labour had produced no return. It was, in every sense, a wasted month, and it had been an amply provoking one.

He who can hope a second time as he did the first, is of a more fortunate constitution than some of our people seemed to be. The despondent could not conceal their feelings; though of the greater number, I am bound to say that their contentedness, or rather resignation, exceeded what I had anticipated. It was my business to show them the brighter side of this picture by recapitulating our success in discovery, the excellent condition of our ship, the comfortable home which we had now learned to make of it, our ample stock of provisions, our good health and peace, and the better harbour which we should now secure, as this was one whence it would prove much more easy to extricate ourselves hereafter. But the bright side of life is not easily seen through the dark one; and I had, therefore, to trust to time and habit, and to hope that between our own resources and the communication of the natives, supplied, as we expected to be by them, with fresh provisions, and before long, with the power of renewing our expeditions by land, time would pass on, and the present evils become lighter.

October 1st. The labour of sawing our way through the bay ice toward harbour was renewed, and with rather better success. The thermometer was 12° at night.

October 3rd. We were obliged to persevere in the same tedious toil; and the whole gain was but sixteen feet which, however, released us from the pressure of the icebergs. This had been very inconvenient, if not more; since they rose above her gunwale and also lifted her up in such a manner as to suspend her three or four feet higher than the water which she drew.

October 5th. We advanced eighteen feet. At daylight on the sixth, the weather was fine, and the breezes had broken up the new bay ice to the northward, so as again to show some clear water. The ship was cut in as far as twenty feet more; being thus much nearer to our intended position for the winter.

October 10th. It was now apparent that we should soon be obliged to adopt the negative scale of the thermometer as well as the positive. It stood at zero this morning; and it had not reached that point last year till the 19th of the same month. We were thus obliged again to labour on Sunday; since another forty-eight hours of such frost would render it extremely difficult to cut the ship in; as the new ice around her was even now three and four feet thick. Nor had we made more than the half of our needful voyage toward safe harbour; while it was absolutely necessary for her safety that she should be removed to a place where she could float, which was not less than a hundred yards off. We gained but thirty feet by all our exertions.

October 17th. A week, a second week, had done little for us, and we were obliged to make Sunday once more a day of work, thus advancing forty feet. A gale, which had arisen the night before, continued till noon. We gained twenty more on the Monday. The following day our progress was thirty; while the ice was so heavy that we were obliged to heave the pieces up by means of the capstan.

October 24th. It was necessary again to occupy Sunday, as before; and the work was harder than usual, since the drift ice was now about sixteen feet thick. It was too heavy, therefore, to lift, even when it was cut, nor could we sink it; so that we were obliged to cut a space for the fragments in the thinner surrounding field of bay ice, that we might lodge them on it, and thus make room to pass by.

The summary of October can be little but the abstract of our labours, since the whole month had been employed in making a worse than tortoise progress, the entire amount of which, after all our toils, was but eight hundred and fifty feet. We had not even, with all this, reached the place that we had intended; we were, however, not very far from it and were compelled to be as content as we could. I believe that some of us could not help calculating the number of centuries it would require to make a single north-west passage at this rate; as others speculated on the premiums that might be demanded at Lloyd's on such a voyage, could indeed one man have been found to "write it."

If our place was not very unsafe, it was by no means a desirable one. Yet, comparatively, it was a great gain; since had we remained in the shallow water, suspended on icebergs, the ship would have been almost uninhabitable from her motions and change of position, and might also have been destroyed.

If the gradually increasing thickness of the ice which had to be cut, and the often severe weather, rendered this an unusually laborious month to the people, the toil seemed to call forth the zeal, and display the perseverance of every man. No one's health was affected; and on the whole there had been a not unexpected advantage in this perpetual occupation, since it had diverted their attention from their obvious subject of grievance, and trained them to a new detention for another winter.

November 1st. To commence our winter preparations, the

sails were unbent, and the topmasts unrigged and taken down. The raftering for the ship's roof was commenced.

November 5th. This day the roof was covered with sails. The valleys and ravines on the shore were filled with snow. On Saturday our covering was completed, the deck cleared, and many matters put to rights. Sunday was a day of rest; and the regularity of our church service was re-established.

November 17th. Things were only varied this day by a little snow, and by our men being employed in preparations for the scientific observatory, which they were occupied in constructing during the following day and the next, when it became cold enough to depress the thermometer to minus 30°.

November 22nd. The chief variety of this day was the taking of a black fox in the trap; being the first that we had seen this season. It was young and starved; and immediately devoured what was offered; we gave it the place which had been rendered vacant by the death of a former white one.

November 25th. The thermometer was at 39° minus, and the mercury froze for the first time. The sun did not rise above the southern hills today; and was therefore not seen from the ship, though visible from the higher grounds on shore; it was the first warning of a very long night to come.

November 29th. The morning being mild and fine, I walked to the place where the ship had wintered during the last season. I found that our old harbour was much more hampered with heavy ice than it had been. I certainly thought our present one preferable, independently of the fact of its being so much further to the north, which was our intended direction. It indeed seems trifling to talk of two or three miles as a great space gained; but when it is recollected that we were a month navigating scarcely three hundred yards, and that the lucky chance of being present when and where the ice opens, be that but for an hour or two, may turn the balance between a free escape and a winter's imprisonment in this "thick-ribbed ice," even two miles were a subject of congratulation.

The winter of 1830-31 was a repetition of the previous one and even Ross lost heart a little, as the scanty entries for this period show. By February he and his men were groping desperately for ways to ease their long imprisonment.

27th February. On this day the sun had just power enough to raise the temperature from minus 43° to minus 38°; and after that it subsided to minus 42°. Some hares were seen during the Sunday's walk; and more on the Monday; but nothing was shot. It was little more than a schoolboy's experiment, to fire a ball of frozen mercury through an inch plank; but this had, possibly, not been done before. The month closed with the thermometer at 43° minus.

The summary of this month is more barren than usual. It had been a very cold one, particularly towards the end. The mean proved to have been minus 34°.

Not having yet seen the Esquimaux, we now gave up the hope of their joining us till May, though not well able to account for their absence.

Our sport, if it be sport to snare foxes for dog food, had been unusually successful. Nor must we be accused of wantonness in this; since we had a family of dogs to maintain. It was the stud that we were bound to keep in as good condition as we could afford, for services which were now not far distant.

20th March. The continuance and degree of the cold at this period of the present month began seriously to attract our attention. The thermometer sank on this day, Sunday, to minus 52°; and the average of the twenty-four hours was minus 49°.

Much snow having fallen, nearly the entire surface of the land was a mass of ice and snow. On one occasion only, the latter melted for a short time beneath the influence of the sun on some rocks that were exposed to its rays; yet not many became thus exposed and the effect was of no long duration. In the March of the preceding year, during several days, the water was running down in streams.

It was an adverse prospect as far as our future plans were concerned; and had at times some effect in casting a damp on the men, which their tiresome sameness of occupation had no tendency to remedy. Yet they were in perfect health. There had been none on the sick list, and there was no appearance of scurvy.

Our disappointment in not seeing the Esquimaux continued daily increasing, as their expected arrival was the longer delayed. Their presence would have furnished us with occupation and amusement. We were also in want of seal's flesh for our dogs, which would have starved had it not been for our success in taking foxes; for ourselves too, fresh venison and fish would have been more than acceptable; nor were we so well stocked with skin dresses as not to wish for more. We still looked forward to their visits with hope.

April 17th. The first snow bunting of the season was seen this morning. On Monday the preparations for a sledge journey were complete, and we waited only for weather. A walking party was sent away two miles with the sledge, that they might be ready to start very early in the morning if the weather permitted.

April 20th. The weather being favourable, the main party set off early, and by noon the convoying portion returned, leaving Commander Ross and five men to pursue a journey of exploration. Another sledge and cooking apparatus were in preparation on board. On the twenty-first the temperature increased so much as to reach 31° plus, and we were agreeably surprised by a visit from three of the natives, Neytaknag, Poweytak, and Noyenak.

They came over the western hills with their dogs, and stopped about a quarter of a mile off, holding up their hands to show they were unarmed, and calling out the usual all hail, on which we proceeded to join them. They had been met by Commander Ross, from whom I received a note, informing me that he had purchased two stores of salmon for two knives. This was welcome news, and we arranged to fetch this acceptable supply the next morning.

We welcomed them to dinner and to sleep, and received from them the following information. All their friends were well except Tiagashu, who had died in the winter. This party had killed many deer and taken much fish, and had been expecting us both at Awatutyak and Neitchillee. One of the men was soon to go to this last place, and would convey the news of our present abode.

April 22nd. With the track of the former sledge to direct us, I left the ship at four in the morning, with the surgeon, three seamen, and our Esquimaux guests. We reached their village at eleven. We found there were two packages of fish weighing jointly but 180 pounds; we nevertheless paid the stipulated price. They began immediately to erect us a house, which they finished in forty-five minutes. We were not long in cooking a warm meal, which was very acceptable after a walk of sixteen miles through very rough ice. The men having forgotten their blankets, we were supplied with skins by our good-natured friends.

At noon two of them set off at a great pace, with their sledge and six dogs to fetch a third depot of fish, which we understood to be at a lake far away. They were to have another knife for it;

and it was well worth our while to wait for such a supply. We examined their hut in the meantime, which was large enough for three families, being eighteen feet in diameter; but it was so much decayed as to show that it had been occupied from a very early period in the winter. We were very kindly received by the women and found an old one sick, or thought to be so, to whom the surgeon administered some medicine. She was a woman of many husbands; and she repaid her physic by the stone which is used in striking fire, which was in reality a valuable present to make on her part. They offered us water, which is a scarce article at this season, as it requires much oil to melt any quantity of snow; together with salmon, which we took, that we might not offend them; returning some trifling presents.

Inquiries about families and new-born children were repaid by questions respecting our own people; one of the children had been named Aglugga in compliment apparently to Commander Ross, whose Esquimaux patronymic it was. The presence of fifty sealskins proved that their hunting had been successful; and besides the flesh visible in the hut there were depots in the snow. They had further killed two musk oxen and two bears, hoping that we might come to purchase the former; in defect of which they had been eaten.

One of the natives informed us of some of the affairs of his coterie. The widow of the dead man had immediately obtained a new husband because she had five children. The "because" would not be a very good reason in England where the ready-made family of another is not often a source of much comfort. But here, the five children were a commodity of price, a great fortune, a source of profit instead of loss, and of happiness instead of vexation and torment. Even at eight they begin to be serviceable; in a few years they are able to maintain more than themselves; and when the parents are old, be they step-children or entirely and absolutely adopted, it is on them that the helpless aged depend for that support which is a matter of course. There are no poor-rates in this country.

It is a Utopian state of things when she of five children is the best of wives, and can take her choice of the young men; it is more than Utopian when population is not poverty, but wealth; when men really will labour, and when the labour of a man will support, not only himself, but those who must depend on him till they can, and will, labour for themselves. Let the wise of wiser lands travel hither and take lessons of wisdom from the savages in seal-skins, who drink oil, and eat their fish raw.

Of another portion of their political economy I must not speak with approbation; yet there is some philosophical fitness in it too. We must not pull a system of legislation to pieces, and then say that this or the other single law is a bad one. Let the whole be contemplated in a mass, and looked at in all its bearings, before we presume to decide what is right. It is the custom to interchange wives. The people thus considered that they should have more children. It is a good thing to have good reasons for doing what may not be very right.

Having at last contacted the indispensable Eskimos, the sledging parties again became active and Commander Ross, who led most of them, not only explored much of the remaining unknown area of Boothia, but also located and visited the site of the Magnetic North Pole. As summer drew on, the voyagers again waited, yet with a terrible uncertainty, for the release of the Victory *from her frozen harbour.*

13th August. The Esquimaux returned, wives, children, and all, to the amount of twenty-three, and were regaled by us with a dinner of fish and fat. We purchased some clothing and accompanied them to their tents; glad of even their society, under our present dearth of variety or amusement.

Is there anything that can convey in a stronger manner our utter destitution of all that can interest men, than to confess that we found a relief from the self-converse of our own minds and the society of each other, from the eternal wearisome iteration of thermometrical registers and winds, and tides and ice, and boats, and rigging, and eating, in the converse of these greasy gormandizing specimens of humanity, whose language we could scarcely comprehend?

Let no one suppose that we had not felt the aforementioned miseries during months and years. There were evils of cold, and evils of hunger, and evils of toil; and though we did not die nor lose our limbs as other men have done in those lands, we had to share with the rest of the world the evils of petty sickness which are sufficiently grievous while they exist. Had we not also undergone abundance of anxiety and care; of the sufferings of disappointed hope; of those longings after our far-distant friends and our native land, from which who that has voyaged far from that home and those friends has ever been exempt? And who more than we, to whom it could not but often have occurred that we might never again see those friends and that home? Yet was there a pain even beyond all this; and that grievance seldom ceased. We were weary for want of occupation, for want of variety, for want of the means of mental exertion, for want of thought, and (why should I not say it?) for want of society. Today was as yesterday and, as was today, so would be tomorrow. Is it wonderful then that even the visits of barbarians were welcome, or can anything more strongly show the nature of our pleasures than the confession that these visits were as delightful as the society of London might be amid the business of London?

In the night which succeeded to this day, the thermometer fell to 36°. Of course the ice remained unaltered. It is difficult to convey to my readers the impression produced by this stationary condition of a sea thus impracticably frozen. When the winter has once in reality set in, our minds become made up on the subject; like the dormouse (though we may not sleep, which would be the most desirable condition by far), we wrap ourselves up in a sort of furry contentment, since better cannot be, and wait for the times to come. It was a far other thing to be ever awake, waiting to rise and become active, yet ever to find that all nature was still asleep and that we had nothing more to do than to wish, and groan, and – hope as we best might.

In a visit to the Esquimaux tents, we found that the wooden leg was once more ailing, in some manner of which I did not particularly inquire, since the carpenter-doctor was at hand to examine into the grievance, and was ready to repair it as he best knew how.

August 14th. The natives were not permitted to come on board till after church, when the boat was sent for them. The wooden leg had been bound with copper, and was better than ever. We bartered and made presents as usual. The Esquimaux were to divide their party the next day for the purpose of going to Shagavoke and to Neitchillee, and promised to bring us venison in the winter. A seal was shot today; it was a sport in which we had hitherto found no success.

August 25th. The weather was much the same, but the ice near us was in motion. The whale boat was jammed between the ship's side and a large piece of these never-ending ice-rocks which, float away as they might, only departed to be succeeded by as bad, or worse, since the storehouse which supplied them was inexhaustible. "Till the rocks melt with the sun" is held an impossible event, in one of the songs of my native land, and I believe we began at last to think that it would never melt those ice rocks; which even at this late period of the year continued to beset us in every shape which their beautiful, yet hateful crystal could assume. Oh! for a fire to melt these refractory masses, was our hourly wish, even though it had burnt up all the surrounding region.

August 28th. The wind blew strong from the westward on the twenty-seventh, and the ice began to drift out of the bay to the eastward. But it was evening before a passage was practicable. The ship was then warped a quarter of a mile to the south-west, into a convenient place for taking advantage of the first opening. As soon as this was done we got under sail, but, unfortunately carrying away the mizzen boom, could not weather a piece of ice. She was thus brought about by it, and equally failed in weathering a large iceberg on the other tack, which was grounded; by which means she took the ground herself. We soon, however, hove her off by hawsers to the shore; and though her bottom did not prove to be damaged, the lower rudder iron was broken so that there was an end to our progress for this day.

August 29th. Early in the morning the rudder was repaired, and the wind remained steady and strong at west, with occasional snow. It was the very wind that we wanted; and after much doubt and anxiety we felt that we were at last liberated: liberated, though not yet free. We cast off soon after four, and with a reefed topsail, stood for some islands through what appeared to be loose ice. Unluckily, when about two-thirds over, the wind came to the northwest and we were unable to fetch within a mile to the eastward of them; after which, shifting to the north with a snow squall, it brought the ice down along the north shore. At nine it backed again to the north-west, and we were soon close to shore after having run four miles.

We had passed two bays when a heavy shower of snow coming on, we were obliged to stand in for a little bay where a baffling breeze nearly laid us on the rocks.

We warped to the head of this new harbour, where a small river entered, and immediately made fast to the shore with two hawsers. No sooner had we done this than a violent gale came on from the north with a heavy fall of snow, which compelled us to carry out more hawsers. We here saw the ice passing to the south-west with considerable rapidity, and had occasion to be very thankful that we were so secure. Under this feeling, the hard labour which every one had undergone was soon forgotten.

August 31st. The wind fell, and we went on shore to examine the state of things in the strait; when we found everything blocked up with ice; it was impassable. The month of August was ended, and we had sailed four miles.

September 10th to 13th. Our harbour was even more completely sheeted with bay ice and, in the offing, all was motionless. Nature did not permit Sunday to be other than a day of rest, even had we been inclined to transgress its laws. On Monday it blew hard and the ice was worse packed than ever, if that could be.

September 15th, 16th, 17th. There was now no open water to be seen from the hill. The general temperature was 32°, but it did not freeze in the sun; a petty consolation indeed. It is little to notice, but much where there was nothing else to remark, that a great many ptarmigan had been killed in the last week. In such a life as ours even the capture of an Arctic mouse was an event; and if it is the custom now for navigators to tell everything, to write without materials, what could we do but follow the fashion, and conform to the established usages?

September 23rd. On this day we were able to carry the ship to an edge of the outer ice, doing this under the chance that the following day might favour our escape. This it did not choose to do. There was the usual hope, if wishes can be called by that name, and that was all. For the present we were "hard and fast"; I do not well know who expected anything better to follow. If any one was silly enough to do this, he was disappointed.

The end of the month found us exactly in the same condition, with our prospects of freedom becoming less every day. I may indeed say that they had ceased. It was impossible to expect any further progress under such a mass and weight of winter as that which surrounded us. The worse part of the prospect, however, was the distant one; it seemed likely that the ship would never be extricated, and that we should eventually be compelled to abandon her with all that was on board.

The first of our future objects was to economize in provisions, still more in fuel; and of course, to take all possible care of the health of the men. Their spirits were to be kept up as might best be, and we could at least point out that we were really on our return, and had made some progress; while there was no reason why the return should not be complete in the following year. There were still before us the *Fury*'s remaining stores; and there were boats to carry us into Davis's Strait (should we be obliged to abandon the ship) where we should either meet a whaler, or reach the Danish settlements in Greenland. If more was said than I here repeat, the usual result followed; the hopeful did not hope more, and the despondent continued to despair.

October 12th, 13th, 14th. The unrigging and stowing on shore went on, and a chain was passed twice round the vessel "amid-ships." It was our intention to sink the vessel the following spring, or rather, as she must sink in no long time in consequence of her leaks, to provide the means of raising her again, should any vessel hereafter return to the place where she was thus deposited. Of the wisdom of this provision for a future as unlikely to occur as that of a season of spring and roses in Boothia Felix, I have not much to say; but it is probably our nursery education which induces us to do all that we can in prevention of waste.

October 25th. There was a storm on the twenty-fifth, and it blew so violently as to tear into rags the canvas of our housing, which had now gone through a long service. We could not even attempt to save it, from the great danger of exposing the men to the cold.

The summary of October cannot be much, in detail, and is of as little moment in point of interest. Some preparations for sinking the ship in spring had been made, as I have already noticed, under our project of travelling by land and by boats to the place of the *Fury*'s stores. Everything except the provisions and stores indispensable for our use had been landed; and the two boats had been placed in such a position as to admit of the construction of sledges under them.

November 27th to 30th. Our allowance of bread had been necessarily reduced, but so was that of salt meat; notwithstanding which last alteration, and the use of spruce beer, six men were slightly afflicted with scurvy; which, however, was checked by means of lemon-juice. Their despondency seemed to have ceased.

December 25th. Christmas-day was made a holiday in all senses. For the cabin dinner, the only fact worth remarking was a round of beef which had been in the *Fury*'s stores for eight years, and which, with some veal and some vegetables, was as good as the day on which it was cooked.

The men were much reduced in strength, but the scurvy had

been kept in check. One man alone, Dixon, being afflicted with a complication of disorders, was not expected to live very long.

1832. January 31st. Our medical report now begins to be very different from what it had hitherto been. All were much enfeebled; and there was a good deal of ailment without any marked diseases. An old wound in my own side had broken out, with bleeding; and I knew too well that this was one of the indications of scurvy. That all were in a very anxious state, needs not be said: and he on whom all the responsibility fell was not least the victim of anxiety. But men must be thus situated before they can appreciate the feelings of any of us.

February 1st to 4th. The month began with a furious storm, which continued for two days, and subsided on the third. The ice was cut through, and its thickness found to be five feet and upwards. We were sufficiently prisoners by the hopeless state of the ship; but it seemed destined that she should be really our prison, as the stormy and cold weather rendered it seldom possible to show ourselves beyond the roof or deck. It is not wonderful if we were dull.

February 19th and 20th. Sunday was stormy and cold, and Monday was much worse. In the morning, a wolverine came on board and began to devour the dogs' meat. It was an inhospitable reception to kill the poor starving wretch, but it was the first specimen of this creature which we had been able to obtain. Are the life and happiness of an animal to be compared with our own pleasure in seeing its skin stuffed with straw and exhibited in a glass case?

This month of February was severe. If the thermometer did not range as much as during the same one in preceding years, the temperature was more uniformly low, while the frequent storms rendered it also bitterly felt.

The thickness of the ice round the ship was such as to prevent all hopes of her liberation, even though we should continue with her, which was impossible from the state of our provisions and that of the health of the crew. The seaman, Buck, who had unexpectedly suffered the recurrence of epilepsy with an unusual degree of violence, had become blind.

The carpenter had nearly finished the sledges for the boats, and was about to make some more for carrying the provisions. It is a brief summary for this month: and others must try to imagine what we felt, and what they can never see.

March, like February, was a very cold month to the feelings, in consequence of the frequent winds; while it is certainly also true that our comparative weakness and the alteration in our diet, made us feel it more severely.

This had retarded the work on the sledges; but we had been busy on board in arranging and concentrating our several travelling necessaries; a work of some consideration, since besides provisions, arms, ammunition, and tools, we had fuel to carry, had it even been but to thaw snow for drinking, besides instruments and all else that belonged to our personal accommodations.

In our crew we had now one blind man; and the mate, Taylor, was so lame that he could walk but a very little way; besides which there were three other men in very indifferent health; while no one was as strong as in the preceding year. On my part, the prudent conduct, as it concerned this state of things, now seemed to be to restore the whole to full food allowance; and this was accordingly done.

April 1st to 7th, 1832. It blew so hard that the men were imprisoned after divine service. On Monday it was more moderate, and the people were employed in cutting round the *Krusenstern*, preparatory to hauling her up. On Saturday the thermometer rose on a sudden to plus 7°; not having passed zero before for 136 days. I do not believe there is another record of such a continuous low temperature; and it was a state of things, most certainly, to confirm us in our resolution of leaving the ship to her helpless fate, and attempting to save ourselves in the best manner that we could.

April 15th to 21st. The fifteenth and two following days were mild so that our work went on. On the eighteenth the cold weather brought us to a stand out of doors; but on the next day the boats were drawn on the sledges a short distance and they were found to answer as well as we had expected. We were ready to start our foot journey to the north on the following day but were prevented by the snow falling thick, with a temperature of 28° minus, even at noon, and were therefore obliged to end the week as we were.

April 22nd. We could have done nothing on this day, even had it not been Sunday, as the thermometer was at minus 30° in the morning. I must explain that our present object was to proceed to a certain distance with a stock of provisions and the boats, and there to deposit them for the purpose of advancing more easily later in the season. The abandonment of the vessel had long ceased to be a matter of hesitation; and the object now was to proceed to Fury beach, not only for supplies, but to get possession of the boats there; failing which, our own would be put into a position on which we could fall back.

April 23rd. Though the temperature was equally low, it was clear and calm. We therefore set out at nine, reaching the nearest boat, which had already been carried about four miles from the ship; after which we drew her to the other boat and store of provisions which was two miles further. The weights were then divided equally, and we proceeded with great labour and difficulty, through rough ice, so that we were at length obliged to carry on but one boat at a time, returning for the other alternately; in consequence of which we did not gain more than a mile, after five hours' work. It then began to blow so hard, with drift snow, that we were obliged to halt and build snow huts. These were covered with canvas, and by means of the deer-skin beds and our cooking apparatus, the whole party of fourteen was well accommodated, though the temperature of our house at night was minus 15°.

April 28th. We could not proceed in consequence of another gale; and as this became worse on Sunday, we decided on securing the boats and returning to the ship, as the wind was behind us, and could thus be encountered with little hazard. We reached the huts that we had first built, in the evening; and on the following day succeeded in returning to the ship about noon. The total result of this journey was that we had each walked a hundred and ten miles, and had advanced, in real distance, but eighteen: while it would be necessary to go over this space three times more before everything from the ship could be even thus far advanced in a journey which was destined ultimately to be three hundred miles.

May 7th. We set out with our remaining provisions and bedding and reached the second station of eighteen miles, at three in the afternoon; having succeeded at last in bringing hither two boats and five weeks' provisions, besides a present supply for ten days more. Our labour was much too serious and anxious to allow of any jesting; yet we could not help feeling that our travelling resembled that of the person in the algebraic equation, whose business it is to convey eggs to a point, one at a time.

May 8th. A severe fall of snow imprisoned us all the day; but if it gave us rest, it alarmed us for the state of our road. The following day was much worse, with an easterly gale; yet the thoughtless sailors slept and enjoyed themselves as if there was nothing else for them to do, leaving the anxiety and the sleeplessness to him who held all the responsibility. On the tenth, however, there being no cessation of the gale and the drift, they appeared to become wearied of this rest in a hut so small that it was impossible to change the position which had first been adopted. At midnight the gale fell, but the thermometer was at zero.

Much of land-jesting there has been, in the prose of the Joe Millers and the songs of the Dibdin race, on the peculiarities of sailors, and on a character which these "land-lubbers" have themselves contrived, as unlike to that of a "British sailor" or any other sailor, as it is to that of a Chickasaw or a Chinese. The animal has a character of its own, that is certain; but it is far from that which the public believes. How far it is worse, I ought not to say; in what respects it is better or different, it is not here within my limits to detail, but this at least is universal; let anything, provisions or water be in doubt, a gale or hurricane, the ship's course lost, the sails or the rigging ruined and irreplaceable, or even the vessel on a lee shore in a storm, it is always "the captain's business." The men obey their orders, it is true, and what they will attempt and execute, no landsman will believe: but the watch at an end, they sleep as sound as if nothing was amiss: it is "the captain's business." Our own men had, in our present voyage, seen perhaps enough to have acquired some thoughts of their own, and possibly too they sometimes considered of matters for which "the captain" ought not to have been exclusively responsible; yet the radical feeling for ever broke out, and whatever there was of unusual and new to be projected and done, their tranquility remained unaltered; it might have been wrong or right, but it was "the captain's business," not theirs – a happy responsibility on his part, it cannot be denied.

May 21st. Arriving on board the ship again we found another month's provisions ready, but we ascertained it would require a week to repair the sledges and put the men in condition to draw them. We had so far travelled 329 miles to move our depot about 30 in a direct line.

May 29th. We had now secured everything on shore which could be of use to us in case of our being forced to return, or which, if we did not, would prove of use to the natives. The colours were therefore hoisted and nailed to the mast, we drank a parting glass to our poor ship, and having seen every man out I took my own adieu of the *Victory*, which had deserved a better fate. It was the first vessel that I had ever been obliged to abandon, after having served in thirty-six during a period of forty-two years. It was like the last parting with an old friend; and I did not pass the point where she ceased to be visible without stopping to take a sketch of this melancholy desert, rendered more melancholy by the solitary, abandoned, helpless home of our past years, fixed in immovable ice, till time should perform on her his usual work.

May 30th. As we proceeded we found the snow harder and our road improved; yet the heavy loads made our progress slow, and we did not arrive at the twelve-mile snow huts till noon. At one on the following morning we proceeded, but could not long carry forward more than two sledges at once, up the hills; so that we did not gain the next post, only eight miles off, under ten hours. We ended the month of May at this halting place.

I may now explain the plan of the journey we had thus undertaken. This was to carry both the boats on to Elizabeth harbour, with provisions for six weeks at full allowance, there to deposit the boats and half the provisions, and to proceed with the sledges and the other half of the provisions till we reached the latitude of 71°, whence we should send a light party of five to ascertain the state of things at Fury beach. If the state of things there seemed satisfactory the whole party would continue on to that place, but if we were forced to retreat we could fall back on the depot at Elizabeth harbour.

This month had brought us to 70° 21′ latitude, leaving us sixteen miles more to Elizabeth harbour; and though our crew were in a very indifferent condition for work, all, even the blind man and the lame, were obliged to exert themselves in some manner, under which, with a revival of hope, they contrived to keep up their spirits.

The state of the ice at this period, and it was now a late one, was incredibly bad. The sea was everywhere one solid mass of the heaviest pieces as far as the eye could reach in every direction. All was rock; it seemed as if there was never to be water again: but whenever this might happen, it was now but too plain that the result could not be to liberate the ship which we had left. It was at least satisfactory to find that there was no rashness in our proceedings, and that nothing but what we were doing could have been done.

June 3rd. We reached the next huts this day with the remainder of our provisions. The men seemed then much fatigued, and the mate Blanky, being deputed by them, intimated their desire to abandon the boats and spare provisions at this place, and proceed direct to Fury point. I had already suspected something of this nature; but as we should thus leave our resources in a place to which it was impossible to return, I not only expressed my refusal, but ordered the party to proceed, in a manner not easily misunderstood, and by an argument too peremptory to be disputed.* It was the first symptom approaching to mutiny which had yet occurred.

June 8th and 9th. We were imprisoned by a storm on the eighth; but on the following day everything was brought forward to the depot in Elizabeth harbour. Here we ascended the hill, so as to examine the state of the ice; the extremely bad aspect of which made us conclude that it would be impossible to carry the boats any further. As they were now within reach, in case we should be compelled to return, I determined to proceed with the people, and three weeks' provisions, for twenty or thirty miles; leaving the rest of the supplies here as a reserve, and sending an advance party on to Fury beach.

On the twelfth preparations were made for the advance of Commander Ross, with Abernethy and Park, who departed for Fury point, taking with them a sledge, fifteen days' provisions, a tent, and such other things as were indispensable. Their directions were to leave a note at every place where they slept, which we calculated on reaching in double their time, with our loads, so as to be advanced about seventy miles when they should have reached to their journey's end, now a hundred and fifty miles away.

June 22nd. While the men slept, I proceeded to examine the land, as we had not before been able to survey this part of the country; and after this we proceeded in the evening as usual, till we arrived at the south Grimble islands where I found Commander Ross's cairn, being the end of his fourth day's journey. By his observations we were twelve miles and, by mine, eight, from the place where we had first taken possession of this country on the tenth of August, 1829.

June 25th. We continued our journey along shore and soon after met and joined Commander Ross's party. The information

* This particular "argument" seems to have been a loaded gun.

he brought from Fury point was that the sea had risen high and carried three of the boats, with many other things, to the north along the shore and that one of them was seriously damaged. All else was in the same condition as we had left it; and the bread and other provisions were in abundance and in good order. We all pitched for the day and found that with what they had brought, there was enough to last us all on full allowance till we should reach that place.

June 30th. We resumed our journey as usual, being now obliged to carry the lame man, in addition to the rest of our load. The sun had a great effect on the snow, and the aspect of the land was hourly changing; but in the offing the ice seemed as firm and continuous as ever. We had shot several ducks in the last few days, and they were somewhat better than a luxury to us, especially before our allowance had been increased. Finally, we ended the month within hail of Fury beach.

July 1. The water was now, at last, running down the large cracks in the ice, and everything was hourly changing in appearance. Three ravines that we passed were also pouring down their respective torrents but we at length passed them all, and encamped on Fury beach at ten o'clock.

July 2nd. We were once more at home, for a time at least, such home as it was, and however long or short was the time that we were destined to occupy it. There was a feeling of home at least, and that was something. The men, I doubt not, felt this most, after all their fears, and the pleasure was little diminished to them by any anticipations of what might yet be to come.

The first measure which I adopted was to send them all to rest for the night, that we might once more bring back the regularity of our days; and after this we proceeded to take a survey of the stores. Being scattered in every direction, it was, however, difficult to prevent the half-starved men from getting access to them; in consequence of which, and in spite of all orders and advice, many suffered smartly for their imprudence. Excepting the damage done by the high rise of the sea, the only important one we discovered was the loss of candles, by the foxes, which had opened some of the boxes and devoured the contents.

As soon as the men were rested they were appointed to their several tasks. The first thing to be done was to construct a house, which was planned at thirty-one by sixteen feet, and seven feet in height, to be covered with canvas; and by evening the frame was erected.

July 4th. The house was finished, and received the nickname of Somerset House. It snowed on the fifth; and this ended in a clear northerly gale, so cold that the rain which had fallen, froze. As it snowed again all the night, the land was completely covered on the following morning as ever it had been during the winter.

The carpenters were set to work on the *Fury*'s boats; the plan for which was that each of them should be strengthened by means of two bulkheads and two strong beams. The house, which we now proceeded to occupy, was divided into two rooms, one for the men, and another, containing four small cabins, for the officers; at present the cook's department was a tent.

August 1st. On the last day of the preceding month, the ice had unexpectedly broken up, so far as to leave some navigable clear water, and as the boats were also ready, we prepared to depart with the hope of being able to quit this strait and reach Baffin's bay before the departure of the whaling vessels. The boats were stored with provisions to last till the first of October, besides the bedding and other needful things; and each carried seven men, with an officer. Commander Ross and I exchanged copies of our charts and narratives in case of separation; and a bottle was buried in the house, containing a short account of our proceedings.

We left the beach at four in the afternoon, but found the channels in the ice very crooked and much impeded by floating pieces, so that it was with difficulty we could use our oars. Our progress was therefore slow; and having passed two rivers, off which there was much heavy ice, we were stopped at nine o'clock under the very precipice where the *Fury* was wrecked. The boats were unloaded as quickly as possible, and hauled up on the beach.

It was not a minute too soon; since the ice immediately came down, and two floes near us were broken to pieces with a violent crash, so as to form a ridge of hummocks close to the shore. The distance which we had thus made was eight miles; and it was a singular coincidence that we experienced this narrow escape, not only where the *Fury* was wrecked, but on the same day that she was lost eight years before.

August 2nd. We were obliged to haul still higher, and to cut a dock for the boats in a large hummock. Some rain in the course of the day loosened stones from the precipices, one of which struck a boat's mast; and we found, from the fragments below, that the vicinity of this precipice, which was four hundred and seventy feet high, was a place of danger.

This seems but a cool remark to make, where such a cliff rising to such an altitude impended over our heads, and when we knew, what all know, the effects of a thaw in throwing down those rocks which the previous ice has split. In reality it was a position of the utmost danger: we might all have been overwhelmed without notice, as the state of the beach below testified, or the brains of any individual among us might have been "knocked out" before he could have suspected any such accident. But I believe that we were fully tried by hazards, and had become somewhat careless.

August 13th. As there was no change today, Mr. Thom was sent with a boat to Fury beach for three weeks' provisions; there being open water in that direction, though there was none to the north of us.

August 25th. A cold northerly wind sprung up, and the tide rose eight feet, but without any effect on the ice. On the following day it fell to 25°, and the breeze was much stronger; it was left to us to guess whether this cold belonged to the old winter or was the commencement of a new one.

August 28th. The gale of the last few days moderated at noon, and we embarked, proceeding under sail along shore, and exposed to very heavy squalls from the precipices, which rendered extreme care necessary. Passing Batty bay, we reached Elwin bay at midnight. We then stood for a beach about a mile further north, and as it was now blowing a whole gale, pitched our tents amid a storm of snow which, in the night, covered all the land.

August 29th. It moderated towards morning and we put to sea, standing for the edge of the packed ice in the direction of Cape York. We then ran along it in hopes of finding some passage; but it continued to lead us out of our course, till it joined to Leopold's island, so as to embay us; and as the wind was again increasing, it was with great difficulty we weathered it.

August 30th. We were obliged to sleep in our boats, in no comfortable position; and as our place was not tenable we re-embarked at six in the morning with a southerly wind. We soon met with the ice pack and ran along it up Barrow's strait; but to no purpose, as there was no exit anywhere. We therefore stood back to the shore near Cape Clarence and found a good position for pitching the tents and hauling up the boats.

August 31st. It snowed all the morning and we removed the boats to the ground ice for the sake of launching them more easily. We found here many remains of Esquimaux huts, and some fox-traps; and as we saw many seals, the reason for the natives fixing in this place was apparent. All the sea to the north was hence seen to be completely full of solid ice.

August had been a month of peculiar anxiety, and a succession of hopes and disappointments severely tried the patience of all. On quitting Fury beach, appearances were so favourable that every advance to bay, or point, or cape, along the coast flattered us with the prospect of soon reaching the northern edge of the ice, and then of surmounting the greatest difficulty in the way, that of making a passage across Prince Regent's inlet. However, by the time that we had reached 73° we were detained so long by the state of the ice that it became doubtful if we should succeed during the present season.

Here was one of the main trials of our patience, and a look-out house, built in the cliffs by the men, became the chief thing which afforded them any amusement, while that consisted only in watching for the changes in the ice. Our allowance of food consisted of half a pound of meat, with a pound of bread and a pint of cocoa, divided into breakfast and supper. All game was considered as an extra and luxurious allowance; but what we obtained was very little since it amounted but to three foxes and as many hares, with a couple of ducks. All the waterfowl had disappeared about the end of the month.

The boats, being made of mahogany, proved so heavy that it gave us great trouble to haul them up on the beach; so that the whole party was required to draw up one, while even this often required the assistance of tackle.

September 2nd and 3rd. Monday I ascended the mountain near our camp which is in reality the north-east point of America,* whence I obtained a sight of Cape Warrender on one side and, on the other of Cape York, with three headlands beyond it to the east. Barrow's strait was an unbroken field of ice; there was not even a pool of water to be seen.

September 17th. Some ice moved off the land, under a north-westerly wind, but it closed again on the following day. Two

* Ross did not know of the existence of Bellot Strait, which makes the northern half of Boothia Felix into an island.

foxes were killed, with some ptarmigans; and we thus had game enough for the different messes. In the beginning of our sojourn in this country we had thought the fox bad eating; but it was now preferred to any other meat.

September 19th. It was still colder, the thermometer falling to 18°, and not rising above 25°; but as the ice appeared to be loosening on the twentieth, we embarked our things, leaving an account of our proceedings in a tin case beneath a cairn. Putting off at noon we reached the pack edge of the ice at the junction of Barrow's strait and Prince Regent's inlet. It was found to be a continuous solid mass, giving no hopes of breaking up during the present season. The land was equally blocked up by heavy ice; so that we were obliged to return whence we had come; though not effecting this without much difficulty, and not landing a minute too soon, as the ice immediately came down on the shore with great force. If any one still hoped to get through this great obstacle, I was willing to wait here for a further trial, though it seemed utterly useless.

September 21st to 24th. We accordingly remained three days. On the twenty-fourth everyone agreed that all hope was at an end, and that it only remained for us to return to Fury beach.

September 26th. Attempting to cross Elwin bay we were stopped by the floes, and were finally obliged to haul into a cove in the ice, when we pitched our tent on it. The ice became more loose on the next day, and we departed, making a very slow progress through heavy bay ice; when a gale coming on at ten in the morning, increased so fast that we could carry no sail by mid-day and were obliged to put ashore on the land ice.

We were, unfortunately, under the most terrific precipice that we had yet seen, two miles from the north cape of Batty bay; having but six feet of beach beneath cliffs which rose five hundred feet above us. A speedy removal was therefore absolutely necessary; but an easterly wind bringing the bay ice on us, we were detained the next day; our only consolation in the meantime being the shooting of three foxes, with some ducks and gulls. We were now reduced to half allowance of provisions, having long been on two-thirds.

Anxious as the preceding months had been owing to the impending prospect of our deliverance from that miserable country in which we had been so long imprisoned, and to the difficulties which had beset our attempts to extricate ourselves, the present one had passed in even greater anxiety, and had been a period of more frequent and more provoking disappointment. Yet we found some occupation for our minds in the discussion of our chances and hopes.

These also were occasionally sources of amusement, (deficient as we were in all others) since we could extract this even from the acrimony which these disputes often engendered. Nor was it a small advantage that these debates served to keep up our spirits; the sanguine, in the heat of their arguments, magnifying our prospects of success, and the timid and desponding thus gaining some courage, and admitting some brighter gleams of hope, from the very speculations and anticipations which they were opposing.

Each of our three tents thus formed a kind of separate deliberative party, or a little society. Among them, Commander Ross, who had always been the most sanguine, was still the leader of the hopeful. The contrary opinion prevailed in the party of Mr. Thom, whose estimable qualities in all other points were not accompanied by a spirit of confidence. My own tent alone was one of divided opinions; and it afforded, therefore, the greater opportunities for these discussions.

It was my wish (I believe it my best policy) to conceal my opinions, and to interfere with none of their debates; and thus, not only to see what their several tempers were on this subject, but to profit by that knowledge.

During the last days of our detention in this place, when, in addition to what we believed the impossibility of succeeding in our attempt to leave this country, it had further become doubtful whether the state of the ice would allow us to return to Fury beach, or even to surmount a small part of the way to this only hope that remained for us, our situation had become truly serious, not simply critical.

At this time it was that we began to experience the greatest sufferings we had yet endured from the cold. We had been unable to carry with us our usual quantity of clothes and of canvas, so that we were most in want of protection from the weather when we were least able to bear up against its severity.

October 2nd. The carpenter began to make sledges out of the empty bread casks; and his chips became very welcome fuel, serving to cook a couple of foxes in aid of our short commons which, during the whole of this expedition, had been distributed into two meals, breakfast and supper. That work was not finished till the fourth amid very heavy snow; when the sleds were loaded with our tents and whatever else might be wanted at Fury beach. There could be no further hope of getting back there in the boats. We therefore determined to leave them here for the next year's use and to proceed with sledges in the best manner that we could.

We found this attempt almost insuperably difficult; and the whole progress that we could make was but four miles. The way was rendered nearly impassable by the deep and loose snow which had been falling; and to increase our troubles, the lame man, Taylor, could neither walk with his crutches nor ride on the sledges, which were perpetually upsetting upon the rough ice. In some manner or other, however, we gained a bad resting place at seven; when it was already dark, with the thermometer at zero.

October 5th. We passed a miserably cold night, but fortunately escaped frost-bites. In the morning, one of our three sledges being broken, we were compelled to leave here some stores; taking nothing but the provisions, tents, and beds, on the other two, and thus having stronger parties to draw them than on the preceding day. We thus gained seven miles on this day's journey, in spite of a strong cold wind and constant snow, and were enabled to carry Taylor, by returning for him with an empty sledge. Burdened and obstructed as we already were, this was a great additional grievance; but they who were inclined to murmur had at least the satisfaction of reflecting that their case was better than his.

It was a difficulty of another kind which we had to encounter on the next day; as the heavy ice was pressed up to the precipices along the shore, and we were often obliged to quit a tolerable track to get round them in the best manner that we could. But the labour kept us warm; and by noon, arriving within eighteen miles of Fury beach, the men acquired fresh courage; when having made eleven miles we pitched within sight of our winter home, killing several foxes on the way.

October 7th. Sunday morning found us a few hours more of similar work; and this being over we reached Somerset House, our labours at an end, and ourselves once more at home.

We found our house occupied by a fox, which soon made its escape. Everything was as we left it; and as we were not less hungry than cold, having finished our last morsel at breakfast, the men were treated with a good meal. Two of the men were found to have frost-bites, and I had been deeply cut in the leg.

October 13th. There was no cessation to a most uncommon storm which had been blowing since the 10th. After promising to lull about noon, it blew harder than ever and the canvas roof being too weak to bear it, the snow gained admission to our beds, and everything was frozen. We had great difficulty in keeping ourselves warm by crowding round the stove; but had the good fortune to take three foxes in the traps; a matter now beginning to be a subject of great congratulation.

October 27th. A snow wall, four feet thick, was built round our house; and further spars and ropes were applied to support the roof, for the purpose of covering it with snow. A continuance of storms on the three following days rendered all work impracticable. On the last days of this week it was milder, and we were able to continue our operations.

October 28th. The men had their last dinner on full allowance, as it now became necessary to retrench. We found a roasted fox to be a very good dish. Thus at least we then thought. However I have had reason to doubt, since my return to the beef and mutton of England, whether I might not have overrated the flavour of fox.

With respect to the present rations, the men were allowed pea-soup, alternately with one made of carrots and turnips, out of the stores of the *Fury*. Instead of bread, which we could not now furnish to a sufficient extent, they were provided with dumplings of flour and water. They were, indeed, sufficiently fed, since it was observed that they had become in much better condition since our return to this place.

During the very severe month of November, the men, not having clothes to withstand the cold, could seldom work in the open air, but we at length succeeded in making our house tolerably comfortable, so that the temperature inside was about 45°, excepting near the enclosing walls where it was, of course, below freezing point; as were our cabins. The men had each a bed place with a canvas bottom, and a thrummed mat for a bed, while in addition to a blanket each, we were about to make mats as further coverings.

The mean temperature of December was 1° below any previous record; and the cold was very severely felt by us in our frozen habitation; but by increasing the mass of snow and ice on the outside, and by flooring the house, we made it more comfortable. Half a dozen foxes were taken, and afforded us an excellent meal on Sundays and on Christmas day; which was the first that we had spent without tasting spirits or wine; these luxuries having been now utterly exhausted. Thomas, the carpenter was now the only person on the sick list, and it was a matter of considerable regret to me, not less on his account than for the interests of all of us, and the credit of our medical treatment, that the scurvy under which he now at length suffered, did not yield to our great specific, lime-juice, which really seemed as if it had lost its anti-scorbutic virtues.

1833. February 10th to 16th. The carpenter being now in a hopeless state, an appropriate sermon was read on the present Sunday. On the following Saturday morning he died. The thermometer being at minus 45°, the ground was so hard that we had great difficulty in making a grave.

My own condition, from the state of ancient wounds brought into troublesome action by a tendency to scurvy, was at this time somewhat threatening. I had now, indeed, some reason to suppose that I might not be ultimately able to surmount all the present circumstances.

The state of the ice could not have been worse than it was at the end of February, and the hills were entirely covered with snow. It was so deep about the place of our compulsory residence that our miserable abode was almost hidden by it, like the snow hut of an Esquimaux in winter; and as to our course of life and feelings, these are things which poetry might tell once, but which neither poetry nor prose can repeat forever with the hope that any one can listen, and understand, and feel.

Throughout March a want of sufficient employment, short allowance of food, and the inevitable lowness of spirits produced by the unbroken sight of this dull, melancholy, uniform waste of snow and ice, combined to reduce us all to a state of very indifferent health.

We were all very weary of this miserable home. If those of the least active minds dozed away their time in waking stupefaction, they were the most fortunate of the party. Those among us who had the enviable talent of sleeping at all times, whether they were anxious or not, fared best.

April 21st. Our present plan now was to carry forward to the boats, by stages, sufficient provisions to last us from the first of July till the first of October. On Tuesday, Commander Ross and the parties set off with two loads of various articles, and returned about mid-day on the twenty-fourth. On their way back, they saw a bear, and killed a seal; and, in the evening, another bear, approaching the house, was killed. It had been at our flagstaff which it had pulled down.

During April we succeeded in getting all our provisions forward eight miles, or a quarter of the distance towards the place of the boats in Batty bay. The transportation of them onwards to that depot was calculated to be work enough for May, because the parties would be compelled to travel the same ground eight times, so as to make the total distance 256 miles. Consequently it was not till May the twenty-fourth that we arrived with the first load near the place of the boats; which we could not at first discover, so deeply was the ground covered with snow. To dig for them and the concealed stores occupied the greater part of the day. The weather had been variable, and often very snowy during this period; and the consequence was to add much to the difficulties of this already miserable and tedious travelling.

June 1st. Having carried forward to the boats all that could be spared from our actual wants, that everything might be in readiness for moving whenever the ice should open, we had now to occupy ourselves as best we could at our Somerset House till it was time to move again. This apparently premature advance was absolutely necessary; because at a later period, when it should be time for the boats to move and make the attempt to navigate the frozen strait, the roads from our winter residence to their place would not only be much worse, but might prove impassable for such loads under the little power that we had at command.

July 4th. Our preserved meat was expended; and we had now no other fresh animal food than what we could procure by our guns, which was not much as yet, since it consisted but of a few ducks and dovekies. Some spare grates were made for the house, and the roof was repaired and strengthened, in case we should be obliged to return to it for the ensuing winter; though we were somewhat at a loss to know how we were to subsist under such an unfortunate event.

July 8th. On Monday everything was ready, and we too were as prepared as we were anxious to quit this dreary place, as we hoped, for ever. Yet with those hopes there were mingled many fears; enough to render it still but too doubtful in all our minds whether we might not yet be compelled to return; to return once more to despair, and perhaps, to return but to die.

The sick, who formed our great difficulty, bore the first journey well, and we reached our first station before mid-day. In the afternoon we proceeded again with infinite toil through nearly impassable ways, which were rendered more difficult to us by the care which the sick required; and so hard was the labour that even here, and at night, we were obliged to work in our shirts. We gained but two miles by midnight, and were glad to rest.

July 19th. Sunday at Batty bay, whence we had at last arrived, was made a day of rest. On the following day the ice was examined from the hills, but was not yet breaking in the offing. The men were employed in repairing the boats, and in preparations for embarking. About a hundred dovekies were killed, so that our supply of fresh meat was respectable, if not great.

August 1st, 1833. The prevailing nature of the wind was northeasterly; and the consequence was to block up the shore with ice, and to keep us closely imprisoned to our beach and our boats. On the third, indeed, we made an attempt to move round the southern point of the bay; but being unable to effect this we returned, as there was nothing to gain by this project.

But even this fruitless labour was not without its use. The result of it was to do something to keep up the spirits and hopes of the people. The Highland squire who makes Boswell haul on the backstay in a gale of wind, displays more knowledge than a landsman has any right to possess.

I know not what we should have done, what would have "become of us," as the phrase is, had we not made work when we had ceased to find it. "An idle man is a pillow for the devil" says a Spanish or Italian proverb; it was not good that our men should have been pillowed in this manner; better was it that they should work themselves into utter weariness, that they should so hunger as to think only of their stomachs, fall asleep and dream of nothing but a better dinner.

The shooting of waterfowl furnished some occupation to those who were worthy of being trusted with powder and shot; but I believe the best occupation, to a set of such starved wretches as we were, was to eat the game, not to shoot it. Every morning now we rose on the hopes of a good supper; if that came, it was more than welcome; and when it did not, why then there was the chance of one tomorrow.

August 14th. It was on the fourteenth that hope became anxiety, when a lane of water was for the first time seen, leading to the northward; and not many, I believe, slept, under the anticipation of what the next day might bring.

The 15th, all were employed in cutting the ice which obstructed the shore. Then, the tide having risen, with a fine westerly breeze, we launched the boats, embarked the stores and the sick, and at eight o'clock were under way.

We really were under way at last; and it was our business to forget that we had been in the same circumstances the year before, in the same place; to feel that the time for exertion was now come, and those exertions to be at length rewarded; to see, in the mind's eye, the whole strait open before us, and our little fleet sailing with a fair wind through that bay which was now, in our views, England and home.

August 16th. We soon rounded the north cape of Batty bay and, finding a lane of water, crossed Elwin's bay at midnight; reaching, on the sixteenth, that spot where we had pitched our tents on the twenty-eighth of August in the preceding year. The difference in time was but twelve days; and should those days pass as they had done in the former year, it might still be our fate to return to our last winter's home, and there to end our toils.

We found no passage to the eastward, but the lane of water still extended towards the north; so that our stay was of no longer duration than was indispensable for the rest. As we proceeded, the open water increased in breadth; and at eight in the evening we reached our former position on the north-eastern cape of America. A view from the hill here showed that the ice to the northward and north-eastward was in such a state as to admit of sailing through it; but as it blew too hard to venture among it in the night, we pitched our tents for rest.

August 17th. At three in the morning we embarked once more. It was calm, and we held on to the eastward by rowing, until at noon we reached the edge of the packed ice, through many streams of floating pieces. A southerly breeze then springing up, enabled us to round it; when, finding the water open, we stood on through it, and reached the eastern shore of Prince Regent's strait at three in the afternoon. In a few hours we had at length effected that for which we had formerly waited in vain so many days, and which, it is likely, could not have been effected in any of the previous years that we had been imprisoned in this country.

Accustomed as we were to the ice, to its caprices, and to its sudden and unexpected alterations, it was a change like that of magic to find that solid mass of ocean which we had looked at for so many years suddenly converted into water; navigable, and navigable to us, who had almost forgotten what it was to float at freedom on the seas. It was at times scarcely to be believed: and he who dozed to awake again, had for a moment to renew the conviction that he was at length a seaman on his own element, that his boat once more rose on the waves beneath him, and that when the winds blew it obeyed his will and his hand.

Thus we ran quickly along the shore as the breeze increased; to take shelter on the beach twelve miles west of Cape York; having made, on this day, a run of seventy-two miles.

August 18th. The wind moderating, and at length becoming calm, we were obliged in the morning to take to the oars; and finding no ice to obstruct us, rowed along to the eastward. At midnight we rested for a short time at the cape to the east of Admiralty inlet. The next day we were halfway between this place and Navy-board inlet, when the men being exhausted with nearly twenty hours' rowing, we stopped on the beach and pitched our tents.

We were soon driven from this exposed place by the coming on of an easterly wind; and taking once more to our oars, we rowed along among icebergs till we arrived at an excellent harbour. We had thus gained five miles more; and were within eighty of Possession bay.

August 20th. It began to blow hard last night with a heavy sea, which continued this day, blocking us up completely, but allowing us to haul up the boats for repair.

August 22nd. It had become prudent to reduce ourselves, once more, to a two-thirds allowance; and thus we were imprisoned on the twenty-third and twenty-fourth, by a continuance of the gale, with fog and rain.

August 26th. At four in the morning, when all were asleep, the look-out man, David Wood, thought he discovered a sail in the offing, and immediately informed Commander Ross who, by means of his glass, soon saw that it was in reality a ship. All hands were immediately out of their tents and on the beach, discussing her rig, quality, and course; though there were still some despairers who maintained that it was only an iceberg.

No time was however lost; the boats were launched and signals made by burning wet powder; when, completing our embarkation, we left our little harbour at six o'clock. Our progress was tedious, owing to alternate calms and light airs blowing in every direction; yet we made way towards the vessel, and if it had remained calm where she was, should soon have been alongside.

Unluckily, a breeze just then sprang up, and she made all sail to the southeastward; by which means the boat that was foremost was soon left astern.

About ten o'clock we saw another sail to the northward, which appeared to be lying-to for her boats; we thinking at one time, when she hove to, that she had seen us. That, however, proved not to be the case as she soon bore up under all sail. In no long time it was apparent that she was fast leaving us; and it was the most anxious moment that we had yet experienced, to find that we were near to no less than two ships, either of which would have put an end to all our fears and all our toils, and that we should probably reach neither.

It was necessary, however, to keep up the courage of the men by assuring them from time to time, that we were coming up with her; when, most fortunately, it fell calm, and we really gained so fast that at eleven o'clock we saw her heave-to with all sails aback, and lower down a boat which rowed immediately toward our own.

Her boat was soon alongside, when the mate in command addressed us by presuming that we had met with some misfortune and lost our ship. This being answered in the affirmative, I requested to know the name of his vessel, and expressed our wish to be taken on board. I was answered that it was the *Isabella* of Hull, once commanded by Captain Ross:* on which I stated that I was the identical man in question, and my people the crew of the *Victory*. That the mate, who commanded this boat, was as much astonished at this information as he appeared to be, I do not doubt; while with the usual blunderheadedness of men on such occasions, he assured me that I had been dead two years. I easily convinced him, however, that what ought to have been true according to his estimate, was a somewhat premature conclusion.

He immediately went off in his boat to communicate his information on board; repeating that we had long been given up as lost, not by them alone, but by all England.

As we approached slowly after him to the ship, he jumped up the side, and in a minute the rigging was manned, while we were saluted with three cheers as we came within cable's length, and were not long in getting on board of my old vessel where we were

* She had been Ross's vessel on his rediscovery of Baffin Bay in 1818.

all received by Captain Humphreys with a hearty seaman's welcome.

Never was seen a more miserable-looking people than our party. No beggar that wanders in Ireland could have outdone us in exciting the repugnance of those who have not known what poverty can be. Unshaven since I know not when, dirty, dressed in the rags of wild beasts instead of the tatters of civilization, and starved to the very bones, our gaunt and grim looks, when contrasted with those of the well-dressed and well-fed men around us, made us all feel, I believe for the first time, what we really were, as well as what we seemed to others.

But the ludicrous soon took the place of all other feelings. In such a crowd and such confusion, all serious thought was impossible, while the new buoyancy of our spirits made us abundantly willing to be amused by the scene which now opened. Every man was hungry and was to be fed, all were ragged and were to be clothed, there was not one to whom washing was not indispensable, nor one whom his beard did not deprive of all English semblance. All, everything too, was to be done at once; it was washing, dressing, shaving, eating, all intermingled, it was all the materials of each jumbled together; while, in the midst of all, there were interminable questions to be asked and answered on all sides, the adventures of the *Victory*, our own escapes, the politics of England, and the news which was now four years old. But all subsided into peace at last. The sick were accommodated, the seamen disposed of, and all was done for all of us which care and kindness could perform. Night at length brought quiet and serious thoughts; and I trust there was not one man among us who did not then express, where it was due, his gratitude for that interposition which had raised us all from a despair which none could now forget, and had brought us back from the very borders of a not distant grave, to life and friends and civilization.

With the memory of all the earlier voyages strong upon us, it is just barely possible to realize the magnitude of John Ross's accomplishment in bringing home alive nineteen of the twenty-two men who had left England with him four years earlier. To lead them through such a never-ending sequence of disasters clearly required a man of heroic proportions. Ross was that. He was also honest beyond most of his contemporaries (and many of his successors too), for he made no secret of his fears and of his own decaying hope, and, in so doing, he brought upon himself additional opprobrium, for it is one of our more idiotic axioms that a truly brave man never for an instant admits to human frailties.

Andrew Taylor, a particularly competent modern student of the Arctic, recently wrote: "History has judged Ross harshly, and he has been given only grudging credit for such of his accomplishments as have been accepted. Others among his achievements have been completely forgotten."

In truth, since Parry condemned him in 1819, it has been habitual to speak of Ross — when he is mentioned at all — in a derogatory manner, as an incompetent sort of fellow who can have no claim upon our admiration. But those who have read his story will, I think, recognize John Ross as one of the greatest Arctic voyagers of all time.

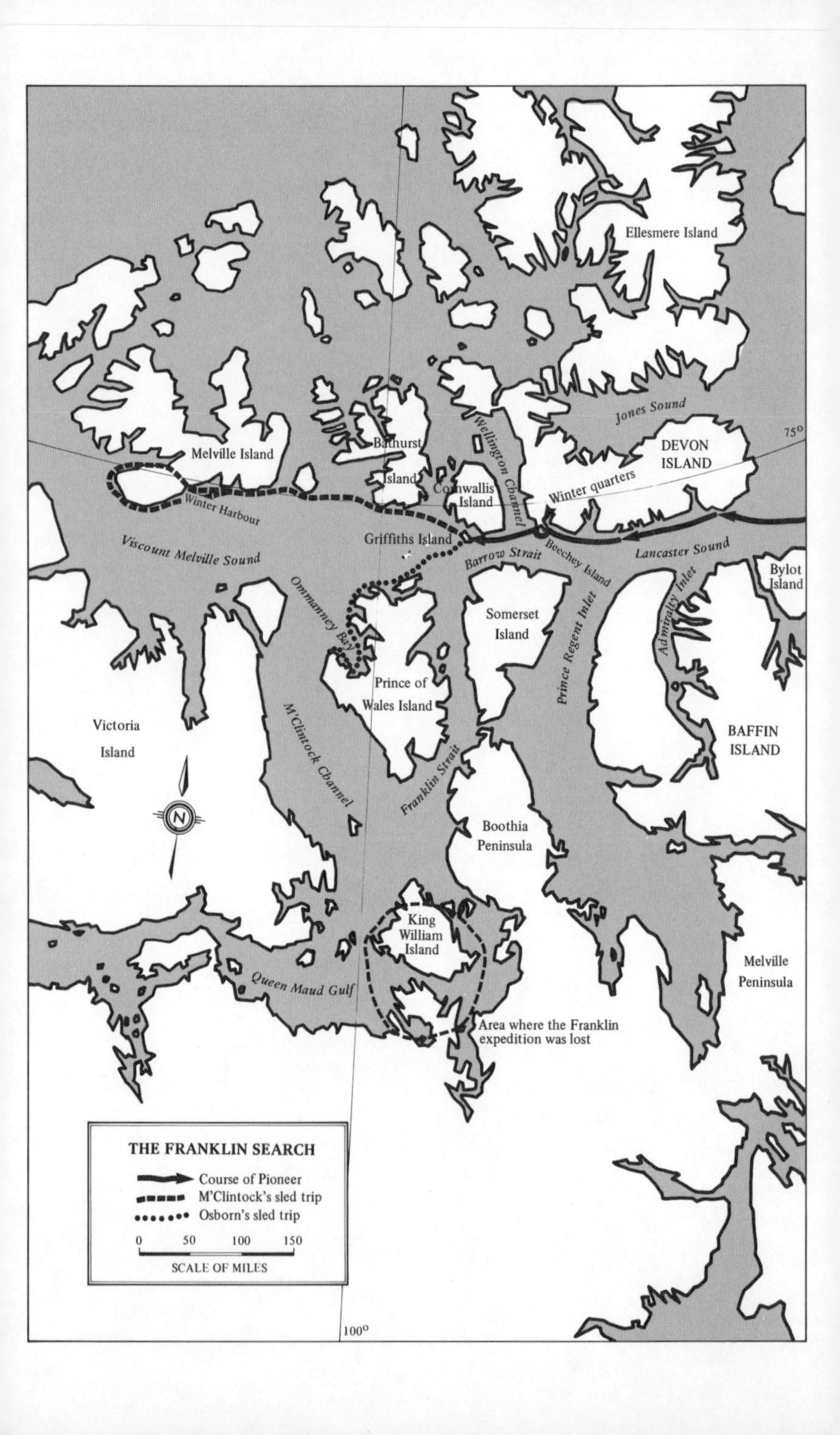

Ellesmere Island
Jones Sound
75°
DEVON
ISLAND
Melville Island
Bathurst
Island
Cornwallis
Island
Wellington Channel
Winter quarters
Winter Harbour
Viscount Melville Sound
Griffiths Island
Barrow Strait
Beechey Island
Lancaster Sound
Bylot
Island
Ommanney Bay
Somerset
Island
Prince Regent Inlet
Admiralty Inlet
Prince of
Wales Island
Victoria
Island
BAFFIN
ISLAND
M'Clintock Channel
Franklin Strait
N
Boothia
Peninsula
King
William
Island
Queen Maud Gulf
Melville
Peninsula
Area where the Franklin
expedition was lost
THE FRANKLIN SEARCH
Course of Pioneer
M'Clintock's sled trip
Osborn's sled trip
0 50 100 150
SCALE OF MILES
100°

IX

The Vanished Ships

News of the rescue of John Ross roused incredulity in England, for his prolonged absence, coupled with his undeserved reputation for incompetence, had convinced officialdom that he must have perished. His apparently miraculous return to England (and consequent return to public favour) had a galvanic effect upon his detractors, for he had demonstrated the error in the Admiralty's opinion that nothing new or useful could be accomplished in the Arctic. The Admiralty now reacted to this implicit challenge by launching a new assault against the ice.

This second act in the story of Naval Arctic exploration began in 1836 when George Back, commanding H.M.S. Terror, *sailed for Hudson Bay to complete Parry's partial survey of Foxe Basin. The voyage was a tragedy of errors and ineptitude. On the outward journey Back allowed his ship to become beset in the pack near Southampton Island, and the* Terror *drifted helplessly and uselessly all that winter and through the following spring until the ice eventually released her in Hudson Strait. Captain Back headed straight home for England, his ship a wreck, and his crew incapacitated by scurvy. Three men had died of this disease after a single winter in the ice; and their loss was in sharp contrast to the single death from scurvy suffered by Ross's expedition during its four years of Arctic isolation. Ross's demonstration that scurvy could be restrained and even conquered by eating fresh-killed local meat had, along with his other innovations about how to live and travel in the north, been totally ignored. The Navy was pro-Parry almost to a man and as such was incapable of learning anything from Ross.*

It was to pay a stiff price for this intransigence.

In 1845 the Admiralty dispatched the best-found expedition it had ever sent to Arctic waters, one designed to find and sail straight through the Northwest Passage.

Sir John Franklin, who had made his reputation as an explorer primarily by conducting two overland expeditions through northwestern Canada to the Arctic coast, was given command of two especially fitted vessels, the Erebus, *and the re-built* Terror, *both of which were equipped with steam auxiliary power. Under him Franklin had a hundred and twenty-nine officers and men, rigorously selected, and proudly acclaimed as the pick of the Royal Navy both in physical condition and in ability and initiative. The ships were stored for four years on full rations, and nothing which the professional explorers of the period thought might conceivably be of value to the expedition was missing from the manifests.*

It was accepted as a certainty that Franklin would succeed. Yet, after speaking to some whalers off Greenland in July of 1845, he, with his two ships and all their people, vanished from the known world.

During the succeeding fourteen years the attempts to solve the mystery of their disappearance resulted in an assault upon the Arctic which was not to be equalled in weight or intensity until the late 1940's brought the U.S. Navy steaming north to take de facto *possession of Canadian Arctic waters.*

The Franklin search by sea really began in 1848 when James Clark Ross (John Ross's nephew) was sent out in command of what was nominally a "supporting" expedition consisting of two ships, H.M.S. Enterprise *and H.M.S.* Investigator. *This squadron wintered at Port Leopold on Somerset Island; but though Ross's two juniors, Leopold M'Clintock and Robert M'Clure, made several sled journeys in the vicinity, no trace of the Franklin expedition was encountered.*

In the following year a "relief" squadron, also consisting of two ships, was sent through Bering Strait in the confident belief that Franklin would be found on the Arctic coast east of the Mackenzie River. No trace of the missing ships or men was found.

By 1850 the Admiralty could no longer evade recognition of the probability that Franklin's party had become the victims of a major tragedy. Consequently a massive search program was mounted in that year. Four naval ships under Captain Austin were sent to Lancaster Sound. Captain Penny, a whaling skipper, was despatched by the British Government in command of two small brigantines to search Jones Sound and Wellington Channel. Meanwhile Captains Collinson and M'Clure, R.N., were ordered to attempt a North-East passage into Lancaster Sound from Bering Strait. Nor was this all. Henry Grinnell, an American millionaire, outfitted two relief ships under Lieutenant De Haven, U.S.N., while Lady Franklin equipped the ninety-ton Prince Albert *to search the vicinity of Boothia. Finally, Sir John Ross himself, then seventy-four years old, fitted out two tiny vessels by public subscription, and sailed once more into the north-west.*

More than a score of books resulted from the efforts of these many ships and men, but almost all of them are blurred by the pompous and desiccated style of writing which had become de rigeur *for respectable explorers of that era. However, there is one amongst these accounts, written by a young Royal Navy Lieutenant named Sherard Osborn, which stands out in welcome contrast to the rest. Though it is hardly an heroic tale, it is a human story which at least touches on the feelings and experiences of ordinary men in conflict with the ice.*

Osborn's account is of value for another reason too, for the ship which he commanded in Captain Austin's flotilla, H.M.S. Pioneer, *together with her sister, the* Intrepid, *were the first real steamers to meet the ice and to show what steam-power could accomplish. Their voyage marks the beginning of a new era in the age-old struggle with the Arctic pack.*

STRAY LEAVES FROM AN ARCTIC JOURNAL

The *Resolute* and *Assistance** were rigged as barks; their hulls strengthened according to the most orthodox Arctic rules until, instead of presenting the appearance of a body intended for progress through the water, they resembled nothing so much as very ungainly snuffboxes; and their bows formed a buttress which rather pushed the water before it than passed through it. The remark made by an old seaman who had grown grey amongst the ice was often recalled to my mind as, with an aching heart, for many a long mile I dragged the clumsy *Resolute* along. "Lord, Sir! you would think by the quantity of wood they are putting into them ships, that the dock yard maties believed they could stop the Almighty from moving the floes in Baffin's Bay! Every pound of African oak they put into them, the less likely they are to rise to pressure; and you must rise in the ice, or sink. If the floe cannot pass under the ship it will go over it."

Internally the fittings of the ships were most perfect; nothing had been spared to render them the most comfortable vessels that ever went out to winter in the Polar ice. Hot air was distributed by means of an ingenious apparatus throughout lower deck and cabins. Double bulkheads and doors prevented the ingress of unnecessary cold air. A cooking battery, as the French say, promised abundance of room for roasting, boiling, baking, and thawing snow to make water for daily consumption. The mess places of the crew

* Sailing ships, and the senior vessels of Austin's four-ship flotilla.

were neatly fitted in man-of-war style; and the well laden shelves of crockery and hardware showed that Jack, as well as jolly marine, had spent a portion of his money in securing his comfort in the long voyage before them. A long tier of cabins on either side showed how large a proportion of officers these vessels carried.

The vessels chosen to be the first* to carry the novel agent steam into Hyperborean climes were the *Pioneer* and *Intrepid*, sister vessels, belonging originally to a cattle conveyance company; they were propelled by screws, and were of sixty horsepower each; about 150 feet long, of 400 tons burden, and rigged as three-masted schooners. Over the whole of their original frames, tough planking called doubling was placed, varying from three to six inches in thickness. The decks were likewise doubled; and, as may be supposed from such numerous fastenings passing through the original timbers of a merchant-man, every timber was perforated with so many holes as to be weakened and rendered useless; indeed, the vessels may have been considered as what is termed "bread and butter built," the two layers of planking constituting, with the decks, the actual strength of the vessels.

For the voyage out the men were confined to a little place in the bows of the vessel and, from thence to the cabins of the officers, all was coal: a dead weight of 260 tons being originally carried from England, which we increased to 300 tons at the Whale Islands. This, at an average consumption of seven tons per diem, would enable us to tow the ships 3000 miles, or steam alone full 5000 miles, carrying twelve or eighteen months' provisions.

We left the Whale Islands in late June, 1850, and, on rounding an inner islet of the Women's Group, saw a straggling assemblage of Esquimaux huts, with a black and red storehouse or two, which denoted the northernmost of the present Danish settlements, as well as the site of an ancient Scandinavian port — a fact assured by the recent discovery of a stone pillar on one of the adjacent islands bearing the following inscription:

> *Elling Sigvatson, Bjarne Thordason, and Endride Oddson erected these memorial stones and cleared this place on Saturday before Gagndag (25th April), in the year 1135.*

This was exactly four hundred and fifty-two years before the place was rediscovered by our countryman, Davis.

* Poor John Ross was not even to be allowed this honour.

We box-hauled about in the offing until we received the disagreeable intelligence that all the English whalers were blocked up by ice some thirty miles to the northward. Captain Penny had been unable to advance, and the season was far from a promising one! Squaring our yards we again bore up for the northward. In a few hours a strong reflected light to the westward and northward showed we were fast approaching the ice-fields of Baffin's Bay.*

June 26. In the first watch Penny's brigs *Lady Franklin* and *Sophia* were seen fast between loose floe pieces, to seaward of which we continued to flirt. The *Intrepid* and *Pioneer* were now slyly trying their bows upon every bit of ice we could get near, without getting into a scrape with the Commodore; and from the ease with which they cut through the rotten stuff around our position, I already foresaw a fresh era in Arctic history, and that the "fine bows" would soon beat the antidiluvian "bluffs" out of the field.

Thursday, 27th June, 1850. The barometer falling, we were ordered to make fast to icebergs, every one choosing his own. This operation is a very useful one in Arctic regions, and saves much unnecessary wear and tear of men and vessel when progress in the required direction is no longer possible.

The bergs, from their enormous depths, are usually aground, except at spring-tides, and the seaman thus succeeds in anchoring his vessel in 200 fathoms without any other trouble than digging a hole in the iceberg, placing a special anchor in it (which one man can lift) and, with a whale-line, his ship rides out under the lee of this natural breakwater even in severe gales, and often escapes being beset in a lee pack.

Fastening to a berg has its risks and dangers; sometimes the first stroke of the man setting the ice-anchor, by its concussion, causes the iceberg to break up, and the people so employed run great risk of being injured. Other times vessels have had pieces

* In early summer the whole central portion of Baffin Bay is almost filled by an immense body of pack ice which drifts slowly southward but is constantly being replenished by more ice from Smith Sound. The currents set this almost solid mass close to the Baffin Island shore, thereby preventing a vessel from sailing north along that coast. Thus the only way in which ships of those times could reach Lancaster Sound was by clawing through the shore floes along the west Greenland coast, past Melville Bay, and then cutting west across the narrowest and loosest portion of the Baffin pack.

detach themselves from overhead and materially injure the ship and spars; and again, the projecting masses called tongues (which form under water at the base of the berg), have been known to break off and strike a vessel so severely as to sink her.

Monday, July 1st, 1850. At last the hoped-for signal "take ships in tow" was made; and, with a leaping heart, we entered a lead having the *Resolute* fast by the nose with a six-inch hawser. What looked impassable at ten miles distance was an open lead when close to. Difficulties vanish when they are faced; and the very calm which rendered the sailing ships unable to take advantage of a loose shore pack, was just the thing for steamers. Away we went past berg, past floe, winding in and out quietly, yet steadily – and the whalers were soon astern.

A block of ice brought us up after a tow of some twenty-five miles and, each vessel picking up a convenient iceberg, we made fast to wait an opening.

We here despatched a boat to a headland where many seabirds had been seen. The boat's crew returned at about four o'clock next morning without any birds, although all the powder and shot had been expended.

I sent for old Abbot, the Captain of the forecastle who had been away in charge of the sportsmen and asked how he had contrived to fire one pound of powder and four of small shot, without bringing home some birds. Hanging his head, and looking uncommonly bashful, he answered, "If you please, sir, we fired it all into a bear!" "Into a bear?" I exclaimed, "What! shoot a bear with No. 4 shot?" "Yes, sir," replied Abbot; "and if it hadn't have been for two or three who were afeared of him, we would have brought him aboard too." Sending my bear-hunting friend about his business for neglecting my orders to obtain fresh food for the crew, I afterwards found out that on passing a small island my boat's crew had observed a bear watching some seals, and it was voted immediately that to be the first to bring a bear home would immortalize the *Pioneer*.

A determined onslaught was therefore made on Bruin: No. 4 shot being poured into him most ruthlessly. He growled and snapped his teeth, trotted round the island, and was still followed and fired at until, finding the fun all on one side, the brute plunged into the water and swam for some broken-up ice. My heroes followed and, for lack of ball, fired at him a waistcoat button and the blade of a knife which, by great ingenuity, they had contrived to cram down one of their muskets. This very naturally, as they described it, "made the beast jump again!" He reached the ice bleeding all over, but not severely injured; and whilst the bear was endeavouring to get on the floe, a spirited contest ensued between him and old Abbot, the latter trying to become possessor of a skin, which the former gallantly defended.

Ammunition expended, and nothing but boathooks and stretchers left as defensive weapons, there seemed some chance of the tables being reversed, and the boat's crew very properly obliged the captain of the forecastle to beat a retreat; the bear, equally well pleased to be rid of such visitors, made off. Old Abbot asserted that if he had had his way, the bear would have been brought aboard the *Pioneer* and tamed to do a good deal of the dragging work of the sledges; and whenever he heard, in the winter ahead, any of the young hands growling at the labour of sledging over snow or ice, he created a roar of laughter by muttering, "Ah! if you had taken my advice, we'd have had that 'ere bear to do this work for us!"

Saturday, July 6th. By 6 a.m. we were alongside of Penny's squadron which was placed at the head of the lane of water up which we had also advanced; and so keen was he not to lose the post of honour that, as we closed, I smiled to see the Aberdonians move their vessels up into the very "nip." In the course of the day some fourteen whalers caught us up, and a long line of masts and hulls dotted the floe-edge.

The ice was hard, affording good exercise for pedestrians. To novices, of whom there were many amongst us, the idea of walking about on the frozen surface of the sea was not a little charming. In all directions groups of three and four persons were seen trudging about, and the constant puffs of smoke, which rose in the clear atmosphere, showed that shooting for the table was kept in view.

The dinner bell rang, and having a very intelligent gentleman who commands a whaler, as a guest, we were much interested in listening to his description of the strange life led by men like himself engaged in the adventurous pursuit of the whale. Mr. S. assured us that he had not seen corn grow, or eaten fresh gooseberries for thirty years, although he had been at home every winter.

A report from deck that the ice was coming in before a southerly gale, finished our dinner very abruptly; and the alteration that had taken place in a couple of hours was striking. A blue sky had changed to one of a dusky colour – a moaning gale sent before it a low brown vapour under which the ice gleamed fiercely; the floes were rapidly pressing together. Two whalers were already nipped severely, and their people were getting the boats and clothing out ready for an accident.

"The sooner we are all in dock the better," said Captain S. as he hurried away to get his own vessel into safety. Almost as quickly as I can tell it, a scene of exciting interest commenced – that of cutting bays or "docks" in the fixed ice, called the land-floe, so the ships could avoid the pressure which would occur at its edge by the body of free ice to seaward being forced against it by the fast rising gale. Smart things are done in the Navy, but I do not think anything could excel the alacrity with which the floe was suddenly peopled by about 500 men, and the long saws used for cutting the ice were manned. A hundred songs resounded through the gale; the sharp chipping of the saws told that the work was flying; and the loud laugh or broad witticisms of the crews mingled with the words of command and encouragement to exertion given by the officers.

The pencil of a Wilkie could hardly convey the characteristics of such a scene, and it is far beyond my humble pen to tell of the stirring animation exhibited by some twenty ships' companies who knew that on their own exertions depended the safety of their vessels and the success of their voyage. The ice was of an average thickness of three feet and, to cut this, saws of ten feet long were used. A little powder was used to break up the pieces that were cut, so as to get them easily out of the mouth of the dock, an operation which the officers of our vessels performed whilst the men cut away with the saws. In a very short time all the vessels were in safety, the pressure of the pack expending itself on a chain of bergs to the north of our present position. The unequal contest between floe and iceberg exhibited itself there in a fearful manner, for the former pressing onward against the huge grounded masses was torn into shreds and thrown back piecemeal, layer on layer of many feet in elevation, as if it was mere shreds of some flimsy material, instead of solid, hard ice, every cubic yard of which weighed nearly a ton.

At five o'clock in the morning of the 12th of July a headland called Cape Walker opened fast to view. The quartermaster grinned as he made his report that he was sure we were in what was a fair lead into the North Water!

Hope is not prophecy, and so they will find who labour in the North; for how changed was the prospect when I went on deck after a short sleep. A south wind had sprung up. We were under sail. The pack was coming in fast, and the signal "Prepare to take the ice," flying from the Commodore's masthead. We did take it, as the pack came against the land-floe, and in a few hours the "nip" took place. The *Intrepid* and *Pioneer* having gone into a natural dock together, were secure enough until the projecting points of the land-floe gave way, when the weight of the pressure came on the vessels, and then we felt for the first time a Melville Bay squeeze. The vessels, lifted by the floes, shot alternately ahead of one another, and rode down the floe for some fifty yards until firmly imbedded in ice which, in many layers, formed a perfect cradle under their bottoms. We, of course, were passive spectators, beyond taking the precaution to have a few men following the vessels over the ice with two or three boats in case of a fatal nip.

The ice slackening a little formed what are called "holes of water," and in these we soon observed a shoal of narwhals, or unicorn fish, to be blowing and enjoying themselves. By extraordinary luck one of the officers of the *Intrepid* happened to hit one in a vital part, and the brute was captured; his horn forming a handsome trophy for the sportsman. The result of this was that the unfortunate narwhals got no peace; directly they showed themselves, a shower of balls was poured into them.

This fish is found throughout the fishing-ground of Baffin's Bay, but is not particularly sought for by our people. The Esquimaux kill it with ease, and its flesh and skin are eaten as luxuries; the latter especially, as an anti-scorbutic, even by the whalers, and some of our crews partook of the extremely greasy looking substance – one man vowing it was very like chestnuts. I did not attempt to judge for myself; but I have no doubt it would form good food to a really hungry person. The use of the horn is a matter of controversy amongst the fishermen: it is almost too blunt for offence, and its point, for about four inches, is always found well-polished, whilst the remainder of it is usually covered with slime and greenish seaweed. Some maintain that it roots up food from the bottom of the sea with this horn; others, that it probes the clefts and fissures of the floating ice with it, to drive out the small fish which are said to be its prey.

Penny had passed a long way inside of the spot the steamers had been beset and nipped in; and he witnessed a sight which, although constantly taking place, is seldom seen – the entire dissolution of an enormous iceberg.

This iceberg had been observed by our squadron, and remarked for its huge size and massiveness, giving good promise of resisting a century of sun and thaw. All on board the *Lady Franklin* described as a most wonderful spectacle this iceberg, without any warning, falling as it were to pieces; the sea around it resembled a seething cauldron from the violent plunging of the masses as they broke and rebroke in a thousand pieces! The floes, torn up for a distance of ten miles by the violent action of the rollers, threatened to destroy any vessel that had been amongst it; and they congratulated themselves on being sufficiently removed from the scene of danger to see, without incurring any immediate risk.

The fog again lifted for a short time. Penny went up to my "crow's nest," as well as into the *Resolute*'s, and soon gave us the disagreeable intelligence that the land-floe had broken up, and we were in the pack, instead of having, as we had fancied, "fast ice" to hold on by; and as he remarked, "We can do nothing but push for it–it's all broken ice–and push we must in-shore, or else away we go with the loose floes to the south."

With this feeling, the six vessels started in the night, in an indifferent and cross lead, we towing the *Resolute* and *Lady Franklin*, – the *Intrepid*, with *Assistance* and *Sophia*, astern. Breaking through two light barriers of ice, the prospect was improving; and, as they said from the "crow's nest" that eight miles of water was beyond a neck of ice ahead, I cast off the vessel in tow in order to charge the ice. At first the *Pioneer* did well, but the floe was nearly six feet thick, hard and sound, and a pressure on it besides. The *Pioneer* was again caught, and the squadron anchored in the floe to await an opening.

On the morning of the 20th we were again beset, and a south gale threatened to increase the pressure; escape was, however, impossible, and "Fear not but trust in Providence" is a necessary motto for Arctic seamen. My faith in this axiom was soon put to the proof. After a short sleep I was called on deck, as the vessel was suffering from great pressure. My own senses soon made it evident; every timber and plank was cracking and groaning, the vessel was thrown considerably over on her side and lifted bodily, the bulkheads cracking, and treenails and bolts breaking with small reports. On reaching the deck I saw indeed that the poor *Pioneer* was in sad peril; the deck was arching with the pressure on her sides, and a quiver of agony wrung my craft's frame from stem to taffrail whilst the floe, as if impatient to overwhelm its victim, had piled up as high as the bulwark in many places.

The men who, whaler-fashion, had without orders brought their clothes on deck, ready to save their property, stood in knots waiting for directions from the officers who, with anxious eye, watched the floe-edge as it ground past the side to see whether the strain was easing; suddenly it did so, and we were safe! But a deep dent in the *Pioneer*'s side, extending for some forty feet, and the fact of twenty-one timbers being broken upon one side, proved that her trial had been a severe one.

The sailing ships, generally the *Resolute*, kept the lead in our subsequent heaving and warping operations through the pack; and leaving a small portion of the crews to keep the other vessels close up under her stern, the majority of the officers and men laboured at the headmost ship to move her through the ice. Heaving ahead with stout hawsers, blasting with gunpowder, cutting with ice-saws, and chipping with ice-chisels, was perseveringly carried on; but the progress fell far short of the labour expended and the bluff-bowed *Resolute* slipped back out of the nip instead of wedging it open. Warping the *Resolute* through a barrier of ice by lines out of her hawse-holes, put me in mind of trying to do the same with a cask by a line through the bung-hole: she slid and swerved every way but the right one. I often saw her bring dead up, as if a wall had stopped her. After a search some one would exclaim, "Here is the piece that jams her!" and a knock with a two-pound chisel would bring up a piece of ice two or three inches thick! In short, all or nearly all of us soon learnt to see that the fine bow was the one to get ahead in these regions; and the daily increasing advantage which Penny had over us with his fine-bowed ships, was a proof which the most obstinate could not dispute.

Friday the 9th of August arrived. Captain Penny's squadron was gone out of sight in a lane of water towards Cape York. Sir John Ross's schooner and ketch were passing us: caution yielded to the grim necessity of a push for our very honour's sake: the *Resolute* was dropped out of the nip and the *Pioneer* was at last allowed to put her wedge-bow, aided by steam, to the crack. In one hour we were past the barrier which had checked our advance for three long weary days. All was joy and excitement; the steamers themselves seemed to feel and know their work, and exceeded even our sanguine expectations; and to everyone's delight we in the screws were this evening allowed to carry on with this system of ice-breaking. As an example of how it was done, a piece of a floe two or three hundred yards broad and three feet thick, prevented our progress. The weakest and narrowest part being ascertained, the sailing ships were secured as close as possible without obstructing the steam vessels, the major part of the crews being despatched to line where the cut was to be made, with tools, and gunpowder for blasting, and plenty of short hand-lines and claws.

The *Pioneer* and *Intrepid* in turn then rushed at the floe, breaking their way through it until the impetus gained in the open water was lost by the resistance of the ice. The word "Stop her! Back, easy!" was then given, and the screw vessel went astern carrying with her tons of ice by means of numerous lines which the bluejackets, who attended on the forecastle, held on by. As the one vessel went astern with her tow of fragments, the other flew ahead to her work. The operation was aided by the explosions of powder; but altogether it was a fresh laurel in the screw's wreath. The *Intrepid* gave a coup-de-grâce to the mass, which sent it coach-wheeling round, as it is termed; and the whole of the squadron taking the nip, as Arctic ships should do, we were next morning in the true lead, and our troubles in Melville Bay were at an end.

It was now the 10th of August. By heavens, I shall never forget the lightheartedness of that day. Forty days had we been beset in the ice, and one day of fair application of steam, powder, and men, and the much-talked-of bay was mastered.

August 22nd, 1850. The *Resolute* in company, and steering a course up Lancaster Sound.

The great gateway, within whose portals we were now fast entering, has much in it that is interesting in its associations to an English seaman. Across its mouth the bold navigator Baffin, 200 years before, had steered. About thirty-five years ago it was converted into a bay by Sir John Ross; and within eighteen months afterwards, Parry sailed through this very bay and discovered new lands extending half of the distance towards Bering's Straits, or about 600 miles. To complete the remaining 600 miles of unknown region, Sir John Franklin and his gallant followers had devoted themselves – with what resolution, with what devotion, is best told by their long absence and our anxiety.

On the 26th of August Cape York gleamed through an angry sky, and as Regent's Inlet opened to the southward there was little doubt but we should soon be caught in an Arctic gale. We however cared little, provided there was plenty of open water ahead, though of that there appeared strong reasons for entertaining doubts, as both the temperature of the air and water was fast falling.

That night the wind piped merrily, and we rolled most cruelly; the long and narrow *Pioneer* threatened to pitch every spar over the side, and refused all the manoeuvring upon the part of her shaken officers and men to comfort and quiet her.

Fast increasing daylight showed us to have been thrown considerably to the northward; and as we sailed to the south the ice showed itself in far from pleasing proximity under the lee – boiling, for so the edge of a pack appears to do in a gale of wind. It was a wild sight, but we felt that at any rate it was optional with a screw steamer whether she ran into the pack or kept the sea. Our tough old quartermaster – an ex-whaler – whose weather-beaten face peered anxiously over the lee, was watching the *Resolute* beating, and I heard him growl out, "Wull, since they are off a lee-pack edge, the sooner they make up their mind to run into it the better!" "Why so, Hall?" I inquired. "Because, sir," replied the old man, "that ship is going two feet to leeward for one she is going ahead, and she would never work off nothing!"

"Perhaps," I said, "you have occasionally been caught in worse vessels off such a pack, or a lee shore, and still not been lost?"

"Oh! Lord, sir! we have some rum craft in the whaling ships, but I don't think anything as sluggish as the *Resolute*. Howsomever, they gets put to it now and then. Why it was only last year we were down near Cumberland Sound. About the 10th of October it came on to blow, sir, from the southward, and sent in a sea upon us which nearly drowned us. We tried to keep an offing, but it was no use; we couldn't show a rag; everything was blown away, and it was perishing cold. But our captain was a smart man and he said, 'Well, boys, we must run for Hangman's Cove, altho' it's late in the day. If we don't, I won't answer where we'll be in the morning.'

"So up we put the helm, sir, to run for a place like a hole in a wall, with nothing but a close reefed topsail set, and the sky as thick as pea-soup. It looked a bad job, I do assure you, sir. Just as it was dark we found ourselves right up against the cliffs, and we did not know whether we were lost or saved until by good luck we shot into dead smooth water in a little cove, and let go our anchor. Next day a calm set in and the young ice made round the ship; we couldn't cut it, and we couldn't tow the vessel through it. We had not three months' provisions, and we made certain sure of being starved to death; when the wind came strong off the land and, by working for our lives, we escaped and went home directly out of the country."

August 28th. The sun was fast dipping behind North Devon and a beautiful moon (the first we had found any use for since passing Cape Farewell on the 28th of May) was cheerfully accepted as a substitute, when the report of a boat being seen from the masthead startled us and excited general anxiety. The boat proved to be the *Sophia*'s, and in her Captain Stewart and Dr. Sutherland. They went on board the *Resolute* and shortly afterwards the interesting intelligence they then communicated was made known to me.

It was this – the *Assistance* and *Intrepid* had visited Wolstenholme Sound and from thence they had examined the north shore of Lancaster Sound as far as Cape Riley, without discovering anything. On landing there, however, numerous traces of English seamen having visited the spot were discovered in sundry pieces of rag, rope, broken bottles, and a long-handled instrument intended to rake up things from the bottom of the sea. Marks of a tent-place were likewise visible. A cairn was next seen on Beechey Island; to this the *Intrepid* proceeded.

The steamer having approached close under the island, a boatful of officers and men proceeded on shore. On landing, some relics of European visitors were found; and we can picture the anxiety with which the steep slope was scaled and the cairn torn down, every stone turned over, the ground underneath dug up a little, and yet, alas! no document or record found.

The boat had gone away from the *Intrepid* without arms of any description, and the people on top of the cliff now saw to their dismay a large white bear advancing rapidly in the direction of the boat. The two men left in charge of the boat happily caught sight of Bruin before he caught hold of them, and launching it they hurried off to the steamer, whilst the observers left on the cliff were not sorry to see the bear chase the boat a short way and then turn towards the packed ice in the offing. This event, together with some risk of the ice separating the two vessels, induced the party to return on board where a general impression was created in the minds of the people belonging to the two ships, that what they had found must be the traces of a retreating or shipwrecked party from the *Erebus* and *Terror*.

Whilst the *Assistance* (Captain Ommanney) and *Intrepid* were so employed, the American squadron, and that under Captain Penny, were fast approaching. The Americans first communicated with Captain Ommanney's division, and heard of their discovery of the first traces of Sir John Franklin. The Americans then informed Penny, who was pushing for Wellington Channel. Captain Penny at once returned, as he figuratively expressed it, "to take up the search from Cape Riley like a blood-hound," and richly was he rewarded for doing so.

At Cape Spencer he discovered the ground-plan of a tent, the floor of which was neatly and carefully paved with small smooth stones. Around the tent a number of birds' bones, as well as remnants of meat canisters, led him to imagine that it had been inhabited for some time as a shooting station and a look-out place, for which latter purpose it was admirably chosen, commanding a good view of Barrow's Strait and Wellington Channel. This opinion was confirmed by the discovery of a piece of paper on which was written "to be called" – evidently the fragment of an officer's night orders.

Some sledge marks pointed northward from this neighbourhood; and the American squadron, being unable to advance up the strait (in consequence of the ice resting firmly against the land close to Cape Innis), Lieutenant de Haven despatched parties on foot to follow these sledge marks, whilst Penny's squadron returned to re-examine Beechey Island. The American officers found the sledge tracks very distinct for some miles, but before they had got as far as Cape Bowden the trail ceased, and one empty bottle and a piece of newspaper were the last things found in that direction.

Not so Captain Penny's squadron: making fast to the ice between Beechey Island and Cape Spencer, in what is now called Union Bay, and in which they found Sir John Ross's *Felix* schooner to be likewise lying, parties from the *Lady Franklin* and *Sophia* started towards Beechey Island.

A long point of land slopes gradually from the southern bluffs of this now deeply interesting island, until it almost connects itself with the land of North Devon, forming on either side of it two good and commodious bays. On this slope a multitude of preserved meat tins were strewed about, and near them and on the ridge of the slope a carefully constructed cairn was discovered; it consisted of layers of meat tins filled with gravel and placed to form a firm and solid foundation; beyond this and along the northern shore of Beechey Island, the following traces were then quickly discovered – the embankment of a house with carpenter and armourer's working-places, washing-tubs, coal-bags, pieces of old clothing, rope, and lastly, the graves of three of the crew of the *Erebus* and *Terror* – placing it beyond all doubt that the missing ships had indeed been there, and bearing the date of the winter of 1845-46.

We therefore now had ascertained the first winter quarters of Sir John Franklin! Here fell to the ground all the evil forebodings of those who had, in England, consigned his expedition to the depths of Baffin's Bay on its outward voyage. Our first prayer had been granted by a beneficent Providence; and we had now a certain assurance of Franklin having reached thus far without shipwreck or disaster.

As the *Pioneer* slowly steamed through the loose ice which lay off Beechey Island, the cairn erected by Franklin's people on the height above us was an object of deep interest and conversation. It seemed to say to the beating heart, "Follow them that erected me!"

However, no further trace of Franklin's expedition was found before the onset of winter brought the season's navigation to an end. Captain Austin's flotilla remained in the ice close to Griffith's Island.

September 11th, 1850. The winter of the Arctic regions had now come on us, in its character of darkness, gale, cold, and snow. The leader of the American expedition, I heard, finding farther progress hopeless, intended in obedience to his orders to return to New York. This he was the more justified in doing, as no preparation or equipment for travelling-parties had been made by them, and their fittings for wintering in the Arctic regions were, compared with ours, very deficient.

September passed; winter and frost had undoubted dominion over earth and sea; already the slopes of Griffith's Island and the land north of us were covered with snow; the water in sight was like a thread, and occasionally disappeared altogether. Fires all day, and candles for long nights, were in general requisition. Some disagreements in the different messes were taking place as the individuals suffered more or less from the cold. Plethoric ones, who became red-hot with a run up the ladder, exclaimed against fires and called zero charming weather; the long and lethargic talked of cold draughts and Sir Hugh Willoughby's fate;* the testy bemoaned the impure ventilation.

A fox or two was occasionally seen scenting around the ships, and a fox hunt enlivened the floe with men and officers who chased the unlucky brute as if they had all come to Griffith's Island especially for fox skins. And the last of the feathered tribe, in the shape of a wounded burgomaster gull shivered, half frozen, as it came for its daily food.

On Thursday, the 10th of October, we started with our tent, a runner-sledge, and five days' provisions on a short sled trip.

Three hours' sharp dragging brought us to Cape Martyr where we turned to the westward and commenced searching the beach and neighbouring headlands.

I had taken a short stroll by myself along one of the terraces which swept around the base of the higher ground when, to my astonishment, a mass of stone-work and what at first looked exactly like a cairn, came in view. It required no spur to make me hasten to it, and to discover I was mistaken in supposing it to have been anything constructed so recently as Franklin's visit. The ruin proved to be a conical-shaped building, the apex of which had fallen in. Its circumference at the base was about twenty feet, and the height of the remaining wall was five feet six inches. Those who had constructed it appeared well acquainted with the strength of an arched roof to withstand the pressure of the heavy falls of snow of these regions; and much skill and nicety was displayed in the arrangements of the slabs of slatey limestone in order that the conical form of the building might be preserved throughout.

We removed the stones that had fallen into the building but found nothing to repay our labour. Indeed, from the quantity of moss adhering to the walls, and filling up the interstices of the masses which formed the edifice, I conjectured it was many years since it was constructed.†

* He and two ships' crews starved to death, or died of cold on the east coast of Lapland in 1554, in an attempt to discover the North East Passage.

† The origin of this ruin has never been satisfactorily accounted for, but some authorities believe it may have been built by the Norse voyagers from Greenland.

No pen can tell of the unredeemed loneliness of an October evening in this part of the polar world; the monotonous, rounded outline of the adjacent hills, as well as the flat, unmeaning valleys, were of one uniform colour, either deadly white with snow, or striped with brown where too steep for the winter mantle as yet to find a holding ground. You felt pity for the shivering blade of grass which was already drooping under the cold and icy hand that would press it down to mother earth for nine long months.

Then, "Pemmican is all ready, sir!" reports our man Soyer. In troth, appetite need wait on one, for the greasy compound would pall on moderate taste or hunger. Tradition said that it was composed of the best rump-steaks and suet, and cost 1s. 6d. per pound; but we generally voted it composed of broken-down horses and Russian tallow. If not sweet in savour, it was strong in nourishment, and after six tablespoonfuls, the most ravenous feeder might have cried, hold! enough!

The meal done, the tent was carefully swept out, the last careful arrangements of the pebbles, termed "picking the feathers" was made, and then a waterproof sheet spread, to prevent our warm bodies melting the frozen ground and wetting us through. Then every man his blanket bag, a general popping thereinto of the legs and body, in order that the operation of undressing might be decently performed; the jacket and wet boots carefully arranged for a pillow; the wolf-skin robes (Oh, that the contractor may be haunted by the aroma of the said robes for his life-time!) brought along both over and under the party, who lie down alternately, head and feet in a row, across the tent. Pipes are lighted, the evening's glass of grog served out; and whilst the cook is washing up and preparing his things ready for the morning meal, as well as securing the food on the sledge from foxes or a hungry bear, many a tough yarn is told, or joke made, which keep all hands laughing until the cook comes in, hooks up the door, tucks in the fur robe; and seven jolly mortals with a brown-holland tent over their heads, and a winter's gale without, try to nestle their sides amongst the softest stones, and at last drop into such a sleep as only those enjoy who drag a sledge all day with the temperature 30° below freezing point.

Captain Penny expressed it as his opinion that the Americans had not escaped out of Barrow's Straits, in consequence of a sudden gale springing up from the southward shortly after they had passed his winter quarters. This supposition we afterwards found to be true, although at the time we all used to speak of the Americans as being safe and snug in New York, instead of drifting about in the ice within a few miles of us, as was really the case.*

Our upper decks were now covered in; stoves and warming apparatus set at work; boats secured on the ice; all the disposable gear taken off the upper decks to clear them for exercise in bad weather; masts and yards made as snug as possible; rows of posts placed to show the road, in the darkness and snow-storms, from ship to ship; holes cut through the ice into the sea to secure a ready supply of water in the event of fire; arrangements made to insure cleanliness of ships and crews, and a winter routine entered upon.

The building of snow-walls, posts, houses, &c. was at first a source of amusement to the men, and gave them a great field in which to exercise their skill and ingenuity. People at home would have been delighted to see the pretty and tasteful things cut out of snow; obelisks, sphinxes, vases, cannon, and lastly, a stately Britannia looking to the westward, enlivened the floe and gave voluntary occupation to the crews of the vessels. These, however, only served for a while; and as the Arctic night of months closed in, every one's wits were exerted to the utmost to invent occupation and entertainment for our little community.

A theatre, a casino, a saloon, two Arctic newspapers (one of them illustrated), evening-schools, and instructive lectures, gave no one an excuse for being idle. Vocalists and musicians practised and persevered until an instrumental band and glee-club were formed. Officers and men sung who never sang before, and maybe, except under similar circumstances, will never sing again; maskers had to construct their own masks, and sew their own dresses, the signal flags serving in lieu of a supply from the milliners; and, with wonderful ingenuity, a fancy dress ball was got up which, in variety and tastefulness of costume, would have borne comparison with any in Europe.

Here, editors exhibited French ingenuity in saying their say without bringing themselves within the grasp of the censors; over here, rough contributors, whose hands, more accustomed to the tar-brush than the pen, turned flowing sentences by the aid of old and well-thumbed dictionaries. There, on wooden stools, leaning

* In fact De Haven's ships drifted in the ice until June of 1851, by which time they were back in Davis Strait.

over long tables, were a row of serious and anxious faces which put one in mind of the days of cane and birch – an Arctic school. Tough old marines curving "pothooks and hangers," as if their very lives depended on their performances, with an occasional burst of petulance, such as, "D - - the pen, it won't write! I beg pardon, sir; this 'ere pen will splutter!" which set the scholars in a roar. Then some big-whiskered top-man, with slate in hand, reciting his multiplication-table; whilst a "scholar," as the cleverest were termed, gave the instructor a hard task to preserve his learned superiority.

The recognition of Nature's beauties richly rewarded us for our isolation from the world of our fellow-men as, from the heights of Griffith's Island, we looked down on our squadron, whose masts alone pierced the broad white expanse over Barrow's Straits, and threw long shadows across the floe.

Imagine yourself on the edge of a lofty table-land which, dipping suddenly at your feet, sloped again to the sea of ice at a distance of some 500 feet below; fancy a vast plain of ice and snow on which four lone barks, atoms in the extensive landscape, mark the observers' home; and beyond them, on the horizon, sweeping in many a bay and headland, the coast of Cornwallis Island, now bursting upon the eye in startling distinctness, then receding into shadow and gloom.

A few bears, perhaps eight in all, visited our ships during the closing period of 1850. Whenever an unlucky brute was seen, the severe competition as to who should possess his skin entailed no small risk of life upon the hunters as well as the bear; and crossing the line of fire was recklessly performed in a manner to have shocked a Woolwich artilleryman. One brute was alone bagged, although a good many were very much frightened. An instance of what risks the community ran, whilst the furor for skins was at its height, occurred when two unconscious mortals who had got on a hummock to look around, were mistaken in the twilight for bears, and promptly drew enthusiastic, if happily inaccurate rifle fire. And one day a respectable individual, trotting among the snow ridges, was horrified to see on a piece of canvas, in large letters, "Beware of spring-guns!" Picture his feelings. How was he to escape? The next tread of his foot might discharge the murderous barrel secreted for a bear. Fate decreed otherwise however, and the spring gun was banished to some lonely ravine from which the proprietor daily anticipated a dead bear, and I, a dead shipmate;

some of whom, pining for forlorn damsels at home, were led to sentimentalize in retired places.

Old Abbot, my captain of the forecastle, whose sporting propensities I have elsewhere noted, cured me of a momentary mania for trophies of the chase. A large bear and cub were fired at by three officers with guns, but only one of the three barrels went off, wounding the cub which, with its mother, made for Griffith's Island. I chased it, followed by some of the men, the foremost of whom was my ancient mariner, who kept close to my heels urging me on by declaring we were fast catching the brutes. We decidedly had done so. By the time I reached the island both bears were within shot, climbing up with cat-like agility the steep face of the cliffs. Again and again I failed to get my gun to go off; and as the she-bear looked at one time inclined to come down and see who the bipeds were that chased her, I looked round at my supporters, who were vehemently exclaiming that "we should have her in a minute!" They consisted of old Abbot, armed with a snow-knife, and a few unarmed men who ran because they saw others doing so. Now a snow-knife consists of nothing more than a piece of old iron beaten out on an anvil, having an edge which, when I anxiously asked if it was sharp, I was figuratively told, "The owner, John Abbot, could have ridden to the devil upon it without injury to his person." Yet with only this I verily believe the old seaman would have entered the list against the teeth and talons of Mistress Bruin. I objected, however, and allowed her to escape with becoming thankfulness.

January 1851. That we were all paler was perceptible to everyone; but only a few had lost flesh. A very little exercise was found to tire one very soon, and appetites were generally on the decrease. For four hours a day, we all, men and officers, made a point of facing the external air, let the temperature be what it would, and this rule was carefully adhered to until the return of the sun induced us to lengthen our excursions.

Much later in the winter – indeed in the month of March – a succession of furious gales quite smothered us; the drift piled up as high as the top of the winter housing which was fifteen feet above the deck, and then blew over to leeward, filling up on that side likewise; whilst we, unable to face the storm without, could only prevent the housing from being broken in by placing props of planks and spars to support the weight. We had actually to dig our way out of the vessel; and I know not how we should have freed the poor smothered craft, had not nature assisted us by the breaking down of the floe.

This at first threatened to injure the *Pioneer*, for, firmly held as she was all round, the vessel was immersed some two feet deeper than she ought to have been, by the subsiding ice. We set to work however to try and liberate her, when one night a series of loud reports awakened me, and the quartermaster at the same time ran down to say that "she was a-going off!" a fact of which there was no doubt as, with sudden surges, the *Pioneer* overcame the hold the floe had taken of her poor sides, and after some time she floated again at her true water line; whilst the mountain of snow around us had sunk to the level of the floe, and at first formed enormously thick ice; but this in time, by the action of the under-currents of warmer water, reduced itself to the ordinary thickness of the adjoining floe.

Before we enter upon the subject of returning spring, and the new occupations and excitement which it called forth, let me try to convey an idea of a day spent in winter darkness.

Fancy the lower deck and cabins of a ship lighted entirely by candles and oil lamps; every aperture by which external air could enter, unless under control, carefully secured; and all doors doubled to prevent draughts. It is breakfast time, and reeking hot cocoa from every mess table is sending up a dense vapour which, in addition to the breath of so many souls, fills the space between decks with mist and fog. Should you go on deck (and remember you go from 50° above zero to 40° below it, in eight short steps) a column of smoke will be seen rising through certain ventilators, whilst others are supplying a current of pure air. Breakfast done – and, from the jokes and merriment, it has been a good one – there is a general pulling on of warm clothing, and the major part of the officers and men go on deck. A few remain to clean and clear up, arrange for the dinner, and remove any damp or ice that may have formed in holes or corners during the sleeping hours. This done, a muster of all took place. Officers inspected the men, and every part of the ship, to see both were clean, and then they dispersed to their several duties, which at this severe season were very light; confined mainly to supply the cook with snow to melt for water, keeping the fire-hole in the floe open, and sweeping the decks. Knots of two or three would, if there was not a strong gale blowing, be seen taking exercise at a distance from the vessels; and others, strolling under the lee, discussed the past and prophesied as to the future. At noon, soups, preserved meats, or salt horse, formed the seamen's dinner, with the addition of preserved potatoes, a treat which the gallant fellows duly appreciated. A little afternoon exercise was then taken, and the evening meal, of tea, next partaken of. If it was school night, the voluntary pupils went to their tasks, the masters to their posts; reading men produced their books, writing men their desks, artists painted by candle-light, and cards, chess, or draughts, combined with conversation and an evening's glass of grog, and a cigar or pipe, served to bring round bed-time again.

Monotony was our enemy, and to kill time our endeavour; hardship there was none; for all we underwent in winter quarters in the shape of cold, hunger, or danger, was voluntary. Monotony, as I again repeat, was the only disagreeable part of our wintering at Griffith's Island.

Signal rockets, in the calm evenings of early winter, were fired with great effect; in proof of which signals were several times exchanged, both in the autumn and spring, between Assistance Harbour and our squadron, by the aid of these useful projectiles, although the distance was twenty miles.

Balloons, as a more novel attempt for intercommunication, were a subject of deep interest. The plan was simple and ingenious; the merit of the idea, as applicable to the relief of Sir John Franklin, by communicating to him intelligence of the position of the Searching Parties, being due to Mr. Shepperd. It was as follows: a balloon of oiled silk capable of raising about a pound weight when inflated, was filled with hydrogen evolved from a strong cask, in which a certain quantity of zinc filings and sulphuric acid had been introduced. To the base of the inflated balloon a piece of fuse five feet long was attached, its lower end being lighted. Along this fuse, at intervals, pieces of coloured paper and silk were secured with thread, and on them the information as to our position and intended lines of search were printed. The balloon sailed rapidly along and as the match burnt, the papers were gradually detached, and falling, spread themselves on the snow, where their glaring colours would soon attract notice should they happily fall near the poor fellows in the *Erebus* and *Terror*.

Next as a means of communication, came carrier pigeons. When first proposed in 1850, many laughed at the idea of a bird doing any service in such a cause. In our Expedition none of these birds had been taken; but on board the *Felix* Sir John Ross had a couple of brace. I plead guilty myself to having joined in the laugh at the poor creatures when, with feathers in a half-moulted state, I heard it proposed to despatch them from Beechey Island to Ayr, in Scotland, even though they were to be slung to a balloon for a part of the journey. At any rate it was tried, I think on the 6th October, 1850, from Assistance Harbour. Two birds, duly freighted with intelligence, and notes from the married men, were put in a basket which was attached to a balloon in such a manner that, after combustion of a certain quantity of fuse, the carrier pigeons would be launched into the air to commence their flight. The wind was then blowing fresh from the north-west, and the temperature below zero.

When we in the squadron off Griffith's Island heard of the departure of the mail, the opinion prevalent was that the birds would be frozen to death. We were mistaken; for in about 120 hours, one of these birds, as verified by the lady to whom it had originally belonged, reached her house in Ayr, and flew to the nest in which it had been hatched in the pigeon loft. This marvellous flight of 3000 miles is the longest on record.

Lastly, we carried out, more I believe from amusement than from any idea of being useful, a plan which had suggested itself to the people of Sir James Ross's expedition when wintering in Leopold Harbour in 1848-49, that of enclosing information in a collar secured to the necks of the Arctic foxes, caught in traps, and then liberated. Several animals thus entrusted with despatches or records were liberated by different ships; but as the truth must be told, I fear in many cases the next night saw the poor "postman" in another trap, out of which he would be taken, killed, the skin taken off and packed away to ornament at some future day the neck of some fair Dulcinea. As a "sub,"* I was admitted into this secret mystery, or otherwise I with others might have accounted for the disappearance of the collared foxes by believing them busy on their honourable mission. In order that the crime of killing the "postman" may be recognized in its true light, it is but fair that I should say that the brutes, having partaken once of the good cheer on board or around the ships, seldom seemed satisfied with the empty honours of a copper collar, and returned to be caught over and over again. Strict laws were laid down for their safety, such as an edict that no fox taken alive in a trap was to be killed: of

* A junior officer.

course no fox was after this taken alive; they were all unaccountably dead, unless it was some unfortunate wight whose brush and coat were worthless: in such case he lived either to drag about a quantity of information in a copper collar for the rest of his days, or else to die a slow death, as being intended for Lord Derby's menagerie in England.

The departure of a "postman" was a scene of no small merriment; all hands, from the captain to the cook, were out to chase the fox who, half frightened out of his wits, seemed to doubt which way to run; whilst loud shouts and roars of laughter were heard from ship to ship as the fox-hunters swelled in numbers from all sides, and those that could not run mounted some neighbouring hummock of ice and gave a view halloo.

February 7th, 1851. The stentorian lungs of the *Resolute* boatswain hailed to say the sun was in sight from the masthead; and in all the vessels the rigging was soon manned to get the first glimpse of the returning day. For ninety-six days the sun had not gladdened us, and now its return put fresh life into our night-wearied bodies. For a whole hour we feasted ourselves with admiring the sphere of fire, which illumined without warming us; and indeed the cold now increased, rather than otherwise, and our lowest temperature and severest weather did not occur until March.

Preparations for spring sledge travelling were now hastened. Everyone commenced to "harden-up" for the labour before them. Zealous individuals might be daily seen trying all sorts of patents. Out of their hard-earned wages some of the men bought and made sails of peculiar cut for their sledges; others, after the "working hours" were over, constructed water-bottles, velocipedes, cooking tins, in fact neither pains nor trouble were spared – officers and men vying in zeal.

The sledges, constructed of tough and well-seasoned wood, had been made in Woolwich Dockyard. They were shod with iron, and the cross-bars or battens which connected the two runners and formed the floor upon which the load was placed, were lashed into place. At the four corners of the sledges light iron stanchions dropped into sockets, and formed the support for the sides of a species of boat, capable of serving to ferry the sledge crew across water in an emergency, as well as to keep the provisions and clothing in it dry.

The daily scale of provision for the sledge parties, as ordered by Captain Austin, for each man was to be as follows:

Pemmican	1 lb.
Boiled pork	6 oz.
Biscuit	12 oz.
Rum, concentrated	¾ gill
Tobacco	½ oz.
Biscuit dust	1 oz.
Tea and sugar	¾ oz.
Chocolate and sugar (alternate days)	1¾ oz.
Lime juice (for 10 days)	½ oz.

The fuel allowed to cook with for a party of seven men amounted to one pint and one gill of spirits of wine, or 1 lb. 8 oz. of tallow a day.

A little calculation soon showed that about forty days' provision was as much as any one sledge could take with it, which, at an average distance of ten miles per diem, could only give an extent of coast line examined by any one sledge of 200 miles, and return to base.

Fifteen sledges, manned by 105 men and officers, were equipped for the search and on the 12th of April, the day calm and some 50° below freezing point, a scene of bustle and merriment showed that the sledges were mustering previous to being taken to the starting point.

Our sense of decorum was constantly overthrown by the gambols of divers dogs, given to us by Captain Penny, with small sledges attached to them, which were racing about, entangling themselves, howling for assistance, or else running between the men's legs and capsizing them on the snow, amidst shouts of laughter.

Reaching the assembly place luncheon was served out, and all of us inspected, approved of, ordered to fall in, and a speech was made which, as was afterwards remarked, buttered us all up admirably.

At two o'clock on the following morning we reached much piled-up ice; and in the hope of clearer weather in the evening, the word to halt and pitch the tents was given. The seven sledges of our division, picking out the smoothest spots, were soon secured. The tents fluttering in the breeze, a little tea was cooked, and then each man got into his blanket-bag and dreamt of a fine day and of finding Sir John Franklin.

In the evening the weather was still thick as pea-soup, with a double-reef topsail breeze blowing in our teeth; but detention was impossible so we again packed up after a meal of chocolate and biscuit and, facing towards Cape Walker, we carried the hummocks by storm. Ignorance was bliss. Straight ahead, over and through everything was the only way; and, fresh, hearty, and strong, we surmounted tier after tier, which more light and a clearer view might only have frightened us from attempting.

A hard night's toil cleared all obstacles, and nothing but a fair smooth floe was before us, sweeping with a curve to the base of Cape Walker. But a fresh difficulty was then met with. The total absence of hummocks or berg-pieces made it most difficult to preserve a course in the thick foggy weather that lasted whilst a warm south wind blew. Imagine, kind reader, a greyish haze, with fast-falling snow; a constant wind in the face, and yourself trying to steer a straight course where floe and sky were of one uniform colour. A hand wind-vane was found the best guide, for of course is was impossible to keep a compass constantly in hand: and the officers, forming in a line ahead so as just to keep a good sight of one another, were followed by the sledges. The sledge crews soon learnt that the easiest mode of travelling, and the most equal division of labour, consisted in marching directly after one another; and as the leading sledge had the extra work of forming the road through the snow, and straining the men's eyes in keeping sight of the officers, the foremost sledge was changed every half hour.

It will be seen that we travelled at night, and hoped by such means to avoid the glare of the sun and consequent snow-blindness. It entailed, however, at this early season of the year, great suffering in the shape of cold; the people being exposed to the weather during the severest part of the day. From the 15th to the 19th the weather was of the same nature – constant gales in our faces, snow-storms and heavy drift against which we struggled, helped somewhat by a rising temperature that we flattered ourselves would end in summer – a mistake for which we afterwards suffered bitterly.

Easter Sunday came in gloomily, with the wind inclined to veer to the northward, and with every appearance of bad weather. Setting our sails on the sledges, and kites likewise when the wind served, the division hurried on for Cape Walker which loomed now and then through the snow-drift ahead of us. The rapidity of the pace at which we now advanced – thanks to the help afforded by the sails – threw all into a profuse perspiration, especially the seamen, who really looked as if they were toiling under a tropical sun rather than in an Arctic night.

During the sleeping hours the increased attention to the fur covering, and the carefully closed door, told us that the temperature was falling; and the poor cook, with a rueful countenance, announced that it was below zero as he prepared the morning meal. More than usual difficulty was found in pulling on our stiffly-frozen boots, stockings, and outer garments; and when the men went out of the tent they soon found their clothing becoming perfectly hard from the action of the intense cold on what had been for several days saturated with perspiration. To march briskly was now the only safety, and in double quick time tents were down, and sledges moving. A nor'-wester was fast turning up, and as the night of Easter Monday closed around us the cold increased with alarming rapidity. One of those magnificent conglomerations of halos common to these regions lit up the northern heavens, and by the brilliancy of colouring and startling number of false suns seemed to be mocking the sufferings of our gallant fellows who, with faces averted and bended bodies, strained every nerve to reach the land in hopes of obtaining more shelter than the naked floe afforded from the cutting gale. Every moment some fresh case of frost-bite would occur. The man would fall out from his sledge, restore the circulation of the affected part, (generally the face), and then hasten back to his post. Constant questions of "How are your feet?" were heard on all sides, with the general response, "Oh! I hope they are all right; but I've not felt them since I pulled my boots on."

One halt was made to remove and change all leather boots which, in consequence of our late warm weather, had been taken into use, but were now no longer safe. And then the piled-up floe around the cliffs of Cape Walker was reached. Cold and hungry as we were, it must have been a heavy barrier indeed to have stopped our men from taking their sledges to the land; and piled as the floe was against the Cape full fifty feet high, we carried our craft over it in safety, and just in time too, for the north-west wind rushed down upon us as if to dispute our right to intrude on its dominion.

Hastily securing the tents, we hurried in to change our boots and to see whether our feet were frost-bitten or not; for it was only by ocular proof that one could be satisfied of their safety, sensation having long ceased. I shall not easily forget my painful feelings when one gallant fellow of my party, the captain of the sledge, exclaimed, "Both feet gone, sir," and sure enough they were, white as two lumps of ice, and equally cold; for as we of the tent party anxiously in turn placed our warm hands on the frost-bitten feet the heat was extracted in a marvellously short time, and our half-frozen hands had to be succeeded by fresh ones as quickly as possible. With returning circulation the poor fellow's agonies must have been intense; and some hours afterwards large blisters formed over the frost-bitten parts as if the feet had been severely scalded.

Sadly cramped as we were for room, much worse was it when a sick man was amongst our number. Sleep was out of the question; and to roll up in the smallest possible compass and try to think of something else than the cold, which pierced to the very marrow in one's bones, was our only resource.

As it is not my intention to give a detailed account of the operations of the Southern Sledge Division, but merely to tell of those events which will convey to the reader a general idea of the incidents connected with this kind of Arctic travelling, I shall without further comment give these, leaving to the curious in the minutiae of the journeys the amusement of reading in the Admiralty Blue Books the details of when we ate, drank, slept, or marched.

Every mile that we advanced showed us that the coast was one which could only be approachable by ships at extraordinary seasons; the ice appeared to be the accumulation of many years. Then we passed into a region with still more aged features: there the inequalities on the surface, occasioned by the repeated snows of winter and thaws of summer, gave it the appearance of a constant succession of hill and dale. Entangled amongst it, our men laboured with untiring energy, up steep acclivities and through pigmy ravines in which the loose snow caused them to sink deeply, and sadly increased their toil. To avoid this description of ice, amongst which a lengthened journey became perfectly hopeless, we struck in for the land, preferring the heavy snow that encumbered the beach to such a heart-breaking struggle as that on the floe.

The injury had, however, been done during our last day's labour amongst the hummocks; a fine clear evening had given us the full effects of a powerful sunlight upon the pure snow; the painful effect of which, those alone can conceive who have experienced it. All was white, brilliant and dazzling; the eye in vain turned from earth to heaven for rest or shade — there was none;

an unclouded sunlight poured through the calm and frosty air with merciless power, and the sun, being exactly in our faces, increased the intensity of its effects.

That day several complained of a dull aching sensation in the eyeball, and on the morrow blindness was rapidly coming on. From experience I can speak of the mental anxiety which also supervened at the thought of one's entire helplessness, and the encumbrance one had become to others who, God knows, had troubles and labour enough of their own. Gradually the film spread itself, objects became dimmer and dimmer, and at last all was darkness, with an intense horror of the slightest ray of sunlight.

Unable to advance, in consequence of a severe gale which raged for six-and-thirty hours, we found, on the 1st of May, that sixteen men and one officer were more or less snow-blind and otherwise unwell; a large proportion out of the entire number of thirty souls. To be ill in any place is trying enough; but such an hospital as a brown-holland tent, with the thermometer in it at 18° below zero, the snow for a bed, your very breath forming into a small snow called "barber" which penetrated into your very innermost garments, and no water to be procured to assuage the thirst of fever until snow had been melted for the purpose, called for much patience on the part of the sufferers. Happily, the effects of snow-blindness are not lasting, for we recovered as suddenly as we had been struck down. The gale blew itself out leaving all calm and still, and again we plodded onwards, parting from the last supporting sledge on the 6th of May.

It was under such unprofitable labour that the sterling value of our men the more conspicuously showed itself. Captain Ommanney, myself, and Mr. Webb, were now the only three officers; we were consequently thrown much into the society of the men, and I feel assured I am not singular in saying that that intercourse served much to raise our opinion of the character and indomitable spirit of our seamen and marines. On them fell the hard labour, to us fell the honours of the enterprise, and to our chief the reward; yet none equalled the men in cheerfulness and hopefulness of a successful issue. Gallant fellows! they met our commiseration with a smile, and a vow that they could do far more. They spoke of cold as "Jack Frost," a real tangible foe with whom they could combat and would master. Hunger was met with a laugh, and a chuckle at some future feast, or recollections told, in rough terms, of bygone good cheer; and often, standing on some neighbouring pile of ice and scanning the horizon for those we sought, have I heard a rough voice encouraging the sledge crew by saying, "Keep step, boys! keep step! she (the sledge) is coming along almost by herself; there's the *Erebus*'s masts showing over the point ahead! Keep step, boys! keep step!"

We had our moments of pleasure too – plenty of them in spite of the cold and fatigue. There was an honest congratulation after a good day's work; there was the time after the pemmican had been eaten, and each one, drawing up his blanket-bag around him sat, pannikin in hand, and received from the cook the half gill of grog; and after drinking it there was sometimes an hour's conversation in which there was more hearty merriment, I trow, than in many a palace – dry witticisms or caustic remarks which made one's sides ache with laughter. An old marine, mayhap, telling a giddy lamby of a seaman to take his advice and never to be more than a simple private; for, as he philosophically argued, "Whilst you're that, do you see, you have to think of nothing; there are petty officers, officers, captains, and admirals paid for looking after you and taking care of you!"

On the 17th May the "Reliance" and "True Blue" sledges parted company, each having provisions left to enable them to advance for a further period of five days. Captain Ommanney generously allowing me, his junior, to take the search up in a westerly direction, whilst he went down the channel to the southward, which after all ended in a blind bay.* I went some fifty miles farther and, finding the coast trend to the south, endeavoured to march in a westerly direction across the floe. The sledge was light, with only ten days' provision, and the men were well inured to their work; but I saw from the severe strains which were brought on the fastenings of the sledge that wood, iron, and lashings would not long stand it; and as, every foot we advanced, progress became more laborious, and risk greater, I desisted in the attempt. Situated as we were, nigh three hundred miles from our ship, the breaking down of the sledge would have entailed fearful misery, if not destruction, to my party.

The journey homeward was light work since the sledges were now half emptied; and by forced marches we succeeded in making

* Now Ommanney Bay.

two days' journey in one, thereby giving ourselves a double quantity of food to consume.

At last Griffith's Island rose above the horizon; a five-and-twenty-mile march brought us to it, and another heavy drag through the melting snow carried us to our ships on the 12th of June, after a journey of five hundred miles in direct lines, in fifty-eight days.

The floes around our ships were entirely covered with the water of the melted snow, in some places full four feet in depth, eating its way rapidly through in all directions, when at last Lieutenant M'Clintock's sledge, the "Perseverance" hove in sight, having been out exactly eighty days. Lieutenant M'Clintock had been to Winter Harbour on Melville Island and visited all the points known to Parry's squadron, but found no traces of Franklin. He had, however, brought substantial proofs of the extraordinary abundance of animal life in that remote region, in the hides and heads of musk-oxen, the meat of which had helped to bring back his crew in wonderful condition.

Lieutenant M'Clintock had fairly won the palm — in eighty days he had travelled eight hundred miles, and heartily did we congratulate him on his success.

All of the eastern search groups returned to their home ports during the summer of 1851, having added nothing to the solution of the Franklin mystery other than the discovery of the wintering place on Beechey Island. In the west, however, Collinson and M'Clure kept their two ships in the ice, and with some remarkable results.

To the south and east Collinson penetrated the channels between the mainland and the off-lying Arctic islands as far as Cambridge Bay where he was within a few hundred miles of demonstrating the existence of a Northwest Passage in these relatively southern waters. After spending three winters in the ice, Collinson finally managed to extricate his ship and turn westward for home.

Meanwhile, M'Clure had worked farther to the north, following Prince of Wales Strait (between Banks and Victoria Islands) until the ice stopped him just short of Melville Sound. Here his ship, H.M.S. Investigator, *was trapped even as Ross's* Victory *had been fatally trapped in Victoria Harbour. Realizing that he could never free her from the ice, M'Clure set out by sled in the spring of 1852, in a desperate bid to find assistance. He made his way to Winter Harbour on Melville Island (first reached by Parry's ships from the east in 1819, and revisited by M'Clintock, by sled, in 1851) but found no sign of human life. He did not know that the whole eastern armada had already returned to England, and this may have been as well for his peace of mind. But if he found no help, M'Clure at least had the cold comfort of knowing that he had established the existence of a Northwest Passage in this direction, even though it was permanently ice-blocked, and impassable to vessels of those times. Leaving a message at Winter Harbour he returned to his ship and spent another scurvy-ridden winter in the ice. He and his men would certainly have perished the following year but for the message left at Winter Harbour.*

So ended the most formidable single assault that the Arctic ice had yet sustained. Much had been discovered about the island complex – but nothing had been discovered about Franklin's fate. The prime reason for this lack of success lay in the fact that the Admiralty, with almost inconceivable stupidity, had chosen to ignore its own original orders to Franklin – that he should attempt to find a passage to the south *of Lancaster Sound – and had instructed the search expeditions to concentrate on the Sound itself, and on the waters to the* north *of it. Coupled with the severe ice conditions which prevented the searchers from sailing past Cornwallis Island in 1850, the Admiralty's incomprehensible instructions virtually ensured the expedition's failure.*

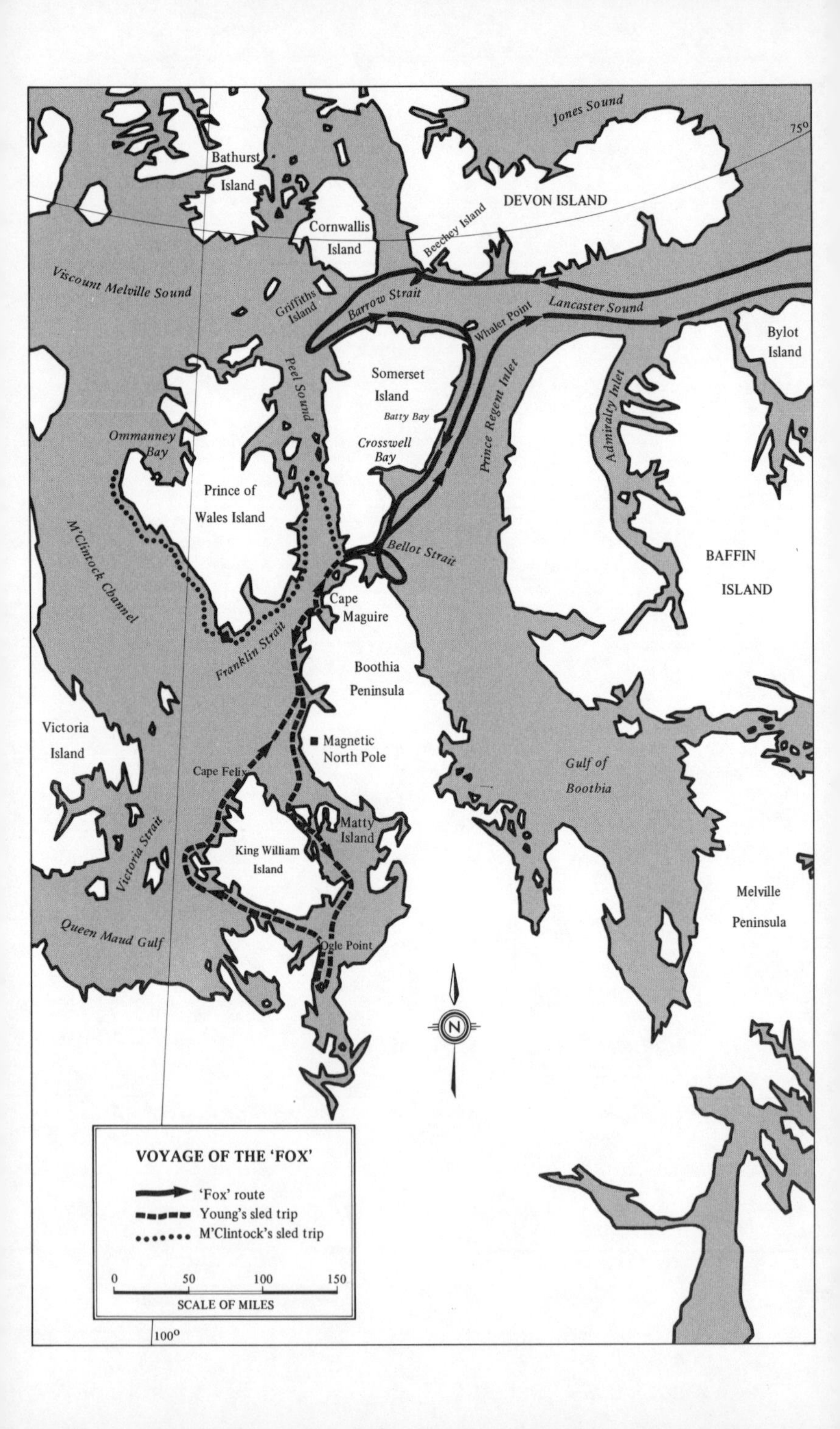
Jones Sound
75°
Bathurst Island
Cornwallis Island
DEVON ISLAND
Beechey Island
Viscount Melville Sound
Griffiths Island
Barrow Strait
Lancaster Sound
Whaler Point
Bylot Island
Somerset Island
Batty Bay
Crosswell Bay
Peel Sound
Prince Regent Inlet
Admiralty Inlet
Ommanney Bay
Prince of Wales Island
M'Clintock Channel
Bellot Strait
BAFFIN ISLAND
Cape Maguire
Franklin Strait
Boothia Peninsula
Victoria Island
Magnetic North Pole
Cape Felix
Gulf of Boothia
Matty Island
King William Island
Victoria Strait
Queen Maud Gulf
Ogle Point
Melville Peninsula
N
VOYAGE OF THE 'FOX'
'Fox' route
Young's sled trip
M'Clintock's sled trip
0
50
100
150
SCALE OF MILES
100°

X

The Fate of Franklin

A solution to the Franklin mystery continued to be unlikely while there was no change in the character of the official rescue effort. Although Lady Franklin, supported by a number of Arctic travellers who were outside the pale of Admiralty approval, maintained that the search should be concentrated to the south of Lancaster Sound, the Sea Lords ignored her pleas. Thus, when the Admiralty mounted its final effort in 1852, it again sent the searchers in the wrong directions.

In that year Sir Edward Belcher, who seems to have been one of the most incompetent dunderheads on record, was placed in command of a two-pronged expedition to finally resolve the mystery. The same four ships used by Austin in 1850 were engaged. Resolute, *and* Pioneer *(with Osborn still in command of her), were directed up Wellington Channel, while* Assistance *and* Intrepid *(the latter commanded by M'Clintock) were ordered west down Lancaster Sound to Melville Sound. These last two vessels actually reached Winter Harbour, but decided not to remain there, and pulled back to the west without discovering M'Clure's message. Fortunately, one of their sledging parties, sent out in the spring of 1883, again visited Winter Harbour, found the message, and was the means of saving M'Clure and his men. When a sledging team reached the* Investigator *it was to find almost all of those aboard in an advanced state of scurvy.* Investigator *was abandoned and her people taken to* Assistance *and* Intrepid.

The crews of these two ships, under the command of Captain Henry Kellett, were responsible for a magnificent series of sled explorations which surveyed the coasts of Melville and Prince Patrick Islands during the two winters that the expedition remained in the ice. It was another thrust to the north-west, but in quite the wrong direction to reveal anything new about Franklin.

Belcher, meanwhile, had been poking about in Wellington Channel, and getting almost as far from the area of Franklin's instructions as Kellett was. Then, in the spring of 1854, Belcher quite incomprehensibly ordered the abandonment of all four *of his search ships, recalled all their people to Beechey Island, loaded them aboard some transports there, and sailed hurriedly for England. It was an ironic comment on this panic-stricken flight that, some sixteen months after she was abandoned, Belcher's flag-ship, the old* Resolute, *piloted* herself *out of the ice, made her way quite without human aid more than a thousand miles to Cape Dyer in Davis Strait, and there fell in with an American whaling vessel. When the whalers recovered from the shock of meeting her, they put a crew aboard, and in due course she sailed majestically back across the Western Sea to England, where her arrival must have had an interesting effect on Belcher.*

With the Belcher debacle, the official search for Franklin was concluded. Although it had brought no aid to the vanished men it had resulted in the exploration of a vast area of Arctic sea and islands. And, equally important, it had helped to give birth to a brand new kind of Arctic traveller.

This new breed of Arctic venturer was exemplified by two men: John Rae and Leopold M'Clintock.

On behalf of the Hudson's Bay Company, Rae had made two extraordinary overland journeys into the Arctic prior to 1852, and he had been quick to understand that survival in the north had to be on the land's own terms. He was the first to reach the obvious conclusion that, since Eskimos could live, travel and prosper in the Arctic, explorers would do well to imitate the Eskimos.

M'Clintock was also groping toward a realization of this fact, and both men had demonstrated a flexibility which none of the earlier explorers, except possibly John Ross, apparently possessed. In the years following Belcher's massive failure, these two men were to drive home the point that victory in the Arctic could not be achieved by force.

Rae led the way. In 1853-54 he was engaged in searching the west coast of Boothia, travelling by dog-sled in native style, when he encountered a group of Eskimos from whom he heard the first reports of a ghastly catastrophe which had overwhelmed a large group of white men — clearly the Franklin party — on and near King William's Island. Rae did not personally visit the site of the tragedy but hastened south with his news — appalling and macabre news, which reached England in the early winter of 1854.

England's reaction was electric. The public was scandalized and horrified to hear that the entire Franklin expedition had evidently perished of starvation and exposure, and, even worse, that its members had apparently engaged in cannibalism during their final hours. Public opinion turned savagely against Rae, preferring to believe that Eskimos had killed and eaten the ship-wrecked men, rather than that they had died as the result of the inflexibility and incompetence of their leaders.

Lady Franklin, still hoping, and still magnificently striving (after having spent most of her personal fortune on three fruitless private expeditions) took no stand in this unpalatable controversy; but she insisted that it was imperative that an expedition should be sent immediately to King William's Island in order to discover the whole truth of what had happened.

The Admiralty, and indeed all official circles, turned their backs upon her. They had lost interest in the Franklin affair and, it may be, were only too anxious to forget it. Nevertheless, Lady Franklin still had sympathizers, and foremost amongst these was Leopold M'Clintock.

As a young Lieutenant in the Navy, M'Clintock had first gone north with the earliest Franklin "relief" party, the James Ross expedition of 1848-49, during which he did considerable sledge travelling in the then-fashionable manner, with sailors pulling heavily overladen sleds while the officers kept themselves aloof from work; and where there was little or no reliance upon living off the land. M'Clintock at once recognized the basic stupidity of this procedure and, during his next Arctic voyage, with Captain Austin's expedition in 1850, he began to experiment, not only with new and lighter sleds and equipment, but with the general possibilities of adapting himself and his material to the real nature of the country. Though still relying on man-power, his experiments were so successful that, as we have seen, he was able to sledge from Cornwallis Island to Melville Island; a return journey of eight hundred miles accomplished in eighty-one days.

Between 1852 and 1854 he was in the north again with Kellett's division of Belcher's squadron; and this time he surpassed himself by successfully completing one of the greatest sled journeys of all time, during which he travelled more than fourteen hundred miles in a hundred and five days, incidentally discovering nearly eight hundred miles of previously unknown coastline.

Perceptive, flexible, possessed of a saving sense of humour, and with an unparallelled experience in Arctic travel, he was the obvious man for Lady Franklin to turn to in this, her final attempt to lay the ghosts of the Franklin expedition.

THE VOYAGE OF THE *FOX* IN THE ARCTIC SEAS

Outward Bound

On the 18th of April, 1857, Lady Franklin did me the honour to offer me the command of the proposed expedition.

I applied to the Admiralty for leave of absence and on the 23rd received a telegraphic message from Lady Franklin: "Your leave is granted; the *Fox* is mine; the refit will commence immediately." She had already purchased the screw-yacht *Fox*, of 177 tons burthen, and now placed her, together with the necessary funds, at my disposal.

Let me explain what is here implied by the simple word refit. The velvet hangings and splendid furniture of the yacht, and also everything not constituting a part of the vessel's strengthening, were to be removed. The whole vessel was to be externally sheathed with stout planking, and internally fortified by strong cross-beams, the slender brass propeller replaced by a massive iron one, and the sharp stem to be cased in iron until it resembled a ponderous chisel set up edgeways. Eventually, like the Paris omnibuses, we were *tout complet*, and quite as anxious to make a start.

Ample provisions for twenty-eight months were embarked, including preserved vegetables, lemon-juice and pickles for daily consumption; and preserved meats for every third day; also as much of Messrs. Allsopp's stoutest ale as we could find room for.

On the night of the 2nd July we passed through the Pentland Firth. The bleak wild shores of Orkney, the still wilder pilot's crew, and their hoarse screams and unintelligible dialect, the shrill cry of innumerable sea-birds, the howling breeze and angry sea, made us feel as if we had suddenly awoke in Greenland, the southern extremity of which ice-locked continent itself became visible on the 12th. It is quaintly named Cape Farewell; but whether by some sanguine outward-bound adventurer who fancied that in leaving Greenland behind him he had already secured his passage to Cathay; or whether by the wearied homesick mariner, feebly escaping from the grasp of winter in his shattered bark, and firmly purposing to bid a long farewell to this cheerless land, history altogether fails to enlighten us.

For trading purposes Greenland is monopolized by the Danish government. The Esquimaux are not subject to Danish laws, but although proud of their nominal independence, they are sincerely attached to the Danes, and with abundant reason; a Lutheran clergyman, a doctor, and a schoolmaster, whose duty it is to give gratuitous instruction and relief, are paid by the Government, and attached to each district, and when the Esquimaux are in distress, which not infrequently happens during the long winters, provisions are issued to them free of cost.

Have we English done more, or as much, for the aborigines in any of our numerous colonies, and especially for the Esquimaux within our own territories of Labrador and Hudson's Bay?

On July 31st we anchored at Godhaven on Disko Island, and here I met with the late commanders of the whalers *Gipsy* and *Undaunted* of Peterhead, which had been crushed by the ice in Melville Bay five or six weeks previously. Here also a young Esquimaux named Christian volunteered his services as our dog-driver, and was accepted. The men soon thoroughly washed and cropped him (soap and scissors being novelties to an Esquimaux); they then rigged him in sailor's clothes. He was evidently not at home in them, but was not the less proud of his improved appearance, as reflected in the admiring glances of his countrymen.

5th August. A pleasant fair wind carries us rapidly northward from Disko, passing many icebergs. Our rigging is richly garnished with split codfish, which we hoped would dry and keep; but a warm day in Disko Fiord, and much rain with a southerly gale in the Waigat, have destroyed it for our own use. It is however still valuable as food for our dogs. I am very anxious to complete my stock of these, our native auxiliaries, as without them we cannot hope to explore all the lands which it is the object of our voyage to search.

7th August. We hove-to off Upernivik. The weather was very bad and rapidly growing worse, therefore our stay was limited to a couple of hours. The last letters for home were landed; fourteen dogs and a quantity of seal's flesh for them embarked, and the ship's head was turned seaward.

Being at last fairly at sea, and the ship under easy sail for the night, I went early to bed in the hope of sleeping. I had been up all the previous night, naturally anxious about the ship threading her way through so many dangers, uncertain about being able to complete the number of our sledge-dogs, and much occupied in closing my correspondence to which there would be an end for at least a year. All this over, the uncertain future loomed ominously before me. The great responsibilities I had undertaken seemed now to fall with all their weight upon me. A mental whirlpool was the consequence, which, backed by the material storm, and the howling of the wretched dogs in concert on deck, together with the tumbling about of everything below, long kept sleep in abeyance.

Now, to the uninitiated, it may be as well to observe that each winter the sea called Baffin's Bay freezes over; in spring this vast body of ice breaks up, and drifting southward in a mass – called the main-pack, or the middle ice – obstructs the passage across from east to west.

The "North Passage" is made by sailing round the north end of this pack; the "Middle Passage" by pushing through it; and the "Southern Passage" by passing round its southern extreme; but seasons occur when none of these routes are practicable.

12th August. We are in Melville Bay; made fast this afternoon to an iceberg which lies aground in 58 fathoms water. We have got thus far without any difficulty, sailing along the edge of the middle ice; but here we find it pressing in against Browne's Islands, and covering the whole bay to the northward.

There is much to excite intense admiration and wonder around us; one cannot at once appreciate the grandeur of the mighty glacier, which here takes the place of a coast line and extends unbroken for forty or fifty miles. Its sea-cliffs, about five or six miles from us, appear comparatively low, yet the icebergs detached from it are of the loftiest description. Here, on the spot, it does not seem incorrect to compare the icebergs to mere chippings off its edge, and the floe-ice to the thinnest shavings.

There is an unusual dearth of birds and seals; everything around us is painfully still, excepting where an occasional iceberg splits off from the parent glacier; then we hear a rumbling crash like distant thunder, and the wave occasioned by the launch reaches us in six or seven minutes, and makes the ship roll lazily.

16th August. One of the loveliest mornings imaginable; the icebergs sparkled in the sun, and the breeze was just sufficiently strong to ripple the patches of dark blue sea; beyond this there was nothing to cheer one in the prospect from the crow's-nest at four o'clock, for little change had taken place in the ice which blocked a northern passage, and I therefore determined to run back along the pack-edge to the south-westward in the hope that some favourable change might have taken place further off shore.

As we steamed on, the ice was found to have opened considerably. By noon a S.E. wind reached us; all sail was set, the leads or lanes of water became wider, and our hopes of speedily crossing Melville Bay rose in proportion as our speed increased. We are pursuing our course without let or hindrance.

19th August. Continued strong S.E. winds, pressing the ice closely together, dark sky and snow; everything wears a wintry and threatening aspect; we are closely hemmed in, and have our rudder and screw unshipped. This recommencement of S.E. winds and rapid ebbing of the small remaining portion of summer makes me more anxious about the future than the present. Yesterday the weather improved, and by working for thirteen hours we got the ship out of a small ice-creek into a larger space of water and in so doing advanced a mile and a half.

20th August. No favourable ice-drift; this detention has become most painful. There is no relative motion in the floes of ice, except a gradual closing together, the small spaces and streaks of water being still further diminished. The temperature has fallen, and is usually below the freezing point. I feel most keenly the difficulty of my position; we cannot afford to lose many more days.

The men enjoy a game of rounders on the ice each evening; Petersen, our interpreter, and Christian, our Eskimo lad, are constantly on the look-out for seals. If in good condition and killed instantaneously, the seals float; several have already been shot; the liver fried with bacon is excellent.

24th August. Fine weather with very light northerly winds. We have drifted 7 miles to the west in the last two days. The ice is now a close pack, so close that one may walk for many miles over it in any direction. My frequent visits to the crow's-nest are not inspiriting: how absolutely distressing this imprisonment is to me, no one without similar experience can form any idea. As yet the crew have but little suspicion how blighted our prospects are.

The Winter in the Pack

27th August. The dreaded reality of wintering in the pack of Baffin's Bay is gradually forcing itself upon my mind – but I must not write on this subject, it is bad enough to brood over it unceasingly. We can see the land all round Melville Bay, from Cape Walker nearly to Cape York. Petersen is indefatigable at seal-shooting, he is so anxious to secure them for our dogs. He says they must be hit in the head; "If you hit him in the beef that is not good," meaning that a flesh-wound does not prevent their escaping under the ice.

30th August. Yesterday we set to work as usual to warp the ship along, and moved her ten feet; an insignificant hummock then blocked up the narrow passage. As we could not push it before us, a two-pound blasting charge was exploded and the surface ice was shattered, but such an immense quantity of broken ice came up from beneath that the difficulty was greatly increased instead of being removed. This is one of the many instances in which our small vessel labours under very great disadvantages in ice-navigation – we have neither sufficient manual power, steam power, nor impetus to force the floes asunder.

13th September. Thermometer has fallen to 17° at noon. We have drifted 18 miles to the W. in the last week. Forty-three seals have been secured for the dogs; one dog is missing, the remaining twenty-nine devoured their two days' allowance of seal's flesh (60 or 65 lbs.) in forty-two seconds! It contained no bone and had been cut up into small pieces and spread out upon the snow before they were permitted to rush to dinner; in this way the weak enjoy a fair chance, and there is no time for fighting.

18th September. Lanes of water in all directions; but the nearest is half a mile from us. They come too late, as do also the N.W. winds which have now succeeded the fatal south-easters. The temperature fell to 2° below zero last night. We are now at length in the "North Water"; the old ice has spread out in all directions, but the young ice – formed within the last fortnight – detains us prisoners here.

We are doomed to pass a long winter of absolute inutility, if not of idleness, in comparative peril and privation; nevertheless the men seem very happy – thoughtless, of course, as true sailors always are.

27th September. Our salt meat is usually soaked for some days before being used; for this purpose it is put into a net and lowered through a hole in the ice. This morning the net had been torn, and only a fragment of it remained. We supposed our twenty-two pounds of salt meat had been devoured by a shark; it would be curious to know how such fare agrees with him, as a full meal of salted provision will kill an Esquimaux dog, which thrives on almost anything.

It is said that Esquimaux dogs will eat everything except fox and raven. There are exceptions however; one of ours, old "Harness Jack," devoured a raven with much gusto some days ago. All the other dogs allow their harness to be taken off when they are brought on board; but old Jack will not permit himself to be unrobed; when this is attempted he very plainly threatens to use his teeth. This canine oddity suddenly became immensely popular by constituting himself protecting head of the establishment when one of his tribe littered; he took up a most uncomfortable position on top of the family cask (our impromptu kennel), and prevented the approach of all the other dogs. But for his timely interference on behalf of the poor little puppies, I verily believe they would all have been stolen and devoured. Dogs may do even worse than eat raven.

24th October. Furious N.W. and S.E. gales have alternated of late; the ship is housed over to keep out the driving snow. So high is the snow carried in the air that a little box perforated with small holes and triced up 50 feet high on the mast is soon filled up.

28th October – Midnight. This evening, to our great astonishment, there occurred a disruption and movement of the ice within 200 yards of the ship. As I sit now in my cabin I can distinctly hear the ice crushing; it resembles the continued roar of distant surf, and there are many other occasional sounds; some of them remind one of the low moaning of the wind, others are loud and harsh, as if trains of heavy wagons with ungreased axles were slowly labouring along. Upon a less-favoured night these sounds might be appalling; even as it is, they are sufficiently ominous to invite reflection.

2nd November. Having observed some days ago that a few of the dogs were falling away (from some cause or other not having put on their winter clothing before the recent cold weather set in) they were all allowed on board and given a good extra meal. Since then we can scarcely keep them out. One calm night they made a charge and boarded the ship so suddenly that several of the men rushed up very scantily clothed so see what was the matter. Vigorous measures were adopted to expel the intruders, and there was desperate chasing round the deck with broomsticks, &c. Many of them retreated into holes and corners, and two hours elapsed before they were all driven out; but though the chase was hot, it was cold enough work for the half-clad men.

16th November. A renewal of ice-crushing within a few hundred yards of us. I can hear it in my bed. The ordinary sound resembles the roar of distant surf breaking heavily and continuously; but when heavy masses come in collision, it fully realizes the justness of Dr. Kane's descriptive epithet, "ice artillery." Fortunately for us, our poor little *Fox* is well within the margin of a stout old floe: we are therefore undisturbed spectators of ice-conflicts which would be irresistible to anything of human construction. Immediately about the ship all is still and, as far as appearances go, she is precisely as she would be in a secure harbour – housed all over, banked up with snow to her gunwales. In fact her winter plumage is so complete that the masts alone are visible. The deck and the now useless sky-lights are covered with hard snow. Below hatches we are warm and dry; all are in excellent health and spirits, looking forward to an active campaign next winter. God grant it may be realized!

Yesterday Young shot the fiftieth seal, an event duly celebrated by our drinking *the* bottle of champagne which had been set apart in more hopeful times to be drunk on reaching the North Water – that unhappy failure, the more keenly felt from being so very unexpected.

Petersen saw and fired a shot into a narwhal, which brought the blubber out. When most Arctic creatures are wounded in the water, blubber more frequently than blood appears, particularly if the wound is superficial – it spreads over the surface of the water like oil.

Bills of fare vary much, even in Greenland. I have inquired of Petersen, and he tells me that the Greenland Esquimaux are not agreed as to which of their animals affords the most delicious foods; some of them prefer reindeer venison, others think more favourably of young dog, the flesh of which, he asserts, is "just like the beef of a sheep." He says a Danish captain who had acquired the taste, provided some for his guests, and they praised his *mutton*, until after dinner he sent for the skin of the animal, which was no other than a large red dog!

Our dogs are fed every second day, when 2 lbs. of seal's flesh – previously thawed when possible – is given to each; the weaker ones get additional food, and they all pick up whatever scraps are thrown out. This is enough to sustain, but not to satisfy them, so they are continually on the look-out for anything eatable. Hobson made one very happy without intending it; he meant only to give him a kick, but his slipper, being down at heel, flew off, and away went the lucky dog in triumph with the prize, which of course was no more seen.

29th November. Nothing to excite conversation, except an occasional inroad of the dogs in search of food; this generally occurs at night. Whenever the deck-light, which burns under the housing, happens to go out, they scale the steep snow banking and rush round the deck like wolves. "Why, bless you, sir, the very moment that there light goes out, and the quartermaster turns his back, they makes a regular sortee, and in they all comes." "But where do they come in, Harvey?" "Where, sir? why everywheres; they makes no more to do, but in they comes, clean over all."

4th December. I have just returned on board from the performance of the most solemn duty a commander can be called upon to fulfill. A funeral at sea is always peculiarly impressive; but this evening at seven o'clock, as we gathered around the sad remains of poor Scott, reposing under a Union Jack, and read the Burial Service by the light of lanterns, the effect could not fail to awaken very serious emotions.

The greater part of the Church Service was read on board under shelter of the housing; the body was then placed upon a sledge, and drawn by the messmates of the deceased to a short distance from the ship where a hole through the ice had been cut; it was then "committed to the deep." What a scene it was! The lonely *Fox*, almost buried in snow, completely isolated from the habitable world, her colours half-mast high, and bell mournfully tolling; our little procession slowly marching over the rough surface of the frozen sea guided by lanterns and direction-posts, amid the dark and dreary depth of Arctic winter, the death-like stillness, the intense cold, and the threatening aspect of a murky, overcast sky; and all this heightened by one of those strange lunar phenomena which are but seldom seen even here, a complete halo encircling the moon, through which passed a horizontal band of pale light that encompassed the heavens. Above the moon appeared the segments of two other halos, and there were also six mock moons. The misty atmosphere lent a very ghastly hue to this singular display, which lasted for rather more than an hour.

Poor Scott fell down a hatchway two days before his death, which was occasioned by the internal injuries then received. He was our engine-driver; we cannot replace him, therefore the whole duty of working the engines will devolve upon the engineer, Mr. Brand.

27th December. Our Christmas was a very cheerful, merry one. The men were supplied with several additional articles such as hams, plum-puddings, preserved gooseberries and apples, nuts, sweetmeats, and Burton ale. After Divine Service they decorated the lower deck with flags, and made an immense display of food. The officers came down with me to see their preparations. We were really astonished! The mess-tables were laid out like the counters in a confectioner's shop, with apple and gooseberry tarts, plum and sponge-cakes in pyramids, besides various other unknown puffs, cakes, and loaves of all sizes and shapes. In the background were nicely-browned hams, meat-pies, cheeses, and other substantial articles. Rum and water in wine glasses, and plum-cake, were handed to us; we wished them a happy Christmas, and complimented them on their taste and spirit in getting up such a display.

28th January, 1858. The upper edge of the sun appeared above the horizon today, after an absence of eighty-nine days; it was a gladdening sight. I sent for the ship's steward and asked what was the custom on such occasions. "To hoist the colours and serve out an extra half-gill, sir," was the ready reply. Accordingly, the Harwich lion soon fluttered in a breeze cool enough to stiffen the limbs of ordinary lions, and in the evening the grog was issued.

15th February, 1858. Daylight reveals to us evidences of vast ice movements having taken place during the dark months when we fancied all was quiet; and we now see how greatly we have been favoured, what innumerable chances of destruction we have unconsciously escaped! A few days ago the ice suddenly cracked within ten yards of the ship and gave her such a smart shock that every one rushed on deck with astonishing alacrity. One of these sudden disruptions occurred between me and the ship when I was returning from an iceberg and I found myself cut off. Had I been on the other side of the crack, I would have loitered to enjoy a refreshing gaze upon this dark streak of water; but after a smart run of about a mile along its edge, and finding no place to cross, visions of a patrol on the floe for the long night of fifteen hours began to obtrude themselves! But at length I reached a place where the jagged edges of the floes met, so crossed and got safely on board.

On the 24th of February there was a fearful gale of wind. Had not our housing been very well secured, it must have been blown away. We are preparing for sea, removing the snow from off the deck and round the ship; our skylights have been dug out and the flood of light which beams down through them is quite charming. How intolerably sooty and smoke-dried everything looks!

23rd March. Yesterday was a very heavy S.E. gale; it blew so furiously, and the snow drift was so dense, that we could neither hear nor see what was going on twenty yards off. At night the ship, becoming suddenly detached from the ice, heeled over to the storm.

25th March. Strong N.W. winds lately, the ship rocking to the breeze and rubbing her poor sides against the ice, producing a creaking sound which is far from pleasant. More ice squeezing, and a further inroad upon our barrier floe; it has yielded slightly, nipping the ship, inclining her to port and lifting her stern about a foot. Occasional groanings within, and surgings of the ice without.

Our boats, provisions, sledges, knapsacks, and equipment, are ready for a hasty departure – beyond this we can do nothing. As long as our friendly ice barrier lasts we need not fear, but who can tell the moment it may be demolished, and the ship exposed to destruction?

6th April. Today we enjoy fine weather, the more so since it comes after a tremendous northerly gale of forty-eight hours' duration. Two days ago our friendly old floe, so long our bulwark of defence, was cracked; the lane of water thus formed soon widened to 60 yards, passed within 30 yards of the *Fox*, and cut off three of our boats which had been put out on the ice. Yesterday morning another crack detached the remaining 30 yards from us and, as it widened, the ship swung at right-angles across the opening. As quickly as we could effect it the ship was again placed alongside the ice and within a projecting point. Had the lane closed only a few feet whilst she lay across it, the consequences to us must have been very serious. Even to effect this slight change of position we were fully occupied for four hours; for the gale blew furiously, and the thermometer stood at 12° below zero, and the cold was very much felt. Our hawsers were frozen so stiff as to be quite unmanageable, and we were obliged to use the chain cables to warp the ship into safety.

12th April. This morning we drifted ingloriously out of Davis Strait and south across the Arctic Circle, and with what very different feelings from those with which we crossed the Circle northbound eight months ago!

18th April. Yesterday morning when I wrote up my journal, I was hoping to hold on quietly to the floe-edge until the wind moderated, when with clear weather we could take advantage of the openings and make some progress towards the clear sea. We were unable to hold on, for the floe-edge broke away, setting us adrift. Some time was occupied in fetching aboard the boats and dogs – five of the latter unfortunately would not allow themselves to be caught. As speedily as possible the rudder was shipped and sail set, and before three o'clock the ship was running fast to the eastward. But during the night the ice closed, and at daylight scarcely any water was visible.

Yesterday three bears, a fulmar petrel, and a snow bunting were seen; today a fine bear came within 150 yards, and was shot by our sportsmen. It seems hardly right to call polar bears *land* animals; they abound here – 120 miles from the nearest land – upon very loose broken-up ice which is steadily drifting into the Atlantic at the rate of 12 or 14 miles daily. To remain upon it would insure their destruction were they not nearly amphibious. They hunt by scent and are constantly running across and against the wind, which prevails from the northward, so that the same instinct which directs their search for prey also serves the important purpose of guiding them in the direction of the land and more solid ice.

I remarked that the upper part of both Bruin's fore-paws were rubbed quite bare; Petersen explains that to surprise the seal a bear crouches down with his fore-paws doubled underneath, and pushes himself noiselessly forward with his hinder legs until within a few yards, when he springs upon the unsuspecting victim, whether in the water or upon the ice.

24th April. Today we have had a strong S.E. breeze, with snow and dark weather. The wind had greatly moderated when the swell reached us about eight o'clock this evening. It is now ten o'clock; the long ocean swell already lifts its crest five feet above the hollow of the sea, causing its thick covering of icy fragments to dash against each other and against us with unpleasant violence. It is, however, very beautiful to look upon, the dear old familiar ocean-swell! It has long been a stranger to us, and is welcome in our solitude. If the *Fox* was as solid as her neighbours, I am quite sure she would enter into this ice-tournament with all their apparent heartiness, instead of audibly making known her sufferings to us. Every considerable surface of ice has been broken into many smaller ones; with feelings of exultation I watched the process from aloft.

Deliverance

26th April. At sea! How am I to describe the events of the last two days?

On Saturday night, the 24th, I went on deck to spend the greater part of it in watching, and to determine what to do. The swell greatly increased; it had evidently been approaching for hours before it reached us, since it rose in proportion as the ice was broken up into smaller pieces. In a short time but few pieces were equal in size to the ship's deck; most of them being not half so large. I knew that near the pack-edge the sea would be very heavy and dangerous; but the wind was now fair and, having auxiliary steampower, I resolved to push out of the ice if possible.

Shortly after midnight the ship was under sail, slowly boring her way to the eastward. At two o'clock on Sunday morning we commenced steaming, the wind having failed. By eight o'clock we had advanced considerably to the eastward and the swell had become dangerously high, the waves rising ten feet above the trough of the sea. The shocks of the ice against the ship were alarmingly heavy; it became necessary to steer exactly head-on to the swell. We slowly passed a small iceberg 60 or 70 feet high; the swell forced it crashing through the pack, leaving a small water-space in its wake, sufficient to allow the seas to break against its cliffs and throw the spray in heavy showers quite over its summit.

The day wore on without change, except that the snow and mists cleared off. Gradually the swell increased, and rolled along more swiftly. The ice often lay so closely packed that we could hardly forge ahead, although the fair wind had again freshened up. Much heavy hummocky ice and large berg-pieces lay dispersed through the pack; a single thump from any of them would have been instant destruction. By five o'clock the ice became more loose, and clear spaces of water could be seen ahead. We went faster, received fewer, though still more severe, shocks until at length we had room to steer clear of the heaviest pieces; and at eight o'clock we emerged from the villainous "pack," and were running fast through straggling pieces into a clear sea. The engines were stopped, and Mr. Brand permitted to rest after eighteen hours' duty, for we now have no one else capable of driving the engines.

Throughout the day I trembled for the safety of the rudder, and screw; deprived of the one or the other, even for half an hour, I think our fate would have been sealed.

Our bow is very strongly fortified, well plated externally with iron, and so very sharp that the ice-masses, repeatedly hurled against the ship by the swell as she rose to meet it, were thus robbed of their destructive force; they struck us obliquely, yet caused the vessel to shake violently, the bells to ring, and almost knocked us off our legs. On many occasions the engines were stopped dead by ice choking the screw; once it was some minutes before it could be got to revolve again. Anxious moments those!

During our 242 days in the packed ice of Baffin's Bay and Davis' Straits we drifted southward 1385 statute miles; it is the longest drift I know of.

We are steering now for Holsteinborg in Greenland, where I intend to refit and refresh the crew.

After refitting at Holsteinborg, M'Clintock slowly forced the Fox *through the ice to Lancaster Sound. It was not until August 10th, however, that he succeeded in working his way into the Sound as far as Beechey Island, that small but famous mound of rock which had been the final point of departure for almost every expedition into the Eastern approaches to the high Arctic, since Franklin wintered there in 1845.*

11th August. Before noon today we anchored inside Cape Riley. I visited Beechey Island house and found the door open; it must have been blown in by an easterly gale long ago, for much ice had accumulated immediately inside it. Most of the biscuit in bags was damaged, but everything else left here by previous expeditions was in perfect order.

Sunday, 15th August. I had found, lying at Godhaven, a marble memorial tablet which had been sent out by Lady Franklin to memorialize her lost husband and his men. It had been sent with an American expedition of 1855 under Captain Hartstein, to be erected at Beechey Island. Circumstances prevented the Americans executing this kindly service, and it fell to my lot to convey it to the site originally intended. I now placed the monument upon the raised flagged square, in the centre of which stands the cenotaph recording the names of those who perished in the Franklin search expedition under Sir Edward Belcher.

17th August. Last night battling westward against a strong foul wind with sea, in rain and fog. Today much loose ice is seen southward of Griffith's Island. The weather improved this afternoon, and we shot gallantly past Limestone Island, and are now steering down Peel Strait on the direct path to King William's Island; all of us in a wild state of excitement – a mingling of anxious hopes and fears!

18th August. For 25 miles last evening we ran unobstructedly down Peel Strait, but then came in sight of unbroken ice extending across it from shore to shore! It was much decayed, and of one year's growth only; yet as the Strait continues to contract for 60 miles further, and it appeared to me to afford so little hope of becoming navigable in the short remainder of the season, I immediately turned back for Prince Regent Inlet and Bellot Strait, as affording a better prospect of a passage into the western sea.

20th August. Noon. Exactly off Fury Point in Prince Regent Inlet. We feel that the crisis of our voyage is near at hand. Does Bellot Strait really exist? If so, is it free of ice?

21st August. On approaching Brentford Bay last evening, packed ice was seen streaming out of it, also much ice in the S.E. The northern point of entrance was landed upon by Sir John Ross in 1829 and named Possession Point. As we rounded it to beat into the Bay, we could distinguish a few stones piled upon a large rock near its highest part – this is his cairn.

At the turn of the tide we perceived that we were being carried, together with the pack, out of the mouth of the Strait and back to the eastward. Every moment our velocity was increased, and presently we were dismayed at seeing grounded ice near us, but were very quickly swept past it at the rate of nearly six miles an hour, though within 200 yards of the rocks, and of instant destruction! As soon as we possibly could we got clear of the packed ice and left it to be wildly hurled about by various whirlpools and rushes of the tide. The ice-masses were large, and dashed violently against each other, and the rocks lay at some distance off the southern shore; we had a fortunate escape from such dangerous company. After anchoring in Depot Bay, a large stock of provisions and a record of our proceedings were landed, as there seems every probability of advancing into the western sea in a very few days.

The appearance of Bellot Strait is precisely that of a Greenland fiord; it is about 20 miles long and scarcely a mile wide in the narrowest part, and within a quarter of a mile of the north shore the depth was ascertained to be 400 feet. Its granitic shores are bold and lofty, with a very respectable sprinkling of vegetation. Some of the hill-ranges rise to about 1500 or 1600 feet above the sea.

23rd August. Yesterday Bellot Strait was again examined, but five miles of close pack occupied precisely the same position as before. Nothing could be effected yet.

24th August. A change of wind led us to hope for a removal of the ice in Bellot Strait, therefore I determined to make another attempt.

When off the table-land, where the depth is not more than from 6 to 10 fathoms and the tides run strongest, the ship hardly moved over the ground, although going 6½ knots through the water! Thus delayed, darkness overtook us, and we anchored at midnight in a small indentation of the north shore, christened by the men Fox's Hole, rather more than half-way through the Strait.

For several hours we have been coquetting with huge rampant ice-masses that wildly surged about in the tideway, or we dashed through boiling eddies, and sometimes almost grazed the tall cliffs. We were therefore naturally glad of a couple or three hours' rest, even in such a very unsafe position. At early dawn we again proceeded west, but for three miles only. The pack again stopped us, and we could perceive that the western sea beyond the Strait was covered with ice. The east wind, which could alone remove it, now gave place to a hard-hearted westerly one.

Last evening's amusement was most exciting, nor was it without its peculiar perils. With cunning and activity worthy of her name, our little craft warily avoided a tilting-match with the stout blue masses which whirled about, as if with wilful impetuosity, through the narrow channel. Some of them were so large as to ground even in 6 or 7 fathoms of water. Many were drawn into eddies and, acquiring considerable velocity in a contrary direction, suddenly broke bounds, charging out into the stream and entering into mighty conflict with their fellows. Nothing but strong hope of success induced me to encounter such dangerous opposition. I not only hoped, but almost felt, that we deserved to succeed.

30th August, 1858. Yesterday I walked over to Possession Point from our old anchorage in Depot Bay, to visit Ross's cairn. I found a few stones piled up on two large boulders, and under each a halfpenny, one of which I pocketed. Upon the ground lay the fragments of a bottle which once contained the record. Having calculated upon finding the bottle sound, I was obliged to make an impromptu record-case of its long neck, into which I thrust my brief document, and consigned it to the safe custody of a small heap of stones.

It was dark before I got on board again. The Strait had meanwhile been reconnoitred from the hills, and was reported to be perfectly clear of ice! This morning therefore we made a fourth attempt to pass through; but Bellot Strait was by no means clear; the same obstruction existed which defeated our last attempt, and in precisely the same place.

5th September. Strong northerly winds have latterly prevailed; Bellot Strait is quite clear of ice; tomorrow morning therefore, we shall make our fifth attempt to get the *Fox* through.

6th September. Steamed through the clear waters of Bellot Strait this morning, and made fast to the ice across its western outlet at a distance of two miles from the shore, and close to a small islet which we have already dubbed Pemmican Rock, having landed upon it a large supply of that substantial traveller's fare, with other provisions for our future sledging parties. If the weather permits, we shall remain here for a few days and watch the effect of winds and tides upon the western ice; but that the ship will get any further now seems improbable.

11th September. Tomorrow we shall return to our harbour and endeavour to procure a few more caribou before they migrate southward.

12th September. We are already in our wintering position, and being without occupation, one day seems most remarkably like another. Although the fondly cherished hope of pushing farther in our ship can no longer be entertained, yet as long as the season continues navigable, it is our duty to be in readiness to avail ourselves of any opportunity, however improbable, of being able to do so.

A few days ago a large cask of biscuit was opened and a living mouse discovered therein. It was small, but mature in years. The cask, a strong watertight one, was packed on shore at Aberdeen in June, 1857, and remained ever afterwards unopened. There was no hole by which the mouse could have got in or out, besides it is the only one ever seen on board. Ship's biscuit is certainly very dry feeding, but who dares assert, after the experience of our mouse, that it is not wonderfully nutritious?

17th September. Of late we have been preparing provisions and equipments for our travelling parties. My scheme of sledge search comprehends three separate routes and parties of four men; to each party a dog-sledge and driver will be attached; Hobson, Young, and I will lead them.

My journey will be to the Great Fish River (Back River), examining the shores of King William's Land in going and returning; Petersen will be with me.

Hobson will explore the western coast of Boothia as far as the magnetic pole, this autumn I hope; and from Gateshead Island westward next spring.

Young will trace the shore of Prince of Wales' Land to Sherard Osborn's farthest, if possible.

Our probable absence will be sixty or seventy days, commencing from about the 20th March.

In this way I trust we shall complete the Franklin search, and the geographical discovery of Arctic America, both left unfinished by the former expeditions.

19th September. Yesterday we steamed once more through Bellot Strait, and took up our former position at the ice-edge, off its western entrance; the ice, hemmed in by islets has not moved.

From the summit of Cape Bird I had a very extensive view this morning: there is now much water in the offing, only separated from us by the belt of islet-girt ice scarcely four miles in width! My conviction is that a strong east wind would remove this remaining barrier; it is not yet too late.

The Second Winter

28th September. The ship was kept available for prosecuting her voyage up to the latest hour; it was only yesterday that we left the western ice, and in consequence of the vast accumulation of young ice in Bellot Strait we had considerable difficulty in returning to the entrance of Port Kennedy. All within was so firmly frozen over that after three hours' steaming and working we only penetrated 100 yards; however, we are now in an excellent position for our wintering place.

Today we are unbending sails and laying up our engines – uncertainty no longer exists – here we are compelled to remain; and if we have not been as successful in our voyaging as a month ago we had good reason to expect, we may still hope that Fortune will smile upon our more humble, yet more arduous, pedestrian explorations – "Hope on, hope ever." In the meantime the sudden transition from mental and physical wear and tear, to the security and quiet of winter quarters, is an immense relief.

8th October. Yesterday an ermine was caught in a trap; hitherto these most active little skirmishers have successfully robbed our fox-traps of their baits as fast as they could be renewed. Today Petersen shot another caribou; it weighs 130 lbs.; many others were seen, also a wolf. Sometimes a few ptarmigan are met with, but hares very rarely.

19th October. All the 17th a N.W. gale blew with fearful violence; yesterday it abated, but not sufficiently to allow our first sledging party to start. But this morning Hobson got away with his nine men and ten dogs. His absence may be from eighteen to twenty days. Autumn travelling is most disagreeable, there is so much wind and snow, the latter being soft, deep and often wet; the sun is almost always obscured by mist, and is powerless for warmth or drying purposes, and the temperature is very variable. Moreover, there are now only eight hours of misty daylight.

Whenever we have a calm night we can hear the crushing sound of the drift-ice in Bellot Strait, which continues open to within 500 yards of the Fox Islands, and emits dark chilling clouds of hateful, pestilent, abominable mist.

2nd November. Very dull times. No amount of ingenuity could make a diary worth the paper it is written on. An occasional raven flies past, a couple more ptarmigan have been shot: another N.W. gale is blowing, with temperature down to –12°.

6th November. Saturday night. The N.W. gale blew without intermission for seventy hours, the temperature being about −15°. We hoped that our absent shipmates of the depot parties might be housed safely in snow huts. This afternoon all doubts respecting them were dispelled by their arrival in good health, but they evidently have suffered from cold and exposure during their absence of nineteen days. For the first six days they journeyed outward successfully; on that night they encamped upon the ice. It was at spring-tide and a N.E. gale sprang up and, blowing off shore, detached the ice and drifted them off! The sea froze over on the cessation of the gale, and two days afterwards they fortunately regained the land near the position from which they were blown off. They have indeed experienced much unusual danger, and suffering from the cold.

I am truly thankful for the safe return of our travellers — all this toil and exposure of ten persons and ten dogs has only advanced the depots 90 miles distant from the ship.

November 7th. Sunday evening. Brief as is the interval since my last entry, yet how awful and, to one of our small company, how fatal it has been! Yesterday Mr. Brand was out shooting as usual, and in robust health; in the evening Hobson sat with him for a little time. Mr. Brand turned the conversation upon our position and employments last year; he called to remembrance poor Robert Scott, and added mournfully, "Poor fellow! no one knows whose turn it may be to go next." He finished his evening pipe and shut his cabin door shortly after nine o'clock. This morning at seven o'clock, his servant found him lying upon the deck, a corpse, having been several hours dead. Apoplexy appears to have been the cause.

We are now without either engineer or engine-driver. We have only two stokers, and they know nothing about the machinery. Our numbers are reduced to twenty-four, including our interpreter and two Greenland Esquimaux.

12th December. Very cold weather: thermometer down to −41°, and the breeze comes to us loaded with mist from the open water, kept free by the tide race in Bellot Strait, which causes the air to feel colder than it otherwise would. Bellot Strait has become a nuisance, not only from this cause, but from the strong winds which seldom cease to blow through it.

Our seal nets have produced nothing; and as there are no seals, we no longer wonder at not seeing bears. Three foxes have been trapped and a hare seen.

The monotony of our lives is vastly increased by want of occupation and by confinement by severe gales to the ship for five days out of every seven. The general health is good, but there is a natural craving for fresh meat and fresh vegetables. But a well-filled letter-bag would be more welcome than anything I know of.

26th December. Our Christmas has been spent with a degree of loyalty to the good old English custom, at once spirited and refreshing. All the good things which could possibly be collected together appeared upon the snow-white deal tables of the men, as the officers and myself walked (by invitation) around the lower deck. Venison, beer, and a fresh stock of clay pipes, appeared to be the most prized luxuries; but the variety and abundance of the eatables, tastefully laid out, was such as might well support the delusion which all seemed desirous of imposing upon themselves – that they were in a land of plenty – in fact, all but at home.

Whilst all was order and merriment within the ship, the scene without was widely different. A fierce north-wester howled loudly through the rigging; the snow-drift rustled swiftly past; no star appeared through the oppressive gloom, and the thermometer varied between 76° and 80° below the freezing point.

9th January, 1859. Another week of uniform temperature of –40°, and confinement to the ship by strong winds. The atmosphere is loaded with enveloping mists which impart a raw and surprisingly keen edge to the chilling blasts; blasts that no human nose can endure without blanching, be its proportions what they may. It is wonderful how the dogs stand it, and without apparent inconvenience, unless their fur happens to be thin. They lie upon the snow under the lee of the ship, with no other protection from the weather.

The Search Begins

Sunday night, 13th February. Tomorrow morning, if it is fine, Young and I set off upon our travels, I to establish contact with the Esquimaux. Young has already advanced a portion of his sledge-load to the west side of Bellot Strait. I have explored a route across by a long lake to the west, and find we can reach it without crossing elevated or uncovered land.

The mean temperature of February up to this date is –33.2°,

being an exact continuation of January. I confess to some anxiety upon this point, as hitherto the winter has been so unusually severe, and the journeys to be performed will occupy more than twenty days. Besides, we shall be earlier in motion than any of the previous travellers on record. Should either Young or myself remain absent beyond the period for which we carry provisions, Hobson is to send a party in search of us.

20th March. Already I have been a week returned from my journey, and so difficult is it to settle down to anything like sedentary occupation, after a period of continued vigorous action, that even now I can scarcely sit still to scribble a brief outline of my trip to Cape Victoria.

On the morning of the 17th February the weather moderated sufficiently for us to set out; the temperature throughout the day varied between −31° and −42½°. Leaving Young's party to pass on through the Strait, I proceeded overland by way of the Long Lake. We built our first snow-hut upon the west coast of Boothia, near Pemmican Rock, after a march of 22 or 23 miles.

On the third day our dogs went lame in consequence of sore feet; the intense cold seems to be the principal, if not the only cause, having hardened the surface-snow beyond what their feet can endure. I was obliged to throw off a part of the provisions; still we could not make more than 14 to 20 miles daily. We of course walked, so that the dogs had only the remaining provisions and clothing to drag, yet several of them repeatedly fell down in fits.

For several days this severe weather continued. The mercury of my artificial horizon remaining frozen (its freezing point is −39°); and our rum, at first thick like treacle, required thawing latterly when the more fluid and stronger part had been used. We travelled each day until dusk, and then were occupied for a couple of hours in building our snow-hut. The four walls were run up 5½ feet high, inclining inwards as much as possible; over these our tent was laid to form a roof.

Our equipment consisted of a very small tent, macintosh floor-cloth, and felt robes. Besides this, each man had a bag of double blanketing and a pair of fur boots to sleep in. We wore moccasins over the pieces of blanket in which our feet were wrapped up and, with the exception of a change of this foot-gear, carried no spare clothes.

The daily routine was as follows: I led the way; Petersen and Thompson followed, conducting their sledges; and in this manner we trudged on for eight or ten hours without halting except when necessary to disentangle the dog-harness. When we halted for the night, Thompson and I usually sawed out the blocks of compact snow and carried them to Petersen who acted as the master-mason in building the snow-hut. The hour and a half or two hours usually employed in erecting the edifice was the most disagreeable part of the day's labour for, in addition to being already well tired, and desiring repose, we became thoroughly chilled whilst standing about. When the hut was finished the dogs were fed, and here the great difficulty was to insure the weaker ones their full share in the scramble for supper. Then commenced the operation of unpacking the sledge, and carrying into our hut everything necessary for ourselves, such as provisions and sleeping gear, as well as all boots, fur mittens, and even the dog-harness, to prevent the dogs from eating them during our sleeping hours. The door was now blocked up with snow, the cooking-lamp lighted, foot-gear changed, diary written up, watches wound, sleeping bags wriggled into, pipes lighted, and the merits of the various dogs discussed until supper was ready. The supper swallowed, the upper robe or coverlet was pulled over, and then to sleep.

Next morning came breakfast, a struggle to get into frozen moccasins, after which the sledges were packed and another day's march commenced.

In these little huts we usually slept warm enough, although latterly, when our blankets and clothes became loaded with ice, we felt the cold severely. When our low doorway was carefully blocked up with snow, and the cooking-lamp alight, the temperature quickly rose so that the walls became glazed and our bedding thawed; but the cooking over, or the doorway partially opened, it as quickly fell again so that it was impossible to sleep or even to hold one's pannikin of tea, without putting one's mitts on, so intense was the cold!

On the first of March we halted to encamp at about the position of the magnetic-pole – for no cairn remains to mark this spot first reached by Sir James Ross. I had almost concluded that my journey would prove to be a work of labour in vain, because hitherto no traces of Esquimaux had been met with and, in consequence of the reduced state of our provisions and the wretched condition of the poor dogs – six out of the fifteen being quite useless – I could only advance one more march.

But we had done nothing more than look ahead. When we halted, and turned round, great indeed was my surprise and joy to see four men walking after us. Petersen and I immediately buckled on our revolvers and advanced to meet them. The natives halted, made fast their dogs, laid down their spears, and received us without any evidence of surprise. They told us they had been out upon a seal hunt on the ice, and were returning home. We proposed to join them, and all were soon in motion again; but another hour brought sunset and we learned that their snow village of eight huts was still a long way off, so we hired them, at the rate of a needle for each Esquimaux, to build us a hut, which they completed in an hour. It was 8 feet in diameter, 5½ feet high, and in it we all passed the night. Perhaps the records of architecture do not furnish another instance of a dwelling-house so cheaply constructed!

We gave them to understand that we were anxious to barter with them, and very cautiously approached the real object of our visit, which was to find out what they knew of the lost expedition. A naval button upon one of their dresses afforded the opportunity; it came, they said, from some white men who had starved upon an island; and the iron of which their knives were made came from the same place. One of these men said he had been to the island to obtain wood and iron, but none of them had seen the white men.

These Esquimaux had nothing to eat, and no other clothing than their ordinary double dresses of fur. They would not eat our biscuit or salt pork, but took a small quantity of bear's blubber and some water. They slept in a sitting posture with their heads leaning forward on their breasts.

Next morning we travelled about 10 miles further; by which time we were close to Cape Victoria. Beyond this I would not go, much as they wished to lead us on; we therefore landed and they built us a commodious snow hut in half an hour. This done, we displayed to them our articles for barter – knives, files, needles, scissors, beads, etc. – expressed our desire to trade with them, and promised to purchase everything which belonged to the starved white men, if they would come to us on the morrow. Notwithstanding that the weather was now stormy and bitterly cold, two of the natives stripped off their outer coats of reindeer skin and bartered them for a knife each.

Next morning the entire village population arrived, amounting to about forty-five souls, from aged people to infants in arms, and bartering commenced very briskly. First of all we purchased all the relics of the lost expedition, consisting of six silver spoons and forks, a silver medal, part of a gold chain, several buttons; and knives made of the iron and wood of the wreck; also bows and arrows constructed of materials obtained from the same source. Having secured these, we purchased a few frozen salmon, some seals' blubber and venison, but could not prevail upon them to part with more than one of their fine dogs.

All the old people recollected the visit of Sir John Ross' *Victory*. I inquired after the man who was furnished with a wooden leg by the carpenter of the *Victory*: no direct answer was given, but his daughter was pointed out to me. Petersen explained to me that they do not like alluding in any way to the dead and that, as my question was not answered, it was certain the man was no longer amongst the living.

None of these people had seen the missing whites alive. One man said he had seen their bones upon the island where they died; but some were buried.

Next morning, 4th March, several natives came to us again. One man told Petersen distinctly that a ship having three masts had been crushed by the ice out in the sea to the west of King William's Island, but that all the people landed safely. However he was not one of those who were eye-witnesses of it. The ship sank, so nothing was obtained by the natives from her; all that they have got, he said, came from the island in the river.*

These Esquimaux were all well clothed in caribou dresses, and looked clean. They appeared to have abundance of provisions, but scarcely a scrap of wood was seen amongst them which had not come from the lost expedition. Their sledges were wretched little affairs, consisting of two frozen rolls of seal-skin coated with ice, and attached to each other by bones which served as the crossbars. The men were stout, hearty fellows, and the women arrant thieves, but all were good-humoured and friendly. The women were decidely plain; in fact, this term would have been flattering to most of them; yet there was a degree of vivacity and gentleness in the manners of some that soon reconciled us to these Arctic specimens of the fair sex. They had fine eyes and teeth, as well as very small

* Montreal Island in Chantrey Inlet.

hands, and the young girls had a fresh rosy hue not often seen in combination with olive complexions.

We now returned toward the ship with all the speed we could command; but stormy weather occasioned two days' delay, so that we did not arrive on board until the 14th of March. Though considerably reduced in flesh, I and my companions were in excellent health, and blessed with insatiable appetites. On washing our faces, which had become perfectly black from the soot of our blubber lamp, sundry scars, relics of frost-bites, appeared; and the tips of our fingers, from constant frost-bites, had become as callous as if seared with hot iron.

In this journey of twenty-five days we travelled 420 miles and completed the discovery of the coast-line of continental America on the West side of Boothia Peninsula, thereby adding about 120 miles to our charts. The mean temperature throughout the journey was 30° below zero, Fahrenheit; or 62° below the freezing point of water.

During this journey I acquired the Arctic accomplishment of eating frozen blubber, in delicate little slices, and vastly preferred it to frozen pork. At the present moment I do not think I could even taste it, but the same privation and hunger which induced me to eat of such food then would doubtless enable me again to partake of it very kindly.

25th March. Hobson's party and my own are now all prepared for our journey to King William's Island, and we propose setting out on the 2nd April – God willing. Young will start a few days after us. All the *Fox*'s winter defences of snow, our porches, our deck-layer, and our external embankment, have been removed. Dr. Walker remains in charge of the ship, with two stewards, a cook, a carpenter, and a stoker. My party, as well as Hobson's, will be provisioned, including the depots, for an absence of about eighty-four days.

The morning of April 2nd was inauspicious, but as the day advanced the weather improved, so that Hobson and I were able to set out upon our journeys. We each had a sledge drawn by four men, besides a dog-sledge and dog-driver. Our five starveling puppies were harnessed, for the first time in their lives, to a small sledge which I drove myself, intending to sell them to the Esquimaux if I could get them to drag their own supply of provisions so far. The procession looked imposing. There were five sledges, twelve men, and seventeen dogs, the latter of all sizes and shapes.

The load for each man to drag was fixed at 200 lbs. and for each dog 100 lbs. Our provisions consisted mainly of pemmican, biscuit, and tea, with a small addition of boiled pork, rum and some tobacco.

The men being untrained to the work, and the sledges heavily laden, our march was fatiguing and slow. We encamped that night upon the long lake. On the second day we reached the western sea, and upon the third, aided by our sledge sails, we advanced some miles beyond Arcedeckne Island.

The various depots carried out with so much difficulty and danger in the autumn, were now gathered up as we advanced, until at length we were so loaded as to be compelled to proceed with one-half at a time, going three times over the same ground. For six days this tedious mode of progression was persevered in.

Hitherto the temperature continued low, often nearly 30° below zero, and at times with cutting north winds, bright sun and intensely strong snow glare. Although we wore coloured spectacles, yet almost all suffered great inconvenience and considerable pain from inflamed eyes.* Our faces were blistered, lips and hands cracked and in fact never were men more disfigured by the combined effects of bright sun and bitterly cold winds. Fortunately no serious frost-bites occurred, but frost-bitten faces and fingers were universal.

On the 20th April we met two families of natives, comprising twelve individuals; their snow-huts were upon the ice three-quarters of a mile off shore, and their occupation was seal-hunting. They were the same people with whom I had communicated at Cape Victoria in February.

After much anxious inquiry we learned that *two* ships had been seen by the natives of King William's Island; one of them was seen to sink in deep water, and nothing was obtained from her (a circumstance at which they expressed much regret). But the other was forced on shore by the ice, where they suppose she still remains; but is much broken.

They told us that the body of a man was found on board the ship; that he must have been a very large man, and had long teeth.

They also told us it was in the fall of the year – that is August or September – when the ships were destroyed, and that all the white people went away to the "large river" (Back River), taking

* Snow-blindness.

a boat or boats with them, and that in the following winter their bones were found there.

Continuing our journey, we crossed a wide bay upon level ice. During the 25th, 26th, and 27th, we were confined to our tents by a very heavy south-east gale with severe cold. Early on the 28th we reached Cape Victoria; here Hobson and I separated. He marched direct for Cape Felix on King William's Island, whilst I kept a more southerly course.

Hobson was unwell when we parted, complaining of stiffness and pain in his legs, but neither of us then suspected that he had scurvy. I gave him directions to search the west coast of King William's Island for the stranded ship and for records, and to act upon such information as he might obtain in this way, or from the natives.

I soon found that my party had to labour across a rough pack; nor was it until the third day that we completed the traverse of the strait, and encamped near to the entrance of Port Parry, on King William's Island.

On May 2nd we set off again briskly; our load being diminished to thirty days' provisions. With the sledge sail set, we soon reached the land, and travelled along it for Cape Sabine. It was very thick weather, and we were unable to see any distance in consequence of the mist and snowdrift. The following day was no better, and the shore, which we dared not leave to cross the bays, was extremely low.

We soon discovered that we had strayed inland; but, guided by the wind, continued our course. Upon May 4th we descended into Wellington Strait, and the weather being tolerably clear, crossed over to the south-west extreme of Matty Island in the hope of meeting with natives, no traces of them having been met with since leaving Cape Victoria. Off this south-west point we found a deserted village of nearly twenty snow huts, besides several others within a few miles upon either side of it; in all of them I found shavings or chips of different kinds of wood from the lost expedition.

There were some considerable islands to the east, but thinking the most southerly of this group, named "Owut-ta" by the Esquimaux, the most likely place to find the natives, I pushed on in that direction until we found another snow-village very recently abandoned, but the sledge tracks from which plainly showing that the inhabitants had gone to the E.N.E. It was now evident that these places of winter resort were deserted, and that here at least we should not find any natives; I was the more sorry at having missed them, as, from the quantity of wood chips about the huts, they probably had visited the stranded ship alluded to by the last Esquimaux we had met.

7th May. To avoid snow-blindness, we commenced night-marching. Crossing back from Matty Island towards the King William's Island shore, we continued our march southward until midnight, when we had the good fortune to arrive at an inhabited snow-village. We found here ten or twelve huts and thirty or forty natives of King William's Island. I do not think any of them had ever seen white people alive before, but they evidently knew us to be friends.

I purchased from them six pieces of silver plate bearing the crests or initials of Franklin, Crozier, Fairholm, and McDonald. The silver spoons and forks were readily sold for four needles each.

Having obtained all the relics they possessed, I purchased some seal's flesh, blubber, frozen venison, dried and frozen salmon, and sold some of my puppies. They told us it was five days' journey to the wreck – one day up the inlet still in sight, and four days overland. This would carry us to the western coast of King William's Land. They added that but little now remained of the wreck which was accessible, their countrymen having carried almost everything away. In answer to an inquiry they said she was without masts; the question gave rise to some laughter amongst them, and they spoke to each other about fire, from which Petersen thought they had burnt the masts through close to the deck in order to get them down.

There had been many books they said, but all had long ago been destroyed by the weather. The ship was forced on shore in the fall of the year by the ice. She had not been visited during this past winter, and an old woman and a boy were shown to us who were the last to visit the wreck. They said they had been at it during the winter of 1857-58.

Petersen questioned the woman closely, and she seemed anxious to give all the information in her power. She said many of the white men dropped by the way as they went to the Back River; that some were buried and some were not. The Esquimaux did not themselves witness this, but discovered their bodies during the winter following.

Bad weather had now fairly set in, accompanied by a most unseasonable degree of cold. On the morning of the 12th May we crossed Point Ogle, and encamped upon the ice in the Back River estuary the same evening. The cold and the darkness of our more southern latitude having obliged us to return to day-travelling. All the 13th we were imprisoned in our tent by a most furious gale, nor was it until late on the morning of the 14th that we could proceed; that evening we encamped near Montreal Island.

On the 18th May we crossed over to the mainland near Point Duncan, but Hampton was complaining of being ill, and I was obliged to encamp. When away from my party, and exploring along the shore towards Elliot Bay, I saw a herd of eight caribou and succeeded in shooting one of them.

On the evening of the 19th we commenced our return journey, but for the three following weeks our route led us over new ground. Hampton being unable to drag, I made over my puppy-team to him, and was thus left free to explore and fully examine every doubtful object along our route. I shall not easily forget the trial my patience underwent during the six weeks that I drove that dog-sledge. The leader of my team, named "Omar Pasha," was very willing, but very lame; little "Rose" was coquettish, and fonder of being caressed than whipped; from some cause or other she ceased growing when only a few months old and she was therefore far too small for heavy work; "Darky" and "Missy" were mere pups; and last of all came two wretched starvelings, reared in the winter, "Foxey" and "Dolly." Each dog had its own harness, formed of strips of canvas, and was attached to the sledge by a single trace 12 feet long. None of them had ever been yoked before, and the amount of cunning and perversity they displayed to avoid both the whip and the work, was quite astonishing. They bit through their traces and hid away under the sledge, or leaped over one another's backs, so as to get into the middle of the team out of the way of my whip, until the traces became plaited up, and the dogs were almost knotted together. The consequence was I had to halt every few minutes, pull off my mitts and, at the risk of frozen fingers, disentangle the lines. I persevered however, and without breaking any of their bones, succeeded in getting a surprising amount of work out of them.

Having unsuccessfully searched the east shore of this part of the mainland for seven or eight miles further north, we crossed over into Barrow's Inlet, and spent a day in its examination, but not a trace of natives was met with.

Regaining the shore of Simpson's Strait, we crossed over to King William's Island again upon the morning of the 24th. The south coast was closely examined as we marched along towards Cape Herschel. Upon a conspicuous point, to the westward of Point Gladman, a cairn nearly five feet high was seen which, although it did not appear to be a recent construction, was taken down stone by stone and carefully examined, the ground beneath being broken up with the pickaxe, but nothing was uncovered.

We were now upon the shore along which Franklin's retreating crews must have marched. My sledges of course travelled upon the sea-ice close along the shore; and although the depth of snow which covered the beach deprived us of almost every hope, yet we kept a very sharp look-out for traces, nor were we unsuccessful. Shortly after midnight of the 24th May, when slowly walking along a gravel ridge near the beach, which the winds kept partially bare of snow, I came upon a human skeleton, partly exposed, with here and there a few fragments of clothing appearing through the snow. The skeleton—now perfectly bleached—was lying upon its face, the limbs and smaller bones either dissevered or gnawed away by small animals.

A most careful examination of the spot was of course made, the snow removed, and every scrap of clothing gathered up. A pocket-book afforded strong grounds of hope that some information might be subsequently obtained respecting the unfortunate owner and the calamitous march of the lost crews, but at the time it was frozen hard. The substance of that which we gleaned upon the spot may thus be summed up:

This victim was a young man, slightly built, and perhaps above the common height; the dress appeared to be that of a steward or officer's servant, the loose bow-knot in which his neck-handkerchief was tied not being used by seamen or officers. In every particular the dress confirmed our conjectures as to his rank or office in the late expedition—the blue jacket with slashed sleeves and braided edging, and the pilot-cloth great-coat with plain covered buttons. We found, also, a clothes-brush near, and a horn pocket-comb. This poor man seems to have selected the bare ridge top as affording the least tiresome walking, and to have fallen upon his face in the position in which we found him.

It was a melancholy truth that the old Esquimaux woman spoke when she said, "they fell down and died as they walked along."

Hobson was also upon the western coast, and I hoped to find a note left for me at Cape Herschel containing some piece of good news. After minutely examining the intervening coastline, it was with strong and reasonable hope I ascended the slope. This summit of Cape Herschel is perhaps 150 feet high, and about a quarter of a mile within the low stoney point which projects from it. Close round this point, or by cutting across it as we did, the retreating parties *must* have passed; and the opportunity afforded by the cairn left here by Simpson* of depositing in a known position – and that, too, where their own discoveries terminated – some record of their own proceedings or, it might be, a portion of their scientific journals, would scarcely have been disregarded.

What now remained of this once "ponderous cairn" was only four feet high; the south side had been pulled down and the central stones removed, as if by persons seeking for something deposited beneath. After removing the snow with which it was filled, and a few loose stones, the men laid bare a large slab of limestone. With difficulty this was removed, then a second, and also a third slab, when they came to the ground. For some time we persevered with a pickaxe in breaking up the frozen earth, but nothing whatever was found, nor any trace of European visitors in its vicinity.

About 12 miles from Cape Herschel I found a small cairn built by Hobson's party, and containing a note for me. He had reached this, his extreme point, six days previously, without having seen anything of the wreck, or of natives, but he had found a record – the record so ardently sought for, of the Franklin Expedition – at Point Victory, on the N.W. coast of King William's Island.

That record is indeed a sad and touching relic of our lost friends and, to simplify its contents I will point out separately the double story it so briefly tells. In the first place, the record paper was one of the printed forms usually supplied to discovery ships for the purpose of being enclosed in bottles and thrown overboard at sea in order to ascertain the set of the currents. Blanks were left for the date and position.

* Thomas Simpson, an H.B.C. explorer, had reached this point in 1839 at the culmination of a 1400-mile small-boat journey along the Arctic coast.

Upon the copy of this form found by Hobson was written as follows:

> *28 of May 1847* | *H.M. ships "Erebus" and "Terror" wintered in the ice in lat. 70° 05′ N.; long. 98° 23′ W.*
> *Having wintered in 1846-7 at Beechey Island, in lat. 74° 43′ 28″ N., long. 91° 39′ 15″ W., after having ascended Wellington Channel to lat. 77°, and returned to the west side of Cornwallis Island.*
>
> *Sir John Franklin commanding the expedition.*
>
> *All well.*
>
> *Party consisting of 2 officers and 6 men left the ships on Monday 24th May, 1847.*
>
> *Gm. Gore, Lieut.*
> *Chas. F. Des Vaeux, Mate.*

There is an error in the above document, namely, that the *Erebus* and *Terror* wintered at Beechey Island in 1846-7. The correct dates should have been 1845-6; a glance at the date at the top and bottom of the record proves this, but in all other respects the tale is told in as few words as possible of their wonderful success up to that date, May 28th, 1847.

Thus we find that, after the last intelligence of Sir John Franklin was received by us (bearing date of July, 1845), from the whalers in Melville Bay, his Expedition passed on to Lancaster Sound and entered Wellington Channel, of which the southern entrance had been discovered by Sir Edward Parry in 1819. The *Erebus* and *Terror* then sailed up that strait for one hundred and fifty miles. Whether Franklin intended to pursue this northern course, and was only stopped by ice in the latitude of 77° north, or purposely relinquished a route which seemed to lead away from the known seas off the coast of America, must be a matter of opinion. But this the document assures us that Sir John Franklin's Expedition, having accomplished this examination, returned southward from latitude 77° north, which is at the head of Wellington Channel, and re-entered Barrow's Strait by a new channel between Bathurst and Cornwallis Islands.

In 1846 they apparently proceeded to the south-west, and eventually reached within twelve miles of the north extreme of King William's Land, when their progress was arrested by the approaching winter of 1846-47. That winter appears to have passed without any serious loss of life; and when, in the spring, Lieutenant Gore left with a party for some especial purpose (very probably to connect the unknown coast-line of King William's Land between Point Victory and Cape Herschel), those on board the *Erebus* and *Terror* were "all well," and the gallant Franklin still commanded.

But, alas! round the margin of the paper upon which Lieutenant Gore in 1847 wrote those words of hope and promise, another hand had subsequently written the following words:

> *April 25, 1848 – H.M. ships "Terror" and "Erebus" were deserted on the 22nd April, 5 leagues N.N.W. of this, having been beset since 12th September, 1846. The officers and crews consisting of 105 souls, under the command of Captain F. R. M. Crozier, landed here. Sir John Franklin died on the 11th June, 1847; and the total loss by deaths in the expedition has been to this date 9 officers and 15 men.*
> *(Signed)*
> *F. R. M. Crozier,* *James Fitzjames,*
> *Captain and Senior Officer,* *Captain H.M.S. Erebus.*
> *and start (on) tomorrow, 26th, for Back's Fish River.*

In the short space of twelve months, how mournful had become the history of Franklin's Expedition; how changed from the cheerful "All well" of Graham Gore! The spring of 1847 found them within 90 miles of the known western sea* off the coast of America; and to men who had already in two seasons sailed over 500 miles of previously unexplored waters, how confident must they have felt that the forthcoming navigable season of 1847 would see their ships pass over so short an intervening space and so complete the Northwest Passage. It was ruled otherwise. Within a month after Lieutenant Gore placed the record on Point Victory, Sir John Franklin was dead; and the following spring found Captain Crozier, upon whom the command had devolved at King William's Island, endeavouring to save his starving men, 105 souls in all, from a terrible death, by retreating to the Hudson Bay territories† up the Back or Great Fish River.

A sad tale was never told in fewer words. There is something

* Queen Maud Gulf, discovered by Simpson.

† Their objective would have been the nearest H.B.C. posts – on Great Slave Lake, more than 1000 miles away!

deeply touching in their extreme simplicity, and they show in the strongest manner that the leaders of this retreating party met, with calmness and decision, the fearful alternative of a last bold struggle for life, rather than perish without effort on board their ships; for we well know that the *Erebus* and *Terror* were only provisioned up to July, 1848.

Lieutenant Hobson's note told me that he found quantities of clothing and articles of all kinds lying about the cairn, as if these men, aware that they were retreating for their lives, had there abandoned everything which they considered superfluous.

Our provisions were running very short, therefore the three remaining puppies were of necessity shot, and their sledge used for fuel. We were also enabled to lengthen our journeys, as we had very smooth ice to travel over, the off-lying islets keeping the rough pack from pressing in upon the shore.

Upon the 29th of May we reached the western extreme of King William's Island. I named it after Captain Crozier of the *Terror*, the gallant leader of that "Forlorn Hope" of which we now had just obtained tidings.

The coast we marched along was extremely low – a mere series of ridges of limestone shingle. The only tracks of animals seen were those of a bear and a few foxes – the only living creatures, a few willow grouse. Traces even of the wandering Esquimaux became much less frequent after leaving Cape Herschel. Here were found only a few circles of stones, the sites of tenting-places, but so moss-grown as to be of great age. The prospect to seaward was not less forbidding – a rugged surface of crushed-up pack, including much heavy ice. In these shallow, ice-covered seas, seals are but seldom found; and it is highly probable that all animal life in them is as scarce as upon the land.

From Cape Crozier the coast-line was found to turn sharply away to the eastward; and early in the morning of the 30th May we encamped alongside a large boat – another melancholy relic which Hobson had found and examined a few days before, as his note left here informed me.

A vast quantity of tattered clothing was lying in her, and this we first examined. Not a single article bore the name of its former owner. The boat was cleared out and carefully swept that nothing might escape us.

This boat measured 28 feet long, and 7 feet 3 inches wide; she was built with a view to lightness and light draught of water, and evidently equipped with the utmost care for the ascent of the Back River. She had neither oars nor rudder; paddles supplying their place, and as a large remnant of light canvas was found, and also a small block for reeving a sheet through, I suppose she had been provided with a sail. A sloping canvas roof or rain-awning had also formed part of her equipment.

The weight of the boat alone was about 700 or 800 lbs., but she was mounted upon a sledge of unusual weight and strength. It was constructed of two oak planks 23 feet 4 inches in length, 8 inches in width, and with an average thickness of 2½ inches.

I have calculated the weight of this sledge to be 650 lbs., it could not have been less, and may have been considerably more. The total weight of boat and sledge may therefore be taken at 1400 lbs. which amounts to a heavy load for seven strong and healthy men.*

But these were later observations; meanwhile there was that in the boat which transfixed us with awe. It was portions of two human skeletons. One was that of a slight young person; the other of a large, strongly-made, middle-aged man. The former was found in the bow of the boat, but in too much disturbed state to enable Hobson to judge whether the sufferer had died there. Large and powerful animals, probably wolves, had destroyed much of this skeleton, which may have been that of an officer. Near it we found the fragment of a pair of hand-worked slippers. The other skeleton was in a somewhat more perfect state and was enveloped with clothes and furs; it lay across the boat, under the after-thwart. Close beside it were found five watches; and there were two double-barrelled guns – one barrel in each loaded and cocked – standing muzzle upwards against the boat's side. It may be imagined with what deep interest these sad relics were scrutinized, and how anxiously every fragment of clothing was turned over in search of pocket-books, journals, or even names. Five or six small books were found, all of them scriptural or devotional works, except *The Vicar of Wakefield*.

* The incredible weight and bulk of the material, most of it quite useless to their endeavour, with which the survivors burdened themselves represents an almost inexplicable, and in the event, suicidal, piece of stupidity. Nevertheless it was part and parcel of the Naval attitude toward the north, and a startling commentary on how little the Navy had learned from Ross, Simpson, and others, who had already demonstrated the essential fact – that survival in the north meant travelling light.

Amongst an amazing quantity of clothing there were seven or eight pairs of boots of various kinds – cloth winter boots, sea boots, heavy ankle boots, and strong shoes. I noted that there were silk handkerchiefs – black, white, and figured – towels, soap, sponge, tooth-brush, and hair-combs. Besides these articles we found twine, nails, saws, files, bristles, wax-ends, sailmakers' palms, powder, bullets, shot, cartridges, wads, leather cartridge-case, knives – clasp and dinner ones – needle and thread cases, slow-match, several bayonet-scabbards cut down into knife-sheaths, two rolls of sheet-lead and, in short, a quantity of articles of one description and another truly astonishing in variety, and such as, for the most part, modern sledge-travellers in these regions would consider a mere accumulation of dead weight, and very likely to break down the strength of the sledge-crews.

The only provisions we could find were tea and chocolate; of the former very little remained, but there were nearly 40 pounds of the latter. These articles alone could never support life in such a climate, and we found neither biscuit nor meat of any kind.

In the after part of the boat we discovered eleven large spoons, eleven forks, and four teaspoons, all of silver. Of these twenty-six pieces of plate eight bore Sir John Franklin's crest, the remainder had the crests or initials of nine different officers.

Sir John Franklin's plate perhaps was issued to the men for their use, as the only means of saving it; and it seems probable that the officers generally did the same, as not a single iron spoon, such as sailors always use, has been found. Of the many men, probably twenty or thirty, who were attached to this boat, it seemed most strange that the remains of only two individuals were found, nor were there any graves upon the neighbouring flat land. Indeed, bearing in mind the season at which these poor fellows left their ships, it should be remembered that the soil was then frozen hard, and the labour of cutting a grave very great indeed.

I was astonished to find that the sledge was directed to the N.E. exactly for the next point of land for which we ourselves were travelling!

A little reflection led me to satisfy my own mind at least, that the boat and her people were returning to the ship: and in no other way can I account for two men having been left in her, than by supposing the party were unable to drag the boat further, and that these two men, not being able to keep pace with their shipmates, were therefore left by them supplied with such provisions as could be spared to last until the return of the others from the ship with a fresh stock.

Whether it was the intention of the retroceding party to await the result of another season in the ships, or to follow the track of the main body to the Back River, is now a matter of conjecture. It seems highly probable that they had purposed revisiting the boat, not only on account of the two men left in charge of it, but also to obtain the chocolate, the five watches, and many other articles which would otherwise scarcely have been left in her.

The same reasons which may be assigned for the return of this detachment from the main body, will also serve to account for their not having come back to their boat. In both instances they appear to have greatly overrated their strength, and the distance they could travel in a given time.

Taking this view of the case, we can understand why their provisions would not last them for anything like the distance they required to travel; and why they would be obliged to send back to the ships for more. Whether all or any of this party ever reached their ships is uncertain. All we know is that they did not revisit the boat (which accounts for the absence of more skeletons in its neighbourhood) and the Esquimaux report that there was no one alive in the ship when she drifted on shore, and that but one human body was found by them on board of her.

I need hardly say that throughout the whole of my journey along the shores of King William's Land I caused a most vigilant look-out to be kept to seaward for any appearance of the stranded ship spoken of by the natives; our search was however fruitless in that respect.

On the morning of 2nd June we reached Point Victory. Here Hobson's note left for me in the cairn informed me that he had not found the slightest trace either of a wreck anywhere upon the coast, or of natives to the north of Cape Crozier.

Hobson's note informed me of his having found a second record, deposited also by Lieutenant Gore in May, 1847, upon the south side of Back Bay, but it afforded me no additional information.

It was found on the ground amongst a few loose stones which had evidently fallen along with it from the top of the cairn. A great quantity and variety of things lay strewed about the cairn, such as even in their three days' march from the ships the retreating crews found it impossible to carry further. Amongst these were four heavy sets of boat's cooking stoves, pickaxes, shovels, iron hoops, old canvas, a large single block, about four feet of a copper lightning conductor, long pieces of hollow brass curtain rods, and a small case of selected medicines containing about twenty-four phials (the contents in a wonderful state of preservation).

The clothing left here by the retreating crews of the *Erebus* and *Terror* formed a huge heap four feet high. Every article was searched, but the pockets were all empty, and not one of all these articles were marked – indeed sailors' warm clothing seldom is.

Here ended my own search for traces of the lost ones. Hobson found two other cairns, and many relics, between this position and Cape Felix. From each place where any trace was discovered the most interesting of the relics were taken away, so that the collection we have made is very considerable.

From Walls' Bay I crossed overland to the eastern shore, and reached my depot near the entrance of Port Perry on the 5th June, after an absence of thirty-four days.

We were then in daily expectation and dread of the thaw, which renders all travelling so very difficult, and we were still 230 miles from our ship.

At one of our depots, a note left by Hobson informed me of his being six days in advance of me, and also of his own serious illness. For many days past he had been unable to walk, and was consequently conveyed upon the sledge. His men were hastening home with all their strength and speed, in order to get him under the Doctor's care. We also were doing our best to push on, lest the bursting out of melting snow from the various ravines should render the ice impassable.

On the 15th of June the snow upon the ice everywhere yielded to the effects of increased temperature. I was, indeed, most thankful at its having remained firm so long. To make any progress at all after this date was of course a very great labour, requiring the utmost efforts of both the men and the dogs; nor was the freezing mixture through which we trudged by any means agreeable; we were often more than knee-deep in it.

We succeeded in reaching False Strait on the morning of the 18th June, and pitched our tent just as heavy rain began to descend; it lasted throughout the greater part of the day. After travelling a few miles upon the Long Lake, further progress was found to be quite impossible, and we were obliged to haul our sledges up off the flooded ice, and commence a march of 16 or 17 miles overland for the ship. The poor dogs were so tired and sore-footed that we could not even induce them to follow us; they remained about the sledges. After a very fatiguing scramble across the hills and through the snow valleys we were refreshed with a sight of our poor dear lonely little *Fox*, and arrived on board in time for a late breakfast on the 19th of June.

Upon my arrival on board, my first inquiries were about Hobson. I found him in a worse state than I expected. He reached the ship on the 14th, unable to walk, or even stand without assistance; but already he was beginning to mend and was in excellent spirits. Christian had shot several ducks, which, with preserved potato, milk, strong ale, and lemon-juice, completed a very respectable dietary for a scurvy-stricken patient. All the rest were tolerably well; slight traces only of scurvy in two or three of the men. The ship was as clean and trim as I could expect, and all had well and cheerfully performed their duties during my absence.

The Doctor now acquainted me with the death of Thomas Blackwell, ship's steward, which occurred only five days previously, and was occasioned by scurvy. This man had scurvy when I left the ship in April, and no means were left untried by the Doctor to promote the recovery and rally his desponding energies; but his mind, unsustained by hope, lost all energy, and at last he had to be forcibly taken upon deck for fresh air.

Too late, his shipmates made it known that he had a dislike to preserved meats, and had lived the whole winter upon salt pork! Yet his death was somewhat unexpected; he went on deck as usual to walk in the middle of the day and, when found there, was quite dead. His remains were buried beside those of our late shipmate, Mr. Brand.

The news of our success to the southward in tracing the footsteps of the lost expedition greatly revived the spirits of my small crew; and we now wished only for the safe and speedy return of Young and his party.

Captain Young had commenced his spring explorations on the 7th of April, with a sledge party of four men, and a second sledge drawn by six dogs under the management of our Greenlander, Samuel. Finding in his progress that a channel* existed between Prince of Wales' Land and Victoria Land, whereby his discovery

* Now named M'Clintock Channel.

and search would be lengthened, he sent back one sledge, the tent, aud four men to the ship, in order to economize provisions; and for forty days journeyed with one man (George Hobday) and the dogs, encamping in such snow lodges as they were able to build.

This great exposure and fatigue, together with extremely bad weather, and a most difficult coastline to trace, greatly injured his health. He was compelled to return to the ship on 7th June for medical aid, but proposing at all hazards to renew his explorations almost immediately. Dr. Walker met this determination by a strong protest, in writing, against his leaving the ship again, his health being quite unequal to it; but after three days Young felt himself somewhat better and, with a zeal which knew no bounds, set off to complete his branch of the search, taking with him both his sledge parties.

The time having elapsed during which Young expected to remain absent, and the difficulties of the transit from the western sea having become greatly increased, I set off early on the 25th June with my four men intending to visit Pemmican Rock in the hope of meeting with him, and of facilitating his return. To our surprise the water had all drained off the frozen surface of the Long Lake, and it therefore afforded excellent travelling. We found the poor dogs lying quietly beside our sledges. They had attacked the pemmican and devoured a small quantity which was not secured in tin, also some blubber, some leather straps, and a gull that I had shot for a specimen; but they had not apparently relished the biscuit. Poor dogs! They have a hard life of it in these regions. Even Petersen, who is generally kind and humane, seems to fancy they must have little or no feeling: one of his theories is that you may knock an Esquimaux dog about the head with any article, however heavy, with perfect impunity to the brutes.

On the 27th I sent three of the men back to the ship and with Thompson and the dogs went on to Pemmican Rock, where, to our great joy, we happily met Young and his party, who had but just returned there, after a long and successful journey.

Young was greatly reduced in flesh and strength, so much weakened indeed that for the last few days he had travelled on the dog sledge; Harvey – also far from well – could just manage to keep pace with the sledge; his malady was scurvy. Their journeys had been very depressing; most dismal weather, low, dreary limestone shores devoid of game, and no traces of the lost expedition. The news of our success in the southern journeys greatly cheered them. On the following day we were all once more on board and indulging in such rapid consumption of eatables as only those can do who have been much reduced by long-continued fatigue and exposure to cold. Venison, ducks, beer, and lemon-juice daily; preserved apples and cranberries three times a week; and pickled whaleskin – a famous anti-scorbutic – ad libitum for all who liked it.

Homeward Bound

1st August, 1859. A long continuance of unusually calm, bright, and warm weather has been favourable to our painting and cleaning the ship, scraping masts, and so forth. The result is that she looks unusually smart and gay, and our impatience to exhibit her and ourselves at home is much increased.

Today the steam was got up, and with the help of our two stokers I worked the engines for a short time.

All are now in good health, but Hobson still a little lame. The issue of lemon-juice has been reduced to the ordinary allowance of half an ounce daily (as we have but little that is really good) lest another winter should become inevitable, which, I can devoutly say, may God forbid!

Wednesday, 10th August. The S.W. wind proved a good friend to us; by the morning of the 9th it had moved the ice off shore, and cleared away a passage for us out of Brentford Bay.

The wind now failed us, and I experienced some little difficulty in the management of the engines and boiler; the latter primed so violently as to send the water over our top gallant yard, and the tail valve of the condenser by some means had got out of its seat, and admitted air to the condenser; but eventually we got the engines to work well, and steamed across Cresswell Bay during the night. Having managed the engines for twenty-four consecutive hours, I was not sorry to get into bed.

26th August. I have been reading over Young's report of his spring journey. It comprises seventy-eight days of sledge-travelling, and certainly under most discouraging circumstances. The extent of coast-line explored by Captain Young amounts to 450 miles, whilst that discovered by Hobson and myself amounts to nearly 500 miles, making a total of 950 miles of new coast-line which we have laid down.

Sunday evening, 29th August. Calm, warm, lovely weather;

and we are thoroughly enjoying it in the quiet security of Lievely harbour, or Godhaven. Although Friday night was dark, we managed to find out the harbour's mouth, and slowly steamed into it. The inhabitants were awakened by Petersen demanding our letters.

It is rather a nervous thing, opening the first letters after a lapse of more than two years. We received them in our beds at three o'clock in the morning; and when we met at breakfast were able, thank God! to congratulate each other upon the receipt of cheering home news.

We sailed all the way home from Greenland without the assistance of the engine, yet the *Fox* made the passage in only nineteen days, arriving in the English Channel on the 20th September.

The relics we have brought home have been deposited in the United Service Institution, and now form a national memento – the most simple and most touching – of those heroic men who perished in the path of duty; but not until they had achieved the grand object of their voyage – the *Discovery of the Northwest Passage.**

M'Clintock's work had resulted in the roughing-in of the outlines of the Franklin tragedy, but the course of events during the last days of the lost expedition still remained obscure. Accordingly, over the years a number of attempts have been made to lighten that obscurity.

In 1879 Lieutenant Schwatka made a remarkable overland journey to King William's Island, by way of Simpson Strait, and found more bones and other relics. He also heard, from the Back River Eskimos, that thirty or thirty-five white men had died on the mainland near Point Richardson, and that, when the Eskimos found them, the bodies had been surrounded by many papers. Starvation Cove, as this lonely and macabre place was later named, was not actually visited by a white man until 1923, when Knud Rasmussen located it and buried the scattered bones. By then, of course, no traces of any documents remained.

* Which they had achieved in essence, if not in reality, by approaching within less than a hundred miles the "farthest east" reached by Simpson during his small-boat voyage along the coast.

In 1931 another group of skeletons was discovered on the Todd Islands in the eastern part of Simpson Strait and, since then, skeletal remains, undoubtedly of Franklin's men, have been found elsewhere in the region. But to this day less than two-thirds of the men who left their ships to seek escape on foot have been accounted for.

Since the bones cannot speak, and since no cache of documents has ever been found, or is likely to be found, the only prospect for any real elucidation of the mystery of what happened both to the missing, and to the known dead, lies, as it has always lain, in an examination of local Eskimo tradition and verbal history.

This was obvious to Charles F. Hall (some of whose adventures are chronicled in the next section of this book), who was the first white man to visit the disaster area after M'Clintock. As a result of seven years of close association with Eskimos, Hall had come to have a very high opinion not only of their veracity but of their incredibly tenacious folk-memory. Consequently, when Hall began his investigations into the Franklin mystery, north and west of Wager Inlet, in the late 1860's, he was fully aware that his best hopes of success lay in plumbing the memories of the local Eskimos.

Essentially, their accounts agreed with what is to be assumed from the mute evidence of the physical relics, but they went a good deal further. According to the Eskimos, the majority of the white men seemed to have been, if not actually afraid of the Eskimos, at least unwilling to learn from them, or in fact to have anything to do with them. The inevitable consequence of this folly was that these doomed fellows, who apparently could not conceive of the possibility that something could be learned from primitive savages, went on trying to live like Europeans until they starved to death.

From what Hall and, to a lesser extent, Lieutenant Schwatka learned from the Eskimos it is possible to reconstruct in some detail the probable events which followed on the abandonment of Erebus *and* Terror.

One of the two ships was evidently crushed by the ice, and sank during the spring of 1848. The other seems to have remained afloat in the ice, but she too was abandoned by her people, and a combined party of a hundred and five men and officers then set out to try to reach Great Slave Lake by way of Back River, according to the intention expressed by Captain Crozier in the document which M'Clintock's party found.

Before reaching Terror Bay with their immense sled loads, the party had already begun to suffer from exhaustion, hunger, and, no doubt, from the prolonged effects of scurvy. Here the entire group seems to have camped for some time and here the over-strained fabric of naval discipline and organization began to come apart. Many men seem to have died at this spot, and three boats, including the one M'Clintock and Hobson found, were abandoned. Eventually Crozier must have decided that to remain any longer at Terror Bay would mean death for all, and so he again set out to the south accompanied by those who were still capable of exertion, or who at any rate believed that there was some use in struggling on. Many of those who remained at Terror Bay died there, but some evidently returned to the remaining ship, and at least five men seem to have survived aboard her through the following winter, abandoning her again in the spring of 1849.

As for the party led by Crozier, it moved painfully along the shores of the island, leaving a pathetic trail of abandoned equipment and unburied dead to mark its passage.

Before reaching the southern shores of the island, the party seems to have divided into two groups. One of these, consisting of about forty men under Crozier, continued to strive for the Back River while the other group turned east. Deluded by inaccurate charts which showed King William's Island as joined to Boothia, those who turned eastward may have hoped to follow John Ross's footsteps to the cache at Fury Beach, and thence to the mouth of Lancaster Sound; or perhaps they hoped to find a rescue expedition along the west shore of Foxe Basin.

Crozier's group, wasting rapidly as summer waned, reached Simpson Strait and, when the ice formed that winter, crossed it via the Todd Islands (where many of them left their bones), and came to the end of their hopeless march in the little bay on the Adelaide Peninsula, since named Starvation Cove. It was here, a year or two later, that the Eskimos found the thirty to thirty-five skeletons, together with the mass of papers which must have been the journals and records of the expedition. It was a gruesome find, for most of the bodies had been eaten – and by men. Many of the bones had been cut through with saws, and the skulls showed gaping holes through which the brains had been removed.

But not all died here. Crozier and four other men survived the summer of 1849 and, giving up the hopeless attempt to escape up the Back River, they turned north-eastward to the Boothia Peninsula where they met, and were succoured by, local Eskimos. They seem to have understood belatedly that their only hope for survival lay in a whole-hearted acceptance of the Eskimo way of life, and to have remained with these Eskimos, moving from camp to camp, and becoming almost Eskimo themselves for two or three years, no doubt always sustained by the hope that a rescue expedition would discover them. But eventually Crozier seems to have given up hope of rescue from that remote place, and he and at least one other man determined to try again to reach the Hudson Bay Territories via the Back River. Equipped with guns, a supply of ammunition, and a folding rubber boat, they left their Eskimo friends on Boothia and moved back toward Chantrey Inlet.

If they had learned the prime lesson of survival in that country (and they appear to have done so) and continued to live an Eskimo way of life and to keep in close contact with the Eskimos along their route, they would have had little difficulty in reaching the Back River estuary. But here they would have learned from the river Eskimos that to attempt a journey to the headwaters of the Back in a flimsy boat was almost suicidal, not only because of the fierce nature of the waterway, but also because of the presence of Indians near the upper reaches — Indians who had waged a bitter war of raids and ambuscades against the Eskimos through many centuries, and who would shoot any intruders appearing from the north long before the strangers could hope to identify themselves as white men.

As an alternative, the Back River Eskimos may well have suggested that Crozier follow one of the well-used overland routes to the Baker Lake-Thelon system, where the two white men would be in the country of the Caribou Eskimos who traded regularly with the Hudson's Bay post at Churchill. That this is what Crozier actually attempted seems fairly certain, for there were subsequent Eskimo reports of Crozier and one other white man having been seen in the Baker Lake area sometime between 1852 and 1858. From this point in space and time, there is no further certain trace of these last two survivors of the southern party. However, in 1948 a very ancient cairn, not of normal Eskimo construction, and containing fragments of a hardwood box with dove-tailed corners, was found by myself and a companion at Angikuni Lake on the Kazan River in central Keewatin, near a famous junction where the Eskimo trade routes between Churchill and the Arctic coasts converge. Considerable research has failed to identify the builder of this cairn. Only one white man, Samuel Hearne, is known to have visited the place at a reasonably distant date, in 1770, and the assumption is that the cairn may have been built by him. But since he makes no mention of it in his journals, the possibility remains that this mute monument was built by Crozier, before he vanished utterly.

As to the group which split off from Crozier's party in the summer of 1848 and headed east, at least four individuals seem to have survived until as late as 1862 or 1863, when they were seen on several occasions by Eskimos, near the north-west corner of Melville Peninsula, probably making for Igloolik where Parry's ships had wintered in 1821-23, and where they might have hoped to meet a whaling ship. Unhappily the local Eskimos mistook the strangers for a far-ranging party of the dreaded Itkilit, *the Barrenlands Indians, and so kept out of sight. A few years after the event the Eskimos concerned were aware that, in their initial panic, they had been mistaken in their identification, but, by the time Hall reached the area in 1868, the only traces still remaining of these, the last of the forgotten wanderers, consisted of no more than an abandoned tent site and a few fire-blackened stones.*

The Eskimo reports on which the foregoing reconstruction of events is based are extremely circumstantial, and in good detail. Like all verbal accounts, they show discrepancies and have some inexplicable elements about them, but there can be no doubt that they are drawn from actual events. However, they have usually been ignored, or condemned outright, by most of the many writers who have set themselves to reconstruct the details of the Franklin story. Officially, therefore, the mystery which surrounds the eventual death or disappearance of the hundred and five men who abandoned the Erebus *and* Terror *still waits for a complete solution.*

Illustrations

1 *Greenland Norse settlers were the first known Europeans to discover and explore parts of North America. Along the east coast of Baffin Island, stretching into Hudson Strait and Ungava Bay and down the east coast of Hudson Bay stands a series of huge stone beacons which were almost certainly built and used by Norse voyagers as navigation beacons. This one stands at the mouth of the Payne River in Ungava Bay.*

11 *On an island at the mouth of the Payne River estuary archaeologist Thomas Lee has excavated and partially restored this stone-built Norse longhouse. It appears to have been built by Norse visitors from Greenland in the 13th century.*

III *The Norse were familiar with Ungava Bay for at least 200 years and they left many traces of their presence there, including several huge longhouses, together with a complete village site on Payne Lake. This monument, believed to represent the Hammer of Thor, stands on the Payne River bank on the route leading to the inland village.*

IV *Martin Frobisher was a typical Elizabethan swashbuckler who fought with Drake against the Armada and dabbled in the legal piracy called privateering. Very much a modern capitalist, he hoped to get rich raping the mineral wealth of the newly discovered continent of North America, while nominally engaged in looking for the Northwest Passage.*

V

Finding what he took to be gold, on his first expedition to south Baffin Island, Frobisher returned to his discovery believing it would make him incredibly wealthy. But, as these miners whom he brought with him soon determined, the gold was fool's gold—iron pyrites, and completely worthless.

VI *With the arrogance toward the natives displayed by most Europeans in all times, Frobisher early managed to pick a fight with the Eskimos and to kill several of them. This skirmish, which took place in Frobisher Bay on August 1, 1577, is believed to have been originally sketched by an eyewitness, one John White.*

VII *Henry Hudson has always been considered a heroic victim of the rascally crew that abandoned him in a boat on Hudson Bay. The truth seems to be that, because of his treatment of his men, he deserved what he got. Here he and his son are seen being forced into the boat before being set adrift.*

VIII *An expedition led by Jens Munk was sent out by King Christian IV of Denmark in 1619, to reaffirm Scandinavian claims to the Hudson Bay region established by two Danish expeditions in the 14th and 15th centuries. One of Munk's little ships was almost lost in a collision with the ice in Hudson Strait.*

IX *Munk established what he hoped would be a permanent Danish settlement at the present site of Churchill, Manitoba. Houses were built, and the ships hauled out, but scurvy decimated his crews and forced the few survivors to flee back to Denmark in the spring of 1620.*

X *Sieur de la Potherie, a courtier and friend of King Louis XIV of France, took part in a French naval expedition into Hudson Bay to expel the Hudson's Bay Company. The expedition came within an ace of succeeding, inflicting a major defeat upon the English.*

XI *When de la Potherie's Flagship, the Pelican, was wrecked, his men managed to get ashore and soon afterwards attacked and overwhelmed the garrison of one of the Hudson's Bay Company forts.*

XII *The Dutch, and later the Scots, whalers explored most of the Arctic seas, including a good part of the Northwest Passage. Official explorers followed in their wakes. The whalers pioneered ice navigation, but at a fantastic cost. More than 400 whaling ships were lost in Baffin Bay and along the east Greenland coast.*

XIII *The whalers' quarry was the slow-moving, plankton-eating bowhead, a huge and normally inoffensive mammal although capable of smashing boats and killing men when harpooned. The species was almost exterminated by the whalers, and not more than 200 remain alive today.*

XIV *The skills of the Arctic whalers were fabulous. Hunting in the ice, away from land for months at a time, they performed miracles of survival. Here the crew of a Scots whaler, which was badly holed by ice below the waterline, have lightened ship and are careening her so they can repair the damage.*

XV *When Sir John Ross was making his attempt on the Northwest Passage in 1818, he was guided through the almost impenetrable ice of Melville Bay by the Scots whaling fleet, seen here with Ross's expedition in the rear. The icebergs are rather fanciful, but the sense of danger they impart in this print was real enough.*

XVI *Sir John Ross was truly entitled to the description "intrepid." The survival of him and his men through four years spent frozen in amongst the Arctic islands was one of the greatest exploits in Arctic exploration. Unlike many of his peers, he respected the Eskimos, made friends with them, and studied their survival methods. Here he is seen making first contact with an Eskimo party in August of 1818.*

XVII *Unable to extricate his ships from the ice, Ross led his men back to safety in a superlatively well-managed boat voyage to the north end of Baffin Island. Here the men met and were rescued by the whaler* Isabella *after four years' absence, during which the world had given up all hope of their survival.*

XVIII *The greatest disaster in the search for the Northwest Passage was the loss of the entire British naval expedition led by Sir John Franklin in 1845-47. More than a dozen other expeditions went in search of Franklin, of which the most important was the Arctic Searching Squadron sent out in 1850. It was unique in that it had two steam auxiliary ships—the first steamers ever seen in the Arctic—one of them commanded by Lieutenant Sherard Osborn. He is shown here (at left) with the rest of the commanders, including Leopold M'Clintock (third from left) who, some years later, was to solve the Franklin mystery.*

XIX *Osborn was a young man at the time and a bit of a rake. He was delighted by the attractions of the Greenland Eskimo girls he visited on the way north, such as these two belles from Godhavn in west Greenland.*

XX *The ships of the Arctic Searching Squadron had little luck forcing their way west in search of Franklin, so they wintered in the ice. On the left is the steam auxiliary* Pioneer, *commanded by Osborn, with the sailing ship* Assistance *on the right.*

XXI *Neither the Arctic Searching Squadron nor any of the other official search expeditions found any trace of Franklin beyond Beechey Island, where stands this weathered grave marker to one of Franklin's young men who died before the expedition vanished into mystery.*

XXII *The discovery of the fate of Franklin and his Northwest Passage expedition was left to Leopold M'Clintock. In the converted steam yacht* Fox, *and sponsored by Lady Franklin, M'Clintock worked his way farther west than anyone save Franklin had reached. The* Fox *was nearly lost a score of times, as on this occasion when she was caught in a tidal bore while surrounded by great masses of ice.*

XXIII *Putting the* Fox *into winter quarters near Port Kennedy, M'Clintock set out on a series of sledge journeys, conducted in British navy style by man power, and eventually reached King William Island where the first traces of the missing Franklin expedition were at last discovered in 1859.*

XXIV *On the frozen shores of Erebus Bay, King William Island, M'Clintock found the wreck of a boat and, inside it, the skeletons of a number of British seamen. These were but a few of the 135 men who starved or froze to death when the Franklin expedition lost both its ships to the Arctic ice.*

XXV *This is the memorial to the lost expedition, sent out by Lady Franklin with M'Clintock, and erected by him on Beechey Island.*

XXVI *When Charles Francis Hall went north in 1860, in a single-handed attempt to continue the search for Franklin survivors, he had no choice but to live like an Eskimo. He seems to have been the first European to overcome his prejudices against the "natives" enough to let him learn to be one of them. In the end, he came to love the Eskimos and to prefer them to civilized men. These kayakers were still pursuing their ancient way of life in 1969, but the kayak and its use is now almost forgotten.*

XXVII *This is an Eskimo family from Baffin Island wearing the style of clothes and carrying the tools and weapons that had endured for thousands of years, and which Hall learned to wear and use.*

XXVIII *The idea that life in an Eskimo house was a hideous ordeal for a civilized man was one that Hall vigorously rejected. Looking at this print one can see that it had its advantages.*

XXIX *The ship that finally made her way through the Northwest Passage was an old Norwegian herring boat with a tiny engine, but mostly powered by sail. The Gjoa had a crew of only six men under command of young Roald Amundsen. She endured incredible ordeals as on this occasion when she was bounced about on a series of rocky reefs for many hours during a hurricane-strength gale.*

XXX *Here is the* Gjoa*'s crew after their arrival at Nome, Alaska. Amundsen went on to become one of the world's greatest polar explorers and became the first man ever to reach the South Pole.*

XXXI *Things have changed almost beyond belief in the methods men have used in their attempts to penetrate the Northwest Passage. Sailing vessels such as these schooners have been replaced by steel giants powered by immense engines . . . ships such as the tanker* Manhattan *and the Canadian government icebreaker* John A. Macdonald *(see next page).*

XXXII *Despite our much-vaunted technological expertise, we are hardly closer to success today than in the days of sail and wooden ships . . . and the Northwest Passage remains almost as far from being a practical reality as it ever was.*

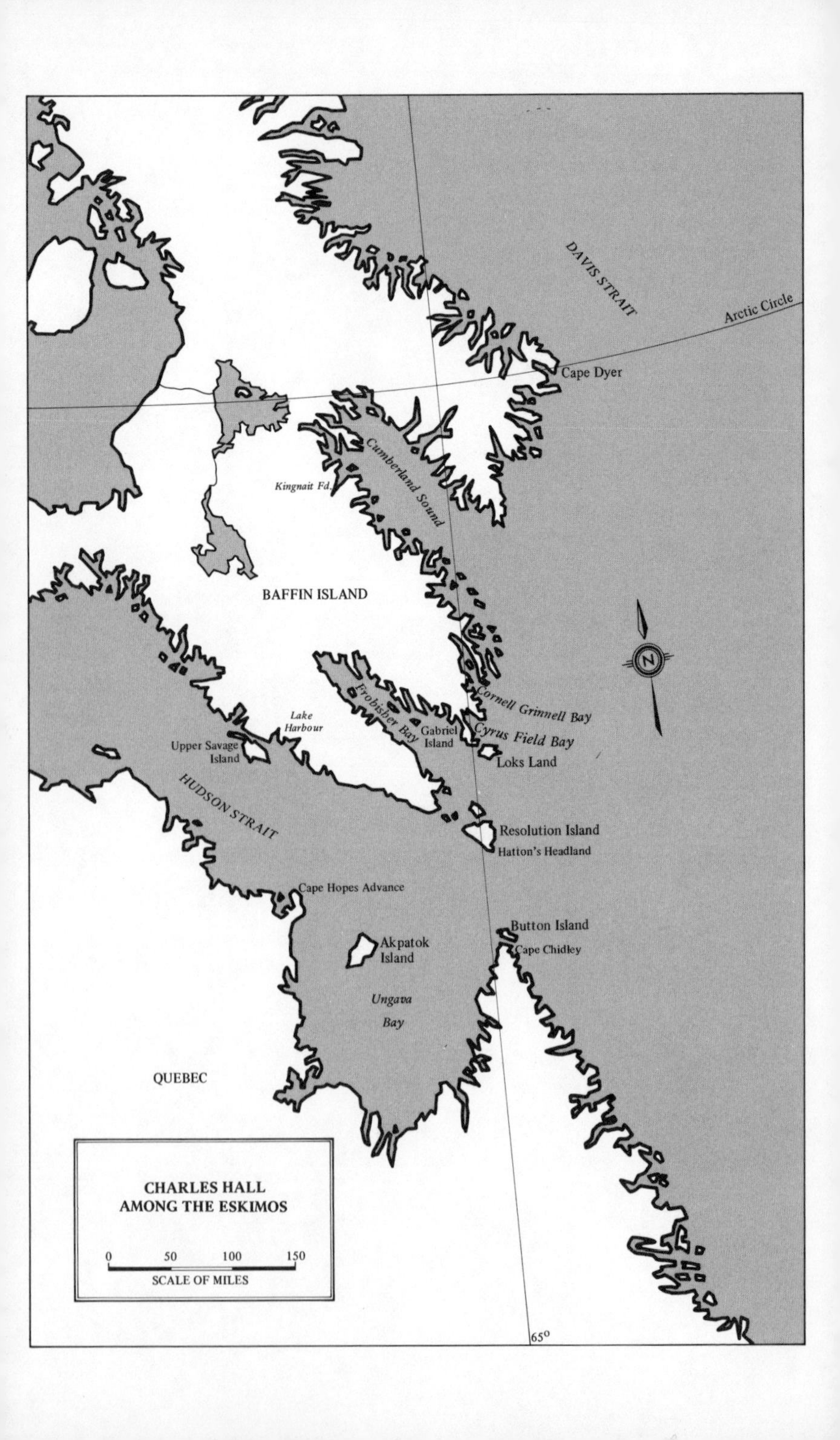
DAVIS STRAIT
Arctic Circle
Cape Dyer
Cumberland Sound
Kingnait Fd.
BAFFIN ISLAND
Cornell Grinnell Bay
Cyrus Field Bay
Frobisher Bay
Gabriel Island
Lake Harbour
Upper Savage Island
Loks Land
HUDSON STRAIT
Resolution Island
Hatton's Headland
Cape Hopes Advance
Button Island
Cape Chidley
Akpatok Island
Ungava Bay
QUEBEC
CHARLES HALL
AMONG THE ESKIMOS
0
50
100
150
SCALE OF MILES
65°

XI
The Almost Eskimo

By 1860 interest in the Northwest Passage had all but ended for, though two possible channels were now known to exist, both were impassable to sailing ships or to the steamers of those times. To contribute to the loss of interest, most of the important blanks in the maps and charts of Arctic North America had now been roughed in; and the Franklin mystery was solved, superficially at least.

In place of these attractions, would-be Arctic adventurers now turned to one of the oldest incentives of them all – to one which had sent ships into the ice as far back as the sixteenth century – the quest for the North Pole itself.

This was to be a fearsome business, filled with tragedy, with colossal blunders, with heroism wasted, with great courage, with chicanery and misery. And, in the end, it was to resolve itself into an acrimonious battle between two Americans, Dr. Cook and Admiral Peary, as to which of them had first attained that insubstantial objective. Since there is strong evidence that neither of them did so, the whole interminable tale ends on a dubious and distasteful note.

However, the desire to be the first to stand upon an ice-floe at 90 degrees north latitude, was not the sole remaining attraction of the North, though it absorbed the attention of most Arctic explorers. One man at least still heard the echoes of the Franklin search.

He was Charles Francis Hall, an American of obscure antecedents, who had been amongst other things a blacksmith's apprentice and the editor of a penny newspaper. He was something of a mystic and given to visions; and during one of these he felt a call of almost religious intensity to continue the now-abandoned search for survivors of the Franklin expedition.

The support that he eventually obtained for this purpose was so meagre that it barely sufficed to provide a small open boat and a completely inadequate stock of supplies — one of the major items of which was a gift of hog-cracklings from a friend in Cincinnati. To get north at all he had to beg free passage aboard a New England whaler which was bound for the east coast of Baffin Island.

East Baffin was a long, hard way from the arena of the Franklin tragedy, but Hall was undismayed. He boarded the whaler George Henry* *in New Bedford in the spring of 1860, determined to leave her when he reached the Baffin coast and then to make his way in his open boat to King William's Island. It was a wild, fantastical scheme — but Hall was a fantastic fellow.*

In the event his little boat was wrecked a short time after the George Henry *reached Baffin Island. This abrupt end to his hopes did not destroy Hall's dream. He at once began making plans for a second expedition (one which was destined to uncover most of the facts about the fate of Franklin's party after it had left its ships). But these plans were for the future, and meanwhile Hall was condemned to spend two years on Baffin Island. He did not intend to waste those years. He seems to have grasped intuitively the cardinal fact which had eluded most of his predecessors, that success could only be achieved in the North if the explorer learned how to become on integral part of the country. He needed knowledge of the land, its beasts, and its people, and Hall went directly to the obvious source of such information, which almost every white man in the Arctic before his time had totally neglected. Hall went to the Eskimos, and became the first white man of whom we have certain knowledge who deliberately chose to live for an extended period as an Eskimo himself.*

The two extracts from his book which follow represent two diametrically opposed attempts to survive the rigours of the Arctic.

* Commanded by the same Captain Budington who had salvaged Belcher's derelict ship, the *Resolute*.

On the one hand there is the harrowing account of the fate of a small band of white men who held the time-honoured attitude which had prevailed until M'Clintock's time, of remaining aliens and intruders in the land; and, on the other, there is the account of Hall's experiences, as he pioneered a totally different approach to the problem of Arctic survival.

LIFE AMONG THE ESQUIMAUX

The Runaways

Tuesday, August 7th, 1860. After dinner I had gone and perched myself up in one of the whale-boats hanging over the ship's side, for the purpose of viewing the mountain scenery as we passed along the Baffinland coast. As I looked easterly, my eye caught a strange black sail. Directing the captain and mate's attention to it, they examined, but could not make out what it was. At length we decided that it was a whale-boat with dark-coloured sails, and approaching us.

In a few moments more the strange boat was near enough to make her crew out for white men, nine in number; and directly they got alongside, a question was put by Captain Budington as to who they were. The steersman promptly answered, "Crew from the *Ansell Gibbs* of New Bedford."

In a few minutes a variety of questions was put as to the number of ships, the whaling, &c. in Cumberland Sound where we conjectured the *Ansell Gibbs* to be; and then the inquiry was made of them, "You are runaways, are you not?" The response immediately was, "Yes, we are!" They then told us that they had left Kingnait, in Cumberland Sound, on August 2nd, and had thus run the distance, 250 miles to where we met them, in less than three days.

The reason they gave for deserting their ship was because of "bad treatment on board," and "not having enough to eat." At all events, they made up their minds to start for the United States on the first chance, and this they did by taking a whale-boat, a "conjuror" (a portable cooking apparatus), two guns and ammunition, a small quantity of provisions, a few blankets, and other trifling things; and this to go a voyage over a tempestuous sea, part of it often full of ice, and along an iron-bound coast, for a distance of say 1,500 miles!

When Captain Budington had asked several questions, the chief of these unfortunate men modestly supplicated for some food, as they were all very hungry. This was immediately responded to by the captain saying "Come and eat"; but at first they hesitated, fearing they might be arrested. But hunger prevailed and, making secure their boat, they entered the ship and fell-to upon the salt junk and biscuit like hungry wolves. Never before did I see men eat with such avidity and relish. To them it was a feast, having had only half a biscuit each and one small duck among the whole number during the past day.

I found that nothing would alter their purpose as to proceeding on their desperate voyage. They meant to strike for York Factory in Hudson's Bay; but on my showing them a chart and the course to Resolution Island, thence across Hudson's Strait to Labrador, this latter course was decided upon, with the hope that fishermen might pick them up.

The captain kindly gave them some beef and pork, powder and shot, and a chart. To this I also added some ammunition and caps.

They remained with us about two hours, and then, after deciding to go on instead of landing for the night (perhaps they were still fearful of being captured), they got into their boat, and with many thanks to us started on their perilous voyage. I watched them long as they passed away from us bending to their oars.

Before I pass from this strange occurrence, it will be better to give the sequel of their history. The following particulars I gleaned at St. John's, Newfoundland, on my way home in the fall of 1862.

It seems that a Captain Nathan Norman, who does business in Labrador and is also a magistrate, encountered the survivors of this boat's crew and, hearing their tale, demanded from them a statement in writing; whereupon one of them drew up an account, the original of which is in my possession:

"My name is John F. Sullivan. I left my home in South Hadley Falls, Mass., about the 1st of March, 1860, for Boston. I remained in Boston until the 20th of the same month. I applied at different offices for a chance to ship. Being a stranger in the place, and a green hand, I found it very difficult to get a berth to suit me. At last I got a little discouraged and that day signed my name at No. 172 Commercial Street, Boston, and left for New Bedford, Mass. Next morning I shipped to go aboard of the ship *Daniel Webster*, then laying at New Bedford, but to sail the same day on a whaling cruise to Davis' Straits, to be gone 18 months.

"I left New Bedford in the *Daniel Webster* on the 21st March, 1860. There were forty of us in the crew, all told. We had very rough weather for many days after leaving, which caused many of us to be sea-sick. I suffered from it about three weeks; after that time I began to recruit. There was nothing happened of any consequence worth mentioning until we passed Cape Farewell, about the last of May. After that we had quite a hard time working the ship through the ice. However, we made out to get her through, and came to anchor,* July 6th, 1860.

"We spoke many vessels going in. I will name some of them; the *Hannibal*, of New London; the *Black Eagle* and *Antelope*, of New Bedford; the *Ansell Gibbs*, of Fair Haven; the *Pioneer*, of New London. These vessels were anchored very close to one another in the harbour; the crews were at liberty sometimes to pay visits to each other; each one would tell how he was treated. Several complained of very bad treatment, especially the crew of the *Ansell Gibbs;* they were planning some way of running away for a long time, but they found no opportunity till the 4th of August.

"My shipmate, whose name was Warren Dutton, was aboard that day and heard a little of the conversation, and he joined in with them, and said he would go, and perhaps one or two more of his crew. He immediately came aboard and informed me; and he pictured everything out so nice that I finally consented to go with him. We had no great reason for leaving our vessel; we could not complain of very bad treatment aboard; all we could complain of was that we were very badly fitted out for such a climate; and, after we arrived there, hearing of so many men that died there the last winter of scurvy, we were afraid to remain there for fear that we might get it. We thought that by running away we would be all right, but we were sadly mistaken.

* In Kingnait Fiord, Cumberland Sound.

"After it was agreed upon to leave, each one was busy making preparations for a start. I, with my shipmate, packed what few things we thought would be necessary into a travelling bag which belonged to me; we then crept into the hold and filled a small bag and a pair of drawers with hard bread, and waited for an opportunity to hide it on deck, unknown to the watch. After we succeeded in that we made a signal to the other crew that we were ready. It being boats' crew watches aboard the *Ansell Gibbs,* they found no difficulty in lowering away the boat, which after they did so they lowered themselves easily into her, and soon paddled under our bows; we then dropped our traps into her, and, taking with us two guns and a little ammunition, got into her, and soon pulled around a small point out of sight of the vessels. The names of the crew that left the *Ansell Gibbs* are as follows: John Giles, boat-steerer; John Martin, Hiram J. Davis, Williard Hawkins, Thomas Colwell, Joseph Fisher and Samuel J. Fisher.

"At 11 o'clock at night, on the 4th of August, we left the vessels in Cumberland Straits, about five miles from Penny's Harbour. Although it being a little foggy, with a fair wind, we stood across the Straits. When about half way across we dumped overboard a tub of towline to lighten the boat some. We had nothing but a small boat-compass to guide us; we had no opportunity of getting a chart before we left, and not much of anything else.

"We made the other side of the Straits by morning; then, by taking the spy-glass, we thought we could perceive a sail in chase of us, but we soon lost sight of her. The other crew were depending mostly on us for bread, as my shipmate informed them that we had a better chance to get it out of the hold. Their bread lay close to the cabin; so what bread they had, with ours, would not exceed more than twenty pounds. We all saw that the bread would not last long, so each one desired to be put on allowance of one biscuit a day to each man. We hoped by the time that was gone to reach some place where we could find help. We made a very good run the first three days, sleeping at night in the boat. On the fourth day out we fell in with the barque *George Henry*, Captain Budington, of New London. He asked us aboard; the boat-steerer acted as spokesman. The captain told us we were very foolish to leave the vessels to undertake so long a trip. I believe he would have taken us all if we wished to stay; but as we had left a whaler, we did not like to go on board another, as he was also going to remain there through the winter; so we were determined to push along, as we had been foolish enough to start in the first place.

"Before we left he gave us a small bag of bread, a piece of salt pork and some ammunition; also a chart. We then bade him good-by, and set off again.

"That night we made a 'lee,' found some moss, and made a fire. Before we ran in we shot a small duck, which made a good stew for all hands. Two days after this we shot a white bear; he was in the water when we shot him, and there being a heavy sea on at the time we could get no more than his hind quarters in; this we skinned – the rest we could not save. That night we managed between us to cook it, as we were divided into watches, two in each watch; by doing so we could watch the boat and keep her with the tide. We kept on in this way, always tracking the shore, and at night going ashore to lay on the rocks, with our boat's sail over us for shelter.

"We had very rough weather in crossing Hudson's Straits. We were on Resolution Island four days, waiting for a fair wind; we got it at last, but so strong that it came very near swamping our little boat many times through the night. It kept two of us bailing water out all the time and we were glad to reach the land after being in the boat thirty hours, wet to the skin. What bear's meat and bread we had was most gone by this time; there was nothing left but a few crumbs in the bottom of the bag. There was nine parts made of the crumbs; then they were caked off, each man taking his share.

"On the 16th of August we made Cape Chidley on Labrador. On the 20th we divided the last crumbs; after that we picked up what we could find to eat. We found a few berries and mushrooms. We suffered very much from the cold, very seldom having a dry rag upon us.

"We continued on in this condition until the 3rd of September, when, to add to our misfortune, William Hawkins and Hiram J. Davis (who we called 'the doctor') ran away from us that night, and took with them everything that was of any use to us; they even took the boat's compass and left us in a miserable condition with our boat broadside on the beach. It being their watch, they made out to get off. We thought it was useless to make chase after them, so we let them go. It then commenced to rain, and there was a heavy sea rolling in, and, weak as we were, we found some difficulty in shoving the boat off. However, after a hard tug, we succeeded, and then pulled out some ways; we then put up sail. It was not up long before it blew so strong that it carried away the mast. We then ran in under a jib, and made a lee.

"About half an hour after we landed my shipmate died of starvation. The evening he died, Samuel Fisher proposed to eat him; he took his knife and cut a piece off the thigh, and held it over the fire until it was cooked. Then, next morning, each one followed his example; after that the meat was taken off the bones, and each man took a share.

"We stopped here three days. We then made a start; but the wind being ahead, we were obliged to put back. Here we stopped two more days. During that time the bones were broken up small and boiled in a pot or kettle we had; also the skull was broken open, the brains taken out, and cooked. We then got a fair wind, but as we got around a point we had the wind very fresh off shore. We could hardly manage the boat; at last we drove on to an island some ways out to sea; we got the boat under the lee of it; but the same night we had a large hole stove into her. Being unable to haul her up, we were obliged to remain here eight days: it was on this island they tried to murder me.

"The third day we stopped here, I was out as usual picking berries, or anything I could find to eat. Coming in I chanced to pick up a mushroom. I brought it in with me; also an armful of wood. While kneeling down to cook the mushroom, I received a heavy blow of a club from Joseph Fisher, and before I could get to my feet I got three more blows. I then managed to get to my feet, when Samuel Fisher got hold of my right arm; then Joseph Fisher struck me three more blows on the arm. I somehow got away from them and, being half crazy, I did not know what to do. They made for me again. I kept begging of them, for God's sake to spare my life, but they would not listen to my cries. They said they wanted some meat, and were bound to kill me. I had nothing I could defend myself with but a small knife; this I held in my hand until they approached me. Samuel Fisher was the first to come toward me; he had a large dirk-knife in his hand; his cousin was coming from another direction with a club and a stone. Samuel came on and grasped me by the shoulder, and had his knife raised to stab me. I then raised my knife and stabbed him in the throat. He immediately fell, and I then made a step for Joe; he dropped his club, and then went where the rest was. I then stooped down to see if Samuel was dead; he was still alive. I did not know what to do. At this time I began to cry; after a little while the rest told me to come up; they would see there was nothing more done to me. I received four deep cuts on the head. One of the fellows dressed them for me and washed the blood off my face. Next day Samuel Fisher died; his cousin was the first one to cut him up; his body was used up the same as my unfortunate shipmate's.

"After a while we managed to repair the boat and left this island. We ran in where we thought was main land, but it proved to be an island. Here we left the boat and proceeded on foot, walking about one mile a day. At last we reached the other side of the island in four days; then put back again to the boat. It took us four days to get back again. When we got there we found the boat was stove very bad since we left her. We tried to get around the island in her, but she sunk when we got into her; we then left her and went back again to the other side of the island, to remain there until we would die or be picked up.

"We ate our boots, belts, and sheaths, and a number of bear-skin and seal-skin articles we had with us. To add to our misery it commenced to rain, and kept up for three days; it then began to snow. In this miserable condition we were picked up by a boat's crew of Esquimaux on the 29th of September, and brought to Okoke on the 3rd of October. The missionaries did all that lay in their power to help us along, and provided us with food and clothing, then sent us on to Nain where we met 'the doctor' who was picked up three days before we were. He reported that his companion died, and told many false stories after he was picked up.

"The missionaries of Nain helped us on to Hopedale; from there we were sent on to Kibokok, where two of us remained through the winter. One stopped with a settler named John Lane, between Nain and Hopedale; 'the doctor' stopped with John Walker until March, when he left for Indian Harbour; the remaining two, Joseph Fisher and Thomas Colwell, also stopped with settlers around Indian Harbour. Mr. Bell, the agent at Kibokok, kept two of us until we could find an opportunity of leaving the coast. We left his place about the 10th of July, and came to Macovie, waiting a chance to get off.

"Captain Duntan has been kind enough to give me a passage; my companion was taken by Captain Hamilton, of the *Wild Rover*. We have had a very pleasant passage so far, and I hope it will continue so.

"Sir, I hope you may make it out; it is very poor writing, and was written in haste.

John F. Sullivan."

We pick up Hall's narrative again, after the wreck of his boat.

On Going Native

Having a great desire to do something in the way of exploring, and particularly to accustom myself to actual life among the Innuits, I at length determined to venture on an excursion by sledge and dogs to Cornelius Grinnell Bay, whither Ugarng* had already gone.

The following account of the first day's journey is from my journal, as written every evening in an igloo:

"Thursday, January 10th, 1861—Thermometer 30° below zero. My company consists of self, Ebierbing, his wife Tookoolito, and Koodloo. By 4 a.m. I was up and called Ebierbing and his wife. They arose and at once proceeded to gather up whatever things they would require during our stay. I then returned to the ship and packed up my own material. The outfit for this trip consisted, in provisions, of 1½ lb. preserved boiled mutton in cans, 3 lbs. raw salt pork, 15 cakes (4 lbs.) sea-bread, ¼ lb. pepper, 2 lbs. ground burnt coffee, 1 quart molasses, 1 quart corn-meal, and 3 lbs. Cincinnati cracklings for soup. For bedding, 1 double wool blanket, 1 sleeping-bag, 1 cloak and 1 shawl for bed-covering. For clothing, besides my native dress upon me, I took 1 extra under-shirt, 1 woollen shirt, 2 pairs extra stockings, 1 pair extra pants, 2 towels and 2 pairs mittens. My books were Bowditch's *Navigator*, Burrit's *Geography and Atlas of the Heavens*, Gillespie's *Land Surveying, Nautical Almanac for 1861*, a Bible, and *Daily Food*. My instruments were, 1 telescope, 1 self-registering thermometer, 1 pocket sextant, 2 magnetic compasses, and 1 marine glass. I had also a rifle and ammunition, oil for lamp, and a hand-saw, besides paper, ink, pens, memorandum and journal book.

* Ugarng was a remarkably intelligent man and a very good mechanic. He had several excellent traits of character, besides some not at all commendable.

In 1854-5 he was on a visit to the States, and among his reminiscences of that visit, he said about New York, "G--d--! too much horse—too much house—too much white people. Women? ah! Women great many—good!"

—C. F. H.

"At 10 a.m. we were in readiness – Ebierbing with the loaded sledge and team of dogs (five of his and five of my Greenland dogs). Tookoolito was gaily dressed in a new caribou skirt, caribou pants, jacket, &c. Bidding adieu to our friends on board, we then started. Tookoolito leading the way – tracking for the dogs – for about one mile to the shore, in a north-easterly direction. Thence our course was that which Ugarng had evidently taken the day before. Over hill and mountain, through vale and valley, away we went. Sometimes, when on a descent, our speed was rapid. Now and then we all got on the sledge for a ride. My spirits were high, for this was my first sledge-travelling trip. I think I never perspired so profusely as I have this day. Some of the events during our journey have been most amusing. Once we were descending a steep incline, all of the company holding on to the sledge so as to prevent its too great speed downward when, one of my feet breaking through the treacherous snow-crust, headlong I went and, like a hoop, trundled to the bottom of the hill. Tookoolito hastened to my relief, and seeing a frostbite on my face, she instantly applied her warm hand, the Innuit way, till all was right again.

"By 3 p.m. we neared the frozen waters of the ocean, after passing over some very abrupt and rocky ground. On the margin of the sea the cliffs were almost perpendicular, and it was necessary to lower the sledge down to the ice below. Accordingly the dogs were detached and while Tookoolito, whip in hand, held on by their traces, which were from twenty to thirty feet long, we lowered the sledge. However, the tide was out, and it caused some difficulty in getting on to the main ice. At length all was safely accomplished, and once more we started on our way, Tookoolito again leading. We proceeded for about five miles when we came to an igloo out on the ice, which had evidently been erected and occupied the night before by Ugarng and his party."

Ebierbing and Koodloo at once commenced sawing out snow-blocks while I carried them to a suitable spot for erecting the igloo, which took us one hour to make. As soon as the igloo was completed, Tookoolito entered and commenced placing the stone lamp in its proper position. It was then trimmed, and soon a kettle of snow was over it making water for coffee and soup. She then proceeded to place several pieces of board we had brought with us on the snow platform where our beds were to be made. Upon these pieces was spread the canvas containing some small dry shrubs.

Over this went the caribou skins, and thus our sleeping accommodations were complete.

The drying of whatever has been worn during the day, or whatever has become wet with perspiration, falls on the lot of the "igloo wife." She places the things on a net over the fire-lamp, and through the night attends to the turning of them, as occasion requires. Her other duties consist in the repairing of such clothing as may be needed. Nothing is allowed to go one day without repair. Everything, where care is required, even to pipes and tobacco, is placed in the igloo wife's hands – in this case, Tookoolito's.

Presently our evening meal was ready. It consisted of Cincinnati crackling soup, a small piece of raw salt pork for each of us, half a biscuit, and coffee. Tookoolito proved herself an excellent cook; and I soon felt convinced that no party should think of travelling in these regions without an Innuit man and his wife, for the latter, above everything, is the "all in all," or at least the "better half."

After supper, myself and the two male Esquimaux had each a pipe, and then turned in, my position being between the hot-blooded Innuits Ebierbing and Koodloo.

I slept as well as I would ever wish, and on the following morning, after breakfast and repacking the sledge, we again started. Our proper course was due north but owing to hummocky ice we could not follow it. In truth, sometimes we were obliged to make a retrograde movement to get out of "a fix" that we were occasionally in among icebergs and hummocks. Owing to this we made but five miles direct toward our destination during the day.

It had been expected that we could reach Cornelius Grinnell Bay in one day from the vessel, but too many obstacles existed to allow it, and thus a second night came upon us while still upon the frozen sea. A storm was also gathering, and its darkness, with the howling wind, which had changed from off the land to right upon it, was foreboding. We were likewise much wearied with the day's labours, and it was some time after we stopped before a suitable place was found and our second igloo erected. At length, though long after dark, we were comfortably located, enjoying a hot supper beneath the snowy dome, the foundation of which rested on the frozen bosom of the mighty deep. But not too soon were we under shelter. The storm had burst in all its fury and we could hear the wind roaring outside as we warmed ourselves within.

All night long the gale continued, and the next morning it was found impossible to go on. It was blowing a strong gale and continued so all day, with snow of an impenetrable thickness. We were therefore obliged to keep inside our shelter, wrapped in furs.

While thus detained I took the opportunity to have my hair cut by Tookoolito. It had grown to a great length, even to my shoulders, and I now found it very inconvenient. My beard whiskers, and moustache were also shorn close to my face. In mosquito time they were serviceable, but now they had become quite an evil, owing to the masses of ice that clung to them. Indeed, on the previous night I had to lose a portion of my whiskers. They had become so ice-locked that I could not well get my caribou jacket off over my head, therefore I used my knife and cut longer attachments to them.

I may here mention that when we vacated the snow-house, our dogs rushed in to devour whatever they could find, digestible or not, and my locks were a portion of what they seized. In went my discarded hair to fill up their empty stomachs! A few days later I saw the very same hirsute material, just as clipped from my head, lining a step leading to another igloo, having passed through the labyrinthian way from a dog's mouth onward.

About 4 p.m. Ebierbing ventured outside to see how matters looked, but he soon returned with the astounding news that the ice was breaking, and water had appeared not more than ten rods south of us! I looked and, to my dismay, found that a crack or opening extended east and west to the land, distant about three miles! The gale had evidently set the sea in heavy motion somewhere, and its convulsive throbs were now at work underneath the ice close to and around us. It still blew very hard, but as yet the wind was easterly, and so far good, because, if a nearer disruption took place we should be forced toward the land, but if it changed to north or north-west, away to sea we must go and perish!

Seriously alarmed, we consulted as to what was best to do — whether at once to hasten shoreward, or remain in the igloo and stand the chance. On shore nothing but rugged precipices and steep mountains presented themselves; on the ice we were in danger of our foundation being broken up, or else driven to sea. At length we decided to remain while the wind lasted in its present quarter and, to guard as much as possible from any sudden movement taking us unawares, I kept within sight my delicately-poised compass needle, so that the slightest shifting of the ice on which we were encamped might be known.

In the evening the gale abated and by 10 p.m. it was calm, but the heavy sea kept the ice creaking, screaming, and thundering, as it actually danced to and fro! It was to me a new but fearful sight. When I retired to bed I laid down with strange thoughts in my mind.

The night passed away without alarm, and in the morning Koodloo made an opening with a snow-knife through the dome of the igloo for peering out at the weather. He reported all clear and safe and, after a hot breakfast, we packed and started, though under great difficulty and hazard.

The ice had given way and was on the move in every direction. The snow was also very deep — sometimes above our knees — and moreover very treacherous. We could hardly get along; and the poor dogs, which had been near starving since we had left the ship (Esquimaux dogs endure starvation, and yet work amazingly), had to be assisted by us in pushing and hauling the sledge, while constant precaution was needed against falling through some snow-covered ice-crack. Every now and then we came to openings made by the gale and heaving sea. Some of these were so wide that our sledge could hardly bridge them, and a detour would have to be made for a better spot. At other places we had to overcome obstructions caused by high rugged ice that had been thrown up when masses had been crushed together by the tremendous power of the late storm.

To guard against and extricate ourselves from these dangers, yet find a track amid the hummocks, each of us by turns took the lead, and in this manner we proceeded on our way; but it was evident we had hardly strength enough to persevere in reaching our destination that night. By 2 p.m. we were so exhausted that I deemed it best to make a halt and use a little more of the slender stock of provisions I had with me, and which, owing to our being so much longer on the way than expected, had become very low. Each of us, therefore, had a slice of raw salt pork and a quarter of a biscuit. This, however trifling, gave renewed strength, and again we pushed forward, hauling, scrambling, tumbling, and struggling almost for our lives.

It was dark ere we got near the locality where our next encampment was to be made, and where in fact we intended to remain a while for the purpose of hunting and sealing, and myself exploring.

At length we caught sight of an igloo which afterward proved to be Ugarng's. As soon as we saw it, fresh efforts were made to get nearer, but we found our passage more and more obstructed by the broken, upturned ice. Often the sledge was carried onward by making it lean over these impediments, sometimes from one point of ice to another, and at others down and up among the broken pieces. Finally we succeeded in reaching the shore ice which we found all safe and sound, and in a short time more we were alongside of Ugarng's igloo, encamped on the south-west side of Roger's Island, overlooking Cornelius Grinnell Bay and the mountains surrounding it.

Immediately I ran into Ugarng's igloo and obtained some water to drink, for I must mention that all day long we had been famishing on account of thirst. The material to make water had been abundant around us – beneath our feet, here, there, and everywhere – but not a drop could be obtained owing to our fire-lamp not being in use. Thus it was most thankfully I received the warm-hearted welcome given me by Nikujar, family wife No. 1 of Ugarng, as she handed me a cup of refreshing cold water. Then I remembered how, on one occasion at the ship, this same woman with her infant came and asked *me* for water, which I gladly gave to her, with something else. Now *she* gave it to me.

I should mention that, in winter, water is most precious to the natives. It is made only by melting snow or ice over the ikkumer (fire-lamp), which is an expensive heat and light when oil and blubber become scarce; and in this case our materials for fuel were all expended.

While our own igloo was being erected, Ugarng and his second wife arrived from sealing and, to the joy of all, brought with him a fine seal. He generously supplied us with what we wanted, and thus an excellent supper was added to the cheerful light and genial warmth from the now well-fed lamp.

My fourth night in an igloo was spent more comfortably than the previous two had been, and on the following morning I rose greatly refreshed and strengthened. As I looked upon the expanse over which we had passed, I was startled to find the ice all gone out to sea. This was confirmed by a view shortly afterward obtained from the top of a mountain behind our igloo, and I felt truly grateful to heaven for having so preserved us.

During the day I took a walk on shore, and the two Esquimaux went sealing. They returned at night with a fine prize which made us an excellent feast; and as my own stock of provisions was exhausted, except a trifle I reserved in case of sickness, this supply was most timely.

On the following day, January 15th, Ebierbing and Koodloo departed with a sledge and dogs on a hunting excursion, and I went away to examine the locality around.

While rambling about, I fortunately preserved myself from a severe frost-bite in the face by taking the precaution of carrying a small pocket mirror which belonged to Tookoolito. I had asked the loan of it, knowing how necessary it was when one is alone in those regions to have a detector of frost-bites; and I found the use of a mirror in such a case equivalent to the companionship of another person.

That night I was alone with Tookoolito and Punnie; the latter Ugarng's third wife, she having come to our igloo to keep company with us until the husbands returned. It was very cold – the thermometer down to 57° below freezing point. Now my usual sleeping-place was between Ebierbing and Koodloo; but they being absent, I had to lay on the general bed, wrapped in my furs and blankets. During the early part of the night my feet were almost frozen. I tried all I could to keep them warm, but in vain. At last a smooth low voice reached my ear:

"Are you cold, Mr. Hall?"

I answered "My feet are almost frozen. I cannot get them comfortable."

Quick as thought, Tookoolito, who was distant from me just the space occupied by little Punnie (that is, Punnie slept in the middle), got down to the foot of the bed; thence she made passage for her hands directly across my feet, seizing them and drawing them aslant to her side. My modesty, however, was quieted when she exclaimed, "You feet are like ice, and must be warmed Innuit fashion!"

Tookoolito then resumed her place beneath her tuktoo furs, intermingling her hot feet with the ice-cold ones of mine. Soon the same musical voice said, "Do your feet feel better?"

I responded, "They do, and many thanks to you."

She then said, "Well, keep them where they are. Good-night again, sir."

My feet now were not only glowing warm, but hot through the remainder of the night. When I awoke in the morning, as near as I could guess, there were no less than three pairs of warm feet all woven and interwoven, so that some difficulty was experienced to tell which were my own.

Ebierbing and Koodloo did not return until the next evening, bringing with them some black skin and krang* – all the success attending them – which was obtained from a cache made the previous fall by the natives when our ship was in the bay. The black skin was compelled to be our food as nothing better could be had; and at supper I ate heartily of the raw frozen whale hide.

The following noon a very heavy snow-storm came on and continued throughout the next and two following days, confining us almost entirely to the igloo, obliged to live on black skin, krang, and seal.

On Sunday, the 20th of January, ten days after leaving the ship, we found ourselves in a sad state from actual want of food. The weather continued so bad that it was impossible to procure any by hunting, and all we had hitherto obtained was now consumed, except a very small portion held in reserve. I had intended sending Koodloo back to the ship for supplies but waited for more suitable weather. This morning, however, it was absolutely necessary an attempt should be made, and as Koodloo refused to go alone, I decided upon proceeding with him.

We expected to be obliged to make one night's encampment on the sea ice, now again (so far as we knew from that around us) compact, and we hoped to reach the ship on the following day. My only preparation was a sleeping bag and shawl with a carpet sack of sundries, and half a pound of baked mutton, which I had carefully preserved to the present moment.

At 8 a.m. we were in readiness with a sledge and team of 12 dogs, most of them nearly starved. Bidding adieu to Ebierbing and Tookoolito, Koodloo and I started on our journey.

At first much hummocky ice impeded the way, but this we got through, and I anticipated a speedy trip. I was, however, disappointed. Soon deep snow appeared; and though we struggled for some miles due south, it was at length evident that to go on like that would be impossible. Occasionally the sledge and dogs contrived to get forward pretty well, but often they were so buried as to be almost out of sight. Koodloo seemed to think of giving it up, and I was so weak as to be hardly capable of dragging myself along. While in this dilemma as to what we should do – go

* Black whale skin, and whale meat.

on, or return to the igloo – I perceived Ebierbing and Ugarng on their way toward us.

They had noticed my difficulty, and Ebierbing now came on snow-shoes to offer his services in going to the ship in my stead. I accepted the proposal, and he, with Koodloo, went forward. Ugarng going in another direction seeking for seal-holes while I, slowly and with difficulty owing to my weakness, returned to the igloo. I was a long time getting back, and when I arrived there was obliged to throw myself on the snow platform quite exhausted.

Toward evening, the weather then being fine, I walked on to a hill that overlooked the bay, and with my glass saw Ebierbing and Koodloo slowly wending their way along near where our second igloo had been erected. The night and the following day I was hardly able to move. My weak state, owing to want of food – all my daily fare being a small piece of black or whale skin – had become very serious.

In the evening I went to Ugarng's. He had just returned from sealing, having been out two days and one night over a seal-hole. All the reward he had, however, for his patient exertions was the seal coming up and giving a puff; then away it went leaving Ugarng a disappointed Innuit. But he bore his disappointment very philosophically. He said, in his native tongue, "Away I go tomorrow morning again!"

The next morning, which was very fine, Ugarng went out sealing again. The following day he returned once more unsuccessful, though he had remained all night over the seal-hole. This was very bad for the whole of us. We could not now have even a fire-light until another seal was captured; and when I called at Ugarng's, I found they were in the same condition. His wife Nikujar was alone, except her infant and Kookooyer, their daughter by another man. They were without light. Her child was restless, and she said the cause was hunger. "Me got no milk – meat all gone – blubber too – nothing to eat – no more light – no heat – must wait till get seal."

While I waited, the second wife came in and said Ugarng was still watching over a seal-hole. Jack, another Esquimaux man, soon afterwards returned without success. Sad – very sad! My own state was bad enough, and I felt it severely; but I could not bear to witness the wants of the poor people around me, having no power to relieve them unless Ebierbing should soon come back with some provisions from the ship. All that I had to eat was my piece of black skin, and this I relished. Indeed, I could have eaten anything that would have gone towards keeping up the caloric within me, and make bone and flesh.

One night I asked Tookoolito if I might try the taste of some blackened scraps that hung up. I knew that she had reserved these for the dogs, but nevertheless I had an uncontrollable longing for them. I was very hungry. Tookoolito replied that she could not think of my eating them – the idea made her almost sick; therefore I did not urge the matter more; but soon afterward I saw they were gone, Punnie (Ugarng's third wife) having taken them and passed the whole into her own stomach!

Ugarng came in late, again unsuccessful, and Tookoolito gave him a cup of tea, such as it was, for owing to the absence of proper light and fuel it could not be well made. Directly he had it, off he went once more to try for seal.

The next morning Ebierbing had not returned, and we were all at our wits' end to find something to eat. At length Tookoolito made out to cut off some of the white from a piece of black skin. From it she "tried" out sufficient oil to use for heating some snow-water which, when warmed, was thickened with Indian meal, a few handfuls having been found remaining of the small quantity I had brought with me. The quantity of meal did not weigh above two ounces, yet it seemed to "loom up" as it was incorporated in the tepid water, and the incident strongly reminded me of the good woman and Elijah of Bible history. Tookoolito, with whom I shared the meal, thought the "pudding" excellent, and so did I. Indeed I shall not readily forget that breakfast even – as I wrote at the time – "if I live to enjoy a thousand more dainty ones in my native home."

At this time, though I kept in general good health and spirits, I was fast losing flesh. But almost worse than want of food was the want of light and fuel. On several occasions the only way I had to keep myself from freezing was by sitting in bed with plenty of caribou furs around me. The writing of my journal was done with the thermometer 15° to less than 0, while outside it was from –25° to –52°. During the day I several times went up the hill to look for Ebierbing's reappearance from the vessel, but no signs of him met my eye, and the night of January 24th (fourteen days from the ship) saw us with our last ration of food, viz., a piece of "black skin" 1¼ inches wide, 2 inches long, and ¾ of an inch thick. It was under these circumstances I went to sleep, hoping to dream of better things, even if I could not partake of them.

At midnight I heard footsteps within the passage-way to our igloo. I sprang out of bed and drew back the snow-block door. There was Jack, his spear covered with pierced seal-blubber hanging in strips like string-dried apples. I had allowed my poor starving dog "Merok" to sleep within the igloo that night, and directly I had opened the door, on his scenting the luscious fat, quicker than thought he gave one leap, a desperate one, as if the strength of a dozen well-fed animals were in him. In an instant I grappled with the dog and made great efforts to save the precious material; but though I actually thrust my hands into his mouth, and though Tookoolito and Punnie also battled with him, Merok conquered, and instantly devoured that portion he seized.

This misfortune was not single. Before Jack could get his well-loaded spear and himself into the igloo, all the other dogs about the place were around him, fighting for a share of what was left. They succeeded in obtaining nearly all before we could drive them away, and thus the good portion intended for us from what Jack had procured was lost to us, but not to the dogs! Jack, who was of Ugarng's party, and had brought this as a present, returned to his own igloo and left us disconsolate to ours. "Better things," therefore in that case were not for us.

Not before 9 a.m. did I again leave my bed and go outside the igloo to look around. Naturally and longingly my first glance was in the direction whence I expected Ebierbing. In a moment my eyes caught something black upon the almost universal whiteness. I looked again and again. It moved, and immediately my heart leaped with joy as I cried in loud tones to Tookoolito within, "Ebierbing! Ebierbing! He is coming! He is coming!" The response was, "That is good," and I bounded away as fast as my enfeebled body would allow.

I soon found, however, that if progress was to be made toward him, I must do it by slow degrees and patient steps. "Black skin," in homeopathic quantities, daily taken for food, had but kept my stomach in sufficient action to support life. All the strength I now had was mostly from the beef-steaks of dear Ohio, eaten and moulded into human fat, muscle, and bones before leaving my native home. But this remaining strength was very, very small, and thus my efforts to get on nearly exhausted me.

After a great struggle through the deep snow, I at last got

within hailing distance, and sang out to know if it was really Ebierbing, as the party I had seen was no longer advancing. No reply came to my question and I immediately hastened my feeble steps to see the cause. A moment or two brought me near enough to be convinced. It *was* Ebierbing with the sledge and dogs, but so exhausted with his labours that he had been obliged to throw himself down, completely overpowered. Soon I was by his side grasping his hand and, with a grateful heart, thanking him for the really good deed he had performed in thus coming alone with the relief I saw before me.

In a short time the loaded sledge was examined, and I found a box of sundries sent from the ship, as also a very fine seal, caught that morning by Ebierbing himself. There was likewise a quantity of whale-meat brought from Rescue Harbour for the use of our dogs.

Directly Ebierbing could renew his journey, we started together; but the dogs and both of us were hardly able to get the sledge along. Finally we reached the shore ice, and here we were so exhausted that not one inch farther could we drag the loaded sledge. Kunniu, wife No. 2 of Ugarng, seeing our condition, hastened to give assistance, and with her strong arms and our small help, the sledge was soon placed high on the shore by the side of the igloos.

Ebierbing's first and most earnest call was for water. This was supplied to him, and then we commenced storing our new supplies. The seal was taken into the igloo and the sledge, with its contents, was properly attended to. Of course the news of Ebierbing's arrival with a seal spread like wildfire, and in our quiet little village, consisting of three igloos, all the inhabitants with exhausted stomachs – including my own – were prepared for wide distension.

The seal weighed, I should say, about 200 lbs. and was with young. According to Innuit custom an immediate invitation was given by the successful hunter's family for every one to attend a "seal feast." This was speedily done, and our igloo was soon crowded. My station was on the dais, or bed-place, behind several Innuit women, but so that I could see over them and watch what was going on.

The first thing done was to consecrate the seal, the ceremony being to sprinkle water over it, when the stalwart host and his assistant proceeded to separate the "blanket" – that is, the blubber, with skin – from the solid meat and skeleton of the seal. The body was then opened and the blood scooped out. The blood is considered very precious, and forms an important item of the food consumed by Esquimaux. Next came the liver which was cut into pieces and distributed all around, myself getting and eating a share. Of course it was eaten raw – for this was a raw-meat feast – its eating being accompanied by taking into the mouth at the same time a small portion of delicate white blubber which answered the same as butter with bread. Then followed distributing the ribs of the seal for social picking. I joined in all this, doing as they did, and becoming quite an Innuit save in the quantity eaten. This I might challenge *any* white man to do. No human stomach but an Innuit's could possibly hold what I saw these men and women devour.

Directly the "feast" was ended all the company dispersed. Tookoolito then sent around bountiful gifts of seal-blubber for fire-lamps; also some seal meat and blood. This is the usual custom among the Innuits, and undoubtedly is a virtue to be commended. They share each other's successes, and bear each other's wants. Generally, if it is found that one is short of provisions, it may be known that all are. When one has a supply, all have.

After the feast and the gifts were over, we had leisure to attend to ourselves, and in what great good humour we were soon to be found! Our lamps were all aglow, and our hunger sated. I then took up the letter sent to me by Captain Budington which added to my pleasure in its perusal.

It appeared, by what I read, that every one on board the ship, as also the natives in the two nearby villages, had given us up for lost during the gale we encountered when encamped on the ice. From the long absence of all information about us, and the fact that the same gale had broken up the ice in Field Bay, it was concluded that we had been driven out to sea and probably had perished. Koodloo's wife never expected to see him again; and old Ookijoxy Ninoo, the grandmother of Ebierbing, said she dreamt about him in such a way that his death was almost assured her.

My information from the ship told me that the natives in both villages were badly off, not having caught one seal since our departure.

I must now mention how Ebierbing obtained the fine seal he brought with him. On his way to the ship he discovered a seal-hole but, being hurried for time, he merely erected a small pile of snow near at hand, and squirted tobacco-juice as a mark upon it. On his return he readily found the hole by this mark and, though he felt the necessity of hastening on to our relief, and had received instructions from the captain to hurry forward, yet he determined to try for the prize by spending the night in attempting to gain it. Accordingly, binding my shawl and various furs around his feet and legs, he took his position, spear in hand, over the seal-hole. This hole was buried in two feet of snow and had been first detected by the keen sagacity of one of the dogs with him. Ebierbing first thrust the spindle shank of a spear a score of times down through the snow until he finally hit the small aperture leading through the ice. It was a dark night, and this made it the more difficult, for in striking at a seal it will not do to miss the exact spot where the animal comes to breathe – no, not by a quarter of an inch. But, to make sure of being right when aiming, Ebierbing put some dark caribou hair directly over the right spot, and thus, after patiently watching the whole night long, he was rewarded in the early morning by hearing the seal blow. In a moment more he captured it by the well-directed aim of his spear.

The next morning, January 25th, the Innuits Ugarng, Ebierbing, and Jack all separated for some place where they hoped to get seals. I supplied them as liberally as I could with my provisions.

The rations sent me from the ship were examined and placed in safety from the dogs, but not from the truly honest Innuits, for such precautions were not needed; and then I tried to go on with some work. But it was colder than we had yet experienced, the thermometer being that night (the seventeenth of my igloo life) 75° below the freezing point! Remembering that our sealers were out on the ice, I shuddered, fully expecting they must be frozen to death; but what was my surprise and pleasure in the afternoon to see Jack and Ebierbing return, each with a seal – the one captured about midnight, the other early in the morning.

Ebierbing admitted that he had felt the cold very much while watching and, though well wrapped in furs tied around him, could hardly prevent his feet from freezing. As to his nose, that *did* get touched by the frost, but he soon remedied it by smoking a Yankee clay pipe loaded with Virginia tobacco.

Another seal feast was of course made, and on this occasion I supped on seal soup, with about two yards of frozen seal's entrails (very good eating) as a finish to the affair.

These seal suppers I found to be most excellent. The seal-meat is cooked in a pan suspended for three or four hours over the fire-lamp. Generally it is boiled in fluid – half sea water and half blood. When ready, it is served up by first giving to each person a piece of the meat. This is followed by a dish of smoking-hot soup in which the seal has been cooked; and I challenge any one to find more palatable food in the world. It is ambrosia and nectar! Once tasted, the cry is sure to be "More! more!"

The seal-meat is eaten by holding it in both hands, the fingers and the dental "mill" supplying the offices of both knife and fork. This mode of eating was known before such instruments were thought of. Among the Innuits generally, the following practice prevails: before the igloo wife hands any one a piece of meat, she "soups" it all over, that is, sucks out all the fluid from the meat that would probably otherwise drip out. Furthermore, if there be any foreign matter upon it such as seal, dog, or caribou hairs, she licks them all off with her pliant tongue.

On January 29th we had the cold so severe that the thermometer showed, during the night and in the morning, 82° below the freezing point! Yet, strangely, I had experienced more severe sensations of cold when the temperature was at zero than at this low state. Still it was cold, and bitingly cold! How Ebierbing and the other men – who had again left on the previous evening – could keep to their watch during that cold night was to me marvellous; yet they did so; and when Ebierbing returned about 9 a.m. without success, he told me that he was unwearied in his watchfulness all through the dreary time. At midnight a seal had come to breathe, but he was not so ready or so smart – probably was too much frozen – as to strike in time, and therefore lost it.

Sometimes the wives accompany their husbands sealing, even in such weather.

Recording my own experience of igloo life at this time, I may here say that, having then spent twenty nights in a snow house, I enjoyed it exceedingly. Now, as I look back at the past, I find no reason to utter anything different. I was as happy as circumstances permitted, even though with Innuits only for my companions. Life has charms everywhere, and I must confess that Innuit life possesses those charms to a great degree for me.

On the 31st we had a stranger visit us – a boy called Noo-ok-kong – who arrived from a spot one mile west of where our first igloo had been erected. He had found us out, and stated that he left behind, at the stopping place, Mingumailo the angeko,* with his two wives. They had started for that spot a short time preceding us, but now, having been a long while without food, he came to see if we could supply him. The lad had an abundance given him, and never before did I see such an amount of gorging as I did by that boy.

Next morning Ugarng departed on a visit to the ship with sundry presents of seal-meat, &c. from Ebierbing to his aged grandmother and friends. I also sent a letter to Captain Budington, preferring to remain here until I had completed all my observations. While taking some of these I "burned" my fingers most sadly by laying hold of my brass pocket sextant with my bare hand. I say burned them, because the effect was precisely the same as if I had touched red-hot iron. The ends of my finger-nails were like burnt bone or horn; and the fleshy part of the tips of my fingers and thumbs were, in appearance and feeling, as if suddenly burnt by fire.

On the 3rd of February we caught sight of some caribou on the ice, making their way slowly in single file northward, and eventually coming within a quarter of a mile of our igloos. I had given my rifle to Ebierbing on the first sight of them, that he might try his skill in killing one; but owing to the charge of powder being too small, he missed, and the caribou alarmed, darted off with the speed of the wind, much to our regret.

That night, about 12 o'clock, we were aroused by a call from someone evidently in distress. The cry came from the passage-way just without the igloo, and was at once responded to by Ebierbing telling the stranger to come in. He did so, and who should stand before us but Mingumailo the angeko! He spoke feebly, and said that he was very ill, thirsty and hungry; and that he, with his family, had had nothing to eat for nearly one month. Immediately a pile of frozen seal-meat was pointed out to him, with permission to eat some, and quick as lightning the famished man sprang to it like a starving bear. But how he did gorge! He swallowed enough, I thought, to have *killed* six white men, yet he took it without any apparent discomfort. Water was supplied to him, and of this he drank copiously – two quarts went down his camel stomach without drawing breath! Seeing his tremendous attack upon our precious pile of fresh provisions, I really felt alarmed

* Medicine man, or shaman.

lest he meant to demolish the whole and leave us without any. To feed a hungry man was well enough, and a ready act on the part of all of us; but then for him to have a stomach as huge and voracious as any polar bear, and to try to fill that stomach from our limited supply of food, was more than we could reasonably stand. I grew impatient; but finally the angeko gave in. He really had no power to stow away one piece more. He was full to repletion; and throwing himself flat on the igloo floor, he resigned himself to the heavy task Nature now had to perform in the process of digesting the monstrous heap he had taken within.

After a time the angeko told us that one of his wives had accompanied him, but had gone into another igloo. The other wife kept with them as far as she could, when he was obliged to leave her till means of relief could be found. He had built an igloo for her, and then hastened on to our snow village. In the morning Noo-ok-kong, the Innuit lad, went with some food to her, and soon afterward brought her in, thus making an addition of no less than four hungry mouths to aid in consuming our supplies. To add to our dilemma, Ugarng returned on the following day bringing with him *three* more fasting beings besides himself. They were his mother, Ookijoxy Ninoo, his nephew Eterloong, and his niece Ookoodlear, all related to Ebierbing.

Ugarng, however, brought for me additional supplies from the ship; but I saw quite clearly that, whatever I might feel inclined to do for my late companions in their need, it would never answer to begin supplying all strangers that arrived, particularly the angeko. Therefore I determined to stop this as speedily as possible. The angeko, however, left us in a day or two for another place, where he and his wives were afterward found, again starving.

After this arrival, the usual daily incidents of our life were unvaried for some time. Occasionally seals were obtained, principally by Ugarng and Ebierbing, and then a grand feast of raw food took place.

Ebierbing was the most persevering and indefatigable sealer. During that season he caught more seals than any other man; and on one occasion, by the aid of my rifle which I had loaned to him, he succeeded in bringing back four seals, after having taken six, but two were lost.

When Ebierbing returned with the four seals he merely stayed long enough for the feast, and was off again, with the understanding to look out for me, as I purposed following him. This

I did on the 16th day of February, being the thirty-eighth of my departure from the ship, and of my living thus wholly among the Innuits. The Innuit Jack was my companion.

We arrived at Ugarng's igloo about 7 p.m. and were welcomed by Kunniu, Ugarng himself being out sealing. Here I stayed until the 18th, aiding them as far as I could, and curiously watching the various efforts made to sustain and enjoy life by these singular people of the North.

I had now been forty-two nights in an igloo, living with the natives most of the time on their food and according to their own customs. I therefore considered that I had gained some experience in the matter, and having made several observations for determining the locality of places, prepared for my return.

I bade adieu to my Innuit friends in the village, and on the 21st of February left what I then called "My Northern Home" for the ship. I was accompanied by Ebierbing, Ugarng, and Kunniu, and we had the sledge and dogs with us. The parting from Tookoolito was affecting. She evidently felt it; but the hope of herself and her husband soon being with me again on my future excursions removed much of the disappointment she then felt at my going away. In fact, both she and Ebierbing were as children to me, and I felt toward them like what a parent would.

It was a fine day when we left the village and rapid progress was made. As we moved out into the bay, a glow of red light suffused the heavens at the eastern part of the horizon, and when we had made about four miles south the sun began to lift his glorious face. Occasionally I looked back to the igloos where I had spent so many days – far from uncomfortable ones – among my Innuit friends; but soon they were out of sight, and my thoughts now turned wholly to the warm hearts that I hoped to meet on board that night.

At 9 a.m. we reached new ice, which started the sealers to try their hands once more for a prize. In ten minutes more Ebierbing had found a hole and actually secured a seal! He hailed me to come and, on reaching the spot, I was asked to pull the seal up while he enlarged the hole, that it might be drawn on to the ice. I did so; and as the beautiful eloquent eyes of the victim met my sight, I felt a sort of shudder come over me, for it seemed to say, "Why disturb me here? I do no harm. Do not kill me!" But the great sealer Ebierbing, with his spear, had already enlarged the hole, and, hauling the prize higher up, speedily ended its life by a few well-directed thrusts midway between the seal's fore-flippers. Not a struggle did the victim make. Its end was as peaceful as that of a lamb.

Ugarng had been unsuccessful; but the one prize of Ebierbing was something and, after properly securing it to the sledge, away we went on our course again. At 10 a.m. we lunched on frozen seal, and our dinner was the same. We reached the land at 3 p.m. and crossed in two hours and forty-five minutes to Field Bay. A half hour's travelling upon the ice brought us to the ship, where I found all the crew ready to welcome me with outstretched hands. For a moment, on once more standing upon the ship's deck, I felt myself overpowered; but speedily recovering, I returned the congratulations offered and, after seeing my companions were attended to, I descended to the cabin where numerous comforts of civilization awaited me. A warm supper was most acceptable. I was much fatigued with my journey; and soon retired. Once more, then, did I enter my own little domicile, where I did not forget to return thanks to Him who had so preserved me in health and safety during that, my first experience of personal life among the native Innuit tribes of the icy North.

For nearly two years Hall continued to live and travel with the Eskimos on Baffin Island. Although he made no startling geographical discoveries he did solve one long-standing mystery of the Arctic by rediscovering and correctly identifying Frobisher's Strait (incidentally proving that it was actually a bay) and thereby transferring it back to its correct location from a mythical position on the map of South Greenland. Hall also unearthed a number of relics of the Frobisher expedition – a matter which delighted his romantic soul.

But the major result of his stay on Baffin Island was that Hall conclusively demonstrated how best to surmount the basic problems of existing in the Arctic. The knowledge and experience which he gained by actually living as an Eskimo made it clear that the secret of survival lay in adapting oneself to the conditions of that hard land; in abandoning, in effect, the entire superstructure of "civilized" attitudes and methods. It was a conclusion which would have meant salvation to scores of expeditions from the time of Jens Munk to that of Franklin, had those earlier explorers been able to arrive at it. Yet the principle behind it, that of acquiescing to existing conditions, rather than of attempting a conquest by brute force, was one that few of Hall's predecessors could have accepted or even tolerated. It was to be a different matter with his successors. Most of the major victories gained over the Arctic during the next half century were to be accomplished by an adherence to the principle which Hall had demonstrated. It was a principle that was to be applied even to the major problem of surmounting that last and most formidable barrier of all — the polar ice itself.

As for Hall, his discovery of the key to Arctic travel served him well during his second expedition — a five-year journey through the area where the Franklin party perished. That it did not serve him on his third and last expedition was no fault of his.

This final venture of Hall's to the Arctic was made in 1871, when he took a converted U.S. Navy tugboat named the Polaris *up through Baffin Bay in an attempt to reach the pole. It was an ill-starred voyage. Hall was accompanied by a crowd of cowards, incompetents, and worse, and though he was able to force a recalcitrant crew to sail his little ship farther north than any other vessel had ever reached before, he did so only at the price of signing his own death warrant. Shortly after* Polaris *reached a winter berth in Hall Basin, almost on the lip of the central polar sea, Hall died — suddenly and mysteriously. There is no doubt but that he was poisoned with arsenic by a dissident portion of his crew who neither shared his ambitions nor his belief in the safety of his new methods of coping with the defences of the Arctic.*

Hall and his works have been publicly ignored by most subsequent Arctic explorers (many of whom made their reputations by applying his methods) and by most Arctic historians. These grave professionals seem to have resented him because he was, first of all, an incurable romantic, and, secondly, because he accomplished so much by such unorthodox methods. Yet he was as great a figure as any who have faced the ice, before his time or after.

He is almost forgotten now in his own country, but he is still remembered by the Eskimos of Baffin Island and of Boothia, who still tell tales, passed on from generation to generation, of the white man who became one of them, and who was a man *amongst them.*

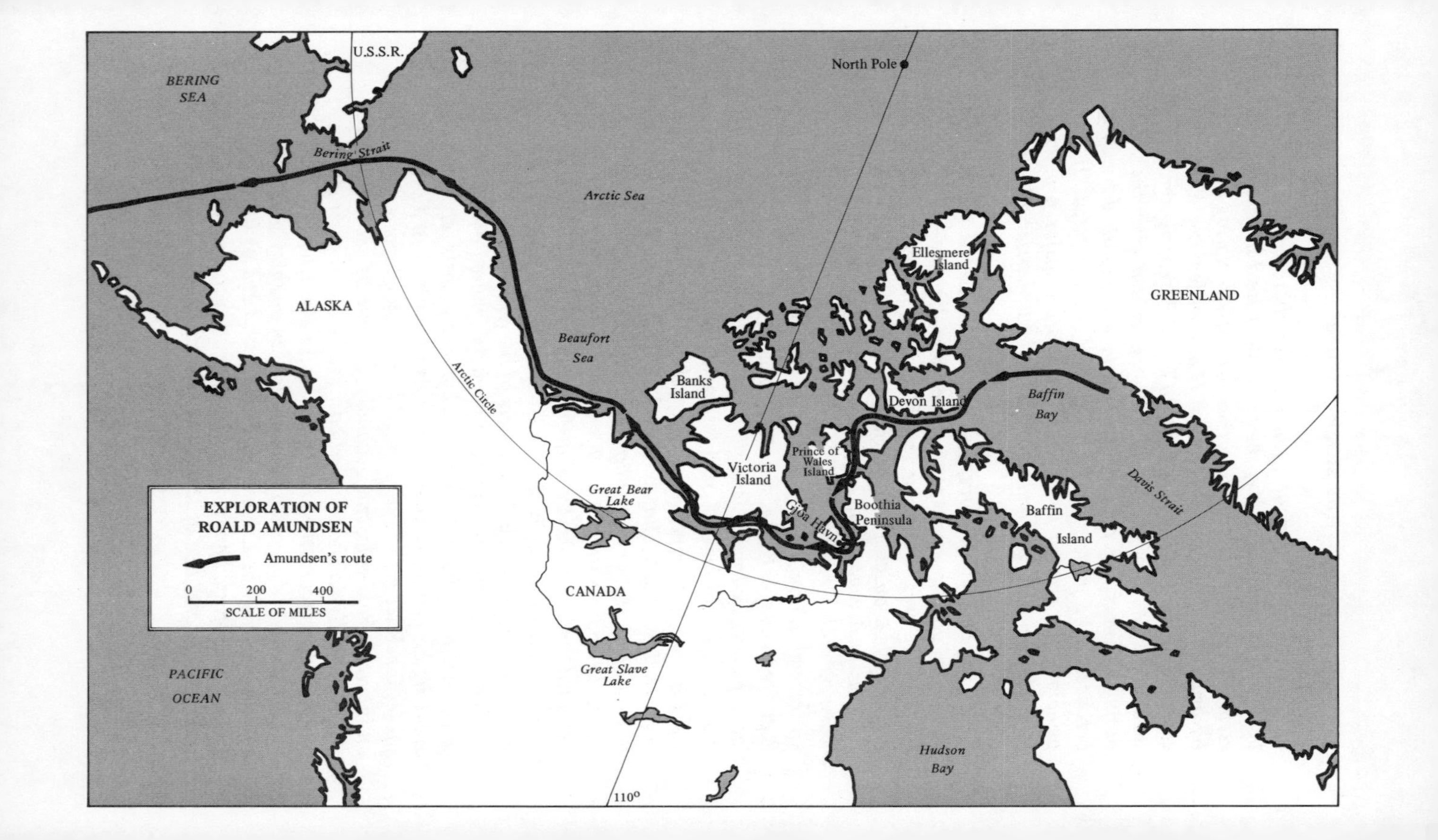
EXPLORATION OF
ROALD AMUNDSEN
Amundsen's route
0
200
400
SCALE OF MILES
U.S.S.R.
BERING SEA
Bering Strait
North Pole
Arctic Sea
ALASKA
Beaufort Sea
Arctic Circle
Banks Island
Victoria Island
Prince of Wales Island
Gjöa Havn
Boothia Peninsula
Ellesmere Island
Devon Island
GREENLAND
Baffin Bay
Davis Strait
Baffin Island
Great Bear Lake
CANADA
Great Slave Lake
PACIFIC OCEAN
Hudson Bay
110°

XII
The Passage West

During the final third of the nineteenth century there was a further hiatus in exploratory ventures to the ice-filled waters of the Arctic island archipelago. Although a Northwest Passage was now known to exist, the cost of its discovery had dulled men's enthusiasm for the age-old dream of voyaging through it to the west. Those who still chose to venture to the Arctic now turned their eyes toward a different goal. For fifty years the major magnet in the north was to be the pole itself. Attainment of this goal did not depend directly upon the success of ships against the ice, but rather upon the success of men travelling over-ice on foot, and so, for a time, the battle between ships and ice sank into relative inactivity, at least as far as exploration was concerned.

Only the whalers still maintained the battle. As steam replaced sail, the Scots whalers in particular extended their field until it included not only the whole of Baffin Bay, but Smith and Jones Sounds, Lancaster Sound west to Melville Island, Prince Regent Inlet, and Wellington Channel. American whalers, meanwhile, fished in Hudson Bay and wintered at Marble Island, where scurvy killed them by the score – and where their bones now lie beside those of Captain Knight. Ships and men of the whaling trade still took to the ice with their old bravado – and paid as high a price as ever. Of the more than sixty big steam whalers which sailed out of Dundee and Peterhead during the last quarter of the century, fifty-three died in the ice before the new century was born.

Then, in the year 1893, a new and unique venture to the ice took place. In that year a young Norwegian named Fridtjof Nansen brought to bear upon the problems of ice-navigation the same attitude which Hall had brought to the problem of Arctic land-travel and survival. Embracing Hall's principle that guile and acquiescence would succeed where force would not, Nansen designed one of the oddest little vessels ever to be launched. She was named the Fram *and she was conceived and constructed for one single purpose — to cheat the polar pack and to stay alive throughout a voyage which was intended to take her into the very heart of the impregnable ice continent.*

Barely a hundred feet in length, but as stout as a dropsical old woman, Fram *did not rely for victory on aggressiveness, but on elusiveness. She was so designed that no "nip" could get a grip on her bulbous bottom, and so that ice pressure would only serve to lift her clear of danger. For it was Nansen's startling plan to work the* Fram *deliberately into the edge of the polar pack until she was totally beset, and then to let the Arctic currents do the work and carry her, immobile in her ice-cradle, through the perpetually frozen sea that had defied every other ship before her.*

With a twelve-man crew aboard, Fram *took the ice near the New Siberian Islands in November of 1893, and, having surrendered herself to the old enemy, she drifted in its grip until August of 1896, when the ice finally released her not far from the Spitzbergen group. By then she had drifted across almost a quarter of the floating continent, and had, at one point, approached to within 350 miles of the pole itself.*

The significance of this victory did not escape the attention of one of Nansen's fellow Norwegians, a young man named Roald Amundsen. Seven years after the safe return of the Fram, *Amundsen set about the task of finally bringing to fruition the ancient dream of making a passage west, by applying to it Hall's and Nansen's principle of submission to the primordial defender.*

Amundsen's vessel, the Gjoa, *was an awkward-looking Norwegian herring boat, only seventy-five feet long, and thirty years of age. Much of her life had been spent in Arctic waters where she had been subjected to wear and tear that would have been the death of any lesser ship. But she was one of those rare vessels into which, through some miracle of craftsmanship (or perhaps by some inexplicable accident) the heart of greatness had been implanted. She was great in a special sense.*

Her master on the passage was her equal. Roald Amundsen, who became one of the most commanding figures in the history of polar exploration, reached manhood in the mundane guise of a medical student. But all through his childhood and his youth the north was a ferment in his blood, and at the turn of the century he abandoned a life of mediocrity and gave himself up to the ice.

It was not easily done. He was without the technical background that was the hallmark of the professional explorers of the period. He had no money and small influence. But his will was inexorable. By means which, in a lesser man might have been considered a little dubious, he scraped together the wherewithal to follow Franklin north.

When the Gjoa *sailed, she did so not only under an atmospheric cloud, but under a figurative one as well, for she put to sea in filthy weather mainly to escape a bevy of angry creditors whom Amundsen's zeal had hypnotized into supporting his venture.*

The voyage was intended to accomplish two major objectives: the passage itself and, equally important, to enable Amundsen to make a thorough study of earth magnetism in the vicinity of the magnetic pole.

The selections which follow are chiefly concerned with the voyage, but some revealing excerpts from the story of the two winters spent on King William Island have been included.

THE NORTHWEST PASSAGE

The Voyage to Gjoahavn

We knew there was a sea passage round Northern America, but we did not know whether this passage was practicable for ships, and no one had ever yet navigated it throughout. So knowledge as to this strip of open sea to the west would remain inadequate until this passage had been traced from end to end by one ship's keel.

The little ship to whose lot this task fell was the *Gjoa*. Little was it dreamt when she was being built, for a herring boat, that she was to achieve this triumph, though it is hard to say what they do not dream of up there in the fjords. She was built in 1872. After she had been used for many years as a herring boat along the coast, she sailed the Polar Sea for some years. She was not spared there, but had ample opportunities of proving herself an uncommonly well-built boat.

In May, 1902, the *Gjoa* hoisted her flag and bade farewell to what for many years had been her home port. I put in to Trondheim to have some necessary ironwork on board executed. Petroleum tanks were built to the shape of the boat. Our little motor – a 13 H.P. of the "Dan" type – which was connected to everything that could possibly be driven with its aid, was easy to work and practical in every part. The motor was the pet of everyone on board. When it was not working we seemed to miss a good comrade.

The only thing that showed a visible sign of emotion at our departure was the sky. But this it did emphatically. When we cast off on the night of June 16th, 1903, the rain fell in torrents. Only those who were nearest and dearest were gathered on the quay to say good-bye to us seven participants in the expedition.

All was hushed and quiet on board; the navigation was attended to for the time by the steam tug at our bows. The watch was entrusted to the helmsman – and our six dogs. The dogs had formerly done service in the second *Fram* expedition, which had brought them home. Poor creatures! It would have been better to have let them remain in ice and snow than to drag them here, where they suffered sorely, especially this spring, which was unusually warm. They were now tied up along the rail and looked wretched in the rain – the greatest infliction to an Arctic dog.

In the North Sea we encountered a couple of gales, none too agreeable to those who were not sea-proof. The dogs were now let loose and jumped about as they liked. On days when we had heavy seas and the *Gjoa* rolled – and she can roll – they would go about studying the faces of the various members of the expedition. The rations they had – one dry cod and two pints of water – were not sufficient to satisfy their appetites, and they resorted to every possible expedient to get an extra meal.

On June 25th we passed between Fair Isle and the Orkneys out into the Atlantic. The many who had predicted our destruction ere we reached here should have seen us now, under full sail and a fresh breeze from the south-east, making at high speed for the west. Everything was now in good trim and running smoothly. When the motor was operating, the engineers were mostly in the engine-room. Yet they were always ready to help us deck hands at a pinch. The old feud between deck and engine-room hands was unknown on board the *Gjoa*. We all worked with a common object, and willingly and cheerfully took part in everything.

On July 11th we sighted land a little to the west of Cape Farewell. The high, craggy mountain landscape of Greenland stood out splendidly. The ice seemed to lie quite close up to the shore. Following the advice of the Scots whale fishers, Milne and Adams, I stood well off the shore to avoid getting into the ice. On the 13th we met the first icebergs, two solitary majestic masses. Those of us who had not seen such things before were naturally much interested, and the telescopes were in great demand.

On July 15th, our hunters tasted their first blood. We made that day a short detour into the ice and shot four big crested seals. The fresh flesh tasted excellent. Lindstrom, our cook, talked volubly of rolled meat, brawn, and sausages till our mouths watered. He bragged of his culinary exploits as chef on the *Fram*. Unfortunately, his tale concerned only the past, and we expected and hoped to see his deeds in the present. But, so far, in vain.

It was, however, not only we men who relished fresh meat. The dogs stuffed till they were as tight as drums; especially did Lurven distinguish himself. He was now a sorry sight, smeared all over with fat and blood. And the scavengers, who had hard work at the best of times during every watch, more than earned their wages in clearing up after such a feast. Every sailor is familiar with *that* result of having a dog on board. So just imagine several dogs at once, quite devoid of any polite training.

July 24th was a beautiful day, dead calm and dazzlingly bright. It was the first real summer day we had had since our departure. We seized the opportunity to bring up into the air all the bread which we had brought fresh from home, and had spread out below in the hold. Much of it was spoilt; but we cut the mould away and aired what was left whenever we had a chance.

"A sail ahead!" is the sudden cry; and there was life aboard. All telescopes – and we had a lot aboard the *Gjoa* – came out.

"A full-rigged ship!" someone exclaimed.

"I see clearly, it is a brig."

"It is probably one of the Royal Danish Greenland Trading Company's ships, on her way home."

"There's another!" shouts one with a telescope to his eye.

It is beginning suddenly to be populous here in the ice waste. And we stroll up and down the deck and mutter in very high spirits what a surprise we shall be for the new arrivals. We must admit that we even smartened up the deck a little. We might have a visit.

Then there was a telescope that was shut up in a decisive manner, followed by a burst of laughter.

"Well?"

"Gentlemen," says Lieutenant Hansen, "it is an iceberg!"

Then followed indignant protests, spying through the glasses and discussion, while we continued to approach the object of dispute. The heat of discussion disappeared, the full-rigged ship is abandoned, and after it the brig. The schooner still had one adherent even when we had advanced near enough to see clearly before us a great gathering of icebergs; they seemed to be aground on the Big Halibut Bank.

On August 6th we were abreast of Upernivik in west Greenland, twelve miles off. Here hundreds of icebergs had collected. Of drift ice we had not yet seen a trace, and we began to entertain the hope of slipping unhindered across Melville Bay. On August 8th we were off Holms Island and were about to begin the voyage across Melville Bay. This is the most dreaded stretch in that part of the Arctic Ocean. Many are the vessels that have made their last voyage here. It is, however, earlier in the year that the conditions are especially dangerous. In June and July, when the ice breaks up and the whale fishers go north – it is, of course, important to be first in the field – they often have a severe struggle with the ice. The outer part of the ice in the bay breaks first, and the inner part remains quite whole. This is what is called shore ice or fast ice. Along its edge the whalers seek a passage, and the wise ones among them do not quit it till they are out in the open water on the north side of the bay. On the borders of the shore ice there are often formed natural havens where vessels can run in for shelter when the drift ice sets in. If there be no natural dock, most of the whalers have sufficient crews to cut their way into the ice in a comparatively short time. It is the Scots who reign supreme in these waters; and there is no doubt that these Scots whalers, under dangerous and difficult conditions, have become some of the doughtiest Arctic seamen of our time.

We now set all sail and put the motor at full speed. It is important to get as quickly as possible across the bay and to spare nothing. At midnight the ice slackened and let us slip in without any particular trouble. At the same time a fog set in, pitch dark. Those who have not seen the ice fog of the Arctic Ocean do not know what fog is. London fog is nothing to it. We could not see the ship's length. But we held our course with the aid of the compass, and the ice politely made room for us.

On August 13th, at half-past two in the morning, I stood at the helm shivering with cold. Perhaps, as an Arctic traveller, I ought not to admit this, but anyhow, I did feel perishing with cold. My two companions in the watch strolled about the deck and tried to keep warm as best they could. The fog settled down and drenched everything it came in contact with; it was sheer misery in the early morning. The watch below were now enjoying steaming hot coffee which they well deserved after a spell of six hours' duty. Suddenly a gleam of light broke through the fog and, as if by enchantment, there opened up before me a wide view out into the bright daylight; right in front of us, and seemingly quite near, the wild, rugged landscape of Cape York appeared suddenly like a scene from fairyland. We all three cried out simultaneously with surprise and delight. The watch below came rushing up from their coffee. To the east the whole interior of Melville Bay lay before us. Right inside, in the farthest background, we could see several mountain tops. An impenetrable mass of ice filled the bay; mighty icebergs rose here and there from out of the mass of ice. When at last we looked back, we saw the fog out of which we had suddenly slipped, lying thick like a wall behind us.

At four o'clock on August 15th we reached Dalrymple Rock, where the Scots whalers, Captains Milne and Adams, had deposited considerable stores for us.

"Two kayaks ahead!" suddenly bawled the look-out atop. In a trice all hands were on deck. I stopped the engine and the kayaks came close alongside. We were very anxious to make the acquaintance of the North Greenland Eskimos, of whom many strange things are reported. They were two really good-looking men.

Their costume seemed to us somewhat strange at first sight, and there was no end of laughter when one of them stooped to pick up a knife he had dropped, and in doing so showed that a stitch in time might have saved nine. A pretty bow, indeed! They were extremely lively, jabbered both together, threw their arms about, and gesticulated.

The depot lay among big stones on a slope of a ridge, and was surrounded on all sides with barbed wire. At the end of the ridge a footing of old ice projected out into the sea and formed the most beautiful natural quay. We therefore decided to rig up our derrick on the quay as a crane, and with its aid to put the cases right into the boat after we had brought them up in sledges. We snatched a hasty supper, and at 10 o'clock we set to work. Lieutenant Hansen remained on board to superintend. I myself undertook the work on shore with the kind assistance of some Eskimos. The whole depot, 105 cases, had to be taken as deck cargo.

I now had four Eskimos to help me. It has often been said that the Eskimos are lazy, unwilling, and possessed of all other bad qualities under the sun. Certainly this was not true as to these four helpers of mine. They handled our cases, many of which weighed nearly 4 cwt., with an ease and skill which would be hard to match. Instead of the oaths and execrations which among "civilized" workmen are wont to accompany such work, these children of Nature carried out their task with song and merriment.

We were now heavily laden. Our stock of petroleum on leaving Dalrymple Rock was 4,245 gallons. The deck was down to the waterline, and the cases were piled almost up to the main boom. The dogs got on the tops of the cases and waylaid each other.

At 2:30 in the morning of August 17th we continued our voyage. Greenland now began to dwindle away and we stood westward towards Cape Horsburgh, the northern entrance to Lancaster Sound. Luckily the weather kept calm and clear. Loaded down as the *Gjoa* was, we were not fit to battle with a storm. And the *Gjoa* was not a flier when travelling under engine power. At last on August 20th, we rounded the cape and got into Lancaster Sound. After rather hard tacking we reached Beechey Island on August 22nd, and anchored in Erebus Bay.

By the time the anchor was down and the vessel hove to, most of us had turned in to enjoy a night of unbroken sleep. It was about 10 o'clock when twilight came on. I was sitting on one of the chain lockers looking towards the land, with a deep, solemn feeling that I was on holy ground; Franklin's last safe winter harbour. My thoughts wandered back – far back. I pictured to myself the splendidly equipped Franklin expedition heading into the harbour and anchoring there. The *Erebus* and *Terror* in all their splendour; the English colours flying at the masthead and the two fine vessels full of bustle – officers in dazzling uniforms, boatswains with their pipes, blue-clad sailors; proud representatives of the world's first seafaring nation up here in the unknown ice waste!

At the breaking up of the ice in 1846, the *Erebus* and *Terror* again stood out to sea. Once more resounds the merry song of the sailors, and the vessels pass out between Cape Riley and Beechey. Once more waves England's proud flag; it is the farewell of the Franklin expedition. From this point it passed into darkness – and death.

Later we all assembled at the old Franklin search expedition's depot and went carefully through everything, to see if there was still anything we might have any use for.

Several of my crew had set their fancy on an old hand-cart, and were anxious that we should take it with us. On being asked whether they would take it into their bunks, they gave in. Of course, they understood that we had no room. But the smith had made a discovery which sent him into the wildest raptures, a very ancient anvil. To dissuade him from taking it with him was impossible. The expedition would simply go to the bottom if we did not have the anvil with us. But we never had any use for it.

With the departure from Beechey, a new chapter opened in our expedition. We knew the course we were to take; the die was cast, and we only had to push on and make headway. Our voyage now assumed a new character. Hitherto we had been sailing in safe and known waters where many others had preceded us. Now we were making our way through waters never sailed in, save, possibly, by a couple of vessels, and were hoping to reach still farther where no keel had ever ploughed. We were very sanguine. In fact, I may almost say we felt certain that we should make our way through, having been fortunate enough to get thus far already. The ice conditions had been unusually favourable. We had made headway with ease, and almost without hindrance, where our predecessors had had to endure the most terrible struggles against ice and storms.

Between Sherard Head, on Prince of Wales' Land, and Cape Court on North Somerset Island, we encountered the first large accumulation of ice. Having the sun in our eyes, we took it, in the mirror-like glitter of the calm sea, to be a compact mass of ice extending from shore to shore. It seemed evident to me that we had now reached the point whence so many of our predecessors had been compelled to return – the border of solid unbroken ice.

As we drew nearer, the sparkling pieces of ice and the bright water seemed to part. The "mass of ice" proved to be simply old drifted-out fjord ice which was quite loose. Between the ice and the land, on either side, there were large and perfectly clear channels through which we passed easily and unimpeded. We were soon out again in open water, having escaped with nothing worse than a fright.

We were soon off Prescott Island in Franklin Strait. This island became a landmark on our voyage. The needle of the compass now absolutely declined to act. We were thus reduced to steering by the stars, like our forefathers the Vikings. This mode of navigation is of doubtful security even in ordinary waters, but it is worse here, where the sky, for two-thirds of the time, is veiled in impenetrable fog.

We were now fast approaching the De La Roquette Islands. This was the point that Sir Allen Young reached with the *Pandora* in 1875,* but here he encountered an invincible barrier of ice. Were we and the *Gjoa* to meet the same fate?

As I walked the deck I felt an irregular lurching motion, and I stopped in surprise. The sea all around was smooth and calm. I continued my promenade, but had not gone many steps before the sensation came again, and this time so distinctly that I could not be mistaken; there was a slight irregular motion in the ship. I would not have sold this slight motion for any amount of money. It was a swell under the boat, a swell – a message from the open sea. The water to the south was open, the impenetrable wall of ice was not there.

I cast my eyes over our little *Gjoa* from stem to stern, from deck to the mast-top and smiled. Would the *Gjoa* victoriously carry us all, and the flag of our native land, in spite of scornful predictions, over waters which had been long ago abandoned as hopeless? Soon the swell became more perceptible, and high glee shone on all our faces.

* This is the same Young who had been with M'Clintock in 1857-59. In 1875 he attempted to navigate the Passage, following Franklin's route, but failed.

When I awoke at 1:30 next morning – it still amazes me that I could go to my berth and sleep like a top into the bargain that night – the swell had become so heavy that I had to sit down to put my clothes on. I had never liked a swell; there is something very uncomfortable about it, with its memories of nausea and headache, dating back to my earliest days of seafaring life. But this swell, at this place and time, was a rapture that filled me to the soul. When I came on deck it was rather dark, but on our beam, not far off, we could faintly discern the outlines of the De La Roquette Islands. And now we had reached the critical point, the *Gjoa* was heading into virgin waters. Now, it seemed we had really commenced our task in earnest.

The next doubtful point was to pass the western mouth of Bellot Strait, where M'Clintock lay for so long waiting for a chance to get through. But the fairly heavy swell indicated an open sea for many miles to the south, and as Bellot Strait was not far ahead, our anxiety was not very great. At 8 a.m. we passed the strait. The only thing we met was a very narrow strip of broken land ice. The strait itself was densely fog-bound. At 5:30 p.m. we met a quantity of ice off Cape Maguire; beyond this we could see clear water. However, the fog settled down as thick as a wall just as we were about to make for the ice, and enveloped everything in its grey darkness. I decided to put back along the shore and wait till the fog lifted. The night was getting dark, and without a compass as we were, we ran the risk of getting into difficulties that might be pretty serious. So we lay to; but in the darkness of the night we felt many a heavy bump from the ice, and on the whole were far from comfortable.

Hitherto the land along which we sailed had presented a mild and genial aspect, with luxuriant vegetation, but the Tasmania Islands looked stern and bare. For once we were now favoured with a good wind and with the engine working at full power we went splendidly towards James Ross Strait. There was ice to the west, but along the land to the south appearances were favourable. I will reproduce here, verbatim, the entries in my journal for the following two days:

"August 30th. Sunday. Made a somewhat faulty course last night, in the gloom and darkness, and became entangled in a large, tightly packed body of drift ice. It took us a couple of hours or so after daybreak to get out of the ice and into the channel. Kept our course along the coast all day, and according to dead reckoning, should have been near Cape Adelaide – the magnetic north pole of James Ross – about noon. Dull weather prevented us from discerning land. Our only means of guidance, the wind, baffled us again and again, as it was very variable. We have had a northerly breeze lately, and made good headway. It is raining, freshening up, and now at 9 p.m. it is pitch dark. It is no easy matter to navigate under these conditions, but still we can manage. We are now in the channel, laying to for the night.

"August 31st. Last night there was a sudden marked fall in the barometer. The wind freshened quickly, and rain began to fall. We lay to at 9 p.m. At midnight we had to reef sails as there was still a fresh breeze. The sea rose quickly and, strangely enough, as we neared the magnetic pole, one or two of the expedition became seasick. At 3 a.m. we made full sail again. We kept close to the wind on the side where we supposed the land lay. At 3:30 the fog lifted for a moment and we sighted a small island a little to leeward. Icebergs and highly piled pack-ice soon showed me that this island was lying out towards the ocean itself. It was presumably the most northerly of the Beaufort group. We were sailing close to the wind, as we supposed to the south. It subsequently appeared that the wind had veered to the east, and this had caused us to drift a good deal towards west. The fog parted several times but we saw nothing of the land. At 8 a.m. I retired to my berth. We continued to keep close to the wind, bearing south and intending to make for Matty Island. At 11 o'clock I was awakened by a violent shock and was on deck in an instant. We were aground just off a very low island, which on further observation proved to be the southernmost of the Beaufort Islands. The vessel had struck amidships on a bank. We set all sail and started the engine at full speed and threw out the kedge. The vessel struck very hard several times, and some splinters of the false keel floated up. The pumps were sounded, but all was in order. After we got off we bore eastward towards Boothia.

"We are now lying at anchor for the night under the lee of the land, in six fathoms of water. It is so dark at night that we can discern nothing; and when, added to this, your course is an unknown one, it is not surprising that the gravest errors frequently result."

Here ends my journal entry for the day. From this short extract it will be evident to most people that navigation in waters about the magnetic pole is by no means without its discomforts.

I was sitting at night entering the day's events in my journal, when I heard a shriek – a terrific shriek – which thrilled me to the very marrow. Something extraordinary had happened. In a moment all hands were on deck. In the pitch-dark night, which luckily was perfectly calm, a mighty flame, with thick suffocating smoke, was leaping up from the engine-room skylight. A fire had broken out in the engine-room, right among the tanks holding 2,200 gallons of petroleum. We all knew what would happen if the tanks got heated; the *Gjoa* and everything on board would be blown to atoms like an exploded bomb. We all flew in frantic haste. One man rushed down to the engine-room to assist Wiik, who had stuck to his post from the outbreak of the fire. Our two fire-extinguishing appliances, which were always ready for use, were first brought into play, and we pumped water on that fire for dear life. In an incredibly short time we had mastered it. It had broken out in the cleaning waste that was lying saturated with petroleum on the tanks. The next morning on clearing up the engine-room, we found that it was no chance, but prompt discharge of duty, that had saved us all from certain destruction. Shortly before the fire broke out, Ristvedt had reported to me that one of the full petroleum tanks in the engine-room was leaking. I bade him draw the petroleum from that tank into one of the empty ones, immediately. This order was promptly carried out. On clearing up the engine-room after the fire, we found that the tap of the emptied tank had been wrenched right off during the struggle with the fire. Had my order not been carried out promptly, over 100 gallons of petroleum would have spurted out into the burning engine-room. I need not enlarge upon what would have been the inevitable sequel. But I hold up the man who so promptly obeyed orders as a shining example.

During the following night the wind slackened, and at 4 a.m. we weighed anchor and proceeded. It was my turn at the wheel and I took my stand on the poop so as to have the best possible look-out. Lund and Ristvedt were busy stretching the mainsail. To leeward of us lay a low island with fairly extensive banks projecting to the east. We had seen this shoal from our anchorage so I knew how to steer to get clear of it. It was, therefore, an unpleasant surprise when we ran aground, although I had steered well out. We got off again immediately and I put the helm hard to starboard to sheer off from the bank, as it seemed to me that in spite of my reckoning, we had got in among the shallows jutting out from the islands. This, however, was a mistake, as the shoal where we grounded was situated further to the south and west. Shortly after, we struck again, got off, and grounded again, this time for good. The engine was stopped, as also the work of setting sails. I rushed at once to the crow's nest. The weather was clear and I could see quite well. The bank we had grounded on was a large submerged reef, branching out in all directions. It extended to the west towards Boothia, as far as I could see. The land right to leeward was probably Matty Island.

It was 6 a.m. when we grounded. We immediately launched a boat to take soundings and ascertain the best way to get off again. The shortest way was aft. But as the two banks on which we had already struck lay higher in the water than the reef on which we stood, the prospect of getting back over them was very slight. We were therefore obliged to try forward, to the south. The soundings gave us little hope. The reef shallowed up in that direction, and had not more than six feet of water upon it in the shallowest part. Taking the shortest way ahead, the distance across the reef was about 220 yards. With a few tons of ballast the *Gjoa* had a draft of six feet. Loaded as she was, she drew 10 feet 2 inches. The prospect of getting across was therefore not brilliant, but we had no choice. We were compelled to lighten the vessel as much as possible. First we threw overboard 25 of our heaviest cases. They contained dog's pemmican, and weighed nearly 4 cwt. each. Then we threw out all the other cases of the deck-cargo on one side, to get the vessel to heel over as much as possible.

At 8 a.m. the current set to the north and the water fell one foot. We had grounded at high tide. We now made all preparations for the next high tide. The kedge anchor was put out, and every manoeuvre was tried to make the vessel heel over. High tide was at about 7 p.m. But in spite of all preparations and all our exertions we could not get the vessel to move an inch forward. When darkness set in about 8 o'clock at night we had to give up for the day.

When I came on deck at 2 a.m. next morning it was blowing fresh from the north. At 3 a.m. the vessel began to move, as if in convulsions. I had all hands called up so as to be ready to avail ourselves of any chance that might present itself. The north wind freshened to a gale, accompanied by sleet. We hove on the kedge, time after time, but to no purpose. The vessel pitched violently. I took counsel with my comrades, as I always did in critical situations, and we decided, as a last resource, to try and get her off with the sails. The spray was dashing over the ship and the wind came in gusts, howling through the rigging, but we struggled and toiled and got the sails set. Then we commenced a method of sailing not one of us is ever likely to forget even should he attain the age of Methuselah. The mighty press of sail and the high choppy sea, combined, had the effect of lifting the vessel up and pitching her forward again among the rocks, so that we expected every moment to see her planks scattered on the sea. The false keel was splintered and floated up. All we could do was to watch the course of events and calmly await the issue. As a matter of fact, I cannot say I did feel calm as I stood in the rigging and followed the dance from one rock to another. I stood there with the bitterest self-reproach. If I had set a watch in the crow's nest, this would never have happened, because he would have observed the reef a long way off and reported it. Was my carelessness to wreck our whole undertaking, which had begun so auspiciously? Should we, who had got so much further than anyone before us, now be compelled to stop and turn back crestfallen? Turn back, yes! that might yet be the question. If the vessel broke up, what then? I had to hold fast with all my strength whenever the vessel, after being lifted, pitched down onto the rocks, or I should have been flung into the sea. Supposing she were broken up. There was a very good prospect of it. The water on the reef got shallower, and I noted how the sea broke on the outer edge. It looked as if the raging north wind meant to carry us just to that bitter end. The sails were as taut as drumheads, the rigging trembled, and I expected the mast to go overboard every minute. We were steadily nearing the shallowest part of the reef, and sharper and sharper grew the lash of the spray over the vessel.

I thought it almost impossible the ship could hold together if she got on the outer edge of the reef, which, in fact, was almost lying dry. There was still time to let down a boat and load it with the most indispensable necessaries. I stood up there, in the most terrible agony, struggling for a decision. On me rested every responsibility, and the moment came when I had to make my choice – abandon the *Gjoa*, take to the boats, and let her be smashed up, or to dare the worst, and perchance go to meet death with all souls on board.

I slid as quickly as I could down one of the backstays on to the deck. "We will clear the boats and load them with provisions, rifles, and ammunition." Then Lund, who stood nearest, asked whether we might not make a last attempt by casting the remainder of the deck cargo overboard. This was, in fact, my own secret ardent desire, to which I had not dared to yield, for the sake of the others. Now, all with one accord agreed with Lund, and hey-presto! we went for the deck cargo. We set to in pairs, and cases of 4 cwt. were flung over the rail like trusses of hay. This done, up I climbed into the rigging again. There was not more than a boat's length between us and the shallowest part. The spray and sleet were washing over the vessel, the mast trembled, and the *Gjoa* seemed to pull herself together for a last final leap. She was lifted up high and flung bodily onto the bare rocks, bump, bump – with terrific force.... In my distress I sent up (I honestly confess it) an ardent prayer to the Almighty. Yet another thump, worse than ever, then one more, and we slid off.

I flew up to the top; not a moment was to be lost; everything now depended on our finding a way out among all the shoals which were lying close around us. Lieutenant Hansen stood at the wheel, cool and collected, a splendid fellow. And now he called out: "There is something wrong with the rudder, it will not steer." Should this, after all, be the end; should we drift down on the island there on our lee. Then the boat pitched once more over a crest, and I heard the glad shout: "The rudder is all right again."

A most wonderful thing had happened – the first shock had lifted the rudder so that it rested with the pintles on the mountings. But the last shock had brought it back into its place. It was a rare thing to see any frantic enthusiasm on board the *Gjoa*; we were all pretty quiet and cool by nature. But this time the jubilation could not be controlled and it burst out unrestrained.

Under sail and engine we stood over towards Boothia Felix, where we soon found deeper water. At noon we anchored to leeward of Cape Christian Frederick in five fathoms. A strong breeze was blowing from the north-east. We dropped both anchors at the same time, one with 30, and the other with 45 fathoms of chain. We had to make various repairs after the stranding, and besides, we were all fairly worn out after our toil and the severe mental strain.

At 11 o'clock the watch came and reported that a stiff wind was blowing from the south. When I came on deck it looked uncanny. It was completely dark, and it was impossible to leave our anchorage as the water was so full of shallows. We paid out all the chain and hoped for the best. All hands were called up and we made everything clear in case we should run aground. We expected the anchor chains to part every moment owing to the heavy choppy sea and the force of the gale. The anchorage presented a hard bottom, but luckily one anchor had caught in the cavity of a rock. We filled the flat-bottomed boat and the canvas boats with provisions and other necessaries. Each man had his task assigned to him, and we were ready should the chains snap. The engine was kept working full steam ahead to relieve the strain on the anchors. Fortunately the chains held, but there we lay for five days and nights in terror, while the gale boxed the compass. It was not until 4 a.m. on the 8th that we were able to weigh anchor. A fresh wind was then blowing from the north-west.

According to our reckoning we should, during the following night, have worked our way to the coast of King William Land. Our surprise was therefore great when, as soon as it was daylight, we found we were off the flat coast which we had, on the previous day, taken for Guiche Point. The current had carried us away in spite of sails and engine, and drifted us right in the opposite direction. We again set our course for the high land, and an hour's sailing brought us in sight of it. In other words, we were in the middle of Rae Straits. To our pleasant surprise the soundings showed no bottom, and as we neared King William Land the weather became quite clear, with a fresh breeze from the north.

When we were off Betzold Point I decided to stand in for Petersen's Bay and anchor there for the night. This proved to be a lucky hit. There was perfectly smooth water under the lee, and although we had to tack up the bay, we managed it very quickly. From the deck there was nothing particular to be seen except the large wide bay. But Hansen, who was on the look-out aloft, saw more than we did. He suddenly called out: "I see the finest little harbour in the world." I climbed up to him and true enough I saw a small harbour quite sheltered from the wind, a veritable haven of rest for us weary travellers. We afterwards christened it Gjoahavn.

To the westward Simpson Strait appeared quite free from ice. The Northwest Passage was therefore open to us. But our first and foremost task was to obtain exact data as to the magnetic north pole, and so the Passage, being of less importance, had to be left in abeyance.

As soon as I saw Gjoahavn, I decided to choose it for our winter quarters. It was evident that the autumn storms had set in in earnest, and I knew the waters further west were very shallow. Had the immediate completion of the Northwest Passage been our chief object, it would have been a different matter, and nothing would have prevented us from going further on.

The day after, Lund, Hansen and Ristvedt went ashore to test the chances of sport. In the afternoon they returned with two caribou calves and one doe. They had seen a large herd of caribou and a quantity of birds. Our mouths watered when they told of large flocks of geese. For the rest, they said the country was an ideal one for caribou, being flat, mossy, and abounding in streams and lakes. Eventually on Saturday, September 12th, the north wind fell sufficiently to permit of our venturing in with the aid of the engine. At 8:30 the *Gjoa* was anchored in Gjoahavn.

On Monday, September 14th, we brought the vessel right up to the bank and berthed there, just as we should alongside a quay. We were thus ready to commence preparations for our proposed winter quarters. First came the turn of the dogs, who were all taken ashore in the flat-bottomed boat. The dogs were highly affronted at being thus summarily ejected from the ship, but it was a great relief for us to get rid of them. After this "eviction" we constructed an aerial ropeway to facilitate unloading, as it was my intention to carry all provisions ashore so as to make as much room as possible on board.

We worked from 5 a.m. to 6 p.m. The "eight-hour day" was not yet introduced among us. We had some foretaste of winter in the form of snow and sleet, but we hoped that it would still keep off and give us time to get ready.

By the afternoon of the 17th the work of discharging was finished. Then we began clearing up on board. First of all we set the hold in order. Then the galley, which was amidships, was unscrewed, taken to pieces, and set up again in the hold. Lindstrom was thus in command below, and had his kitchen there from September, 1903, to June, 1905. Afterwards, in order to accomplish as much as possible before the winter set in, we divided ourselves into two parties. First and foremost it was necessary to get our observatory erected, and to procure fresh meat for the winter. Caribou had hitherto shown themselves very rarely in our neighbourhood. Lund and Hansen were therefore sent out on a boat trip to the little Island of Eta which lies in the middle of Simpson Strait, and where I knew from reports that caribou used to come in autumn in large herds. On September 21st they went off in the dory, provisioned for a fortnight. We who remained took the building operations in hand.

Lund and Hansen came back from their hunting expedition late one night. They had been lucky, and the boat was loaded with twenty carcasses of caribou. At a distance barely twelve miles from the harbour, they had found a spot where there were large herds of caribou, but the animals were very shy and difficult to get at. They put up a tent and hunted for several days. This place was near Booth Point, which later on became a familiar spot, as we met Eskimos who had their camp there. The Eskimos told us afterwards that they had seen our huntsmen, but dared not approach them for fear of the guns.

Double skylights were put in, oil-stoves were set up and the ventilation was improved. We made ourselves comfortable in the cabin, and it was very enjoyable after finishing the day's work to come into the cosy well-lighted room and have a good meal. We lounged about on those nights with an exquisite sense of comfort after the rough daily toil. We could not but feel that we had been very fortunate in every way. Finally, on the 29th, the whole vessel was covered in with sailcloth, and we were ready to stand the winter on board.

For the next twenty-three months the little Gjoa *remained at anchor in her haven while Amundsen and his companions carried on their magnetic observations, met and studied the Netchilik Eskimos, and made long exploratory sled journeys up the unknown eastern shore of Victoria Island. The excerpts that follow are vignettes of life at Gjoahavn, taken at random from the events of the two years spent on King William Island.*

Meeting the Eskimos

Early one morning we went dog sledding. In the calm weather we went swimmingly over the plains of King William Land. We were soon down in La Trobe Bay, on the east side. We skimmed smoothly over the even ice in the bay, and after dusk we erected our tent under a hummock. But we had bitter experience of the difference between a tent and a snow hut. We could not get warm even in the sleeping bags, and we passed most of the time turning and twisting about and knocking our feet together. It was pure enjoyment to be on the move again the next day and get warmth into our bodies by means of a little hard marching. Unfortunately, we had spoilt our thermometer, and could not determine the degree of cold. Our petroleum, however, acted as a sort of thermometer. When it was thick and milky white, we knew it was about 58° below zero. We set our course north to reach Matty Island. I had proposed establishing a depot on Cape Christian Frederick.

At 10 o'clock we stopped to lash the sledges tighter, and the conversation turned on the Eskimos, whom M'Clintock met here in 1859; should we find some tribes here still? As we sat, we saw a black dot far out in the ice. Hansen, with his excellent sight, soon concluded it was an Eskimo approaching us. Shortly after, several of them emerged from the hummocks, and very soon we could see thirty-four men and boys at a distance of about 200 yards. They stood still and observed us without any sign of coming nearer. We got our rifles ready, and Hansen kept an eye on them. When we were quite near, I called out "Manik-tu-mi!" and it was as if an electric shock had gone through the whole crowd. A 34-fold "Manik-tu-mi" was heard in reply, and I went straight up to them. Hansen, who saw that there was nothing to fear, abandoned his post and followed me. The Eskimos' delight, nay, enthusiasm, was really touching. They stroked and patted us, laughed and shouted "Manik-tu-mi." They were Nechilli Eskimos. They told us they were on the way to their seal fisheries; each man carried his spear in his hand and had a dog following him on a leash. They were also provided with large snow knives.

When I asked where their camp was, they pointed eastwards beyond the hummocks. I was anxious to make the acquaintance of these people, and told them that I should be happy to accompany them to their camp. They were frantically glad to hear this, and at once set to work to help us with our sledges, harnessing all their own dogs to them. An old fellow came driving along on a little sledge. This was Kagoptinner, i.e. the "grey-haired," who we later got to know was the oldest and best medicine man of his tribe; after a friendly greeting, his three dogs were added to our team, and the old chap himself was set on the top of one of our sledges. The Eskimo dogs were overjoyed at returning home so early, and our own got scent of the camp, and made for it. Then one of them suddenly flew at his neighbour, and before long the whole of one team was engaged in a furious fray. This was more than the other team could stand, and first one, then two, three, and at last the whole lot were engaged in mortal combat. The Eskimos threw themselves among them; snorting dogs and howling Eskimos formed one chaos, until they finally succeeded in getting the dogs parted; the traces were disentangled again, and the journey continued. The men formed a row alongside each team, running, laughing, and shouting unceasingly. They were clumsy and heavy, but looked as if they could keep the pace a long time. In about an hour they began to shout "Igloo! Igloo!" – and sure enough, far ahead among the hummocks, we sighted a crowd of huts shaped like hayricks. Another half-hour and we were there.

The whole place looked quite deserted. We halted a little way off and loosed the dogs. The men made quietly for their huts, and shortly afterwards the fair sex made their appearance. They arranged themselves in single file one behind the other. When all were mustered, the strange procession started running towards us. "Running" hardly expressed the movement; they reminded one of a row of waddling geese. They made straight for us, and I trembled; would they kiss us as a sign of welcome? We had come upon them so abruptly that they had had no time to complete their toilet. Such clothing as one old woman called Auva had on was covered with fat and soot, her face shone with train oil, and her greyish-black hair hung in wild confusion under the hood that had slipped down at the back of her neck. I looked at her with horror as she came nearer and hid myself hastily behind the little-suspecting Hansen to let him take the first shock. Nor was Anana beautiful either – she was covered with dirt and soot, and train oil, but anyone who could survive Auva could easily put up with the other. Now they were up to poor Hansen, and I was just expecting the kissing and embracing to commence when they swerved aside and formed a circle round us, emitting all sorts of weird grunts, and then waddled off back to the camp.

Now that the fright was over, I was able to examine them more calmly, and I must say that my first impressions of Nechilli Eskimo ladies did not redound to their advantage. Whether it was pure accident that just the ugliest of them came to us then, or that my taste altered later, I cannot say; certain it is that afterwards I thought some of them were quite good looking.

Now we had to think about getting our snow hut built. We

selected a spot not far from the others, and set to work. At first, the Eskimos followed us with inquisitive glances. They, no doubt, hardly thought that a "Kabluna" (foreigner) could manage a piece of work which was their own speciality. But they did not wait long before very audibly expressing their views on the point. Hansen and I did something or other they were not used to, and in a trice the whole crowd burst out into noisy exultation. Their laughter was uncontrollable; the tears ran down their cheeks, they writhed with laughter, gasped for breath, and positively shrieked. At last they recovered sufficiently to be able to offer us their assistance. They took the whole work in hand, but had to stop every now and then to have another laugh at the thought of our stupidity. In a short time, however, the most beautiful igloo was ready for us.

I had already noticed one man among the rest out on the ice. He was not like his companions, full of laughter and nonsense, but rather serious. There was also something haughty in his air, almost commanding, yet he could hardly be a chief of any kind, as the others treated him quite as an equal. A fine fellow he was, with raven black hair and, unlike his fellow tribesmen, had a luxuriant growth of beard; he was broad shouldered and somewhat inclined to corpulency. His belongings – clothes, tackle, dogs, etc. – were choice in quality and appearance. When I came out of my hut, he stood at a little distance from the others and regarded me with a look that seemed to intimate that he had something special to tell me. I accordingly went straight up to him, and he bade me go with him to his hut. It looked exceptionally neat outside. Like a courteous host he made me enter first. This, as I am now inclined to think, was an accident, but at the moment it increased my sympathy for the man, as was only right and proper.

His name was Atikleura. He was a son of old Kagoptinner, the medicine man we had met on the ice. He showed himself later to be far superior to all his countrymen in every respect. I followed his suggestion and went inside his igloo. A passage led into the hut proper; this was so low that I had to stoop down. It had two extensions, like quite small huts, and what they served for was not difficult to guess by the odour; there was nothing to see, as the dogs were the scavengers. A hole so small that one had almost to creep through it led into the dwelling room. When I stood upright inside I was speechless with astonishment. It was quite an apartment for festive occasions; it had been constructed the day before, and was therefore still gleaming white. From floor to roof the room measured fully twice a man's height. The blocks in the wall were regular and of equal size, and the inside diameter was not less than fifteen feet. The sleeping shelf was so high one had to swing oneself up onto it, and it was covered with the most delicate reindeer skins. Everything gave the impression of the most perfect order.

Before the fireplace sat the lady of the house. She was strongly Mongolian in type, and by no means beautiful. But she looked clean and tidy. Like most other Eskimo women, she had lovely, shining white teeth and beautiful eyes, brown on a light-blue ground. She was tattooed like the rest on the chin, cheeks, brow and hands. We learnt afterwards that these women also tattooed themselves on other parts of the body. The eldest son, Errera, was a youth of sixteen or seventeen, of the purest Indian type. The absolute dissimilarity between the child and the parents was then inexplicable to me, but it became less so later when I learnt to know their matrimonial relations better. Errera was a well-bred boy, whose polite and pleasing disposition endeared him to us all. The next in age was his exact opposite, a saucy fellow, who had been given as a present to grandfather Kagoptinner, who, in grandfatherly fashion, spoiled him and withdrew him from his mother's good influence. The youngest was Anni, a perfectly charming little chap of five, his parents' darling. The whole family was better clad than the other Eskimos. From what I saw I determined to be on good terms with Atikleura. He was manifestly a man it would be an advantage to know.

As soon as I came in, Atikleura fetched a skin sack, out of which he took a very finely made reindeer-skin garment which he presented to me. In my eagerness I wanted to strike while the iron was hot, and hinted that I should greatly value a suit of underclothing as well. Evidently very pleased at my request, he now brought out some old, worn underclothing, put them on in place of those he was wearing, and handed me the latter with every indication that I was to change there and then. Somewhat surprised I hesitated; I must say I was not in the habit of exchanging underwear with other people, especially in the presence of a lady. But as Atikleura insisted, and his wife, Nalungia, showed the most complete indifference as to what I did, I quickly made my decision, seated myself on the form, veiled my charms as well as I could with the bed clothes, and was soon clad in Atikleura's still-warm underclothing. After this I was regaled with water, frozen raw reindeer meat, and salmon, served with small squares of seal blubber. I did not relish the meat, but the frozen salmon was quite delicious in flavour. For dessert I had frozen reindeer marrow, which did not taste badly.

After this feast of welcome was over, I put on my fine new outer clothing and went out. Outside in front of the hut lay a very fine polar-bear skin; thick-haired and shining white, a really splendid specimen. I stood gazing at it in admiration, but then went hastily over to our own hut to bring some return gifts for my friends. Luckily I had brought with me some sewing needles, spear points, etc., on which the Eskimos set special value, and I think Atikleura and Nalungia had hardly ever been so happy in their lives as when I brought them my gifts – two spear-points for him, and six sewing needles for her. After this I made a round of all the huts, and was everywhere very well received. Old Auva was particularly amiable. When I took leave of her, she presented me with a little bear skin and two reindeer tongues. As the latter were thoroughly filthy and covered with hair, she first picked the coarsest dirt off and then had recourse to the universal Eskimo tool – her tongue. She licked my reindeer tongues so clean that you could see your face in them. On my return to our own hut, Atikleura stood there with his bear skin. He handed it to me, beaming with joy. As a modest young man, I represented to him that I could not possibly accept such great generosity. But Atikleura would not hear of it, and resolutely carried the skin into my hut and laid it there.

Good relations having been established with the Eskimos, the northern natives took to visiting Gjoahavn where they would spend weeks at a time. Social life at the little harbour thus took on new and greater dimensions for the Norwegians.

One evening Ristvedt came over from the Eskimo tent and told us he had refused an invitation to supper there. As he stated that the reason of his refusal was that the food they offered him had even exceeded the limits of what he regarded as eatable, I was very anxious to know how it was prepared. It was a new sort of blood-pudding. Ristvedt was very fond of blood-pudding, and one of his specialities as a cook was something he called blood-dumpling; this was really very good. But the Eskimo pudding, well . . . no thanks, he could not manage it! He had followed the preparation from the moment the deer was shot. It was at once skinned and the blood carefully collected. A portion of the tepid blood was drunk up by itself, then the stomach was taken out of the animal. The Eskimos partook of a portion of the contents by scooping it up with their hands. When the stomach was half empty, they put the blood into it and stirred it round with a thigh bone. The dish thus prepared was blood-pudding à la Eskimo. After they had eaten a portion of the fresh "pudding," they tied up the stomach and put it in a spot exposed to the sun, covering it over with a flat stone; there it lay to "season" until late in winter; it was then ready and "ripe," and was used for banquets.

The Lieutenant had completed his triangulation of the bases. Lund and Hansen had to look after the ship and keep it in repair, and they did this work very thoroughly. Wiik conscientiously carried out the magnetic observations. After the charting work was finished, the Lieutenant offered to increase our zoological collection. We were all interested in this, and got a great deal of material together; the Eskimos also helped us considerably in completing it. Lindstrom gave prizes, principally consisting of old underwear, for which the Eskimos competed eagerly. Later on we met Eskimos on King William Land strutting about in Lindstrom's worn-out pantaloons, etc. Altogether, he worked indefatigably, and he endeavoured to obtain a specimen of every living creature in the region. Even the special kind of *pediculus capitis*,* which the Eskimos rejoiced in, had to be obtained, and Lindstrom offered a prize for specimens. At first very few specimens were obtainable, but when the Eskimos understood that it was really a business matter, they came daily in crowds, bringing specimens to Lindstrom. What had previously been Lindstrom's joy was now his despair, and it required all his energy to put a stop to this business and keep the *pediculi* at a distance, but even then he had enough of all varieties to furnish a good supply to every zoological collection in Europe.

The ice on the more extensive lakes now began to break up, and the Eskimos caught plenty of trout and brought them to us.

* Lice

The ice in the bay was crowded with fishermen, and we made arrangements with one to bring us small fresh cod whenever we required them. We generally had them fried for supper. Reindeer beef was almost invariably served for breakfast. On the whole, the life around us was very pleasant to contemplate. Little tots of five to six years sat with their fishing lines, often through the whole night, and made very good catches, sometimes more than their own weight. The youths and the men undertook the fishing on the lakes. They fished in the small leads close in to the land, where the water was so clear that one could follow every movement of the fishes.

One evening a very tragic event occurred. Umiktuallu, the "Owl's" elder brother, lived with his wife, three children, and a foster-son, in a tent pitched a few paces from us. He had in his possession an old muzzle-loading rifle he had obtained by barter from another Eskimo. He had procured balls, powder, and caps from us. He was accustomed to leave the weapon loaded, which indeed in itself was not very dangerous, but in spite of our repeated advice he had not removed the caps. That evening, when he and his wife were visiting another family, his foster-son and his own eldest son got hold of the rifle. Then followed what so often happens when boys play with weapons without having been shown how to use them properly; they were ignorant of their danger, the gun went off, and Umiktuallu's son, who was only seven years old, fell down dead. The father heard the shot and rushed to the spot. At the sight of his own dead son, and the foster-son sitting with the smoking weapon, he was seized with frenzy. He carried the horror-stricken boy out of the tent, stabbed him three times through the heart with his knife, and then kicked him away. Wiik was a witness of this terrible scene. The seven-year-old lad was an exceptionally bright and clever little fellow; he was really quite a hunter, and with his bow and arrow brought quantities of game to the house. Umiktuallu was exceedingly fond and proud of him. Both boys were buried that night, we did not know where. With time and reflection Umiktuallu calmed down, and was seized with remorse.

One morning we set out on our dog sleds in a southerly direction. At 4 o'clock in the afternoon we reached Navyato, where to our surprise we did not find altogether more than ten huts; considerably less than we had expected. We were, however, very well received by a number of our old acquaintances who were here cod-fishing. Navyato is situated not far from the bottom of Hunger Bay, which owes its name to a large number of skeletons of Franklin's men having been found there, plainly having starved to death on their way to the south. It is an irony of fate that this sinister name has been applied to what is in reality one of the most beautiful and lovely spots on the American north coast. In spring, when the channels are opened, enormous quantities of large fat salmon are met with. A little later the reindeer arrived in countless hordes and remained here throughout the summer, then in the autumn an unlimited quantity of cod can be caught, and yet here – in this Arctic Eden – those brave travellers died of hunger. The truth probably is that they had arrived there when the low land was covered over with snow; overcome by exertions, worn out with sickness, they must have stopped here and seen for miles before them the same disheartening snow-bedecked lowland, where there was no sign indicating the existence of any life, much less riches, where not a living soul met them to cheer them up or give them encouragement and help. Probably there is not another place in the world so abandoned and bare as this is in winter. There when summer comes and millions of flowers brighten up the fields; there where all the waters gleam and all the ponds sing and bubble during the short freedom from the yoke of ice; there where the birds swarm and brood with a thousand glad notes and the first buck stretches his head over the ice harbour; there a heap of bleached skeletons marks the spot where the remains of Franklin's brave crowd drew their last breath in the last act of that sad tragedy.

On this spot, which conceals so many sad mementoes, the Eskimos live gay and happy until darkness comes on and throws its iron cloak over these regions and all within it.

After the lapse of a few days we left Navyato with our sledge fully loaded with fish. Many of the Eskimos accompanied us on our return trip, amongst them being our oldest and best friend, Teraiu. The old fellow had now contracted a severe cold and accompanied us in order to get some medicine. During the trip he had one attack after the other, and coughed up a considerable quantity of blood. Old Auva, the liveliest of them all, we left in a very wretched condition, suffering from some stomach trouble; when we started she was still able to sit by the fireside, but she died a few days afterwards. We passed the first night on one of Todd's Islands in an old snow hut. On these islands a few skeletons and other traces of Franklin's expedition had also been found. Teraiu told me that he had heard tell about all the white men who had lost their lives there. He showed me a large white stone on the island on which we were passing the night that had been set up in memory of the dead.

In accordance with the experience gained during our first winter, we continued our improvements to the *Gjoa*. The winter roof over the boat was better fitted up, and we arranged an inside door so that we had, as it were, a second house. This arrangement had also the advantage that we were better cut off from the Eskimos, which at times was really necessary. Of an evening Lieutenant Hansen locked the door, and there we all sat safely and securely as in a fortress. We placed our American steam bath on the floor. The Lieutenant and I made constant use of this steam bath in the course of the winter; it worked splendidly, and, living as we were in such close quarters, heavily clothed, etc., it was really indispensable to us. We had no dressing-room to spare, but we used an old butter cask turned upside down. What was by no means pleasant was the cold douche which we always obtained from the rime formed on the roof from the frozen steam. Lieutenant Hansen also installed the electric light – three complete lamps. Indeed, he went so far as to install the electric light on deck; thus one sat quite comfortably in the cabin, pressed a button and – yes, we ought to have got light, but there was no light. This was the only fault of Hansen's electric-light installation, it never gave any light; we just had to take our bath in the darkness.

One question that the Lieutenant and I had often discussed was how we could protect ourselves against the Eskimos, in case they should take it into their heads to do anything. There was now a great number of them collected around us and if, for example, they were not very successful in their catches, our provision tent was exposed to them. We had, therefore, to teach them to regard us and ours with the greatest respect, and at last we hit upon a method of accomplishing this. A powerful mine was buried beneath a snow hut at a good distance from the ship, and well covered with snow.

When that was ready, we collected the Eskimos together on board. I spoke to them about the white man's power; that we could spread destruction around us, and even at a great distance accomplish the most extraordinary things. It was, consequently, for them to behave themselves properly and not to expose themselves to our terrible anger. If they should play any tricks on land, for example, over there by the snow huts, then we should merely sit quietly on board and do so.... With a terrific report the igloo blew up, and clouds of snow burst high into the air. This was all that was required.

On Sunday, November 20th, as we sat at breakfast, we were surprised by the visit of an Eskimo: a perfect stranger to us. The manner in which he entered showed that he had been among "people"; his clothes were also quite different from the Nechilli race. Our astonishment was not less when the fellow addressed us in, if not perfect, at least very intelligible English. "Give me 'moke!" We set pipe and tobacco before him and he filled his pipe like a perfect gentleman; he then introduced himself: "I am Mr. Atangala." This began to be very interesting. I sat and observed him, eager to see what his next step would be. I was, however, soon brought to myself and reminded that it was my turn to take the next step. "Might I ask, sir, what is your name?" I blushed at my ill-manners, bowed slightly and gave my name. The introduction being over, he was evidently more at ease. He intimated to me that his family were on deck, and I immediately remedied my previous behaviour by inviting his family down. They did not need to be urged. The woman was a tall, dark, typical Eskimo; her name was Kokko, and she was about thirty years old. Their son was about ten years old, and at first sight one saw that he was an exceptionally unmannerly boy. Atangala told me that he and his family had accompanied three white men from Chesterfield Inlet, in Hudson's Bay, to Coppermine River. From Coppermine River he turned his steps homeward, where he learnt that a vessel was lying in Ogchoktu – a trifle of about a couple of hundred miles away – so he determined to visit us and see if there was any business to be done with us. He boasted a good deal about being able to write, and at his request we brought him pencil and paper, but his skill in this useful art was not very remarkable. After a great deal of trouble and time he managed to sign his name. A few years ago he had accompanied an American whale fisher overland from Hudson Bay to Winnipeg, and during his stay there he had become acquainted with all the latest discoveries such as the telephone, railways, electric light – and whisky. He was especially interested in the last, and asked eagerly about it. I tried to explain to him that the teetotal movement was the latest advance in the region, but he would not listen to it. At last he asked straight out for some spirits, but we did not give him any. It was of the greatest interest to us to learn that two large vessels were at Katiktli (Cape Fullerton). I immediately began to think of getting into postal communication with the outer world by these two ships, and I asked Mr. Atangala if he would be willing to act as post-boy. He appeared willing to accept this position. The boy, however, was an awful nuisance. At one moment this ten-year-old hobbledehoy lay on his mother's breast and took a drop of milk, and then snatched the pipe from his father's mouth and began smoking.

Saturday, May 20th, was a great day on board the *Gjoa*. Wiik came from Magnet Hill, where he had been taking meteorological observations, and told us that some people were coming along on the ice; this was not an unusual occurrence, but as he thought he had noticed, in spite of the great distance, that it was a sledge with a lot of dogs, and that it was travelling very rapidly, I sent out Talurnakto to see what it was. Our Eskimo friends do not as a rule travel "express," and as Talurnakto did not return, we felt sure that it must have been an Eskimo family now stopping to camp for the night. I therefore got into my bunk, but I had not been there very long before I heard hasty and unfamiliar footsteps on deck, and immediately afterwards a man burst into the cabin. "Go' morning! You give me 'moke!" was his greeting. It was Atangala, with his broadest and most triumphal smile. He stood before me and held out his hand, at the same time asking me not to press it too hard as he had hurt it. I cared little for his smile, hand, or 'moke, I merely wanted to see whether he had the mail. "Have you any letters?" "Letters? Yes, out there on the sledge, a whole heap of them." He was both surprised and hurt that we were in such a hurry about these letters, but I hastily put on a few clothes, and we both went outside. In a hurry and scurry everyone got up, and soon we stood beside Atangala's sledge; at last he brought out a neat little soldered tin box from beneath all kinds of odds and ends.

This was the mail!

I shall not endeavour to describe my feelings when holding this tin box in my hands, containing as it did messages from the living tumultuous world. We well knew that there could not be any direct message from the dear ones at home, but here, at least, was news of the great human community to which we all belonged, and from which we had so long been cut off. The simple word "mail" produced an indescribable sensation in us all. We carried our treasure on board and gathered around it. Lund immediately got the soldering-lamp to work, and the box was soon opened. The first I found was a letter from Major Moodie, Chief of the Royal North West Mounted Police, and Chief Commander of *The Arctic*, belonging to the Canadian government. *The Arctic* was investigating the conditions around Hudson Bay, and had wintered off Cape Fullerton, near Rowe's Welcome, an arm of Hudson Bay. In this very friendly letter he offered us every assistance, should we go near him, and he also sent me five sledge dogs. From the Captain of *The Arctic*, Captain Bernier, I also received a long and interesting letter. His information about the American whalers on the north-west coast was very acceptable to me, and of the greatest importance. The Captain also sent us a quantity of newspaper cuttings and photographs, which we greedily devoured.

We sat up late through the night and discussed all this news. In our hurry to get up we had not troubled to dress very much, and, as we sat in eager groups around the letters and newspapers, we formed a very amusing picture. Atangala took advantage of the time and opportunity, and had one " 'moke" after the other. This time he was accompanied by his son Arnana, a young man about twenty-five years old, a very fine fellow. When at last I had time to attend to Mr. Atangala, he told me he had had a very fine trip, although he had run rather short of food until he got near his home at Chesterfield Inlet. Of course, he had to go home first. Here he had encountered some musk-oxen, and had hunted them. One day, when out shooting, one of the cartridges had jammed in the barrel of the gun and, in endeavouring to get it out, the cartridge exploded, with the result that Atangala lost his forefinger. When he reached home his friends and relations tried to persuade him to give up carrying the mails and to remain at home quietly and take care of his finger; but he withstood all temptations and continued his route. The recompense he had in view, after successfully accomplishing it, was an old gun and four hundred cartridges; but I am inclined to believe that it was not merely the payment which impelled him to fulfil his task, but that he was stimulated by a desire to prove that he was a man of his word, and in circumstances like ours, such a man is doubly appreciated. He consequently received a considerable addition to his pay, and during his entire stay with us he was treated as the honoured guest. He was especially delighted at the praise I gave him for his integrity and sense of honour. On May 23rd at 11 o'clock in the morning he started out again for the south, together with the superfluous dogs we were sending back, as also with the return mail. He was to try and reach *The Arctic* before she could sail – that is, before the ice broke up.

On June 1st, 1905, the self-registering instruments were stopped, after nineteen months' uninterrupted working. In the afternoon I collected together all our Eskimo lady friends to enrich them with our empty tins. There were some hundreds of tins, and I had put them together in a large heap in the middle of the hill. Then I had the womenfolk arranged round the heap in a ring and told them that when I had counted three, they might "go for" the heap and get all they could. The men arranged themselves behind their ladies: One! two! three! and in they rushed, using both hands and shovels; they threw the tins out backwards between their legs – they were not hampered by skirts – and the men grabbed hold of the flying tins, and so each collected his lot. Laughter and noise, shrieks and shouts, tins flying, men rushing, and so the heap was cleared.

The Voyage Continues

On July 28th, 1905, for the first time this summer, the harbour was free from ice. Out in the straits we saw that the ice had a bluish tinge, but no cracks were visible. In the previous summer the rivers had been exceptionally full owing to the great quantities of snow. This year they flowed quiet and still, and exerted hardly any influence on the breaking-up of the ice, so we had to depend on the sun and wind. There was hardly any current; but for a long time we had a scorching sun every day, and the prospects were rather bright. Towards the end of July the heat ceased definitely, but now the wind came to our assistance. On the night of July 31st a breeze blew up from the north-east with squalls, and sleet fell so heavily that the whole land was white. We had been very anxious about our departure for some time, and were looking out for this north wind with a good deal of excitement. The best of the summer was now over, and the nights, the worst enemy to our further progress, had begun to be noticeable. The ice out in Simpson's Strait had up to the present kept exceptionally quiet; no channels had formed, and the ice seemed just as compact and impenetrable as it had been the whole winter. The bluish tinge was, however, a sure sign that it would not need much force to break it up. The only spot of open water was outside Ristvedt River, which was like a bay out into the ice, and here the gale would get a good hold and begin the breaking-up in earnest. And so it happened; in the course of a few days the north-east wind worked wonders. The ice went over to the south, and large channels opened in it in many directions.

We were now free to set sail. The hold was almost completely filled with all our collections. Our most important belongings stood in the main hatchway. First and foremost were two large re-soldered iron tanks in which were preserved all the observations we had made during these two years. They were so arranged that if they were thrown overboard they would float; both had been marked with the name of the ship. Round these we arranged stores for fourteen days, as well as ammunition and other articles packed in small cases, ready for removal in the event of our being compelled to leave the ship. Here also each of us had his sack of waterproof and other clothing as well as such necessaries as would be required under the circumstances. All our boats and canvas-covered kayaks were perfectly arranged ready to stand a gale. We all knew that we were going to have a rough time of it, but the splendid relations which had always existed between us so strongly united us that although we were only seven, we were not easily discouraged.

On August 12th we again got a fresh northerly breeze and realized that if we were to get off, we must take advantage of this. The ice was still lying around Todd Islands but we thought we could see open water beyond them. The departure was fixed for 3 o'clock the next morning. Precisely at 3 a.m. on August 13th, the windlass played a lively tune on the deck of the *Gjoa*. The weather was not of the finest – thick fog and a light contrary breeze. We therefore set the motor going full speed ahead when leaving the harbour. The Eskimos had assembled in the early morning on shore to wish us a last good-bye. Talurnakto accompanied us out towards Fram Point, and we could hear him calling out his "God-da! God-da!" (good-day) long after he was lost in the fog.

We jumped, so to speak, right into the same doubtful navigation as before, impenetrable fog, useless compass, and a very changeable breeze, which was therefore a poor guide. The lead was thrown continually. I put Hansen and Lund on the look-out in the crow's nest, they being the best qualified men for the job, for the cards had to be played judiciously in this game if one wished to come out a winner. The Lieutenant and I myself took the helm in turn, from which point we could better survey the route. Ristvedt and Wiik looked after the engine. The man attending to the soundings had his full share of work; the lead flew up and down so rapidly that it was almost a wonder it did not melt. In this manner we groped our way as far as Booth Point, where we were compelled to stop, as we could not see our way clear to get through the ice. We were not far from Todd Islands, consisting of three very low islets, large enough, however, to collect a quantity of ice. It did not look very promising from the masthead. A channel – so narrow that at a distance it seemed barely to afford room for a rowing boat to pass – was all the open space between the main pack and the island. Then it was a question whether the channel was deep enough. "I think we shall get through," Lund called out from the crow's nest. "I notice stones at the bottom, but we can go close to the shore." This was precisely what we had to do, to squeeze through. Fortunately the west coast of the island was perpendicular. But it was only a margin of a few inches, compared with the *Gjoa*'s beam, that prevented us from getting stuck. We all heaved a sigh of relief when we had open water ahead of us to the west.

The Lieutenant and Helmer Hansen, when making a boat trip from Gjoahavn in 1904, had found two skeletons above ground at Hall Point. These were skeletons of white men; two, no doubt, of Franklin's companions. They buried the remains and built a cairn over their grave. We passed the point just as the sun was setting, and with our colours flying in honour of the dead we went by the grave in solemn silence; the sky and the land then glowing with a soft red, golden light. Our victorious little *Gjoa* was honouring her unfortunate predecessors.*

* At least one of Franklin's ships had penetrated almost to this point – a fact about which Amundsen may not have been aware at the time.

The lead was still going, but not so feverishly as during the forenoon. The man at the helm was standing dozing and at ease. We could now give some attention to Manni,* who hitherto had had to look after himself. I handed him over to Ristvedt, who had the afternoon watch looking after the engine, to make him a white-man. Considering the quantity of soap and insect-powder utilized in the process, I was convinced that Manni had had a proper cleansing. We had not the heart to cut his long, magnificent hair, but it was well combed, and we noticed no lice in it afterwards. His get-up became somewhat picturesque; blue stockinet jacket, seal-skin knee-breeches, white stockings, and the Lieutenant's old low-cut dress-shoes. His head was covered with a light-blue bathing-cap which I had at some time or another bought at a watering place. He won everybody's heart from the first start. Manni's laughter banished the most surly airs, and he was undoubtedly pleased with himself too. He had, it is true, reached the paradise of the Eskimo; the place where you eat as much as you can possibly manage to stow away.

During the evening some ice made its appearance from the south, and presently the whole Queen Maud's Sea was full of ice.

At daybreak on August 15th, we had before us a large newly discovered group of islands extending as far as our sight could reach. The position was clear to us. The ice surrounded the whole group, and we could neither get round to the north nor to the south — we had to go straight through. From the aspect of the islands it was obvious that the waters between them were foul and filled with all sorts of nasty things. Although the *Gjoa* was small, she got some good thumps but we got through without much trouble.

As we turned westward, the soundings became alarming, the figures jumped from seventeen to five fathoms. From an even, sandy bottom we came to a ragged, stony one. We were in the midst of a most disconcerting chaos; sharp stones faced us on every side, low-lying rocks of all shapes, and we bungled through zigzag, as if we were drunk. The lead flew up and down, down and up, and the man at the helm had to pay very close attention and keep his eye on the look-out man who jumped about in the crow's nest like a maniac, throwing his arms about for starboard and port, keeping on the move all the time to watch the track.

* A young Netchilik Eskimo who had chosen to accompany the *Gjoa* from King William Island.

Now I see a big shallow extending from one islet right over to the other. We must get up to it and see. The anchors were clear to drop, should the water be too shallow, and we proceeded at a very slow rate. I was at the helm and kept shuffling my feet out of sheer nervousness. We barely managed to scrape over. In the afternoon things got worse than ever; there was such a lot of stones that it was just like sailing through an uncleared field. Though chary of doing so, I was now compelled to lower a boat and take soundings ahead of us. This required all hands on deck, and it was anything but pleasant to have to do without the five hours' sleep obtainable under normal conditions. But it could not be helped. We crawled along in this manner, and by 6 p.m. we had reached Victoria Strait, leaving the crowd of islands behind us.

Victoria Strait was full of ice floes, but loose enough to enable us to get through. Outside Lind Island it was thick, but we managed to slip through a narrow channel, getting out on the other side and reaching open water again. As we were setting sail in the morning our gaff snapped. I then decided to seek refuge in Cambridge Bay, so as to get it repaired.

We anchored on August 17th, on the west side of Cape Colborne, and this was a significant day in the history of our expedition – for we had now sailed the *Gjoa* through the hitherto unsolved link in the Northwest Passage. We now felt we had got back again to fairly known waters, so to speak. A sounding was now and then given on the chart, and we felt much more at ease, knowing that we had waters ahead of us which had been ploughed by a larger vessel.*

At 3 p.m., August 21st, we passed Liston and Sutton Islands, and stood off into Dolphin and Union Strait. My relief at having thus got clear of the last difficult hole in the Northwest Passage was indescribable. I cannot deny that I had felt very nervous during the last few days. The thought that here in these troublesome waters we were running the risk of spoiling the whole of our so-far-successful enterprise was anything but pleasant, but it was always present in my mind. All our precautions and everybody's careful attention notwithstanding, any moment might have some surprise in store for us. I could not eat. At every meal-time I felt a devouring hunger, but I was unable to swallow my food. When finally we got out of our scrapes and I regained my usual calm, I

* Collinson's *H.M.S. Enterprise* in 1850-55.

had a most rapacious hunger to satisfy, and I would rather not mention what I managed to dispose of.

We could now discontinue the laborious watches of eighteen hours a day, and revert to the normal arrangement of six-hour watches.

At 8 a.m. on August 27th, when we were off Nelson Head on Banks Island, my watch was finished and I turned in. When I had been asleep some time, I became conscious of a rushing to and fro on deck. Clearly there was something the matter, and I felt a bit annoyed that they should go on like that for the matter of a bear or a seal. It must be something of that kind, surely. But then Lieutenant Hansen came rushing down into the cabin and called out the ever-memorable words: "Vessel in sight, sir!" He bolted again immediately, and I was alone.

The Northwest Passage had been accomplished – my dream from childhood. This very moment it was fulfilled. I had a peculiar sensation in my throat; I was somewhat overworked and tired, and I suppose it was weakness on my part, but I could feel tears coming to my eyes. "Vessel in sight!" The words were magical. My home and those dear to me there at once appeared to me, as if stretching out their hands – "Vessel in sight!"

I dressed myself in no time. When ready, I stopped a moment before Nansen's portrait on the wall. It seemed as if the picture had come to life, as if he winked at me, nodding. "Just what I thought, my boy!" I nodded back, smiling and happy, and went on deck.

It was a wonderfully fine day. The breeze had veered round somewhat to the east, and with the wind abaft, and all sails set, we made excellent headway. It seemed as if the *Gjoa* understood that the hardest part of the struggle was over, she seemed so wonderfully light in her movements. A heavy, bright swell rocked the vessel pleasantly, and the air was mild and soft. All this was observed in a moment. but it did not arrest our attention for long. The only objects between sky and sea that possessed any interest for us then were the two mastheads on the horizon. All hands had come on deck and all glasses were levelled at the approaching vessel. All faces were wreathed in smiles.

On the closer appearance of the unknown vessel we hoisted our Norwegian flag. It glided slowly up under the gaff, every eye watching it.

The vessels were approaching each other very rapidly.

"There! up goes the American flag," sang out the watchman. We could now all see the Stars and Stripes under the vessel's gaff.

The *Charles Hanson*, of San Francisco, did not seem to be rigged out in a very luxurious manner. We took hold of her chain-wales and crawled on board. Our first impression was most peculiar. Every available space on deck was occupied to such an extent that it was nearly impossible to get along. Eskimo women in red dresses, and Negroes in the most variegated costumes, were mingling together just as in a land of fable.

An elderly man with a white beard advanced towards me on the quarter-deck. He was newly shaven, and nicely dressed, evidently the master of the ship. "Are you Captain Amundsen?" was his first remark. I was quite surprised to hear that we were known so far away, and answered in the affirmative, owning that I was the man. "Is this the first vessel you have met?" the old man asked. And when I admitted it was so, his countenance brightened up. We shook hands long and heartily. "I am exceedingly pleased to be the first one to welcome you on getting through the Northwest Passage."

The success of the Gjoa's *voyage only intensified Amundsen's love for the polar world – that cold and unpassioned mistress. Directly driven, he went back again and again as the years drew down.*

In 1911 he became the first man to reach the South Pole; but even that was not enough. In 1925, accompanied by Lincoln Ellsworth, he made the first attempt to fly over the North Pole. He did not reach the Pole itself, which did not greatly disappoint him, for on this flight he accomplished far more than the mere passage over a non-existent point. After making the first aircraft landing on the polar pack, he sounded the hidden sea beneath and gave us our first knowledge of its tremendous depth. It was still not enough. In 1926, again with Ellsworth, he crossed the north polar basin from Spitzbergen to Alaska in the airship Norge, *and thereby forever scotched the legend of an undiscovered land mass at the top of the world.*

Perhaps this was enough, but the old, cold mistress knew a trick to bring him back once more.

In 1928 the airship Italia *set out from Spitzbergen for the Pole. She reached it safely, but on her return southward she was lost.*

Although her Commander, Nobile, had shown bitter animosity toward Amundsen, the Norwegian held no grudge. As quickly as he could he organized a search and rescue expedition, and on June 20th, 1928, he took off from Tromso in a French-built aircraft. Again he headed into the white world he loved; but from this journey there was no return.

Nobile was rescued by a Swedish pilot; but of Roald Amundsen nothing more was ever heard.

Epilogue

During the first decade of the twentieth century, men and ships of a new nation appeared in northern waters. These were the Canadians, who were belatedly beginning to take an interest in their own Arctic lands and seas. Between 1904 and 1911 Captain J. E. Bernier, in command of the ex-Dundee whaler *Arctic*, made four notable voyages into the ice. Bernier retraced almost all the routes of the earlier ice-voyagers, and he came within a hair's breadth of completing the Northwest Passage by its northern route, through Lancaster Sound, Melville Sound and Prince of Wales Strait. In 1908 the *Arctic* reached the point where M'Clure had abandoned his ship during his attempt to force the passage from the west in 1851. The *Arctic* could probably have completed the passage easily enough, but Bernier carried instructions to go no farther, and to return into eastern waters.

By 1911, when Bernier made his last major voyage into the high Arctic, a new lull in the battle between ships and ice had begun. The whaling trade was finished, and the few whalers which had survived the pack now rusted in their final harbours. The quest for the pole was ended, even though there was considerable doubt that either of the rival claimants had actually reached that nebulous objective. A war was brewing; and for more than a decade there were to be no new exploring voyages out of the Western Sea into the Arctic pack.

The lull was broken in 1922 when the *Arctic*, now a venerable ship, once more came north to begin a series of voyages known as the Eastern Arctic Patrols. For the most part these annual journeys to the ice were unremarkable, though each one was a new struggle and none was routine. In the annals of Arctic voyages the name of the *Arctic* deserves to stand beside Hudson's and Bylot's *Discovery*, M'Clintock's *Fox*, the Royal Navy's *Resolute*, Nansen's *Fram*, and Amundsen's *Gjoa*, as that of one of the outstanding warriors in the conflict with the ice.

When the *Arctic* was eventually retired one other famous ship remained to challenge the supremacy of the pack. She was the Hudson's Bay Company steamer *Nascopie*, a little ship, designed as a sealer and built to spend her life amongst the ice. *Nascopie* made her first voyage into the Eastern Arctic before the First World War and, with only brief interludes, she made a voyage each year thereafter, carrying in merchandise, bringing out furs, and gradually extending her voyages as trading posts and R.C.M.P. stations moved farther north. From 1932 until her death on a reef in 1946, she also took over the duties of the *Arctic* and carried on the Eastern Arctic Patrol. In 1937, at Bellot Strait, she made contact, by prearrangement, with the H.B.C. schooner *Aklavik* (which had come east from the Mackenzie). Supplies were transshipped from the steamer to the schooner, to make this the first occasion on which the Northwest Passage was used for a commercial purpose.

The approach of the Second World War again brought about a pause in Arctic venturing, although during the war years the little R.C.M.P. schooner *St. Roch* under the command of Sergeant Henry Larsen made a name for herself and her commander in the Amundsen style, by wriggling her way through the Northwest Passage, not once but twice; and not only from east to west, but from west to east as well. It was a further proof, if one were needed, that where force could not overmaster force in the battle with the ice, patience and compliance could still win victories.

Still, we are a species which believes intrinsically in force, and it was inevitable that the old outright conflict would some day be renewed, as men pitted the full power of new machines against the ancient resistance of the ice. This renewal of conflict, when it came, was inspired by another kind of war – the cold war between Russia and the United States. It involved Canada and her Arctic regions, willy nilly, since the Americans believed that the northern portion of the continent provided an avenue of approach for possible Russian aggression; and so they set themselves to defend it, with the resultant paradox that they found they had first to conquer the resident defender – the Arctic ice.

In the years following 1948 ship after ship went north, and most of these were U.S. military, naval and coast-guard vessels, for the Americans were quietly assuming *de facto* sovereignty over much of the North American Arctic. Military bases, air-fields, radar and weather stations were built across the mainland tundra and upon the high Arctic islands in order to defend the continental heartland of the U.S.A. Since the materials needed to build and maintain these installations had to be carried to the sites, for the most part, by sea, the old war against the pack took on a new and grimmer meaning.

Canada's control of her own Arctic waters, so laboriously established by Bernier and by the voyages of Hudson's Bay Company and R.C.M.P. vessels, was slipping from her hands. Not until 1956 did she make any real attempt to re-assert her interest, and then her action was largely a symbolic one intended to regain at least the shadow of her diminished control over her own territory. In 1956 she built a special ship to send into the ice. This vessel was H.M.C.S. *Labrador*, and it was to be her pride to be the first large ship to navigate the Northwest Passage, and the first ship in history to navigate it through its northern arm. Hers was a magnificent gesture, for she was a fine ship and her people were concerned to show that Canadians, too, could dare the ice, accept its perils, and do as much as anyone to penetrate its defences.

It was, however, not much more than a gesture. Before two years had passed, the *Labrador* had been taken away from the Navy and given to a government administrative department, doomed to spend the rest of her days in the routine business of servicing such Arctic outposts as Canada still nominally controlled.

The burden of the conflict with the Arctic ice in the northwestern regions now devolved upon the Americans by Canadian default, but the Americans' effort was directed not so much against the ice barriers as at by-passing them, either by aircraft or by submarine. In 1958 the U.S. Navy obtained a remarkable success when its nuclear-powered *Nautilus* crossed the polar basin far beneath the pack and, as her historian grandiloquently put it, "pierced the Pole." No doubt this was a gratifying technical achievement, but it had little if any practical value as far as opening the Northwest Passage was concerned.

The next attempt to burst through the passage did not take place until the 1970's. By then Canada was trying to make up for lost time, partly impelled by a sense of shame for her long neglect of her own northern interests and partly because the men in power were belatedly beginning to realize how valuable the once-neglected and rejected Arctic regions might soon become to whichever nation truly controlled them. Canada began building a fleet of modern ice breakers which would be second only to that of the U.S.S.R. and far superior to anything the U.S.A. possessed. The first of these extraordinarily powerful new ships was the *Sir John A. Macdonald*. She arrived on the scene just in time to go to work – not for Canada, but for the United States!

The *Macdonald* opened the Northwest Passage to the first transit by a commercial vessel . . . the giant tanker *Manhattan* which belonged to a U.S. oil company and was carrying out a trial run to discover whether or not oil from Alaska could be moved to eastern U.S. markets through the territorial waters of Canada's Arctic archipelago. Just why Canada, who had everything to lose in the event of an oil spill, and nothing to gain, should have provided the services of the *Macdonald* is a question which has never been satisfactorily answered. The fact is that the *Macdonald* shepherded the *Manhattan* through the passage; but the huge tanker was badly holed and barely escaped disaster on several occasions and, luckily for Canada, her owners concluded that the route was not practicable.

In the light of recent findings by the Canadian research vessel *Hudson*, it seems probable that the passage will never be useable by such huge, deep-draft bulk transport ships. This is because of the presence of large numbers of lethal pinnacles of frozen mud and ice which lance almost to the surface from the floor of the Beaufort Sea. The discovery of these previously unknown defences has been greeted with relief by the growing multitude of people who believe that massive exploitation of the Canadian Arctic regions would be disastrous.

So it is not yet over. We have not yet won a final victory over that ancient antagonist, the frozen Arctic sea. Perhaps, if we were truly wise, we would learn a lesson from this continuing defeat.

We might learn to rest content with what has already been accomplished instead of seeking still more victories at the expense of the natural world which is the womb of all living things, ourselves included. And perhaps we might learn enough humility from our defeats in the Arctic to persuade us to turn our driving energies away from the work of world destruction, and direct them instead to the work of healing the wounds we have already made. If this should prove to be the case, surely it would be no bad thing.

Index

C

D

E

F

G

H

I

J

K

N

Q

R

Sources and Acknowledgements

The original sources from which the material in this book has been taken are shown below. The section "French Guns Amongst the Ice" is based in great part upon a translation by David R. Keys of the "Letters of La Potherie" which appeared in a volume entitled *Documents Relating to the Early History of Hudson Bay*, by J. B. Tyrrell, and which was published by the Champlain Society. We are indebted to the Society for permitting the material to be used for this purpose.

MARTIN FROBISHER:

Richard Hakluyt, *The Principall Navigations, Voiages and Discoveries of the English Nation*, London, 1589, Bishop and Newberie.

HENRY HUDSON (ALSO DAVIS, BAFFIN AND BYLOT):

T. Rundall, *Narratives of Voyages toward the North-West*, London, 1849, Hakluyt Society.

JENS MUNK:

C. C. A. Gosch (editor), *Danish Arctic Explorations, 1605 to 1620*, Vol. II, London, 1897, Hakluyt Society. (English translation)

THOMAS JAMES:

Strange and Dangerovs Voyage of Captaine Thomas Iames, London, 1633, I. Legatt.

SIEUR DE LA POTHERIE:

J. B. Tyrell, *Documents Relating to the Early History of Hudson Bay*, Toronto, 1931, Champlain Society. (English translation by David Keys)

JAMES KNIGHT:

Samuel Hearne, *A Journey from the Prince of Wales's Fort in Hudson Bay to the Northern Ocean*, London, 1795, A. Strahan and T. Cadell.

WILLIAM SCORESBY:

The Northern Whale-Fishery, London, circa 1835, Religious Tract Society.

JOHN ROSS:

Narrative of a Second Voyage in Search of a Northwest Passage, London, 1835, A. W. Webster.

SHERARD OSBORN:

Stray Leaves from an Arctic Journal, London, 1852, Longmans.

LEOPOLD M'CLINTOCK:

The Voyage of the Fox in the Arctic Sea, London, 1860, John Murray.

CHARLES HALL:

Arctic Researches and Life among the Esquimaux, New York, 1865, Harper.

Picture Credits

I Thomas E. Lee
II Thomas E. Lee
III Thomas E. Lee
IV Courtesy of The New Brunswick Museum's Webster Pictorial Canadiana Collection
V The Arctic Institute of North America
VI The British Museum
VII John Ross Robertson Collection – Metropolitan Toronto Central Library
VIII Metropolitan Toronto Central Library – from *de Veer: Three Voyages of William Barrents*
IX Metropolitan Toronto Central Library – from *Munk: Danish Arctic Expeditions*
X Public Archives of Canada
XI Metropolitan Toronto Central Library – from *Bacqueville de la Potherie: Histoire de l'Amerique Septentrionale*, Vol. I
XII Glenbow-Alberta Archives
XIII Metropolitan Toronto Central Library – from *Scoresby: An Account of the Arctic Regions*, Vol. II
XIV Metropolitan Toronto Central Library – from *Scoresby: An Account of the Arctic Regions*, Vol. I
XV Metropolitan Toronto Central Library – from *Ross' Voyage to Baffin Bay, 1818*

All illustrations appear in a 32-page section following page 333.

ABOUT THE AUTHOR

Farley Mowat was born in Belleville, Ontario, in 1921, and grew up in Belleville, Trenton, Windsor, Saskatoon, Toronto and Richmond Hill. He served in World War II from 1940 until 1945, entering the army as a private and emerging with the rank of captain. He began writing for his living in 1949 after spending two years in the Arctic. Since 1949 he has lived in or visited almost every part of Canada and many other lands, including the distant regions of Siberia. He remains an inveterate traveller with a passion for remote places and peoples. He has twenty-five books to his name, which have been published in translations in over twenty languages in more than sixty countries. They include such internationally known works as *People of the Deer, The Dog Who Wouldn't Be, Never Cry Wolf, Westviking, The Boat Who Wouldn't Float, Sibir, A Whale for the Killing, The Snow Walker* and *And No Birds Sang*. His short stories and articles have appeared in *The Saturday Evening Post, Maclean's, Atlantic Monthly* and other magazines.